Coleridge and Wordsworth

PAUL MAGNUSON

C O L E R I D G E

A N D

W O R D S W O R T H

A Lyrical Dialogue

PRINCETON UNIVERSITY PRESS

PRINCETON UNIVERSITY

Copyright © 1988 by Princeton University Press
Published by Princeton University Press, 41 William Street,
Princeton, New Jersey 08540
In the United Kingdom: Princeton University Press,
Guildford, Surrey

All Rights Reserved
Library of Congress Cataloging in Publication Data will be found on
the last printed page of this book

ISBN 0-691-06732-5

Publication of this work has been supported in part by a grant from
the Abraham and Rebecca Stein Faculty Publications Fund of New
York University, Department of English.

This book has been composed in Linotron Baskerville

Clothbound editions of Princeton University Press books are printed
on acid-free paper, and binding materials are chosen for strength and
durability. Paperbacks, although satisfactory for personal collections,
are not usually suitable for library rebinding

Printed in the United States of America by Princeton University Press,
Princeton, New Jersey

iv

IN MEMORY OF
Harold Einar Magnuson

CONTENTS

P R E F A C E

A reading of the lyrical dialogue formed by Coleridge's and Wordsworth's poetry is made possible by two recent developments in scholarship and criticism. First, the new editions of Coleridge's writing from Princeton University Press and of Wordsworth's poetry from Cornell University Press require more than a reassessment of their individual achievements. They offer the opportunity of developing a new methodology of reading their poetry as an intricately connected whole, of reading their works as a joint canon, and of understanding the generation of their greatest poetry. The proliferation of drafts, early versions, and associated fragments for each work and the shifting contexts for these fragments make it difficult to trace the growth of a single work isolated from the writing that preceded it and the works that were written at the same time. It is also difficult to explain the development of a single work by reference to authorial intention or the metaphor of organic growth Poems take time to develop, in many instances decades, and in the process other voices and texts intrude. What can be made of these various drafts and early versions? How do they fit into the canon, and how do they shape the poetry that follows? What method of reading does justice to their complexity, their fragmentary nature, and their power to generate further texts?

The second development is the proliferation of critical perspectives on a literary work, literary history, and textual relationships. Harold Bloom has offered a view of literature in which poems display the struggle of their own generation. They misread their precursors by various strategies and thus revise what has already been written or envisioned; they turn upon previous poetry. With Bloom's theory of the anxiety of influence, the younger poet must engage in a tormented conflict with a precursor. In lyrical dialogue, however, two poets are speaking simultaneously. Each alludes to the other's poetry as well as to his own, and each poem turns upon a previous one. After listening to the other poet, each has the opportunity of responding. A mutual interchange is formed that resembles the processes of dialogue described by Mikhail Bakhtin, except that the turns of lyrical dialogue do not parody another's text to challenge its authority. On the contrary, the dialogue begins with shared themes and voices. Various other critical approaches have raised questions about the allusiveness of literature, of its complex inter-textual references, which extend the fields of reference of a single work and tend to fragment its unity. Is there an intelligible order that can be seen within the dispersion of texts and the fields of their reference, one that can admit a pattern of sequence, not only in the great moments of the canon, but also in the entire landscape of ut-terance?

I propose a method of reading that takes some preliminary steps toward answering these questions. In the first chapter I describe some ways of reading the canon composed of both Coleridge's and Wordsworth's poetry organized in roughly chronological order. The reading regards their poetry as highly allusive and dialogic, as responding to poems previously written. Dialogue is the essential generative condition of their poetry; it becomes the motive for fur-ther writing. As Coleridge once suggested, the relationship among their poems was similar to that among stanzas of an ode. The dia-logue progresses by the transitions and turns of lyric, and it is pro-gressive in that it generates further writing, whether or not it tends toward a final unity of significance. By itself, lyrical dialogue is open-ended; it tends toward something to be.

The methodology of reading obviously requires the use of the earliest versions of poems and—where relevant—drafts, fragments, and works in progress, many of which are seldom, if ever, discussed in criticism. It considers all poems, whether they are usually consid-ered to be integral works or fragments, to be parts or fragments of the dialogue. A dialogic reading allows one to listen to those sections of poems that allude to previous poems by negation, questioning, and interruption. It permits one to read their joint poetry as an ex-tended lyric sequence. A dialogic reading, in this instance, is a source study only in that the first stanza of a lyric is a source for the following stanza or in which the opening poem in a volume of col-lected poems is the source for the following poems. There are, of course, abundant verbal parallels in their poetry, and sometimes they indicate a dialogic relationship to other poems. But verbal par-allels alone do not always trace the important transitions. As Cole-ridge once said, "Commentators only hunt out verbal Parallelisms—*numen abest*" (*STCL* 2: 866). The dialogue is best mapped through its figures and forms and in its rhetoric that highlights the allusiveness and reference among its various fragments.

In the second chapter I offer partial readings of poems written before Wordsworth and Coleridge's close association began in the summer of 1797. These poems generated later poems and were mutually complementary. In subsequent chapters I discuss pairs or groups of poems by both poets that illustrate the procedures of the dialogue. Chapters 3 and 4 deal with the narrative poems "The Ancient Mariner," "The Discharged Soldier," "The Ruined Cottage," and "Christabel." In the remaining chapters I deal with the lyric poetry beginning with Coleridge's Conversation Poems, to a large extent the motivating texts for much of Wordsworth's poetry, including *The Prelude*.

I have quoted extensively from transcripts of unpublished manuscript material and have reproduced the quotations as they appear in the editions, with the standard editorial symbols. Words in brackets are those that have been supplied by editors. Bracketed words that are preceded by a question mark indicate conjectural readings by editors. Question marks alone within brackets indicate illegible words. Editors have indicated gaps in the manuscript either with empty brackets or simple gaps. I have reproduced the transcriptions as they appeared in the original edition; in a very few instances, which I have noted, I have simplified the transcription.

Such a critical study would have been difficult, if not impossible, without the work of generations of editors of both poets, especially those of the new editions. I would particularly like to thank Stephen Parrish, James Butler, James Averill, and Beth Darlington for generously and patiently responding to my queries and for sharing the results of their work with me. I would also like to thank Laurence Lockridge, Richard Haven, Frederick Garber, and Kathleen Fowler, for thorough readings and thoughtful suggestions, and my editor, Alan M. Schroder, whose attention to detail saved me from many errors. My gratitude also goes to my chairman, John Maynard, who generously granted support for the preparation of this work. In addition, I would like to thank Marilyn Gaull for permission to reprint "The Genesis of Wordsworth's 'Ode'" from *The Wordsworth Circle* (1981) and "The Articulation of 'Michael'; or, Could Michael Talk?" from *The Wordsworth Circle* (1982) copyright © Marilyn Gaull; to New York University Press for permission to reprint "Wordsworth and Spontaneity," from *The Evidence of the Imagination: Studies of Interactions between Life and Art in English Romantic Literature*, edited by Donald H. Reiman et al., copyright © 1978 by New York University; and to the Trustees of Boston University for permission to reprint " 'The Eolian Harp' in Context," from *Studies in Romanticism* copyright © 1985 by the Trustees of Boston University. I am grateful to Oxford University Press for permission to quote from *The Complete Poetical Works of Samuel Taylor Coleridge*, ed. E. H. Coleridge (1912) and from *Collected Letters of Samuel Taylor Coleridge*, ed. Earl Leslie Griggs (1956–71), and to Jonathan Wordsworth and The Wordsworth Trust, Cornell University Press, and The Harvester Press Ltd./Wheatsheaf Books Ltd. to quote from the Cornell Wordsworth series: *The Salisbury Plain Poems*, ed. Stephen Gill, copyright © 1975 by Cornell University; *The Prelude, 1798–99*, ed. Stephen Parrish, copyright © 1977 by Cornell University; *Home at Grasmere*, ed. Beth Darlington, copyright © 1979 by Cornell University; *"The Ruined Cottage" and "The Pedlar,"* ed. James Butler, copyright © 1979 by Cornell University; and *The Borderers*, ed. Robert Osborn, copyright © 1982 by Cornell University, used by permission of the publisher, Cornell University Press.

ABBREVIATIONS

Beer   *Samuel Taylor Coleridge: Poems*. Ed. John Beer. London: J. M. Dent & Sons, 1974.

BL   *Biographia Literaria*. Ed. James Engell and W. Jackson Bate. 2 vols. Vol. 7 of *The Collected Works of Samuel Taylor Coleridge*. Princeton: Princeton University Press, 1983.

Bord.   William Wordsworth, *The Borderers*. Ed. Robert Osborn. The Cornell Wordsworth. Ithaca; Cornell University Press, 1982.

Butler   William Wordsworth, *"The Ruined Cottage" and "The Pedlar."* Ed. James Butler. The Cornell Wordsworth. Ithaca: Cornell University Press, 1979.

CEY   Mark Reed, *Wordsworth: The Chronology of the Early Years, 1770–1799*. Cambridge: Harvard University Press, 1967.

CMY   Mark Reed, *Wordsworth: The Chronology of the Middle Years, 1800–1815*. Cambridge: Harvard University Press, 1975.

CNB   *The Notebooks of Samuel Taylor Coleridge*. Ed. Kathleen Coburn. 3 vols. Princeton: Princeton University Press, 1957–.

CPW   *The Complete Poetical Works of Samuel Taylor Coleridge*. Ed. Ernest Hartley Coleridge. 2 vols. Oxford: Clarendon Press, 1912.

Darlington   William Wordsworth, *"Home at Grasmere": Part First, Book First of "The Recluse."* Ed. Beth Darlington. The Cornell Wordsworth. Ithaca: Cornell University Press, 1977.

DWJ   *Journals of Dorothy Wordsworth*. Ed. Mary Moorman. New York: Oxford University Press, 1971.

EW   William Wordsworth, *An Evening Walk*. Ed. James Averill. The Cornell Wordsworth. Ithaca: Cornell University Press, 1977.

EOT   *Essays on His Times*. Ed. David Erdman. 3 vols. Vol. 3 of *The Collected Works of Samuel Taylor Coleridge*. Princeton: Princeton University Press, 1978.

Friend   *The Friend*. Ed. Barbara Rooke. 2 vols. Vol. 4 of *The Collected Works of Samuel Taylor Coleridge*. Princeton: Princeton University Press, 1969.

Lamb Letters   *The Letters of Charles and Mary Anne Lamb*. Ed. Edwin Marrs, Jr. 3 vols. Ithaca: Cornell University Press, 1975–78.

LB   *Wordsworth & Coleridge: Lyrical Ballads*. Ed. R. L. Brett and A. R. Jones. London: Methuen, 1963.

LEY   *The Letters of William and Dorothy Wordsworth: The Early Years, 1787–1805.* Ed. Ernest de Selincourt, rev. Chester Shaver. Oxford: Clarendon Press, 1967.

LMY   *The Letters of William and Dorothy Wordsworth: The Middle Years, Part I, 1806–1811.* Ed. Ernest de Selincourt, rev. Mary Moorman. *Part II, 1812–1820.* Ed. Ernest de Selincourt, rev. Mary Moorman and Alan G. Hill. Oxford: Clarendon Press, 1969–70.

Moorman   Mary Moorman, *William Wordsworth: A Biography.* 2 vols. Oxford: Clarendon Press, 1957–65.

Parrish   William Wordsworth, *The Prelude, 1798–1799.* Ed. Stephen Parrish. The Cornell Wordsworth. Ithaca: Cornell University Press, 1977.

Prel.   William Wordsworth, *The Prelude: 1799, 1805, 1850.* Ed. Jonathan Wordsworth, M. H. Abrams, and Stephen Gill. New York: W. W. Norton, 1979.

Prose   *The Prose Works of William Wordsworth.* Ed. W.J.B. Owen and Jane Worthington Smyser. 3 vols. Oxford: Clarendon Press, 1974.

PTV   William Wordsworth, Poems, in Two Volumes, *and Other Poems, 1800–1807.* Ed. Jared Curtis. The Cornell Wordsworth. Ithaca: Cornell University Press, 1983.

SPP   *The Salisbury Plain Poems of William Wordsworth.* Ed. Stephen Gill. The Cornell Wordsworth. Ithaca: Cornell University Press, 1975.

STCL   *Collected Letters of Samuel Taylor Coleridge.* Ed. Earl Leslie Griggs. 6 vols. Oxford: Clarendon Press, 1956–71.

WBS   *Bicentenary Wordsworth Studies.* Ed. Jonathan Wordsworth. Ithaca: Cornell University Press, 1970.

WPW   *The Poetical Works of William Wordsworth.* Ed. Ernest de Selincourt and Helen Darbishire. 5 vols. Oxford: Clarendon Press, 1940–49.

Coleridge and Wordsworth

CHAPTER 1

"Our Fears about Amalgamation":

An Introduction

S HORTLY AFTER arriving in Germany in 1798, William and
Dorothy Wordsworth separated from Coleridge and began a
dreary trip to Goslar, where they spent the winter alone.
Coleridge had written to Thomas Poole, his friend and patron, on
September 28 that "Wordsworth & his Sister have determined to
travel on into Saxony, to seek cheaper places" (*STCL* 1: 419), and
Wordsworth himself had informed Poole on October 3 that "we set
off this evening by the diligence for Brunswick" (*LEY* 230). Poole
responded to Coleridge on October 8: "The Wordsworths have left
you—so there is an end to our fears about amalgamation."[1] The
news of their separation was similarly received by Josiah
Wedgwood, who had granted Coleridge an annuity of £150 the

1. Letter of Thomas Poole to Coleridge, Oct. 8, 1798. The letter is in the British
Library, Additional Manuscript 35, 343. Griggs quotes from the letter but mistran-
scribes the phrase as "tease about amalgamation" (*STCL* 1: 419). Poole's letter contin-
ues: "I think you both did perfectly right—it was right for them to find a cheaper
situation—and it was right for you to avoid the expense of travelling, provided you
are where *pure German* is spoken." When Coleridge wrote to John Thelwall on De-
cember 31, 1796, the thought of the amalgamation of his poetry with Wordsworth's
did not bother Coleridge: "I think, that an admirable Poet might be made by *amal-
gamating him & me*. I *think* to much for a *Poet*; he too little for a *great* Poet" (*STCL* 1:
294).

3

previous winter: "I hope that Wordsworth & he will continue separated. I am persuaded that Coleridge will derive great benefit from being thrown into mixed society" (*STCL* 1: 419). Charles Lamb, too, quipped to Southey: "I hear that the Two Noble Englishmen have parted no sooner than they set foot on german Earth, but I have not heard the reason—Possibly to give Moralists an handle to exclaim 'Ah! me! what things are perfect?' " (*Lamb Letters* 1: 152).

Lamb's play on the title of Fletcher's *The Two Noble Kinsmen* implies that the relationship between Coleridge and Wordsworth was one of kinship but also that it was less than an ideal fraternity. There is no evidence, however, that the Wordsworths' decision to seek less expensive lodgings was based on any other than financial considerations. There is no hint of the personal conflicts that led to Coleridge's separation from the Wordsworths on the 1803 Scottish tour, when each complained of the other's hypochondria, and that led to more serious breaks later on. The "amalgamation" must have been a poetic and intellectual one. *Lyrical Ballads* (1798) had just been published, and that volume was just one of the projects for joint publication that they had discussed with Joseph Cottle the previous spring.

Poole's phrase is ambiguous. One cannot be sure whom he included in the phrase "our fears." It certainly includes himself and probably Coleridge, but one cannot be sure whether it included Wordsworth or any of Coleridge's other acquaintances. In May Coleridge had written to Cottle about their proposed publications: "We deem that the volumes offered to you are to a certain degree *one work*, in *kind tho' not in degree*, as an Ode is one work—& that our different poems are as stanzas, good relatively rather than absolutely" (*STCL* 1: 412). If Coleridge's offer to Cottle accurately reflects Wordsworth's opinions, then Wordsworth, too, must have looked upon their poetry as *"one work."* Thus Poole's relief and Wedgwood's hope reflect a commonly held and openly discussed concern about the continued close relationship between Coleridge and Wordsworth in 1798. In the following chapters I examine the relationships between Coleridge's and Wordsworth's texts as though they were *"one work,"* or as though they constituted an extended lyric sequence or lyric dialogue. I will concentrate on their poems rather than their lives and personal relationship, which have been discussed in detail before.

Their personal relationship has been explained from two general points of view. The first, suggested by Coleridge himself in the *Biographia Literaria*, presents Wordsworth as temperamentally the poet and Coleridge as the philosopher and literary critic. Discussing his definitions of imagination and fancy, Coleridge contrasted his interests with Wordsworth's in the 1815 preface: "it is my object to investigate the seminal principle, and then from the kind to deduce the degree. My friend has drawn a masterly sketch of the branches with their *poetic* fruitage" (*BL* 1: 88). Recently, Jonathan Wordsworth, in *The Music of Humanity*, argued that before 1798 Coleridge's early philosophical thought, a combination of pantheism and Berkeley's idea of nature's language as divine language, provided Wordsworth with a philosophical basis for his mature nature myth. Coleridge had "evolved a philosophical belief which Wordsworth assimilated" and "had evolved the doctrine of the One Life, and had pointed the way towards *Tintern Abbey.*"[2] Kenneth Johnston, surveying Wordsworth's lifelong efforts to organize and complete *The Recluse*, describes "Wordsworth's respectful and eager attendance upon Coleridge for a set of notes or other direct indication of a philosophical outline to support his 'pictures of Nature, Man, and Society.' "[3]

A second common account of their personal relationship emphasizes Coleridge's myriad of psychological dependencies upon

2. Jonathan Wordsworth, *The Music of Humanity* (London: Nelson, 1969) 193, 199. He has repeated his view of the relationship: "under Coleridge's influence [Wordsworth] went on . . . to assert a universe of blessedness and love, based on the assumption that the individual could perceive as well as share 'the life of things' " (*William Wordsworth: The Borders of Vision* [Oxford: Clarendon Press, 1982] 23). For a critique of Jonathan Wordsworth's thesis in *The Music of Humanity*, see Norman Fruman's *Coleridge, The Damaged Archangel* (New York: Braziller, 1971) 524, where Fruman argues that before Coleridge's close association with Wordsworth, "*nowhere* do we find those beliefs which, at the middle of 1797, flow so abundantly from his pen." See also H. M. Margoliouth, *Wordsworth and Coleridge 1795–1834* (London: Oxford University Press, 1953) 78: "Without Coleridge Wordsworth would have had no philosophy worthy of the name. As Dorothy opened the eye of his imagination to the small and tender, so Coleridge provided that imagination with structure and order."

3. Kenneth R. Johnston, *Wordsworth and "The Recluse"* (New Haven: Yale University Press, 1984) 16. According to Johnston, the philosophy of *The Recluse* is "a version of Kantian idealism as modified by Schelling and other contemporary German philosophers whom Coleridge in turn sought to modify, affected, on the one hand, by his knowledge of Berkeley's still more radical idealism and the Platonic and Neoplatonic traditions, and, on the other, by his always more respectful awareness of the contrary traditions of British empiricism, of which Hartley's efforts to realize moral ideas in the accumulation of random associations of 'vibratiuncles' in the brain was the most significant contemporary British form" (17).

5

stronger persons and his deep need for support and affection within a circle of friends. The origin of this view is also the *Biographia*, in which he presents Wordsworth as the greatest modern poet, one who provided him with the insights to construct a philosophy of literature. It receives support from Coleridge's letters, in which he informs correspondents again and again that Wordsworth is the greater man. In May 1799 Coleridge wrote to Poole from Germany, just having visited with the Wordsworths on their way back to England:

> I told him plainly, that *you* had been the man in whom *first* and in whom alone, I had felt an *anchor*! With all my other Connections I felt a dim sense of insecurity & uncertainty, terribly uncomfortable/—W. was affected to tears, very much affected; but he deemed the vicinity of a Library absolutely *necessary* to his health, nay to his existence. It is painful to me too to think of not living near him; for he is a *good* and *kind* man, & the only one whom in *all* things I feel my Superior—& you will believe me, when I say, that I have few feelings more pleasurable than to find myself in intellectual Faculties an Inferior/ . . . My many weaknesses are of some advantage to me; they unite me more with the great mass of my fellow-beings—but dear Wordsworth appears to me to have hurtfully segregated & isolated his Being. . . . (*STCL* 1: 491)

John Beer presents a sensible account of their relationship and the anxieties that it contained by noting, in reaction to Harold Bloom's theories of the anxiety of influence, that "anxiety can take many forms, and in Coleridge's case it might be said that he suffered less from an anxiety *of* influence than an anxiety *to be* influenced," and that Coleridge's anxiety was a fear of having no support of influence from a stronger individual and artist. But in the years of his greatest creativity, Beer adds, Coleridge was free from such fears.[4] A more radical view of Coleridge's dependencies in all their forms is presented in Norman Fruman's *Coleridge, The Damaged Archangel*, in which he notes that "Coleridge's life is punctuated by his dependence upon some older, or stronger, or more stable personality." Fruman argues that "the influence of Wordsworth on Coleridge's flowering as a great poet is vastly, perhaps incalculably, more important than has hitherto been allowed—not only as to the general contours and terracings of his poetic landscape, but in the minute texture and

4. John Beer, "Coleridge and Wordsworth: Influence and Confluence," *New Approaches to Coleridge: Biographical and Critical Essays*, ed. Donald Sultana (London: Vision Press; Totowa, N.J.: Barnes and Noble, 1981) 193–94.

grain of his language." To illustrate Wordsworth's influence, Fruman cites Wordsworth's substantial contributions to "The Ancient Mariner" and his influence in the purification and simplification of Coleridge's poetic diction.[5] Finally, it is often argued that Coleridge's dependencies made him so weak, and Wordsworth's independence was so determined, that Coleridge was led, in a moment of depression in March 1801, to write to William Godwin that "if I die, and the Booksellers will give you any thing for my Life, be sure to say—'Wordsworth descended on him . . . , by shewing to him what true Poetry was, he made him know, that he himself was no Poet' " (*STCL* 2: 714). A. M. Buchan exaggerates this approach to argue that Wordsworth's egotism and Coleridge's childlike dependence upon Wordsworth killed Coleridge as a poet.[6]

These two common ways of explaining the relationship are each limited by their pursuit of theses that do not require a full accounting of that relationship. Thomas McFarland's "The Symbiosis of Coleridge and Wordsworth" offers at once a more synthetic and a more systematic account, which recognizes the astonishing similarities of their minds while at the same time recognizing their individuality. Their relationship was "nothing less than a symbiosis, a development of attitude so dialogical and intertwined that in some instances not even the participants themselves could discern their respective contributions." The "structure of symbiosis presupposes a principle of opposition or polarity as the very condition of the urge toward submersion and oneness." McFarland suggests that the dialogue works in several ways. Collaboration, the connections of individual poems as answer and response, and the similarity of theme and language in various poems all suppose a oneness of mind and indicate that the dialogue of the poems and critical statements is based upon actual conversations. He implies that their separate poems are thus incarnations or embodiments of original conversations. Their dialogue proceeds by opposition and disagreement,

---

5. Fruman 266–67.

6. A. M. Buchan, "The Influence of Wordsworth on Coleridge (1795–1800)," *University of Toronto Quarterly* 32 (1963): 346–66. Lucy Newlyn has recently examined the relationships between Coleridge and Wordsworth as a dialogue of public and private allusions in which private disagreement is masked by public declarations of fraternal agreement. In her account there is little unanimity of mind and no threat of amalgamation. The two poets are unique individuals, and Wordsworth, she argues, frees himself from Coleridge's influence in the spring of 1798 and becomes the autogenous poet (*Coleridge, Wordsworth, and the Language of Allusion* [Oxford: Clarendon Press, 1986]).

particularly Coleridge's disagreements with Wordsworth's incipient pantheism and critical statements in the preface to *Lyrical Ballads*. McFarland concludes that "if Wordsworth . . . overshadowed the formidable poetical abilities of Coleridge, the latter, for his part, possessed powers of insight and understanding no less indubitably unique than his friend's poetic gifts."[7]

An account of the "fears about amalgamation" in 1798 and later, the concerns about poetic and intellectual resemblances, should be relatively free from speculation about the lives, moods, and experiences of the two poets. The closer one looks at biographical evidence for a mood or experience that generates poetry, the more difficult it is to be certain whether a particular emotion of either joy or anxiety precedes the writing of a particular poem. Of course, poems are written over periods of time with varying moods. What is there, after all, in any one experience of life that determines that a reaction to a powerful event or intellectual insight be expressed in poetry? Why, for instance, when Wordsworth sees an impoverished girl leading a cow along a dusty road to crop in the sparse roadside weeds does he react as a poet and not a political activist? Why does he exalt the solitary instead of the communal figure? There is nothing in any one experience of life that necessarily leads to poetry rather than picketing, philandering, or religious musings. The simple answer to these questions is that Wordsworth reacts as a poet because he is moved by poetry to be a poet; he expresses his reactions to the events of the day and his reflections upon them in the form of

7. Thomas McFarland, "The Symbiosis of Coleridge and Wordsworth," *Studies in Romanticism* 11 (1972): 263–303; revised and expanded in *Romanticism and the Forms of Ruin* (Princeton: Princeton University Press, 1981) 57, 69, 103, from which I quote. McFarland comments that "Wordsworth and Coleridge largely created and also largely extinguished one another as great poets because such a double effect also characterizes the related *aporia* that consists of displacements of poetic energy into philosophical ambitions (*Romanticism and the Forms of Ruin* 224). Harold Bloom, discussing Tennyson's relationship to Keats, has written that "for the post-Enlightenment poet, identity and opposition are the poles set up by the ephebe's self-defining act in which he creates the hypostasis of the precursor as an Imaginary Other. We can agree with Nietzsche that distinction and difference are humanly preferable to identity and opposition as categories of relationship, but unfortunately strong poets are not free to choose the Nietzschean categories in what has been, increasingly, the most competitive and overcrowded of arts" (*Poetry and Repression* [New Haven: Yale University Press, 1976] 145). The dialogue between Coleridge and Wordsworth begins in the recognition that the initial condition of their dialogue is identity and opposition. It continues in the hope, unfulfilled, that it could realize distinction and difference.

poetry that is provided by previous poems. And if Coleridge's poems in 1797 and 1798 convey a consistent tone, either of joy or anxiety, they do not do so because his mood in those months was consistent. Contrast, for example, his mood of April 1797, "On the Saturday, the Sunday, and the ten days after my arrival at Stowey I felt a depression too dreadful to be described . . ." (*STCL* 1: 319), with Dorothy's description of his exuberant spirits during his visit to Racedown in June. "His conversation teems with soul, mind, and spirit. Then he is so benevolent, so good tempered and cheerful, and, like William, interests himself so much about every little trifle," and "has more of the 'poet's eye in a fine frenzy rolling' than I ever witnessed" (*LEY* 188–89). In my account of the relationship between Coleridge and Wordsworth I have avoided the temptation to account for their poetry by reference to a biography of their moods, except as they are defined in the poetry, and I have tried to look steadily at the dialogue that is conducted through their poetry.

There is a strong temptation, given the two poets' long personal association and the details of their relationship that we possess from Dorothy's journals and their letters, to locate their amalgamation and the unanimity of their spirits in their mutual conversations. Many critics suggest that these conversations stand as a kind of pretext or ur-text for their poetry. McFarland puts it this way:

> In the certainty that much more was discussed between the two friends than is explicitly recorded, one is tempted to extend recognition of the symbiosis still further. An ideal understanding of the mutual interaction would have to go beyond verifiable dates and documentary backing, would be to some extent what Friedrich Schlegel called "a divinatory criticism." Such a criticism, however, would not be made up of irresponsible guesses; it would rather entail something of the same process by which an astronomer deduces the presence of a hidden astral body by interpreting variations in the behavior of a celestial object already known.[8]

McFarland's caution about such criticism could be extended to that caution against an attempted reconstruction of the ur-dialogue from the evidence of the poetry. There is little to be gained and much to be risked in any attempt to recapture the letter of that dia-

8. McFarland (*Romanticism and the Forms of Ruin* 83–84) quotes from the Athenaeum Fragments, number 116. A translation is available in *Friedrich Schlegel's "Lucinde" and the Fragments*, trans. Peter Firchow (Minneapolis: University of Minnesota Press, 1971) 175.

logue when what is important is its moving spirit. The literal conversation is not recoverable. There are pitfalls for a reading of the poetry, as well, in attempts to recover a single moving spirit. The writings of each poet—the celestial objects that are known, with their myriad variations—are the evidence of the prime moving spirit of their dialogue, but the variations argue, in this instance, great variation in the motive itself. To try to find a single or unified spirit in a personal psychological motive or in a shared philosophy from such evidence is to generalize or abstract from the evidence itself. The result may be a set of generalizations, true in themselves and sufficient to account for a broad range of themes in poetry but in many instances inadequate to trace the significant variations and subtleties of poetic utterance and poetic form. I have not, therefore, tried to generalize about a moving spirit in their poetic dialogue. I have, rather, tried to trace the variations in apparently similar statements to account for the discontinuities by which such a dialogue generates poetry.

One of the results of such a reading is a recognition that Coleridge's poetry was the prime influence on Wordsworth's from the first days of their association until the winter of 1799–1800, when Wordsworth began to describe himself as a self-generated poet. Coleridge's influence was not only philosophic but poetic. Johnston has explained in great detail the influence that Coleridge had on *The Recluse* and its organization, but in the early years Coleridge's influence was wider than the suggestions that he made about the organization of Wordsworth's major poem; it came, not only from his plans for Wordsworth's poem, but also from the examples of his own poetry. Coleridge was in 1798 and 1799 a more published and more public figure. Wordsworth had published only *An Evening Walk* (1793) and *Descriptive Sketches* (1793), which displayed, as Coleridge noted, true marks of genius but which Wordsworth recognized immediately as immature and awkward, and which he began revising shortly after publication. Coleridge had not only delivered public lectures on politics and religion and started *The Watchman*, he had also published two volumes of poetry, in 1796 and 1797. While Wordsworth had drafted some of his best poetry, he was incapable of bringing it to a form that satisfied him. As William Heath has phrased it, "after all, in 1795 when Coleridge had written 'The Aeolian Harp' Wordsworth was still working on such poems as 'Guilt and Sorrow,' an imitation of Juvenal (Satire VII), and translations from Catullus. 'This Lime-Tree Bower,' 'Frost at Midnight' and

'The Nightingale' all preceded 'Tintern Abbey.' "9 When Words-
worth needed an opinion on "Adventures on Salisbury Plain," he
had the manuscript delivered to Cottle, who, at Wordsworth's re-
quest, delivered it to Coleridge for judgment.[10] Two years later,
when Coleridge wrote to Cottle proposing joint publication, he
wrote "Wordsworth's name is nothing—to a large number of per-
sons mine *stinks*."[11]

With the completion of *The Prelude* (1799), however, Wordsworth
gained confidence and optimism in his poetic prospects. Jonathan
Wordsworth has said accurately that *The Prelude* (1799) "shows
Wordsworth moving away from Coleridge."[12] At this time of great
optimism, Wordsworth began to construct his myth of being a self-
generated poet, of being his own great original, of reaching what
Leslie Brisman has called his "romantic" origins in autogenesis.[13] It
began in *The Prelude* (1799) when Wordsworth acknowledges a
power

at times
Rebellious, acting in a devious mood,

9. William Heath, *Wordsworth and Coleridge: A Study of Their Literary Relations in
1801–1802* (Oxford: Clarendon Press, 1970) 169–70.
10. Bergen Evans and Hester Pinney, "Racedown and the Wordsworths," *Review of
English Studies* 8 (1932): 1–18.
11. *STCL* 1: 412. G. M. Harper explains that "a group of clever young Tory writers,
in *The Anti-Jacobin*, were assailing, amid general applause, the reputation of poets,
orators, and pamphleteers, who had been so imprudent as to favour the Revolution.
... In the issue for July 9, 1798, Coleridge was distinctly mentioned, and Words-
worth probably alluded to, in the scurrilous verses entitled 'New Morality' " (*William
Wordsworth: His Life, Works, and Influence*, 2 vols. [1929; New York: Russell and Rus-
sell, 1960] 1: 277-78).
12. Jonathan Wordsworth and Stephen Gill, "The Two-Part *Prelude* of 1798–99,"
Journal of English and Germanic Philology 72 (1973): 512.
13. Writing of *The Prelude* (1805) I, 640–53, Brisman says that "this is a *romantic*
myth of origins because it is a myth of autogenesis; it is a *myth* of origins because or-
dinary ideas of the power of the past over the present give way to humanized or su-
perhuman abstractions" (*Romantic Origins* [Ithaca: Cornell University Press, 1978]
280). Brisman's account of romantic origins focuses on the myth of autogenesis. Al-
though he mentions that "one idea of the romance of the origin shared by the two
poets is that moments of revelatory conversation can be themselves seminal spots of
time from which invigorating thoughts can be said to date" (278), he does not locate
a possible myth of origin within Coleridge's writing. Wordsworth's myth of origin
may be, not only a substitution for an irretrievable origin or authority, but also a cov-
ering for an origin or beginning in his ventriloquizing of Coleridge's voice. The pas-
sage that Brisman discusses, "Nor will it seem to thee, my Friend! so prompt / In sym-
pathy, that I have lengthened out, / With fond and feeble tongue a tedious tale,"
displaces Coleridge from authority to submissive reader.

A local spirit of its own, at war
With general tendency, but for the most
Subservient strictly to the external things
With which it communed.

(II, 412–17)

Geoffrey Hartman has documented Wordsworth's growing recognition that his imagination was independent of nature and sometimes in conflict with it, and this recognition parallels Wordsworth's claims of independence of Coleridge's poetic influence.[14]

Sections of "Home at Grasmere" that were written in 1800 imply an independence and self-sufficiency, which is explicit in the second part of *The Prelude* (1799), by suggesting that Grasmere is a "Whole without dependence" (168). His blessing is that he shares that independence. In a section of "Home at Grasmere" that may have been written in 1800, although the date is more probably 1806,[15] Wordsworth makes the claim explicitly:

Possessions have I, wholly, solely mine,
Something within, which yet is shared by none—
Not even the nearest to me and most dear—
Something which power and effort may impart.
I would impart it; I would spread it wide,
Immortal in the world which is to come.

(897-902)

If this passage belongs to 1800, it is followed in the same year by the preface to *Lyrical Ballads*, which echoes its claim in the famous definition of poetry as the "spontaneous overflow of powerful feelings." As I have argued in more detail elsewhere, the word "spontaneous" does not mean "unpremeditated," but rather "self-generated" and "without external stimulation."[16]

14. Geoffrey Hartman, *Wordsworth's Poetry, 1787–1814* (New Haven: Yale University Press, 1964). For a contrary view of the mind's relation to nature, see Thomas McFarland's "Romantic Imagination, Nature, and the Pastoral Ideal," *Coleridge's Imagination*, ed. Richard Gravil, Lucy Newlyn, and Nicholas Roe (Cambridge: Cambridge University Press, 1985) 5–21.

15. Jonathan Wordsworth argues that almost all of "Home at Grasmere" was written in 1800 ("On Man, on Nature, and on Human Life," *Review of English Studies* ns 31 [1980]: 28). I quote from Darlington's edition of MS. B.

16. See my "Wordsworth and Spontaneity," *The Evidence of the Imagination: Studies of Interactions between Life and Art in English Romantic Literature*, ed. Donald H. Reiman, Michael C. Jaye, and Betty T. Bennett (New York: New York University Press, 1978) 101–18.

When Wordsworth returned to work on *The Prelude* in the early months of 1804, he added a section to Book III surveying his theme and repeating the claims of his own poetic uniqueness; his theme, he says, is "genius, power, / Creation, and divinity itself," which is,

> in truth heroic argument,
> And genuine prowess—which I wished to touch,
> With hand however weak—but in the main
> It lies far hidden from the reach of words.
> Points have we all of us within our souls
> Where all stand single . . .
>
> *(Prel.* [1805] III,
> 171–72, 182–87)

In the "Essay, Supplementary to the Preface" (1815) Wordsworth defines one quality of genius in words that originally came from Coleridge: "every author, as far as he is great and at the same time *original*, has had the task of *creating* the taste by which he is to be enjoyed."[17] Wordsworth implies that the original poet creates the standards of literature. In the *Biographia* Coleridge acknowledges that originality when he says that he derived some of his literary judgment from Wordsworth, but he says that "to admire on principle, is the only way to imitate without loss of originality" (*BL* 1: 85). "To admire on principle" is to insist that the principles are prior to the poetry, and the poetry is great only insofar as it measures up to the principles that it has established. Coleridge's comment admits only poetry that conforms to principle. It also suggests that Wordsworth's claims of originality are a bit misleading and hide his earlier dependence upon Coleridge's philosophy, encouragement, and most important, as I will show, Coleridge's poetry.

Yet, too, Coleridge's principles for admiration include those of originality. While he offered Wordsworth the rudiments of a philosophical scheme, he also fostered Wordsworth's myth of autogenesis. On January 15, 1804, two weeks after Wordsworth read to him "the second Part of his divine Self-biography" (*CNB* 1: 1801) just before Coleridge left for Malta, Coleridge wrote to Richard Sharp:

> Wordsworth is a Poet, a most original Poet—he no more resembles Milton than Milton resembles Shakespere—no more resembles Shakespere than Shakespere resembles Milton—he is himself: and I dare af-

17. *Prose* 3: 80. Owen states (*Prose* 3: 102) that Wordsworth attributed the thought to Coleridge in a letter of May 21, 1807 (*LMY* 1: 150).

firm that he will hereafter be admitted as the first & greatest
philosophical Poet. . . . (*STCL* 2: 1034)

Coleridge portrays a Wordsworth who is free from any anxiety of
influence in the months in which he begins the major expansion of
The Prelude; Wordsworth's great work is about to be. Coleridge's en-
couragement is a complex gesture of making Wordsworth into the
great poet that he himself had given up hopes of being and in part
of freeing them both from an anxiety of amalgamation.

After Coleridge's departure for Malta in 1804, when Wordsworth
returned to work on *The Prelude* and to his "heroic argument,"
Wordsworth read his previous work as the exploration of his "ge-
nius." *Genius* has many meanings throughout the eighteenth cen-
tury and into the early nineteenth. To understand the relevance of
Wordsworth's use of it for the dialogue with Coleridge and the
theme of amalgamation, it is helpful to explore just some of them.
One meaning that has received a great deal of commentary and
quotation is Coleridge's in the 1818–19 *Philosophical Lectures*, which
emphasizes the universality of genius and the selflessness of it:

> . . . all genius exists in a participation of a common spirit. In joy indi-
> viduality is lost and it therefore is liveliest in youth. . . . To have a genius
> is to live in the universal, to know no self but that which is reflected not
> only from the faces of all around us, our fellow creatures, but reflected
> from the flowers, the trees, the beasts, yea from the very surface of the
> [*waters and the*] sands of the desert. A man of genius finds a reflex to
> himself, were it only in the mystery of being.

The definition appears in the context of Coleridge's discussion of
Michelangelo and Plato, but as Miss Coburn suggests in a note, he
probably has Shakespeare in mind.[18] Genius is defined by the ideal
that it contemplates, and any intrusion of self is a corruption or dim-
inution of that ideal. In *The Friend* Coleridge defines genius by its
acts: "genius produces the strongest impressions of novelty, while it
rescues the stalest and most admitted truths from the impotence

18. Kathleen Coburn, ed., *The Philosophical Lectures of Samuel Taylor Coleridge* (New
York: Philosophical Library, 1949) 179, 413 n. 10. M. H. Abrams cites this passage in
his explication of the effects of joy in "breaking down the boundaries of the isolated
consciousness" (*Natural Supernaturalism: Tradition and Revolution in Romantic Literature*
[New York: W. W. Norton, 1971] 276). Thomas McFarland discusses the meaning of
genius and its relation to *soul* and individuality in *Originality & Imagination* (Baltimore:
Johns Hopkins University Press, 1985) 181–85.

caused by the very circumstances of their universal admission" (1: 110). It is the creation of newness and novelty that is the polar opposite of the eternally present ideal and acts in dynamic relation with it.

Wordsworth's use of the word in 1804, however, suggests that genius is something other than a "participation of a common spirit"; it is something entirely individual and perhaps close to what Coleridge described in the *Biographia* as the "creative, and self-sufficing power of absolute *Genius*" (*BL* 1: 31), a genius whose self-sufficiency is not an intrusion on the ideal that it contemplates. In 1853 Thomas De Quincey, whose thoughts on genius are surely influenced by both Wordsworth and Coleridge, added to his autobiographical essay "The Nation of London" several notes that emphasize the individuality implied by the word *genius*. First of all, he remarks that "it is clear that from the Roman conception (whencesoever emanating) of the natal Genius, as the secret and central representative of what is most characteristic and individual in the nature of every human being, are derived alike the notion of the *genial* and our modern notion of *genius*." Still stressing the individuality of genius, De Quincey continues: "*genius* differentiates a man from all other men; whereas *talent* is the same in one man as another. . . . In genius . . . no two men were ever duplicates of each other." In words that echo the preface to *Lyrical Ballads*, De Quincey writes that genius "works under a rapture of necessity and spontaneity."[19] Wordsworth's use of the word *genius* in Book III of *The Prelude* to describe the power within "where all stand single" emphasizes the individuality of genius and the generative energy over the qualities of joy and universality which, in different contexts, it often evokes. His use of the word echoes Coleridge's in February 1804 before Coleridge could have seen new work on the extended *Prelude*; Coleridge speaks of Wordsworth's "uniqueness of poetic Genius" (*STCL* 2: 1065). In "Tintern Abbey" when Wordsworth fears the loss of his "genial spirits" he is as much concerned with his poetic individuality and ability to generate more poetry as he is with his ability to participate in a common joy. Similarly, when Coleridge laments the loss of his "genial spirits" in "Dejection: An Ode," he admits that his poetic originality is at stake. In their poetic dialogue each struggles to preserve

19. *The Collected Writings of Thomas De Quincey*, ed. David Masson, 14 vols. (1889) 1: 195.

his "genial spirits" as the saving generative energy that would alleviate fears of amalgamation.

In exploring their poetic dialogue, I have followed the suggestion made to Cottle, with which Wordsworth perhaps agreed, that their poems may be read as *"one work . . . as an Ode is one work."* Coleridge wrote in the dedicatory letter to Thomas Poole for the "Ode to the Departing Year" that "impetuosity of Transition, and the Precipitation of Fancy and Feeling . . . are the *essential* excellencies of the sublimer Ode" (*CPW* 2: 1113–14). Wordsworth defined it exactly the same way in an 1800 note to "Tintern Abbey": "I have not ventured to call this Poem an Ode; but it was written with a hope that in the transitions, and the impassioned music of the versification, would be found the principal requisites of that species of composition" (*WPW* 2: 517). Hugh Blair, whose *Lectures on Rhetoric and Belles Lettres* (1783) Coleridge borrowed from the Bristol Library four months before he offered their poetry to Cottle as one work,[20] defines the ode as verses "intended to be sung, or accompanied with music," and "in the Ode, therefore, Poetry retains its first and most antient form." Blair notes that the ode is not defined by its subject matter: "I know no distinction of subject that belongs to it, except that other Poems are often employed in the recital of actions, whereas sentiments, of one kind or other, form, almost always, the subject of the Ode," which sounds very much like Wordsworth's statement in the preface to *Lyrical Ballads* that "the feeling therein developed gives importance to the action and situation, and not the action and situation to the feeling" (*Prose* 1: 129). The ode, then, to Blair is categorized generally as the original lyric form. Its "peculiar character" is derived from its association with music and from "the enthusiasm that belongs to it, and the liberties it is allowed to take, beyond any other species of Poetry. Hence, that neglect of regularity, those digressions, and that disorder which it is supposed to admit; and which, indeed, most Lyric Poets have not failed sufficiently to exemplify in their practice." Blair's rationalizing temperament leads him to caution against the wildness of the form. The poet

is in great hazard of becoming extravagant. The licentiousness of writing without order, method, or connection, has infected the Ode more

20. George Whalley, "The Bristol Library Borrowings of Southey and Coleridge, 1793–8," *Library* 4 (1949): 114–31. Coleridge took out the second volume of Blair's *Lectures*, from which all the following quotations are taken, from January 29 until February 26, 1798.

than any other species of Poetry. Hence, in the class of Heroic Odes, we find so few that one can read with pleasure. The Poet is out of sight, in a moment. He gets up into the clouds; becomes so abrupt in his transitions; so eccentric and irregular in his motions, and of course so obscure, that we essay in vain to follow him, or to partake his raptures.[21]

In the extravagance that Blair found in abrupt transitions, Coleridge and Wordsworth found the essential qualities of the ode.

Martin Price calls attention to Cowley's similar explanation of the form. In his notes to his paraphrase of Isaiah, Cowley describes the ode:

The manner of the *Prophets* writing, especially of *Isaiah*, seems to me very like that of *Pindar*; they pass from one thing to another with almost *Invisible connexions*, and are full of words and expressions of the highest and boldest flights of *Poetry*, as may be seen in this Chapter, where there are as extraordinary Figures as can be found in any *Poet* whatsoever, and the connexion is so difficult, that I am forced to adde a little, and leave out a great deal to make it seem *Sense* to us, who are not used to that elevated way of expression.

Cowley continues that there is

no Transition from the *subject* to the *similitude*; for the old fashion of writing was like *Disputing* in *Enthymemes*, where half is left out to be supplyed by the Hearer; ours is like *Syllogisms*, where all that is meant is exprest.[22]

Coleridge's equivalent formulation draws upon the ancient writers and his schoolmaster Bowyer: "Poetry, even that of the loftiest, and, seemingly, that of the wildest odes, had a logic of its own, as severe as that of science; and more difficult, because more subtle, more complex, and dependent upon more, and more fugitive causes" (*BL* 1: 9). For Coleridge the logic of figurative language and the logic of poetic structure and transitions is not merely a matter of abbreviated logic; poetry has a logic all its own.

Coleridge's application of the characteristics of the ode to their entire work covers proposed publications, not only of *Lyrical Ballads*, but also of their plays, the Salisbury Plain poems, and their other

21. Hugh Blair, *Lectures on Rhetoric and Belles Lettres*, 2 vols. (1783; Carbondale: Southern Illinois University Press, 1965) 2: 353–56.

22. Martin Price, "The Sublime Poem: Pictures and Powers," *Yale Review* ns 58 (1968–69): 206.

works to the spring of 1798. His remark to Cottle was prophetic, because their subsequent work through 1802 may be read in the same way, and I have regarded their work as capable of such a reading. It is a method of reading that imagines a canon based upon a chronology of writing and publication, somewhat like that presented for Wordsworth in Mark Reed's two volumes of Wordsworth chronology. The Coleridge-Wordsworth canon includes, not only what are usually considered completed and separate poems, but also early versions, fragments, canceled drafts, and poems in progress, such as the new texts currently being published in the Cornell Wordsworth series. All are parts or fragments of a poetic dialogue or poetic dialectic, if that word is understood in its loosest sense and does not imply a logical or linear progress. Each poem or fragment in the dialogue takes its significance from its surrounding context. Whatever its explicit subject, whether the injustice of human suffering, the simple joys of nature, or the more sublime moments of imaginative illumination and recognition, each part of the dialogue has an implicit subject in the intertexts of the dialogue and the problems of amalgamation. The context of each part is the poetry previously written, whether in rough draft or in finished form. The context also may be the form and order in which a poem is first published, the surrounding poems in the volume. At times the subject may be its own first draft or another version of the same episode, as the "Home at Grasmere" lines on the visit to Hart-Leap Well and "Hart-Leap Well," published in the second volume of *Lyrical Ballads* (1800). A dialogic reading sees a Coleridge-Wordsworth canon as a single work. Reading only Coleridge's poetry or only Wordsworth's is somewhat like listening to half a telephone conversation. One gets the general drift of what is being said but misses the particular references and the subtleties of the dialogue.

Their dialogic poetic sequence proceeds by the abrupt transitions that are characteristic of the ode, the turns that are the tropes of form. The etymological origin of *verse* is, of course, *versus* and indicates, quite simply, a turn from what has preceded. The origin of a verse is in its turn from a previous one. In general, the dialogue proceeds by opposition. A later poem or fragment turns abruptly in some important respect from a preceding one. Sometimes, as in the dialogue on dejection in the spring of 1802, the connections among poems and drafts are obvious. They work by the commonly recognized and traditionally valued presence of quotation, allusion, and echo to point to their sources in earlier works. At other times, however, the connections are, as Coleridge said, "more fugitive," depending on the appropriation and transformation of figures, such as Coleridge's use of Margaret's wandering from her cottage in "The Ruined Cottage" for the figure of Christabel's wandering from her castle to pray in the midnight woods. Also, works that often appear at a quick glance to possess a similar theme turn out, upon close examination, to present important differences that emphasize the turns and opposition. Thus, identifying a source or origin for any particular part of the dialogue may involve, not only the discovery of a work that it most resembles, but also a discovery of that with which it may have major differences. Once a poetic dialogue begins (and it may be impossible to identify its precise point of beginning), it proceeds by turns that imply opposition and defy logical representation.

The Coleridge-Wordsworth dialogue is similar to the "double-voiced discourse" described by Mikhail Bakhtin: discourse is "directed both toward the referential object of speech, as in ordinary discourse, and toward *another's discourse*, toward *someone else's speech*."[23] Bakhtin grounds his dialogics on what he calls "metalinguistics" (202), meaning actual dialogic utterances, not a system of language. My dialogic reading shares with Bakhtin's an emphasis on actual utterance, but it is constructed on the formal principles of lyric turn, transition, and sequence. Thus it presents a different view of lyric poetry than Bakhtin's description of poetry as "monologic." My dialogic reading does not employ parody or carnivalization for its progress; to do so, for both poets, would be to resign a voice in their dialogue. The Coleridge-Wordsworth dialogue begins with the threat of amalgamation, which Bakhtin calls "imitation" and which, he writes, "takes the limited material seriously, makes it its own, directly appropriates to itself someone else's discourse. What happens in that case is a complete merging of voices, and if we

---

23. Mikhail Bakhtin, *Problems of Dostoevsky's Poetics*, ed. and trans. Caryl Emerson (Minneapolis: University of Minnesota Press, 1984) 185. As Bakhtin says, dialogue is different from dialectic, which tends to be monologic and moves toward philosophical conclusion: lyric dialogue is dialogic in Bakhtin's sense that "*nothing conclusive has yet taken place in the world, the ultimate word of the world and about the world has not yet been spoken, the world is open and free, everything is still in the future and will always be in the future*" (166). M. L. Rosenthal and Sally Gall have described the modern lyric and the lyric sequence in somewhat similar terms: "*its object is neither to resolve a problem nor to conclude an action but to achieve the keenest, most open realization possible*" (*The Modern Poetic Sequence: The Genius of Modern Poetry* [New York: Oxford University Press, 1983] 11).

do hear another's voice, then it is certainly not one that had figured in to the imitator's plan" (190). The lyric dialogue is what Bakhtin categorizes as active, the "reflected discourse of another" (199), a "hidden dialogicality": "Imagine a dialogue of two persons in which the statements of the second speaker are omitted, but in such a way that the general sense is not at all violated. The second speaker is present invisibly, his words are not there, but deep traces left by these words have a determining influence on all the present and visible words of the first speaker. We sense that this is a conversation . . ." (197).

I have mapped some connections that define the dialogue while at the same time emphasizing the turns that generate the dialogue. Many of the works that I discuss have been considered canonical since their first publication, and in many instances I have used the earliest versions of them, which are infrequently, if ever, read. In other instances I have emphasized minor poems, fragments, and discarded or unused drafts because they often reveal, in ways that published and public poems do not, a greater degree of meditation upon the process of writing itself, the difficulties and impediments that arise in their dialogue, and the occasions for the "fears about amalgamation." Wordsworth's early drafts, in particular, reveal their origins in their repeated quotation and allusion to Coleridge's published poetry, origins that are obscured by later drafts that seem almost designed to hide their beginnings in Coleridge's poetry.

A dialogic reading shifts some emphases in their canon. "Home at Grasmere," to some merely an indication of Wordsworth's wisdom in not publishing it, assumes a crucial role as a response to Coleridge's earlier "Reflections on Having Left a Place of Retirement" and as the text upon which the opening stanzas of "The Immortality Ode" turn. In a similar way, Wordsworth's first version of "The Discharged Soldier" becomes important as his first and best response to "The Rime of the Ancient Mariner." Other poems often identified as responses to "The Ancient Mariner," notably "Peter Bell," have been discussed in criticism, but as John Jordan has said, "Peter Bell" did not begin as an answer to Coleridge's poem.[24] Al-

24. Jordan has written that "the poem did not start as a serious counter–*Ancient Mariner* and degenerate into the comic, as Harper speculated. Nor, I think, did it start as a denial of the supernatural in the *Ancient Mariner*" ("The Hewing of *Peter Bell*," *Studies in English Literature* 7 [1967]: 560). He has reiterated his opinion in "Wordsworth's Most Wonderful as Well as Admirable Poem," *The Wordsworth Circle* 10 (1979): 49–58, and in his introduction to *Peter Bell* (Ithaca: Cornell University

though Coleridge's comment to Cottle was offered at the time the first volume of *Lyrical Ballads* was organized, I have not considered that volume of major significance in the dialogue, except for "Tintern Abbey," because, first, the major poetry written at the time the shorter ballads were written is of vastly greater importance, and, second, because the volume was not generative of further poetry; the ballads themselves are not as influential in the writing of later poetry as "The Ruined Cottage" and "The Pedlar" are. The second volume of *Lyrical Ballads*, however, is of major importance, because Coleridge is excluded and because it contains one of the greatest poems generated by its context, "Michael." I do not pretend to have mapped the entire dialogue, nor even all of its most important parts; I have, rather, attempted to touch some of its most important points and to illustrate some of the methods by which it turns and proceeds.

There are a variety of ways in which the dialogue turns upon itself. All involve, in one way or another, some form of opposition or interruption, and many are found in combination. Single moments of redirection may turn upon several texts, both from the poet's own work and the work of the other poet. Both poets allude to their own work throughout their career. Although I have not emphasized those allusions, since they are often a large part of other critical studies, I have noted that Wordsworth begins, in about 1800, to allude increasingly to his own poetry rather than to Coleridge's, when he feels that he has become the self-generated poet that Coleridge encouraged him to be. Insofar as turns indicate opposition, they come close to what Paul Fry has called the figure of irony, "the figure of thought (which subverts *itself*),"[25] except that the dialogue progresses as it revises its earlier texts, so that subversion—which in a reading of isolated, integral poems may lead to a fatal reduction in

Press, 1985) 20. Mary Jacobus has described the differences between "The Ancient Mariner" and "Peter Bell" as "Coleridge's imaginativeness versus Wordsworth's own matter-of-factness" and noted that the tone of "Peter Bell" suggests that Wordsworth "must at some level have realized that he had been left behind because he was less inspired" (*"Peter Bell* the First," *Essays in Criticism* 24 [1974]: 221).

25. Paul H. Fry, *The Poet's Calling in the English Ode* (New Haven: Yale University Press, 1980) 11. Fry, following Kenneth Burke, equates irony with dialectic (10). In my dialogic reading of Wordsworth's and Coleridge's poetry, subversion is enacted by transition that subverts by rendering an utterance transient. It is a shift from "I feel" to "I felt" rather than a logical denial of the former utterance or a simultaneous denial embedded in a positive utterance. I emphasize the theme of the transience of utterance in Chapter 8.

a poem's initial aspiration—may have a more generative function in the progress of further writing. The varieties discussed below are not intended to be a complete anatomy of possible turns but are simply intended to identify some basic forms, derived from an examination of the poetry, in order to raise some particular problems in the conduct of the dialogue.

The basic form of turn is that of negation or denial, in which the previous text is denied and an alternative offered. It is common in Wordsworth's revisions of his own work. For example, the ending of "Adventures on Salisbury Plain" presents a picture of legalized injustice:

> They left him hung on high in iron case,
> And dissolute men, unthinking and untaught,
> Planted their festive booths beneath his face;
> And to that spot, which idle thousands sought,
> Women and children were by fathers brought;
> And now some kindred sufferer driven, perchance,
> That way when into storm the sky is wrought,
> Upon his swinging corpse his eye may glance
> And drop, as he once dropp'd, in miserable trance.
>
> (*SPP* 154)

The ending of "Guilt and Sorrow" apologizes to the reader for a text to which the reader has no access:

> His fate was pitied. Him in iron case
> (Reader, forgive the intolerable thought)
> They hung not:—no one on *his* form or face
> Could gaze, as on a show by idlers sought;
> No kindred sufferer, to his death-place brought
> By lawless curiosity or chance,
> When into storm the evening sky is wrought,
> Upon his swinging corse an eye can glance,
> And drop, as he once dropped, in miserable trance.
>
> (*SPP* 281–83)

This conclusion is pointless in the context of "Guilt and Sorrow." It serves no purpose whatever in discussion of the sailor's fate. Its sole purpose is for Wordsworth to deny a text that he had previously composed. Coleridge's verse letter to Sara Hutchinson—his response to the opening stanzas of Wordsworth's "Immortality Ode," and the first version of "Dejection: An Ode"—contains several examples of negation and denial that do not use a negative explicitly but clearly involve a denial of Wordsworth's argument. Wordsworth complains that he cannot see what he has seen in the past, and Coleridge counters, "I see, not feel. . . ." Sight thus is of less importance than feeling, the absence of which, to Coleridge, defines dejection. Also, Wordsworth implies that nature has a life of its own, which at one time he could see, and Coleridge again counters with "We receive but what we give. . . ." Explicit or implicit denial is more frequent after 1800, as Coleridge begins to realize that his differences with Wordsworth are greater than before. Negation, however, is never simple denial or skeptical qualification. Michael Cooke has explained Wordsworth's use of negation and litotes. His poetry often "admits, as it denies, the negative possibility; it incorporates potential resistance and rejection in a controlled innocuous form."[26] Doubt is presented only to be overcome within his poetry, but the negation or double negation that signifies a turn within Wordsworth's poetry also signals a turn in the Coleridge-Wordsworth dialogue. Doubt leads to the formulation of counterstatements.

A second common turning point is the question. Wordsworth begins his drafts of *The Prelude* with the question "Was it for this . . . ?" that turns from the previous retrospective poetry in "Tintern Abbey" and "Frost at Midnight" and is followed by the negation of the implied doubt, "Not in vain." Questions may also mark a temporary halt of work on a particular poem, such as the "Whither has fled . . . ?" which comes at the end of the opening stanzas of "The Immortality Ode." As such, it is similar to aposiopesis, the breaking off of a statement because the speaker is unwilling or unable to go on. In "The Immortality Ode" it does not indicate that the speaker is overwhelmed with emotion, as is often the case with aposiopesis, but

---

26. Michael Cooke, "The Mode of Argument in Wordsworth's Poetry," *Acts of Inclusion: Studies Bearing on an Elementary Theory of Romanticism* (New Haven: Yale University Press, 1979) 198. Cooke responds to John Jones's complaint that "Wordsworth carries his delight in negatives to the point of tiresome mannerisms: there are too many double negatives" (*The Egotistical Sublime* [London: Chatto and Windus, 1954] 204). In a review of Harold Bloom's *The Anxiety of Influence* (1973), Thomas Weiskel suggested that the revisionary ratios could be applied to individual poems and the strategies that they use to swerve from their beginnings through forms of apparent negation (*The Wordsworth Circle* 4 [1973]: 181–82). More recently, Tilottama Rajan has written that "the reexamination thus undertaken by the Romantic mind is dialectical in form, in that it uses a process of constant self-negation to generate a momentum toward synthesis" (*The Dark Interpreter: The Discourse of Romanticism* [Ithaca: Cornell University Press, 1980] 29).

rather a confusion of mind when the question recurs at the moment of rejoicing, which it interrupts. A third example comes from the second book of *The Prelude* (1799), when Wordsworth begins to classify his early experiences upon a chronological pattern and then asks, "But who shall parcel out / His intellect by geometric rules . . . ?" The question introduces a radical revision of his presentation of childhood's influence on the poet's imagination as outlined in the first book. This question interrupts the formation of his argument and sets it in a new direction. A similar redirecting occurs in Coleridge's "The Eolian Harp" when he asks, "And what if all of animated nature . . . ?" and in the elegiac "Ah fair Remembrances . . . Where were they?" of the verse letter to Sara Hutchinson.

There are other generative questions within Coleridge's narrative poetry that, as the dialogue shows, apply to Wordsworth's poetry as well. The hermit's question to the mariner, "What manner of man art thou?" and Christabel's similar question to Geraldine, "And who art thou?" both inquire about the presences of figures who cannot be accounted for, whose presence is inexplicable. In a dialogic reading these questions are, not merely a mark of the meeting between common sense and the supernatural, but a questioning of the figures in Wordsworth's poetry and the naturalism with which they are presented. They redirect the context in which they appear. Wordsworth's work on "The Ruined Cottage" and the Pedlar extension done just before Coleridge wrote the first part of "Christabel" had insisted that the Pedlar could "see around me . . . / Things which you cannot see" (Butler 48). That which his worthy eye could see are the "spiritual presences of absent things" (Butler 263). The hermit's and Christabel's questions are certainly the baffled and credulous confusions of the innocent, but they are also questions that challenge Wordsworth's confidence that nature and the figures of landscape can be read with a worthy eye. Coleridge's "Christabel" and Wordsworth's "The Discharged Soldier" are, in part, responses to such questions, which interrupt the calm assurances of the texts to which they respond.

The turns of negation or questioning occur at the borders of poems or fragments to mark their boundaries or at an important turning point within a single poem that marks an abrupt change of mood or thought. There are three other kinds of turn that are not as literally dialogic. They occur within texts when individual figures or structural principles are created to differ from figures and structures of previous poems or fragments. The first of these in the Coleridge-Wordsworth dialogue is best called reduction or exclusion. I do not use the term *reduction* in Kenneth Burke's sense of metonymy, in which the large is reduced in scale, but in a sense closer to Harold Bloom's, in which metonymy is associated with isolation and regression.[27] It is an exclusion of possible counterstatements, a limitation of subject matter that reduces its scope for the purpose of claiming that the reduced ground includes all necessary reference and perfection. Wordsworth's "Home at Grasmere" is such a work in relation to his own previous work on *The Prelude* and to Coleridge's personal and poetic involvement in public affairs, as well as his encouragement to Wordsworth to write the great philosophical poem. There is an exclusion associated with his limitation: "By such forgetfulness the soul becomes— / Words cannot say, how beautiful" (Darlington 62), a regression, perhaps, to the "wise passiveness" of the early lyrical ballads. All that tends to disrupt the peace of seclusion is kept beyond the borders of Grasmere, yet the figures that are excluded always threaten to intrude with their blessings and the consciousness of a world vastly more complex. A somewhat similar reduction comes in Coleridge's verse letter to Sara Hutchinson, in which he views his, at times, voluntary exclusion from the Wordsworth circle, which he sees existing as the perfect unity that Wordsworth anticipated in "Home at Grasmere." His exclusion is not, like Wordsworth's, a determined reduction to simplify and find perfection but is rather less regressive. Laboring under the burden of depression, he struggles to find a voice that can still utter a blessing on those distant from him, even though he is forced to acknowledge a loss of imagination. A somewhat similar reduction comes in Coleridge's letter to John Thelwall of December 17, 1800, after "Christabel" had been excluded from the second volume of *Lyrical Ballads*:

27. Kenneth Burke, *A Grammar of Motives* (1945; Berkeley: University of California Press, 1969) 503–6; Harold Bloom, *A Map of Misreading* (New York: Oxford University Press, 1975) 84–88. In tracing the dialogue between Coleridge and Wordsworth, I am less concerned with tropes or turns as psychic defense mechanisms used by a younger poet to defend himself against the intimidating presence of a precursor, whose work is completed, and more concerned with what John Hollander has called "tropes of form," "an ambiguous phrase" that may refer to "the underlying trope of structural strangeness itself" ("Poetic Misprision," rev. of *A Map of Misreading*, by Harold Bloom, *Poetry* 127 [1976]: 231). In a dialogic reading, the strangeness of the turn or trope is, not only in the illogic of its abrupt transitions, but also in its conspiracy with time that renders a present utterance a thing of the past. By replacing one utterance with another, poetic form tends to limit poems as fragmentary at the same time that it generates further utterances.

"As to Poetry, I have altogether abandoned it, being convinced that I never had the essentials of poetic Genius, & that I mistook a strong desire for original power" (*STCL* 1: 656).

Perhaps the most common act in the dialogue is the appropriation and relocation of a fragment or figure. Often the original text is itself a fragment or canceled draft or a part of a work in progress that as yet has no conclusion or clear direction. "The Ancient Mariner" appropriates lines from the Salisbury Plain poems; Wordsworth's "The Discharged Soldier" reappropriates the figure of the mariner before "The Ancient Mariner" is completed. Relocation revises the figure by placing it within a new context, by situating it within a new landscape and thereby changing its significance. When the originating text is a completed or published poem within the larger context of its publication, the appropriation selects only parts for relocation. Wordsworth's appropriation of lines and figures from Coleridge's Conversation Poems does not imply a use of their entire structure but only of sections of them as though they were fragments. In all relocation there is a strong revisionary impulse to complete a fragment whose direction is unclear. The transformation assumes a different form than Bloom's account of the anxiety of influence because the text upon which these two poets turn is not a complete poem of a precursor, who stands as a father figure and original. It is not based upon the relationship of generations in which priority is easy to assign, for who can claim priority when the beginning is in an ambiguous sketch? The author of the fragment, or the author who brings it to a more perfect form? And is the revision based on a fragment a re-vision of what has been seen before or something seen for the first time? Answers may be possible in a more broadly diachronic reading of literary history.

Finally, the dialogue continues by the tactic of reiteration or reverberation, the insistent return to one theme, or figure, from an earlier period of the dialogue presented in a slightly different form dictated by the present context. By reverberation I do not mean precisely what John Hollander means by echo, which always returns only a fragment of the original, although that is often the case in this dialogue.[28] It is similar to the familiar Wordsworthian repetition and in many instances involves a deafness to what is being said in the present dialogue. Wordsworth's continued and reiterated theme of

28. John Hollander, *The Figure of Echo: A Mode of Allusion in Milton and After* (Berkeley: University of California Press, 1981).

26

the One Life in the face of Coleridge's implicit criticism of it is one example. At points, Wordsworth seems to have forsaken it for a theory in which mind alone is creative. A second example comes in the spring of 1798, when the amalgamation of the two is the closest, when Coleridge begins to question deeply the articulation of nature and likens it to human language and Wordsworth continues for some time not to hear Coleridge's questions and continues to write of nature's language as inarticulate and without the associations of a human language. Reverberation occurs also within an individual poem as repetition or tautology when there is an absence or silence from the failure of language to articulate or from a failure of original sensation from nature or of responding voices in the dialogue. In such instances reverberation is always self-echo, but there are obviously cases in which one poet echoes the other in which the echo is fragmentary and in which reverberation is similar to appropriation and relocation.

A dialogic reading of the Coleridge-Wordsworth canon must view all the individual poems as parts of the larger whole, and in this sense they are all fragments whether they are canceled drafts of five or six lines or longer completed poems. The borders of individual poems are not fixed, particularly with Wordsworth's continuous practice of rewriting, recomposing, and rearranging his lyric fragments. Similarly, what are usually considered individual poems cannot be considered discrete units or integral wholes, since they may have been generated by a previous fragment and may be fragmentary themselves at the moments of their strongest influence in the dialogue. In the context of a continuous dialogue, the individual fragments may be viewed, not only as fragments of a ruined past or pieces of an unreachable ideal, but as parts of a poetic canon evermore about to be, as parts of a generative process.

The location of a fragment within the dialogue is crucial. A dialogic reading must ask not only What does it mean? or What are its affects? but Where is it, and when? and in the case of later editions, Who put it there? Poems have significance, not only in themselves, but also in relation to their surrounding texts, and among those contexts there are many possibilities. What, for instance, is the proper context for "Tintern Abbey"? In what ways is it an appropriate concluding poem for the first volume of *Lyrical Ballads*? What is its significance as the concluding poem in the first volume, when it becomes the turning point to the second volume? What is its significance as a commentary upon "Frost at Midnight," which provides its structure, and for "The Pedlar," which precedes it as Wordsworth's first autobiographical writing? What is its relationship to the early work on *The Prelude* done shortly after? It does not exist in glorious isolation from other works; its borders blend with those of poems it echoes and anticipates, and its resolutions are undone by work that follows.

A radical implication of a dialogic reading insists that individual poems or individual lyric effusions have no meaning in themselves, any more than an individual stanza within an ode or other lyric has meaning in itself, and that significance shifts according to the placement within the lyric. Wordsworth's shuffling and reforming of *The Prelude* material reveals that he realized this. His changing of the context for the "spots of time" passages is only one of the relocations of lyric moments. There are many others. In February 1799 he reflected upon his work to date on the drafts of what was to become *The Prelude*, most of which included childhood recollections and a questioning of their influence:

> Scattering thus
> In passion many a desultory sound,
> I deemed that I had adequately cloathed
> Meanings at which I hardly hinted, thoughts
> And forms of which I scarcely had produced
> A monument and arbitrary sign.
>
> (*Prel.* 495)

His answer to this recognition follows in a second fragment and proposes that the solution to the inadequacy of his "memorials" is the "considerate and laborious work" that provides those fragments with an organization and a context, "Outline and substance, even till it has given / A function kindred to organic power— / The vital spirit of perfect form."[29] Fragments have their meanings only within a poetic "perfect form," and as a result, Wordsworth's work in writing was as much a concern with organization and composition as it was with drafting the spontaneous lyric moments.

The methodology of a dialogic reading underlines a problem of reading in general. If the context grants and determines meaning, then the contrary is also true. The determination of context locates a fragment or poem as a former utterance upon which a later one turns, and to turn from a former utterance is necessarily to limit it

29. See Parrish 163.

and to acknowledge its inadequacy and fragmentary nature. In both individual poems, especially those constructed upon the model of the ode, and in the dialogue as a whole, the turn emphasizes the transient quality of the former utterance; it tends toward illusion in the light of the later utterance. The wild speculation at the beginning of "Religious Musings" and the confident enthusiasm of the opening of "Home at Grasmere" take advantage of the license granted by poetic form and sequence to indulge an extravagant set of hopes. When it is applied to a sequence, lyric form permits individual poems to modify their initial aspirations and permits one poem to turn upon another, which places an utterance in the past and thereby renders it no longer completely true. The urgency of the "timely utterance" in "The Immortality Ode" and Coleridge's responding struggle to utter a blessing with the knowledge and fear of its transience both reflect an awareness of the transience of utterance, which in a poetic dialogue is the temporal equivalent of a fragmentation of spatial or structural form.

The paradoxical implications of location within the dialogue that gives meaning and at the same time qualifies it as approaching fiction do not mean that the dialogue has no meaning or that the sequence becomes a succession of meaningless utterances or a confusion of momentary illusions. It is difficult, after all, to conduct a dialogue with illusions or with statements that have no meaning whatever. A dialogic reading must take account of theme and trace the shifting focus on theme, both as literal statement and as fiction and figure. I have discussed the themes of parts of the dialogue, not as they appear in isolated works, but as they are defined by the surrounding dialogue, although I have not attempted to give either full readings of poems or readings of full poems.

A further implication of a dialogic reading, or any reading that regards a continuous canon as a succession of lyrics, is the presence of new beginnings. The closer one looks at the turns of dialogue, the more difficult it is to identify one text or one moment in which major works begin.[30] Does *The Prelude* have its beginnings in Wordsworth's determination in the spring of 1798 to write a major work called *The Recluse* or in his drafting lines describing the history of the

30. Edward Said has written that "the designation of a beginning generally involves the designation of a consequent *intention*," and he defines "intention" as "a notion that includes everything that later develops out of it, no matter how eccentric the development or inconsistent the result" (*Beginnings: Intention and Method* [New York: Basic Books, 1975] 5, 12).

29

Pedlar, which were later included in *The Prelude*? Or does it begin with the Goslar drafts, or with childhood recollections that form a sequence? Or does it begin in the winter and spring of 1799, when Wordsworth forms these fragments into a more perfect form and when, at the same time, intention seems unclear? Or does it begin when he extends the drafts into a second part in the fall of 1799? Speculation delights in these questions, but they are so complex and the evidence of intention is so obscure that they are probably unanswerable. Not only is it difficult to identify the one moment in which Wordsworth intends the structure of *The Prelude*, its later sections bear such a radically revisionary relationship to earlier sections that they appear to be new beginnings. In Book II, the passage on the blessed babe argues against Book I that the child is not an outcast in the world and that the origins of love and imagination reside with the mother, not nature, which becomes secondary. Structure and intention change in works in progress. Is "The Ancient Mariner" the same poem in 1817 as it was in 1798? Is it an extension and elaboration of the original or a departure from it? Is "Frost at Midnight" the same poem in 1817 when Coleridge returns from the excursion into his past to a "deep calm" as when he returned in 1798 to a "dead calm"? In light of the revisions and changes in direction, it is difficult to argue that the organic metaphor of development, in which the end is implied in the beginning, is of much use.

Although a dialogic reading is grounded in chronology, it escapes being rigidly or reductively linear through reverberation, reiteration, and the rearrangement of texts. In addition, there are times when there are two voices speaking simultaneously. The early months of 1798, when Wordsworth was working on "The Ruined Cottage" and the history of the Pedlar and when Coleridge was writing "Frost at Midnight," "The Nightingale," and "Christabel," the time of their closest amalgamation, is the most important instance of the simultaneity of their voices. In many instances it is impossible to determine who first drafted passages that echo in their poetry. On the one hand, it is a question of the sufficiency of our knowledge of chronology. If only we had more information on the dates of composition, if only Dorothy's journal recorded the precise dates that lines were drafted, we would be able to be more precise on the generative process. But, on the other hand, even if there were such a precise chronology, the time it takes to develop a fragment, to locate it, and to assimilate it into consciousness obviates a strict linear chronology. The chronology of texts does not form a simple plot by cause and effect but remains a sequence of lyric moments and beginnings. The Coleridge poetry that Wordsworth uses in the spring of 1798 is to a large extent the works that he had known in the previous year, "The Eolian Harp," and "This Lime-Tree Bower," not the contemporaneous "Frost at Midnight," although it is so close to his own work on the Pedlar. He seemed unaware of the ways in which "Frost at Midnight" questioned the influence of childhood; only when he came to write "Tintern Abbey" months later did he respond to "Frost at Midnight."

Finally, important lyrics by both poets appear to duplicate their dialogue within individual poems. Criticism has agreed to call Coleridge's most Wordsworthian poems the Conversation Poems, and Wordsworth felt the necessity of addressing his most important poems to Dorothy or Coleridge. Before its publication *The Prelude* was known in the Wordsworth circle as "the poem to Coleridge." These instances suggest a vital and dynamic relationship between speaker and auditor in the poems, but the most important auditor is the speaker himself. The acts prior to speaking and writing are listening and reading, and the responding poetry often interrupts what it hears. Coleridge read Wordsworth's poetry before he met Wordsworth and their dialogue began; Wordsworth read his poetry to Coleridge at their first meeting and later sent Coleridge his manuscripts.

If writing is a dialogic act, the Coleridge-Wordsworth dialogue points to a paradox in the use of the word *genius*. It must be individual, but it cannot be private. De Quincey insists that genius is always individual and traces its origin to the Roman idea of the natal genius. When Wordsworth uses the term in Book III of *The Prelude* and "Home at Grasmere" he is speaking of a private possession, something uniquely his. Read in the context of Wordsworth's poetry, such claims for individual genius indicate a new-found confidence. When they are read in the context of the continuing dialogue with Coleridge, however, they allude to the influence of Coleridge's poetry and intend to deny that his poetry is generated in response to Coleridge's. Mikhail Bakhtin also traces the word *genius* to its Roman use in the *prodigia*, or omens, of autobiography and finds that it is always associated with public deeds. Thus "an unrecognized genius was a *contradictio in adjecto*," a contradiction in terms.[31] There

---

31. *The Dialogic Imagination: Four Essays by M. M. Bakhtin*, ed. Michael Holquist,

cannot be a mute and private genius. Much of the anxiety that Wordsworth felt about his writing came from the fact that much of his early poetry, such as the Salisbury Plain poems, was on public themes but remained private. The paradox suggests that the similar problem of the threat of amalgamation may not be resolved by a turn to pure individuality and genius. There cannot be segregated and isolated utterances. The resolution is the dialogue. Words-worth's claims for pure individuality arise within the course of the dialogue. The dialogue is prior to them and is the enabling condition of their utterance, but it precludes the possibility of their being completely realized. In a reading of the Coleridge-Wordsworth canon, the dialogue itself becomes the important issue.

---

trans. Caryl Emerson and Michael Holquist (Austin: University of Texas Press, 1981) 139.

First Readings:

1793–1797

THE POETIC DIALOGUE between Coleridge and Wordsworth began in earnest in the summer of 1797, when Coleridge visited the Wordsworths at Racedown and arranged, through Thomas Poole, to have the Wordsworths take Alfoxden, a manor house near Nether Stowey, where Coleridge and Poole lived. There had been occasional visits and discussions since their first meeting in August or September 1795, but their poetry did not become mutually influential until their close association in the summer of 1797. Wordsworth's visit to Nether Stowey in the spring of 1797 may have provided him with the opportunity to tell Coleridge about his work on *The Borderers*, which may have influenced Coleridge's *Osorio*, but the documentary evidence of influence is slight. Their independent work in these years, however, is mutually complementary. Both were responding to the political issues raised by the French Revolution, and both took their themes from the plight of the poor and the sufferers. Both aspired to gain a public voice on the issues of the day. They struggled to find an appropriate style within the traditions available to them: the literature of sensibility, the Gothic, and the sublime and visionary poetry of the eighteenth century.

The poetry written before 1797 was important for their later dialogue, not because it was generated in response to earlier poems, but because of Wordsworth's and Coleridge's discovery in 1798 that their poems were complementary. Although "Religious Musings" and *Osorio* were not written in direct response to Wordsworth's Salisbury Plain poems and *The Borderers*, Coleridge knew of them and commented on them. Similarly, Wordsworth commented on Coleridge's poetry, or so Coleridge reported. Their readings in 1798 led to proposals for joint publication in 1798 and to attempts at joint composition. In the failure of their efforts at collaboration on individual poems their dialogue began, with Wordsworth's Salisbury Plain poems leading directly to Coleridge's "The Ancient Mariner."

On March 25, 1796, Azariah Pinney wrote to Wordsworth that he had transmitted Wordsworth's "Adventures on Salisbury Plain" manuscript to the publisher Joseph Cottle and that Cottle in turn had given it to Coleridge, who "interleaved it with white paper to mark down whatever may strike him as worthy your notice and intends forwarding it to you in that form."[1] Pinney implies that he acted on Cottle's, and perhaps Wordsworth's, request to have Coleridge read the manuscript. Plans were made to publish it through the subscription list that Coleridge had compiled for his periodical, *The Watchman*. Wordsworth's desire for a competent reader and a careful criticism before publication originated with his realization that his earlier poems, *An Evening Walk* and *Descriptive Sketches* (1793), suffered from not having such criticism. Before reviews of those poems appeared, Dorothy wrote Jane Pollard: "I regret exceedingly that he did not submit the works to the Inspection of some Friend before their Publication, and he also joins with me in this Regret. Their Faults are such as a young Poet was most likely to fall into and least likely to discover, and what the Suggestions of a Friend would easily have made him see and at once correct."[2]

It is probable that Wordsworth knew of Coleridge's admiration of *An Evening Walk* before he met him in 1795,[3] and when he did meet

1. Bergen Evans and Hester Pinney, "Racedown and the Wordsworths," *Review of English Studies* 8 (1932): 13.

2. *LEY* 89. In the same letter Dorothy says that "My Brother Kitt and I, while he was at Forncett, amused ourselves by analysing every Line and prepared a very bulky Criticism, which he was to transmit to William as soon as he should have [ad]ded to it the [remarks] of his Cambridge Friends." James Averill, the editor of the Cornell Wordsworth edition of *An Evening Walk*, informs me that no record of this criticism survives.

3. Christopher Wordsworth's friendship with Coleridge at Cambridge in 1793 may

him he may have thought of him as the ideal reader that he had been seeking, a critic who could mediate between himself and a reading public, not only as a publicist, as it was later to turn out, but also as a partner in the entire creative effort. Coleridge was to become not only the ideal reader and critic; he was to become the first reader, one who interleaved Wordsworth's poetry with critical commentary and later with his own poetry. In fact, even before he met Wordsworth, Coleridge had woven a number of lines from *An Evening Walk* into his own poetry.[4] Coleridge's enthusiasm for "Salisbury Plain" was immediate in 1795: "There was here, no mark of strained thought, or forced diction, no crowd or turbulence of imagery. . . . The occasional obscurities, which had risen from an imperfect controul over the resources of his native language, had almost wholly disappeared . . ." (*BL* 1: 79). One of the roles that Coleridge filled was that of an editor, alive to style and fully capable of pointing out flaws to a poet who was, perhaps, too inexperienced. But also, since Coleridge later became the first reader of Wordsworth's poems, one can consider the poems to have been written for him. It is not a relationship in which a great original poet has his works edited at points where they are weak and thus retains an unquestioned priority over the editor; it is, rather, a case of a poet and a critic engaging as equals in an unremitting interchange of text with text and of text with criticism.

When Wordsworth selected Coleridge as the ideal reader of "Adventures on Salisbury Plain" in 1796, Coleridge himself had recently completed copy for his volume *Poems on Various Subjects*, published in April (*STCL* 1: 187). While Coleridge immediately became the admiring reader of Wordsworth's poetry, Wordsworth became the admiring reader of Coleridge's as well, particularly "Religious Musings." In spite of their divergent styles, the two poems have similar themes, and although one cannot argue that Coleridge's poem intentionally answers the despair of "Adventures on Salisbury Plain," there are many ways in which it complements that poem.

---

have prompted him to tell William and Dorothy of Coleridge's admiration. See Christopher Wordsworth, *Social Life at the English Universities* (1874) 589. James Averill suggests that Coleridge may have influenced the "bulky Criticism" (*EW* 12).

4. For a summary of Coleridge's borrowings from *An Evening Walk*, see James Averill, "Another Early Coleridge Reference to *An Evening Walk*," *English Language Notes* 13 (1976): 270–73.

Fear and Holy Awe: The Salisbury Plain Poems and "Religious Musings"

Coleridge heard of the Salisbury Plain poems on two different occasions. The first was their meeting in August or September 1795, to which Coleridge refers in the *Biographia*: "I was in my twenty-fourth year, when I had the happiness of knowing Mr. Wordsworth personally, and while memory lasts, I shall hardly forget the sudden effect produced on my mind, by his recitation of a manuscript poem."[5] The second was the manuscript that Wordsworth and Cottle sent to Coleridge in March 1796. When Coleridge first learned of the Salisbury Plain poems is crucial, because the time when he heard of it determined which version he heard, and as I argue in Chapter 3, these manuscripts became seminal for both poets. The version that Coleridge heard in 1795 is now called "Salisbury Plain," a poem written in the summer of 1793 which narrates the misfortunes of a homeless woman, who, having lost father, husband, and children through poverty and the wars of the American Revolution, wanders on a hopeless and endless journey. But the version Coleridge saw in 1796 was a quite different and expanded version. When Wordsworth and Dorothy settled at Racedown in September 1795, he set to work revising the original. The revised version, "Adventures on Salisbury Plain," expands the role of the traveler, formerly almost characterless, to that of a sailor who has been pressed into service and denied his wages upon the completion of his enlistment. When he returns near his home, he robs and kills a stranger, and he is forced into a life of continuous wandering, pursued by reminders of his guilt and tortured by continuous seizures of paralyzing fear.[6]

"Salisbury Plain" presents a theme similar to "Religious Musings": the transformation of fear into hope and the humanization of those who have suffered as a result of their suffering. It opens with a pic-

5. *BL* 1: 78–79. Gill suggests that Coleridge "first encountered the poem" in 1795 when he first met Wordsworth (*SPP* 3).

6. Two manuscripts survive from before 1800. The first, "Salisbury Plain," may have been composed during or immediately after Wordsworth's journey across the plain in 1793 and copied in a notebook at Windy Brow in the spring of 1794. The second, "Adventures on Salisbury Plain," was written in the fall of 1795 at Racedown. The surviving manuscript probably dates from after May 1799, but Stephen Gill argues that although some evidence suggests that "the 1795 poem is now lost to us, there is no doubt that substantially, if not in every detail, it has survived in the poem in MS. 2, *Adventures on Salisbury Plain*" (*SPP* 12). For both I have quoted from *SPP*.

ture of the savage living in fear in the primitive landscape and contrasts the fear that he shares with all his tribe to the fear of the poor in a society split between the oppressed and the affluent. The hospital of charity once built on the plain has become a ruin, "the dead house of the Plain." The woman has taken refuge in that dead house, and when the unnamed traveler arrives, he hears her groans. He reacts with horror, which reinforces his earlier imaginative apprehension of being pursued by demons, but as he meets the woman and hears her story he is moved to sympathy. Her story told, a dawn arises for them both because her tale forges a bond of sympathy between them:

> Along the fiery east the Sun, a show
> More gorgeous still! pursued his proud career
> But human sufferings and that tale of woe
> Had dimmed the traveller's eye with Pity's tear,
> And in the youthful mourner's doom severe
> He half forgot the terrors of the night,
> Striving with counsel sweet her soul to chear,
> Her soul for ever widowed of delight.
> He too had withered young in sorrow's deadly blight.

> (397–405)

Each sympathizes with the other and by so doing replaces fear and terror with pity and hope. But the change is not complete and is the result of the traveler's forgetting. Wordsworth implies that pity and sympathy repress unwanted emotions, just as the sun dispels the gloom of night.

The traveler is characterized no further than the final line in this stanza. We are told that he has experienced sorrow, that before he meets the woman he is beset by cold, hunger, thirst, fear, and despair, and that his burdens are somewhat lightened by the woman's sympathy. Wordsworth's revisions in 1795 expand the role of the traveler to that of a sailor who has committed a crime. The poem shifts its emphasis from the criticism of social conditions to the study of the effects of war, guilt, and sorrow upon the two wanderers. At first Wordsworth seems determined to continue the theme of the sailor's sympathy with the woman. In a separate notebook he drafted notes for either a continuation of the woman's story or a transition between the parts of her story:

> The Woman continues her story
> Her feelings and forlorn situation.

sailor

Sympathy of the ~~traveller~~

and his benevolent exertions

to console her [? distress] [?]

still further exhibiting

the sad choice to which the

he

~~sailor~~ is exposed and his humanity[7]

Wordsworth's deletion of "traveller" and insertion of "sailor" in the third line and his use of "sailor" in the final line indicate that he is early in the process of changing his character and expanding "Salisbury Plain." The theme of human sympathy remains from the original poem, but this note describes a human sympathy that is not possible for the sailor of "Adventures on Salisbury Plain." Unlike the traveler, who merely suffers a vague sorrow, the sailor has committed a crime, and when Wordsworth describes his wanderings, there is a recurrent presence of guilt that prevents the full development of his sympathy.

The first revisions of "Salisbury Plain" were done in blank spaces of the manuscript, and some indicate this new direction. One presents the sailor as incapable of responding to human sorrow because of his guilt; the implication is that the worst effect of war is that it divides society and prevents social sympathy:

> And little grieved he for the sleety shower
> Cold wind and hunger he had long withstood
> Long hunted down by mans confederate power
> Since phrenzy-driven he dipped his hand in blood
> Yet till that hour he had been mild and good
> And when the miserable deed was done
> Such pangs were his as to relenting mood
> Might melt the hardest since   he has run
> For years from place nor place nor known one chearful sun

> Yet oft as Fear her withering grasp forbears
> Such tendency to pleasures loved before
> Does Nature   common cares
> Might to his breast a second spring restore
> The least complaints of wretchedness explore
> His heartstrings trembled with responsive tone
> Trembling the best of human hearts not more

---

7. Gill dates this entry in the Racedown notebook "soon after 26 September 1795" (*SPP* 305–6).

From each excess of pain his days have known
Well has he learned to make all others ills his own.

Yet though to softest sympathy inclined
Most trivial cause will rouse the keenest pang
Of terror and oerwhelm   his mind
For then with scarce distinguishable clang
In the cold wind a sound of irons rang
He looked and saw on a bare gibbet nigh
In moving chains a human body hang
A hovering raven oft did round it fly
A grave the[re] was beneath which he could not descry[8]

In these drafts Wordsworth is wrestling with the effects, not of sorrow, but of guilt. His theme is the wild vacillation between the tranquillity of a restorative "second spring" when "Fear her withering grasp forbears," and abject fear that comes unpredictably, when he is reminded of his guilt by the gibbet or other instance of man's inhumanity to man. The promise of a new dawn held in "Salisbury Plain" is absent in "Adventures on Salisbury Plain." The "keenest pang / Of terror" returns to suspend the moments of joy and sympathy. Whereas in "Salisbury Plain" the process of forgetting permits the traveler's pity and sympathy, here emphasis is placed on the return of terror. Forgetting is an insufficient defense against the continual return of guilt, and that permanent presence promises continuous wandering. The narrative of Coleridge's mariner has its origin in these stanzas and indeed reflects the entire narrative of the Salisbury Plain poems.

In "Adventures on Salisbury Plain" as it was completed in the fall of 1795, there is even little of the "second spring" possible for the sailor. He is gradually overcome by guilt and submits to it. The gibbet, which he sees early in his journey,

> rouzed a train
> Of the mind's phantoms, horrible as vain.
> The stones, as if to sweep him from the day,
> Roll'd at his back along the living plain;
> He fell and without sense or motion lay,
> And when the trance was gone, feebly pursued his way.
>
> (121–26)

8. *SPP* 115–16. The stanzas are also printed in *WPW* 1: 97–98. I have simplified the transcription in *SPP*. Very heavily revised, these stanzas become stanzas 11, 12, and 13 of "Adventures on Salisbury Plain."

Fear was to him "a terrific dream in darkness lost / The dire phantasma . . ." (130–31). When the woman whom he awakens in the roofless and deserted "dead house of the Plain" relates her own story of loss and madness, the effect upon him is similar to that when he sees the gibbet. The first part of her tale ends with her awakening on a British ship "as from a trance restored" (396), but that account of restoration only projects the sailor into another trance:

> She paused—or by excess of grief oppress'd,
> Or that some sign of mortal anguish broke
> In strong convulsion from her comrade's breast—
> She paused and shivering wrapp'd her in her cloak
> Once more a horrid trance his limbs did lock.
> Him through the gloom she could not then discern
> And after a short while again she spoke;
> But he was stretch'd upon the wither'd fern,
> Nor to her friendly summons answer could return.
>
> (397–405)

She began her tale "to natural sympathy resign'd" (259), but its effect is exactly the opposite; the sailor awakens from his trance and says, "Your tale has moved me much and I have been / I know not where" (419–20).

The dislocation and displacements of the sailor are as much mental as they are physical. He has been, it is clear, in a nightmare. Like the Wedding Guest, he "is of sense forlorn." That Wordsworth fully intended to reverse the effect of the woman's story on the sailor is indicated by a comparison of the transitions between the first and second parts of her story in "Salisbury Plain" and "Adventures on Salisbury Plain." First, two stanzas from "Salisbury Plain":

> Here paused she of all present thought forlorn,
> Living once more those hours that sealed her doom.
> Meanwhile *he* looked and saw the smiling morn
> All unconcerned with their unrest resume
> Her progress through the brightening eastern gloom.
> Oh when shall such fair hours their gleams bestow
> To bid the grave its opening clouds illume?
> Fled each fierce blast and hellish fiend, and lo!
> Day fresh from ocean wave uprears his lovely brow.

"Oh come," *he* said, "come after weary night
So ruinous far other scene to view."
So forth she came and eastward look'd. The sight
O'er her moist eyes meek dawn of gladness threw
That tinged with faint red smile her faded hue.
Not lovelier did the morning star appear
Parting the lucid mist and bathed in dew,
The whilst her comrade to her pensive chear
Tempered sweet words of hope and the lark warbled near.

(325–42)

Wordsworth altered the roles, and a comparison of them suggests that the primary referent of those from "Adventures on Salisbury Plain" is "Salisbury Plain." In the earlier version the traveler points to a new dawn, but in the later he is speechless, oblivious to all but the guilt within him. When the woman ends her story in "Salisbury Plain," the traveler's eye is filled with pity, but at the same moment in "Adventures on Salisbury Plain," the sailor "sate and spake not." She, not the sailor, witnesses the dawn:

"But come," *she* cried, "come after weary night
Of such rough storm the breaking day to view."
So forth he came and eastward look'd: the sight
Into his heart a [   ] anguish threw;
His wither'd cheek was ting'd with ashy hue.
He stood and trembled both with grief and fear,
But she felt new delight and solace new,
And, from the opening east, a pensive chear
Came to her weary thoughts while the lark warbled near.[9]

The woman alleviates her sorrow by telling her tale, but the expression that humanizes her only intensifies the sailor's fear. Her story "had sent / Anguish that rankled like a fiery dart" deep into his heart (588–89). She tries to relieve his depression, but "nothing could beguile / His thoughts, still cleaving to the murder'd man" (596–97). Thus there has been a complete reversal of roles in the two versions. In "Salisbury Plain," the narrator tries to lighten the burden that the woman bears. In "Adventures on Salisbury Plain" the woman tries to lighten the sailor's burden. She fails. Two fur-

9. Lines 568–76. The first two stanzas are 37 and 38 of "Salisbury Plain" (*SPP* 31), and the third is stanza 64 of "Adventures on Salisbury Plain" (*SPP* 146–47). I have added the italics.

ther episodes repeat the sailor's depression until he submits to the
law. They find a father beating his child, and the wound on the
child's head is exactly on the spot where the sailor had hit and mur-
dered the stranger. The sailor's reaction displays a moment of hu-
man sympathy that is qualified by his own experience and that does
not lead to a renewal of hope for himself:

> " 'Tis a bad world, and hard is the world's law;
> Each prowls to strip his brother of his fleece;
> Much need have ye that time more closely draw
> The bond of nature, all unkindness cease,
> And that among so few there still be peace:
> Else can ye hope but with such num'rous foes
> Your pains shall ever with your years increase."
>
> (658–66)

Finally, the sailor meets his dying wife. She is relieved to see him and
to be reconciled, but the effect on the sailor is the opposite. She is
comforted; he can utter only, "Oh God that I were dead!" (792).
Both episodes elicit some sympathy from the sailor, but they are also
recurrent reminders of his own guilt, which dominates his con-
sciousness. "Adventures on Salisbury Plain" ends with the sailor's
surrender to justice, contemptuous of its corruption and eager to
end his tormented life, to which the sympathy of others can give no
hope:

> Confirm'd of purpose, fearless and prepared,
> Not without pleasure, to the city strait
> He went and all which he had done declar'd:
> "And from your hands," he added, "now I wait,
> Nor let them linger long, the murderer's fate."
> Nor ineffectual was that piteous claim.
> Blest be for once the stroke which ends, tho' late,
> The pangs which from thy halls of terror came,
> Thou who of Justice bear'st the violated name!
>
> (811–19)

The poem ends as the first part of the poem ended: with the trance
of fear. The second part repeats the implications of the first. Just as
the sailor fell down in a trance before the gibbet, so others, perhaps
guilty of nothing more than thoughtlessness, seeing his corpse
swinging in the wind, repeat his fall in fear.

The end of "Adventures on Salisbury Plain" makes it clear that if there is relief, "a second spring" for the sailor, it is merely an exhausted emotional stillness.[10] The further he goes on his journey, the more persistent are his seizures. There is no progress, but only repetition. The sailor of "Adventures on Salisbury Plain" is exactly the opposite of the person whom Wordsworth briefly sketched in his prose note for the revision of "Salisbury Plain." The traveler had no personal guilt and could sympathize with the woman. He resembles the Pedlar who narrates Margaret's story in "The Ruined Cottage," who felt no crises in his life, "no wild varieties of joy and grief," a line which, in the context of Wordsworth's later poetry, denies that the sailor's pain belongs to the Pedlar. The draft stanzas suggest that the sailor sympathized because he had committed a crime and experienced the vacillations of joy and fear: "From each excess of pain his days have known / Well has he learned to make all others ills his own" (*SPP* 116). Yet when the draft stanzas were revised for "Adventures on Salisbury Plain," these two lines were deleted. When the stanza that claimed that "common cares" might restore a "second spring" was placed in "Adventures on Salisbury Plain," the season of promise was reduced to mere "hours of joy." For a short time, Wordsworth conceived of a character who had been humanized by crime, but he found that he could not fully realize that conception. The sailor has lost most human sympathy; he has not been humanized but has been conquered by fear. His wandering is anything but purgatorial. Sorrow humanizes, but guilt induced by injustice destroys and dehumanizes.[11] By forgetting, sor-

---

10. In "Salisbury Plain" the vagrant's story is preceded by the narrator's use of the phrase "second spring," but there the phrase is negative, and Wordsworth turns upon it in his first revisions:

> And are ye spread ye glittering dews of youth
> For this,—that Frost may gall the tender flower
> In Joy's fair breast with more untimely tooth?
> Unhappy man! thy sole delightful hour
> Flies first; it is thy miserable dower
> Only to taste of joy that thou may'st pine
> A loss, which rolling suns shall ne'er restore.
> New suns roll on and scatter as they shine
> No second spring, but pain, till death release thee, thine.

(217–25)

The stanza does not appear in "Adventures on Salisbury Plain."

11. My reading of these two versions and the various prose and verse drafts differs from recent commentary. Stephen Gill takes the three draft stanzas to represent

CHAPTER 2

row may be repressed, but fear and guilt cannot be forgotten and cannot be transformed into other emotions. They exist merely to return unmodified, as "The Ancient Mariner" was to illustrate in its final sections, where there is a similar unpredictable vacillation between joy and the return of fear.

When Coleridge received the manuscript of "Adventures on Salisbury Plain" at the end of March 1796, he had just completed "Religious Musings" for *Poems on Various Subjects* (1796). He had contracted with Cottle to provide copy for a volume of poems in the summer of 1795 and began to send him poems then, but publication was delayed while he revised and completed "Religious Musings." It was finished as the final poem in the volume only weeks before he received "Adventures on Salisbury Plain."[12] Coleridge reported that "Religious Musings" was the poem that Wordsworth most admired. In a May 13 letter to the atheist John Thelwall, who had complained about Coleridge's including metaphysics and religion in poetry, Coleridge responded that "a very dear friend of mine, who is in my opinion the best poet of the age . . . thinks that the lines [from "Religious Musings"] from 364 to 375 & from 403 to 428 the best in the Volume—indeed worth all the rest—And this man is a Republican & at least a *Semi*-atheist."[13] In *The Prelude* (1850) Wordsworth acknowledges Coleridge's influence in 1795 and 1796:

Wordsworth's thought in "Adventures on Salisbury Plain" and concludes that "the crime and the intensity of suffering that ensued have served to widen the sailor's innate sympathy with the suffering of others. The paradoxical result of the crime that shuts the man off from humankind is that his sensitivity to humanity is increased" (" 'Adventures on Salisbury Plain' and Wordsworth's Poetry of Protest, 1795–97," *Studies in Romanticism* 11 [1972]: 58). Paul Sheats has written that the "prose sketch of the revised plot which occurs early in the notebook Wordsworth used at Racedown . . . in no way departs" from "Adventures on Salisbury Plain" (*The Making of Wordsworth's Poetry, 1785–1798* [Cambridge, Mass.: Harvard University Press, 1973] 271). My argument is that the woman, not the sailor, responds to the dawn and that she leads him forth because he is stunned into silence by her tale.

12. For the dates of composition of "Religious Musings" and the copy for *Poems on Various Subjects* (1796), see Coleridge's letters to Joseph Cottle for February and March 1796 (*STCL* 1: 185–94). I quote from *Poems on Various Subjects* (1796).

13. *STCL* 1: 215–16. The 1796 version of "Religious Musings" is conveniently reprinted in Beer. The line numbering in Coleridge's *Poems* (1796) does not correspond to Beer's numbering because there was an error in the 1796 numbering and because the late-eighteenth-century practice was to count half lines as full lines. The lines that Coleridge refers to in his letter are 356–67 and 395–419 in Beer's edition and correspond roughly to 343–54 and 377–410 in the later version printed in *CPW*. My parenthetical notes follow Beer's numbering.

44

Shall I be mute, ere thou be spoken of?
Thy kindred influence to my heart of hearts
Did also find its way. Thus fear relaxed
Her overweening grasp. . . .

(XIV, 280–83)

Wordsworth echoes a line from the early revisions of "Salisbury Plain" that was included in "Adventures on Salisbury Plain": "Yet oft when Fear her withering grasp foregoes" (100), a conventional phrase, perhaps, but one that indicates Wordsworth's reference quite clearly.

At first sight the Salisbury Plain poems and "Religious Musings" hardly seem comparable, yet both address current social injustice and an uncertain political future. In his second version of the poem, Wordsworth becomes more strident and outraged by the oppression that sank the woman's father into poverty and began her wandering. Coleridge's poem also addresses oppression, poverty, and the brutal carnage of war, but where "Adventures on Salisbury Plain" held little hope for the future and provided little of a saving context for the wanderings of his characters, Coleridge infused his poem with Christian millennial hope and an optimism that faced the horrors of war.

The model for "Religious Musings," originally called "The Nativity" (*STCL* 1: 162), is Milton's "On the Morning of Christ's Nativity." Aside from the numerous verbal parallels, there are structural similarities that are important for Coleridge's poem. Milton asks the Heavenly Muse for a song of celebration. The Hymn is not that song but is the mortal song of a poet who aspires to hear the Muse's song. The Hymn's magnificence is a deceptive thing to its creator, the poet, who seems in the first half of the Hymn unsure as to how to respond and how to understand the birth of Christ. He asks the spheres to "ring out" and "bless our human ears"; he hopes that if the music of the spheres becomes audible, the "holy Song" will "Enwrap our fancy long, / Time will run back, and fetch the age of gold." Such enthusiasm misleads Milton, so the Hymn turns abruptly and rejects the regressive desire for a return to an original paradise.

But wisest Fate says no,
This must not yet be so,
    The Babe lies yet in smiling Infancy,
That on the bitter cross

45

Must redeem our loss;
    So both himself and us to glorify:
Yet first to those ychain'd in sleep,
The wakeful trump of doom must thunder through the deep.[14]

History must run its course through sacrifice and judgment. Instead of remembering a lost Eden, Milton looks forward to the final judgment.

"Religious Musings" extends Milton's structure. Coleridge begins in enthusiastic speculation on the effects of Christ's birth, the immediate renovation of the world and the individual's ascent to God, and a merging of the self with God. But as his speculations become bolder, he, like Milton, is misled and stopped short by a sudden recollection of the historical moment. In an abrupt turn, the sobering reality of war interrupts his speculative ascent: "But first offences needs must come! Even now / . . . THEE to defend . . . / Mistrust and Enmity have burst the bands / Of social Peace" (173–78). Coleridge, in a second section of the poem, catalogues the outrages and their origins. The first part evoked the symbols of the nativity, and the second deplores their misappropriation; the first proclaims the immediate unity of all in God, and the second acknowledges the fragmentation of man against man and class against class. But Coleridge adds a second turn to the poem, in which he confidently predicts the coming of the millennium:

> Rest awhile
> Children of Wretchedness! More groans must rise,
> More blood must steam, or ere your wrongs be full.
> Yet is the day of Retribution nigh:
> The Lamb of God hath open'd the fifth seal:
> And upward rush on swiftest wing of fire
> Th' innumerable multitude of Wrongs
> By man on man inflicted!
>
> (313–20)

The day of retribution inexorably brings the millennium.

Although he gave "Religious Musings" the subtitle "A Desultory Poem," Coleridge thought of it as a sublime ode. The dedication to "Ode on the Departing Year" (1796) defines "the *essential* excellencies of the sublimer Ode" as "impetuosity of Transition" and "Pre-

14. Lines 133–35 and 149–56 in *John Milton: Complete Poems and Major Prose*, ed. Merritt Y. Hughes (New York: Odyssey, 1957).

cipitation of Fancy and Feeling," precisely the characteristics of "Religious Musings." Coleridge wrote Thomas Poole in May 1796 that he thought of "Religious Musings," not as a poem with epic aspirations, but as sublime: "The 'Religious Musings' has more *mind* than the Introduction of B. IId of *Joan of Arc*, but it's versification is not equally rich; it has more passages of sublimity, but it has not that diffused air of severe Dignity which characterizes *my Epic Slice*" (*STCL* 1: 207). Its abrupt turns define the structure of the poem. When Coleridge published ninety-seven lines from the poem as "The Present State of Society" in *The Watchman* for March 9, 1796, he placed the line "Yet is the day of Retribution nigh" in the middle as line 43 so that the extract provides the turn from his depiction of the horrors of war to millennial hope.[15]

If Coleridge thought the essence of the sublime ode rested in its impetuous transitions, we should read his poems with that in mind, and if Milton's Hymn provides a partial paradigm for "Religious Musings," we should be alert to the boldly speculative possibilities of "Religious Musings." To turn, in these poems, is not just to make a leap of logic intelligible only to strong feeling, but it is to turn away from the implications of a previous section because they are immediately recognized to contain either fragmentary or incorrect views. The particular location of lines in a lyric provides a context for their meaning, just as the particular location of a poem provides its context. If lines are placed where they must necessarily be revised in later sections, they cannot be read without that qualifying context. Milton turns back to "fetch the age of gold," and then, under the pressure of fate, faces a future that cannot be denied. Coleridge is not as boldly regressive. He does not hope for a return but for an ascent that immediately escapes the present. "Religious Musings" illustrates both Coleridge's use of the license of lyric and ode form and the later form of the dialogue itself. It permits him to form a sequence of religious speculation and enthusiasm tempered by the reality of the historical moment.

In the first third of the poem, before the first turn, there are several accounts of the purgation of the evil emotions, and these accounts address directly those emotions that the sailor in "Adventures on Salisbury Plain" could not purge in himself. One presents

15. *The Watchman*, ed. Lewis Patton, *The Collected Works of Samuel Taylor Coleridge*, vol. 2 (London: Routledge & Kegan Paul; Princeton: Princeton University Press, 1970) 64–67.

the allegorical figure who reaches the altar and finds tranquillity while "hot pursuing fiends / Yell at a vain distance" (76–77). The traveler in "Salisbury Plain," homeless in a land empty of human life, is pursued: "Till then as if his terror dogged his road / He fled, and often backward cast his face" (127–28). He finds, not an altar, but the "dead house." Coleridge's figure of fear, however, is "transfigured" to a "dreadless awe" and thus prefigures the transformation of fear into awe and wonder in Wordsworth's greatest poetry. In 1797 Coleridge added a note to explain the alteration: "Our evil Passions, under the influence of Religion, become innocent, and may be made to animate our virtue—in the same manner as the thick mist melted by the Sun, increases the light which it had before excluded. In the preceding paragraph, agreeably to this truth, we had allegorically narrated the transfiguration of Fear into holy Awe" (*CPW* 1: 112). Strip Coleridge's verse of the awkward allegory and one has a clear anticipation and interpretation of what Wordsworth describes in the preface to *Lyrical Ballads* as the creative process: the transformation of rudimentary and personal emotion of experience, such as fear and terror, into those emotions of awe and wonder.

Coleridge illustrated this transformation with a picture of a traveler that provides a pattern for the most intense moments of recognition in "A Night-Piece" and the Snowdon episode of *The Prelude*:

> As when a Shepherd on a vernal morn
> Thro' some thick fog creeps tim'rous with slow foot,
> Darkling he fixes on th'immediate road
> His downward eye: all else of fairest kind
> Hid or deform'd. But lo, the bursting Sun!
> Touch'd by th'enchantment of that sudden beam
> Strait the black vapor melteth, and in globes
> Of dewy glitter gems each plant and tree:
> On every leaf, and every blade it hangs!
> Dance glad the new-born intermingling rays,
> And wide around the landscape streams with glory!
>
> (103–13)

The traveler in "Adventures on Salisbury Plain," having his attention directed to the dawn, feels only an anguish that is a false echo of renewal: "His wither'd cheek was ting'd with ashy hue. / He stood and trembled both with grief and fear . . ." (572–73). The traveler

here, however, oblivious to the renovating light, sees only defor-
mation and distortion until the brilliance of the light makes it ob-
vious and irresistible; it is a something shown to Coleridge's traveler
that proclaims its own innocence, not something created by his own
will. Coleridge's simile not only contrasts strongly with "Adventures
on Salisbury Plain," it anticipates the glorious light that gems the
trees and grass as the celestial light of "The Immortality Ode." The
celestial light of "Religious Musings" is, in contrast, the result of a
transformation of the evil passions, the idolatry, and the deforma-
tions that precede it; it is also a restoration of that "glory-streaming
VISION" of the Nativity.

Contemplation of the Nativity and its promise of ultimate victory
lead Coleridge to surmise that salvation is present, and insofar as his
speculations ignore the historical present, they are untimely. Just as
Milton is enchanted by fancy, Coleridge, tempted by sublimity, in-
dulges a willful error, not in the assurance of the effects of the Na-
tivity, nor even in the exercise of metaphysical speculation, but in
the deliberate disregard of political and social circumstance. The
second section of the poem turns from the illusions of the immedi-
ate transformation of pain to joy in order to acknowledge the same
pain and injustice that Wordsworth faced. He describes, as does
Wordsworth, the "childless widows" on the "groaning land" and the
"aged Woman" who with trembling hand reaches for the "morsel
tost by law-forc'd Charity" and dies "so slowly, that none call it mur-
der" (301–2), and the "Widow, who in dreams dost view / Thy Hus-
band's mangled corse" (309–10). If these figures duplicate the fe-
male vagrant in "Salisbury Plain," another doubles the sailor of
"Adventures on Salisbury Plain":

> O thou poor Wretch,
> Who nurs'd in darkness and made wild by want
> Dost roam for prey, yea thy unnatural hand
> Liftest to deeds of blood!
>
> (291–94)

Both Coleridge's and Wordsworth's murderers are driven to des-
peration by the injustice and indifference of society. Most likely
both are conventional figures in the radical Jacobin rhetoric of the
1790s, and it would be too great a claim to assert that they are orig-
inal with either Wordsworth or Coleridge, but their presence in

49

both works suggests that both were facing the same subjects but with vastly different conclusions.

The final section of "Religious Musings" combines the hope that the "day of Retribution" is near with the realization that until that time "more groans must rise." Both sections that Coleridge reported that Wordsworth admired are in the final section of the poem. The first begins in the middle of an elaborate simile in which "seraph-warbled airs" and "odors snatch'd from beds of amaranth" descend from heaven at the time of "some solemn jubilee of Saints" when the gates of heaven are opened. In those lines, "The favor'd good man in his lonely walk / Perceives them, and his silent spirit drinks / Strange bliss which he shall recognize in heaven" (365–67). The "good man" here is the good Samaritan to whom Coleridge referred in the first section when he mentioned the "soft balm the weeping good man pours / Into the lone despoiled trav'ller's wounds" (95–96). Wordsworth admired the presence of the "good man," of human sympathy, at a time of despoliation and deformation, who is guarantee enough to perpetuate millennial hope. The good man will comfort all wanderers. The millennium itself is merely a prefiguration of yet another time in which "time is no more" and in which the surmise, speculation, and allegory of the poem itself, as well as historical contingency, are simply irrelevant. The second section that Wordsworth admired begins with a question that asserts the coming of an end to time but which also admits that it cannot be imagined: "Who of woman born / May image in his wildly-working thought" (404–5) the final apocalyptic moment in which time, which circumscribes the millennium, comes to an end. From such a point of view, "Life is a vision shadowy of Truth" (414).

"Religious Musings" would seem, thus, to be a direct answer to the Salisbury Plain poems. It is difficult to argue such a relationship for the simple reason that parts of it were most likely written before Coleridge saw Wordsworth's poems. Some had been written in January 1795 and by October Coleridge claimed to have finished over three hundred lines, almost three-quarters of the poem (*STCL* 1: 162). The extract "The Present State of Society" had been published before Coleridge received the manuscript of "Adventures on Salisbury Plain." And it is even somewhat uncertain that Wordsworth actually singled out the particular lines for admiration that Coleridge mentioned to Thelwall. In the absence of corroborating evidence from Wordsworth himself, it is risky to take what Coleridge says at face value. But it may, after all, be true that Wordsworth did admire particularly those lines, and if he did, it is easy to see that he saw "Religious Musings" as reflecting an optimism that in 1796 was not his. What perhaps is more likely is that in May 1796 Coleridge read his own poems, published for only one month, in the context of Wordsworth's unpublished ones and began to see that his poems answered their darker views. The letter in which Coleridge identifies those passages was written to the atheist John Thelwall. Coleridge intended those sections of "Religious Musings" to be an answer to Thelwall's radicalism, an answer that is repeated in his public lectures and in *The Watchman* in 1795 and 1796. Whether Coleridge read "Religious Musings" as an answer to Wordsworth or to Thelwall, or to both, it is clear that he read his poem as an answer to the pessimism of the day.

Wordsworth was the private pessimist, the unpublished prophetic voice; Coleridge was the public optimist. To Benjamin Flower, Thomas Poole, and John Thelwall, Coleridge wrote that he rested all his claims for "poetical credit on the *Religious Musings*" (*STCL* 1: 197, 203, 205). In the letter to Thelwall he proclaimed himself "an *Optimist*." In the Gutch memorandum book he defined optimism: "by having no will but the will of Heaven, we call in Omnipotence to fight our battles" (*CNB* 1: 22). Optimism is not necessarily the personal mood in which Coleridge wrote the poem, not a subjective emotion that finds its expression in verse. It is, rather, a public and religious attitude, akin to the virtue of hope, that Coleridge chose to assume in 1796 and the attitude in which he chose to read his and Wordsworth's poems. It matters little what his personal moods and emotions were.

"Our Two Tragedies": The Borderers *and* Osorio

In March 1798, when Coleridge and Wordsworth were considering a number of projects for joint publication, Coleridge wrote to Joseph Cottle, "What *could* you conveniently & *prudently*, and what *would* you, give for . . . Our two Tragedies—with small prefaces containing an analysis of our principal characters" (*STCL* 1: 399–400). When Coleridge visited the Wordsworths in June 1797, Dorothy wrote to Mary Hutchinson that "the first thing that was read after he came was William's new poem *The Ruined Cottage* with which he was much delighted; and after tea he repeated to us two acts and a half of his tragedy *Osorio*. The next morning William read his tragedy *The Borderers*" (*LEY* 189). The work that Coleridge heard was begun in the fall of 1796, and Wordsworth was hard at work on it in

October. Only fragments of the early work survive. The earliest surviving complete draft was copied in 1799 after Wordsworth's return from Germany. It is unlikely that Wordsworth changed much of the play from the end of 1797 to 1799, because he was at work on other projects, so the 1799 manuscript represents the play finished in the fall of 1797 and is most likely close to the play that Coleridge heard that summer (*Bord.* 6).

Coleridge began *Osorio* in April 1797 at the suggestion of Richard Brinsley Sheridan. By May he claimed to have written fifteen hundred lines, and in early June he told John Prior Estlin that he will "have quite finished my Tragedy in a day or two" (*STCL* 1: 327), but it was not finally completed until early September. There is no clear evidence as to what portions of the play were read to Wordsworth; Dorothy does not say that Coleridge read the *first* two and one-half acts or that he had written only two and one-half acts. The version that E. H. Coleridge prints as the one sent to Sheridan totals about 1,750 lines, and if Coleridge was correct about his estimate of having finished fifteen hundred lines in May, he had finished more than two and one-half acts. Emile Legouis once suggested that the last half of *Osorio* was strongly influenced by Coleridge's having heard *The Borderers*,[16] but it is difficult to say precisely where the influence lies. Each began his work independently of the other, yet there may have been some influence. Wordsworth visited Coleridge in Nether Stowey at the beginning of April 1797 just as Coleridge was beginning to write *Osorio*, and he seems to have received the idea of showing the play to Sheridan from Coleridge. It is likely that there was mutual discussion of their plays, since Wordsworth had described his in February as "nearly finished" (*LEY* 177).

16. Emile Legouis wrote that when Coleridge heard *The Borderers* he "became so infatuated with it as to imitate it in the second part of a tragedy, entitled *Osorio*, of which he had already written two acts and a half. Impressed by the character of the villain Oswald, he borrowed his pride and cynical philosophy for the traitor of his own work, a flagrant piece of imitation which begins at the very point in his tragedy where Coleridge had stopped before he became acquainted with *The Borderers*" (*The Early Life of William Wordsworth, 1770–1798*, trans. J. W. Matthews, rev. ed. [1921; New York: Russell and Russell, 1965] 356). Stephen Parrish notes that Coleridge echoed Rivers' soliloquy in *The Borderers*, 1797–99 (II, iii, 231–41), in the third act of *Osorio* (*The Art of the "Lyrical Ballads"* [Cambridge, Mass.: Harvard University Press, 1973] 75). Parrish's comparison of the two plays is astute and useful. (Following Osborn's practice for *The Borderers*, I have noted the Early Version [1797–99] by act, scene, and line, and the Late Version [1842] simply by line number.)

In the instance of "our two Tragedies," the significant relationship between them comes, not from evidence of the possible mutual influence at the time they were conceived and written, but from the readings of them that led Coleridge and Wordsworth to propose them to Cottle for joint publication. Coleridge's comments on *The Borderers* identify the themes of its first version, many of which were obscured in later revision, and prepare for their later reading of both plays as complementary, as *"one work."* Almost immediately after having heard *The Borderers*, Coleridge expressed his enthusiasm to Cottle:

> Wordsworth admires my Tragedy—which gives me great hopes. Wordsworth has written a Tragedy himself. I speak with heart-felt sincerity & (I think) unblinded judgement, when I tell you, that I feel myself a *little man by his* side; & yet do not think myself the less man, than I formerly thought myself.—His Drama is absolutely wonderful. You know, I do not commonly speak in such abrupt & unmingled phrases—& therefore will the more readily believe me.—There are in the piece those *profound* touches of the human heart, which I find three or four times in 'The Robbers' of Schiller, & often in Shakespere—but in Wordsworth there are no *inequalities*. T. Poole's opinion of Wordsworth is—that he is the greatest Man, he ever knew—I coincide. (*STCL* 1: 325)

Coleridge's deep admiration for the *"profound* touches of the human heart," an appreciation of intense human passion, distinguishes his response to Wordsworth's poetry from his response to other contemporary literature in 1797, including simple romance and the excesses of the Gothic. By the time he began *Osorio*, his enthusiasm for the Gothic had waned,[17] but his admiration for the intensity of sublime passion had not. He saw in *The Borderers*, not a poet who was reacting to contemporary political theories or expressing his disillusionment with the French Revolution, but a poet who was able to delve into the grand passions of the human heart.

Coleridge's offer of "our two Tragedies" to Cottle in March 1798 as *"one work"* provides, not an explanation of the genesis of the plays,

17. See, for instance, his review of *The Monk* in the *Monthly Review* for February 1797 in *Coleridge's Miscellaneous Criticism*, ed. Thomas Middleton Raysor (Cambridge, Mass.: Harvard University Press, 1936) 370–76. Coleridge comments that "Figures that shock the imagination, and narratives that mangle the feelings, rarely discover *genius*" (372) and may have influenced Wordsworth's later rejection of sensationalist and Gothic literature.

but a way in which he and Wordsworth read them after they were written. Since the analogy for the *"one work"* is, as Coleridge explained it to Cottle, lyric structure, the rationale for their being offered as a joint publication is, not their similarities or their mutual influence, but their differences. There are, of course, similarities, but they are so general that they could be ascribed to the presence of similar public themes rather than to direct mutual influence. The ability to read the two plays as complementary resides in their sharing themes and in the sharp contrasts between the two works. The essential characteristics of the plays are determined by their being placed in the same context and by their mutually influencing a reading of the other text. Each stands as a counterstatement to the other. By the spring of 1798, the problem of amalgamation had become acute to Coleridge, and his offering of the plays to Cottle with such a definition of their relationships indicates his consciousness of the necessity for individual difference.

Commentary on *The Borderers* has concentrated on the political implications of the play and Wordsworth's growing disillusionment with Godwinian reason as a guide to moral action. It has also focused on the moral issues of the characters' psychology, a delineation of a "philosophical murder," as Emile Legouis has called it, or the portrait of an "intellectual murder," as Geoffrey Hartman has called it.[18] Two notes written in the 1840s link the play with the French Revolution, but the preface, written at the time of the first completed version, does not specifically link it. It merely states that the "general moral intended . . . is to shew the dangerous use which may be made of reason when a man has committed a great crime" (*Bord.* 67). In 1797 Wordsworth understood that reason was merely a disguise for instinct, pride, and the "love of distinction" (*Bord.* 62). Wordsworth's 1797 preface is far more concerned with the perverted passions and with the means by which one is tempted to crime than are either of the 1840 notes. The play published in 1842 makes significant changes in the characters and their reactions to events, in spite of Wordsworth's disavowal of important changes: "not the slightest alteration has been made in the conduct of the

18. Legouis 270 and Geoffrey Hartman, *Wordsworth's Poetry, 1787–1814* (New Haven: Yale University Press, 1964) 125. Since Garrod's *Wordsworth* (Oxford: Clarendon Press, 1923) the play has been read as a reaction against Godwinian reason. Robert Osborn's recent introduction to his edition comments on "Rivers' promise of intellectual independence" (*Bord.* 30).

story, or the composition of the characters; above all, in respect to
the two leading Persons of the Drama, I felt no inducement to make
any change."[19] The 1842 version offers a temptation to an intellec-
tual freedom, but the 1797 version offered the temptation to a
crime, not through liberation of the intellect, but through liberation
of the imagination to reach for sublimity. It is difficult to imagine
that in 1797 Coleridge would have responded to *The Borderers* as
possessing "*profound* touches of the human heart" if the 1797 ver-
sion were substantially the same as the 1842 version, which so many
have read as a play about the use and misuse of the intellect.

Rivers' betrayal of Mortimer resembles Iago's of Othello, yet Riv-
ers' is an explicit temptation to choose sublimity, a sublimity pur-
chased at the price of a violation of Mortimer's dearly held creed of
benevolence and generosity. In the later 1842 version, Rivers ar-
gues that his notion of justice requires the harsh applications of pain
and evil and that Mortimer's benevolence is contemptible. The early
text, however, contains a significantly different version of Rivers'
temptation, in which the moral question is not stated in such clear
terms:

> Benevolence that has not heart to use
> The wholesome ministry of pain and evil
> Is powerless and contemptible: as yet
> Your virtues, the spontaneous growth of instinct,
> From vigorous souls can claim but little praise.
> To day you will assume a character
> More awful and sublime. . . .
>
> (II, i, 72–78)

The text of 1842, which holds no specific promise, is an intentional
obscuring of the "character / More awful and sublime" held as a pos-
sibility in 1797. In 1842 Wordsworth gave Rivers two short lines that
describe the band of outlaws as "Men who are little given to sift and
weigh— / Would wreak on us the passion of the moment" (645–46),
lines that offer the alternatives of intellectually superior individuals,
who are really debased utilitarians, or bands of passionate, unthink-
ing men. But the earlier version gives Rivers a longer speech:

19. *Bord.* 813. Osborn minimizes the differences between the two versions: "In re-
vising *The Borderers* for publication in 1841–42, Wordsworth changed the names of
his characters . . . and introduced various minor plot changes. . . . The most signifi-
cant changes were introduced in V.iii, the final scene of the play" (*Bord.* 16–17).

The eye
Of vulgar men knows not the majesty
With which the mind can clothe the shapes of things:
They look but through the spectacles of forms,
And from success alone they judge of actions.

(II, i, 98–102)

This presents far other alternatives. Rivers suggests that the superiority of great men rests, not in their ability to "sift and weigh," but in their imaginative power to "clothe the shapes of things." He tempts Mortimer with the power to become a poet of supreme majesty. To claim such majesty is to "assume a character / More awful and sublime." In the 1797 preface Wordsworth describes Rivers: "His imagination is powerful, being strengthened by the habit of picturing possible forms of society where his crimes would be no longer crimes, and he would enjoy that estimation to which from his intellectual attainments he deems himself entitled" (*Bord.* 64–65). An important element of the criticism Wordsworth makes of Rivers in the preface is that his imagination requires strong stimulus. Rivers needs "those sudden results which can afford a sufficient stimulus to a troubled mind." His mind requires "constant provocatives" (*Bord.* 63–64). He is thus, in part, a young poet, whose prospective imagination has not outgrown the need for what Wordsworth called in the preface to *Lyrical Ballads* "gross and violent stimulants" (*Prose* 1: 129), and his temptation offers Mortimer, himself quite young, these same shocks to his imagination.

Shortly after this dialogue Mortimer asks Rivers about the means of murdering Herbert, and Rivers replies:

By shewing that you calculate, and look
Beyond the present object of the sense—
A few leagues hence we shall have open field,
And tread on ground as free as the first earth
Which nature gave to man. Before we enter
The barren heath, just half way to the convent
We pass the beetling rock from which there hangs
A ruined castle. . . .

(II, i, 109–16)

The territory depicted in 1842 is a barren landscape, surveyed with a practical, dispassionate eye and judged isolated enough. This earlier text offers an astonishing claim; to claim majesty, Mortimer

56

must look beyond the "present object of the sense" and see things not as they appear to the senses, not merely as a suitable place for crime. To look beyond the sense is to enter the "first earth / Which nature gave to man," a free and natural world. Wordsworth repeats the startling point in the preface: "every time we plan a fresh accumulation of our guilt we have restored to us something like that original state of mind, that perturbed pleasure, which first made the crime attractive" (*Bord.* 67). If ever crime were attractive, this is it. To be told that criminality is purgative, to be informed that it restores freedom and innocence and banishes remorse, and to be assured that it restores our "original state of mind," is to be tempted to become the agent of summary justice. It is not a temptation to stride beyond good and evil and ignore or break moral codes; it is, rather, a temptation to restore an innocence that is a prelude to the excited agitation of a possible new freedom. Rivers' temptation is to perform a sublime act in which the mechanism of forgetting the troubled present existence is implied. Rivers' temptation is a diabolic inversion of the enthusiasm in the opening third of "Religious Musings," which promises a similar reward.

Yet the intention of forgetting and regressing through action turns upon itself and produces an ironic result. Mortimer's contemplation of Herbert's murder directs his thoughts to a childhood different from that presented in Rivers' temptation:

> And yet in plumbing the abyss of vengeance
> Something I strike upon which turns my thoughts
> Back on myself—I think again—my breast
> Concenters all the terrors of the universe,
> I look at him and tremble like a child—
>
> (II, iii, 61–65)

Mortimer finds himself in a mental landscape that is not the unimpeded and free prospect of innocence surveying infinite possibility. Ironically, his view is blocked by the figure of Herbert as a father who reduced him to a terrified child. Wordsworth's portrait of Mortimer becomes more complex than this ironic reversal because the terror that Mortimer finds can become either the paralyzing fear in confronting crime or the terror that can be transformed into a sublimity. In the next act, Mortimer recognizes that

> Deep, deep and vast, vast beyond human thought,
> Yet calm—I could believe that there was here

The only quiet heart on earth.—In terror,
Remembered terror, there is love and peace.

(III, v, 1–4)

The early version of *The Borderers* struggles somewhat crudely with themes that inform the early work on *The Prelude*, the effect of terror in childhood and in a childlike state upon a later state of mind. Mortimer validates Rivers' claims that bold action has its majesty, but it is a majesty that derives from terror in confrontation with a father figure. When Wordsworth composed the stolen-boat episode for Book I of *The Prelude*, with its recollection of childhood terror, and the ninth stanza of "The Immortality Ode," with his recollection of trembling "like a guilty Thing surprised," he retained the Coleridgean motive of transforming fear and terror into awe but excluded the motif of an undeniably criminal action.

If at times Mortimer resembles the Wordsworth of the great poetry, Rivers also resembles him at some points. Tempting Mortimer shortly after Mortimer's soliloquy, Rivers promises that "Your faculties should grow with the occasion" (III, v, 35), and telling Mortimer of his adventures in the East, he speaks in lines that could fit easily into *The Prelude*: "In these my lonely wanderings I perceived / What mighty objects do impress their forms / To build up this our intellectual being" (IV, ii, 133–35). He had become "the master of the better half of wisdom. / I saw unveiled the general shapes of things" (IV, ii, 160–61), lines that were deleted from the 1842 version. Rivers also says

> Enough is done to save you from the curse
> Of living without knowledge that you live.
> You will be taught to think—and step by step,
> Led on from truth to truth, you soon will link
> Pleasure with greatness, and may thus become
> The most magnificent of characters.

(IV, ii, 204–9)

All but the first two lines were deleted in 1842. The earlier version repeats the temptation to sublimity, greatness, and magnificence. Thus both Mortimer and Rivers foreshadow the future Wordsworth, and in this context it is not surprising that Coleridge should find in *The Borderers* "*profound* touches of the human heart."[20]

20. Roger Sharrock reads Wordsworth's play as an exploration of the moral divi-

First Readings

Thus, while the 1842 version stresses the temptation of intellectual freedom and reason of the independent intellect, the 1797 version emphasizes that of a grand visionary freedom that leads to criminal violation of a natural social order. Submitting Herbert to ordeal is a return to medieval law that denies a natural benevolence of the human heart and at the same time calls attention to the ordeals of suffering caused by contemporary war and injustice. In the earliest revisions of "Salisbury Plain," Wordsworth had tried to formulate a character who had been humanized by the suffering caused by his crime. The character was never realized; instead the sailor became locked within his own fear of retribution and remorse, unable to sympathize fully with others. *The Borderers* returns to the same problems left unsolved in the drafted stanzas and prose outline. Mortimer is, ironically, humanized by his crime, but not in the sense that he is able to extend full sympathy to others. His humanization is the product of a new self-awareness. Rivers says Mor-

---

sions within Wordsworth ("*The Borderers*: Wordsworth on the Moral Frontier," *Durham University Journal* 56 [1964]: 170–83). The appeal of Rivers' temptation for Wordsworth the poet is clearly illustrated in an Alfoxden notebook that recomposes Rivers' lines "Enough is done to save you from the curse / Of living without knowledge that you live":

> To gaze
> On that green hill and on those scattered trees
> And feel a pleasant consciousness of life
> In the impression of that loveliness
> Until the sweet sensation called the mind
> Into itself, by image from without
> Unvisited, and all her reflex powers
> Wrapped in a still dream [of] forgetfulness.
>
> I lived without the knowledge that I lived
> Then by those beauteous forms brought back again
> To lose myself again as if my life
> Did ebb and flow with a strange mystery.

> (*WPW* 5: 341)

Wordsworth has transferred Rivers' words to his own meditation upon the inward and outward turnings of his mind, a movement that Coleridge glossed in his notebook entry explaining lines in "Tintern Abbey" (*CNB* 1: 921). See also Michael C. Jaye, "William Wordsworth's Alfoxden Notebook: 1798," *The Evidence of the Imagination: Studies of Interactions between Life and Art in English Romantic Literature*, ed. Donald H. Reiman, Michael C. Jaye, and Betty T. Bennett (New York: New York University Press, 1978) 71–72. Butler presents photographs and transcriptions of the passage (124–25).

59

timer is saved "from the curse / Of living without knowledge that you live" (IV, ii, 204–5), and his self-awareness isolates him from the human community. But Rivers is wrong. Mortimer's fate is a "blank forgetfulness" (V, iii, 275), not a new consciousness but the end of consciousness.

When Coleridge offered "our two Tragedies" to Cottle in March 1798, he did so at Wordsworth's suggestion. Both must have seen the plays as complementary, and there are several ways in which they may be read as such. Each explores the criminal mind as it was manifested in the events of the Revolution. Wordsworth set his at a time of the "absence of established Law & Government—so that the Agents might be at liberty to act on their own impulses" (*Bord.* 814). *Osorio* was set "in the reign of Philip II shortly after the civil war against the Moors, and during the heat of the Persecution which raged against them" (*CPW* 2: 519). While Mortimer's band of outlaws is free to roam between England and Scotland administering their justice in a chaotic time, the Moors suffer from unyielding tyranny and persecution. *The Borderers* deals with the possibilities of human action when all restraints have been removed, and *Osorio* treats the rebellion of the oppressed against tyranny. *The Borderers* studies the fate of individuals in a lawless society; *Osorio* presents the fates of single tyrants and an entire oppressed class at a time of despotism.

Alhadra's revenge, in contrast to Albert's ineffectual attempts to lead Osorio to remorse, is executed without any common mercy. When the band of Moors breaks into the dungeon where Osorio has imprisoned Albert and is about to kill him, Maria begs for mercy for Osorio, and Alhadra replies:

> And is it then
> An enviable lot to waste away
> With inward wounds, and like the spirit of chaos
> To wander on disquietly thro' the earth,
> Cursing all lovely things? to let him live—
> It were a deep revenge.
>
> (V, ii, 295–300)

Her only mercy is to prevent Osorio from the wandering that is Mortimer's fate and that of the sailor in "Adventures on Salisbury Plain." It almost seems that Coleridge has Wordsworth's final lines in mind, because Alhadra does not seem aware of the "inward wounds" of self-consciousness. Her instinct is for unthinking reaction provoked by immediate events. Her lack of self-awareness and thought resembles what Rivers sees as the lack of reflection in the border band. In contrast to Mortimer's neglect of Herbert, her action is a natural rebellion against intolerable oppression, an action that does not hesitate; she is exasperated into reckless action, and her creed is "Great evils ask great passions to redress them, / And whirlwinds fitliest scatter pestilence" (I, i, 231–32). She acts as an heroic member of a society: "The Tyger, that with unquench'd cruelty, / Still thirsts for blood, leaps on the hunter's spear / With prodigal courage" (V, i, 100–102).

At the end of the play, Osorio is surrounded by the Moors and led offstage, presumably to his death, while Mortimer is left alone to wander in the barren landscape. The final words are Alhadra's:

> I thank thee, Heaven! thou hast ordain'd it wisely,
> That still extremes bring their own cure. That point
> In misery which makes the oppressed man
> Regardless of his own life, makes him too
> Lord of the oppressor's! Knew I an hundred men
> Despairing, but not palsied by despair,
> This arm should shake the kingdoms of the world;
> The deep foundations of iniquity
> Should sink away, earth groaning from beneath them;
> The strong holds of the cruel men should fall,
> Their temples and their mountainous towers should fall;
> Till desolation seem'd a beautiful thing,
> And all that were and had the spirit of life
> Sang a new song to him who had gone forth
> Conquering and still to conquer!
>
> (V, ii, 307–21)

Alhadra is the secular agent of what Coleridge in "Religious Musings" called "salutary wrath" (93). In contrast to the death and dispersion of the good and the just in *The Borderers*, *Osorio* presents the victory of the oppressed as a class over the intolerable tyranny of the Inquisition and the proud aristocracy. While the final lines of *The Borderers* present an outcast, the final lines of *Osorio* present a victory, but a victory that results from the frightening fact that rule by extreme terror and violence will be answered by extreme violence. Alhadra's is collective and unreflecting action.

Osorio is politically a strong counterstatement to *The Borderers. The Borderers* presents only the sad, unwitting repetition of events in a cycle of lawless arrogation of power and the perpetuation of justice by ordeal, which ends in lawless wandering. *Osorio*, in contrast, ends with the oppressed in possession of the citadel. If Alhadra's revenge is a call for the poor and oppressed to rise as a class, as it would certainly be if it were staged, it is as radical a statement as Coleridge ever wrote and resembles Wordsworth's cry at the end of "Salisbury Plain" to "uptear / Th'Oppressor's dungeon from its deepest base." It may, however, be more conservatively read merely as a description of the lengths to which individuals are driven under tyranny.[21] In either case, within the play itself there is a victory that ends the social and political conditions that provoked its action.

The contrast of the two plays' political themes is complicated by their emphasis on character. Both placed primary emphasis on the changes that take place within the characters, who live in different historical conditions of oppression and disorder. Commenting on *The Borderers* in 1842, Wordsworth said that "the study of human nature suggests this awful truth, that, as in the trials to which life subjects us, sin and crime are apt to start from their very opposite qualities, so are there no limits to the hardening of the heart, and the perversion of the understanding to which they may carry their slaves" (*Bord.* 813). This explanation for apparently motiveless actions reverses the transformation of the soul that Coleridge described in his 1797 note to "Religious Musings," in which "our evil Passions, under the influence of Religion, become innocent." In Rivers' temptation of Mortimer, evil passions masquerade in the guise of innocence, so that Mortimer's genuine innocence is betrayed into crime. Wordsworth's and Coleridge's early poetry can be read as a continued commentary on the variations in the potential for radical transformation of the soul under various historical and political conditions. Coleridge explains in the preface to *Osorio* that he has a similar concern: "In the character of Osorio I wished to represent a man, who, from his childhood had mistaken constitu-

---

21. Compare Alhadra with Coleridge's characterization of the second class of democrats in *Conciones ad Populum* (1796): "they possess a kind of wild Justice well calculated to spread them among the grossly ignorant. To unenlightened minds, there are terrible charms in the idea of Retribution, however savagely it be inculcated. The Groans of the Oppressors make fearful yet pleasant music to the ear of him, whose mind is darkness, and into whose soul the iron has entered" (*Lectures 1795 On Politics and Religion*, ed. Lewis Patton and Peter Mann, vol. 1 of *The Collected Works of Samuel Taylor Coleridge* [Princeton: Princeton University Press, 1971] 38). Coleridge's lecture predates Wordsworth's rejection of vengeance and hatred in the conclusion to "The Ruined Cottage."

tional abstinence from vices, for strength of character—thro' his pride duped into guilt, and then endeavouring to shield himself from the reproaches of his own mind by misanthropy" (*CPW* 2: 519). Both plays portray characters who are betrayed, duped, seduced, and mistaken; they are misled into crime by others and understand neither themselves nor their society. Wordsworth wrote in his essay "On the Character of Rivers" that Rivers possessed "great intellectual powers" and that his ruling passions were "pride and the love of distinction": "He goes into the world and is betrayed into a great crime" (*Bord.* 62).

In both plays the immediate occasion for the transition in the soul is either a tale that is told or a theatrical event that is staged. In *The Borderers* many, if not all, of the characters tell tales, and the tales are validated by memory and experience.[22] Mortimer confesses to having been enchanted with Matilda's tales of her father's suffering and heroism: "It was my joy to sit and hear Matilda / Repeat her father's terrible adventures . . ." (I, i, 65–66). Matilda's love for her father originated in her hearing his tales of the Crusades and their subsequent wandering. Rivers' purpose is not to tell another tale or to fabricate a contrary history. He intends to cast doubt on the truth contained in the history that Mortimer has heard by hinting that Herbert is an impostor. With evident sarcasm he says that

> For sometimes, in despite of my conviction
> He tempted me to think the story true;
> . . . .
>
> But sure, he loves the girl; and never love
> Could find delight to nurse itself so strangely,
> And thus to plague her with *inventions*!
>
> (I, i, 199–208)

His inventions challenge Mortimer's understanding of the tales and replace Mortimer's original motives with a new suspicion that they were based on misinterpretation and misrepresentation. Rivers does not offer himself as the sole authority for his contrary interpretation but instead stages a scene played by a beggar woman who has been directed to tell Mortimer that Matilda is not Herbert's

22. For a discussion of the telling of tales in *The Borderers* and a discussion of the Wordsworth-Coleridge relationship, see Reeve Parker, " 'Oh Could You Hear His Voice!': Wordsworth, Coleridge, and Ventriloquism," *Romanticism and Language*, ed. Arden Reed (Ithaca: Cornell University Press, 1984) 125–43.

daughter. Rivers leads Mortimer to doubt, not merely Herbert's current motives and intentions, but the entire narrative of their relationship as it has been represented to him in tales and as he had experienced it. Questions are raised by Rivers' suggestions and by his staging events, but the coherence of narrative truth is not finally questioned. Matilda's tale is true and remains so; Mortimer's tragedy is that he is led to disbelieve it. History's tragedy is that events repeat themselves, with the earlier becoming the cause of the latter. Rivers' betrayal by a deception is repeated in his betrayal of Mortimer.

Osorio also contains many tales, but, in contrast to those in *The Borderers*, they do not validate a past. Rather, they are admitted fictions that initiate the action or have little relevance to the plot. The best known is "The Foster Mother's Tale," published in *Lyrical Ballads*. In *Osorio* the tale has no relation to the plot and is used exclusively to present an alternative, natural life to the oppressively institutional life under Spanish rule. Most of the characters in *Osorio* tell their dreams or visions, just as those in *The Borderers* tell their histories. The major difference is that the visions and dreams in *Osorio* have no corresponding reality; they are admitted fictions of wish fulfillment. Maria tells her father that she has created an image of Albert's return, although she has been told that he has been killed, and she imagines that she herself "had died—died, just ere his return." She can thus preserve her emotional stability through conventional melancholy contemplation of Albert's meditating upon her tomb. Velez dreams of events that did not happen; he imagines "the merchant-ship in which my son was captured . . . in sight of land." Albert himself returns thinking that Maria is married, and when he discovers she is not, he dismisses his fears as "a dream, a phantom of my sleep, / A lying dream" (I, 275–76). All the dreams are fictions, the product of desire and not the realities of history.

The Borderers argues that history and narrative form the ground of a reality; *Osorio* suggests the contrary, because human motives become based on human dreams and because human action is based on the confusion of dreams and not on the realities of history. Human motive and human action become discontinuous, as they do in Coleridge's later poetry. Albert returns with a twofold motive: he wishes to revenge himself on his brother and to lead him to repentance through remorse so that he will be saved from his former motives. The means he chooses to bring him to repentance, to consciousness of his act, only lead Osorio to commit the crime that previously had not been committed, to enact the assassination that had never taken place. Albert stages a theatrical event to awaken Osorio's conscience. The purpose of the conjuring is to convince Maria that Albert is in fact dead and thus to encourage her to marry Osorio. Coleridge explains in a marginal note what he intended: "Instead of Maria's portrait, Albert places on the altar a small picture of his attempted assassination. The scene is not wholly without *poetical* merit, but it is miserably undramatic, or rather untragic. A scene of magic is introduced in which no single person on the stage has the least faith—all, though in different ways, think or know it to be a *trick* . . ." (*CPW* 2: 555). Although Maria says "This is some trick—I know, it is a trick," nevertheless she responds to the suggestion in the conjuring that she sees the picture she gave Albert, even though the picture is not there. Coleridge also noted in the margins his intentions for Velez's and Osorio's reactions: "Velez supposes the picture is an innocent contrivance of Osorio's to remove Maria's scruples" (*CPW* 2: 556). Thus, not only do all the characters think the staged presentation is a mere trick, they all see something other than what is actually present, or they all pretend to see something other than what is actually present. Even the painting of the assassination is a representation of an event that never occurred. Thus dreams and visions lead only to more fictions, and the artist who creates them initiates the action.

Later, having seen the painting of the assassination and realizing that it was not the painting he gave Albert, Osorio believes he has been betrayed by Ferdinand. When Osorio arrives at the cave where Ferdinand is hiding, Ferdinand complains to him of having seen Osorio as a hideous monster in his dreams and having dreamed of "falling down that chasm." Shortly, Ferdinand is in fact murdered by being pushed into the chasm. Coleridge noted in the margin that he had attempted by introducing the dream to present something other than a "mere Tragedy-dream," apparently one that predicts future events. His intention was to present a prophetic dream in which "Perception and Imagination insinuate themselves and mix with the forms of Recollection, till the Present appears to exactly correspond with the Past. Whatever is partially like, the Imagination will gradually represent as wholly like" (*CPW* 2: 565–66). The note is interesting if it simply means to banish superstition, but it is more significant in its argument for the workings of perception and imagination that create from the present a past that predicts the present. The present is its own creation, disconnected from narrative and history, and memory is subverted by present imagination. Just as Albert's conjuring is a fiction of the moment, so Ferdinand's fear of Osorio is a creation of the moment, not of the past. The implication that past and present do not form a continuity of cause and effect is repeated in the disjunction between Albert's intention to lead Osorio to repentance and the result, as Albert's artistic conjuring in fact leads to crime.

Thus a volume containing "our two Tragedies" as one publication with the individual plays as mutually complementary would have made a coherent work. Both are documents on the historical present, conditioned by contemporary events and Wordsworth's and Coleridge's observations on the fate of individuals shaped by social and historical events. *The Borderers* presents a lawlessness that betrays individual hopes and makes it possible for evil to masquerade as a reasoning revision of the future. *Osorio* offers two divergent interpretations of the influence of the historical moment. The first, contained in the plot of Alhadra's revenge, presents the oppressed, who are exasperated beyond all restraint, rising in violent rebellion. The second, the story of Albert's conjuring and causing Osorio to commit murder, presents the contrary view that human actions are prompted by dreams, visions, tricks, and admitted fictions, which knowingly misrepresent both the past and the future. Human motive originates in the imaginings of individuals, and furthermore those motives often have effects opposite to those that were intended.

Coleridge's more complex presentation of possibilities has important implications for their future dialogue. In both *Osorio* and "Religious Musings," the dreams and speculations of poets and artists are qualified by their opposites. The speculation that begins "Religious Musings" is recognized as speculation when Coleridge turns to the realities of present events, and the instinctive reaction of the Moors to oppression is contrasted to the disjunction between motive and action in Albert's conjuring. The implication is certainly not that these opposites simply leave a reader in confusion and uncertainty as to an intended interpretation of history and political events as well as the truths of character and psychology. Rather, continuous revision is the initiating condition of dialogue, that which makes continued writing possible. Its fundamental form is lyric, and lyric assumes continued alteration and change of direction in a way that narrative does not. In this case dialogue begins with the mutual reading of both narrative and dramatic works, and insofar as reading is closer to the gestures of lyric than to simple narrative reconstruction, their reading initiates their poetic contributions to the dialogue. Coleridge's reading of the Salisbury Plain poems leads from deep admiration to the wish for collaboration and to an independent effort that incorporates its origins. And Wordsworth's participation in the initial stages of collaboration on "The Ancient Mariner" leads to his composing "The Discharged Soldier." Wordsworth's and Coleridge's recollections of their reading of these early poems—written before intense dialogue begins in the summer of 1797, when *The Borderers*, *Osorio*, and "The Ruined Cottage" were read—continue to contribute to their poetry for years.

"My Own Voice":

"The Ancient Mariner" and "The Discharged Soldier"

THE MUTUAL ADMIRATION that Coleridge and Wordsworth expressed for each others' poetry led in the fall of 1797 to attempts at collaboration in the writing of "The Ancient Mariner." Collaboration proved unsuccessful, but in its failure, poetic dialogue began. "The Ancient Mariner" was at first an attempt to produce one work from their combined efforts, but when Coleridge's imagination was more energetic, the poem became an answer to Wordsworth's Salisbury Plain poems. It obviously employed elements of "Adventures on Salisbury Plain": the act of violation or crime by an innocent or unthinking individual who feels himself persecuted, the resulting endless wandering, which does not purge the effects of the violation, and the fitful, and finally ineffective, return of joy, which is transitory and replaced by the return of guilt and terror. The dialogue does not proceed, however, by simple imitation but by transformation. "The Ancient Mariner," particularly in its earliest published version in *Lyrical Ballads*, redirects "Adventures on Salisbury Plain." Wordsworth's poem ended with the sailor's surrender to justice and with his silence. Coleridge created his mariner as the teller of his own tale, giving a voice to his experience and suffering. Coleridge's redirecting of Wordsworth's poem implies that he read its major theme as the possibility of suffering's finding a voice; in a poetic

68

dialogue the responsive poem defines the theme of the poem from which it departs. The poetic association that begins in collaboration and turns within a matter of a few months into the writing of responsive poems must be conscious that it is a dialogue, that poems are written in the context of previous efforts at collaboration, and that responsive poems take the urgency of their utterance from earlier fragments of the dialogue.

"The Ancient Mariner" alters the Salisbury Plain poems, not only in giving a voice to suffering, but also in characterizing the voice as dissociated from the mariner. Wordsworth's response to Coleridge's figure is "The Discharged Soldier," which portrays the soldier as the returned, yet still wandering, mariner—alone, displaced, and figurative because he corresponds to nothing the poet has seen before and because he has no place either in landscape or society. Like many figures in the literature of the supernatural, he resembles or images nothing and cannot himself be reflected. The soldier is the figure in a landscape that has no familiar location. The soldier, like the mariner, is dissociated from his own tale because he can no longer feel its importance. Wordsworth incorporates Coleridge's figure in his verse in order to naturalize him, to accommodate him to society and landscape, and to give him a voice that both gives thanks and bestows a blessing, a voice that is a direct expression of his character.

The occasion for the writing of "The Ancient Mariner" and Wordsworth's contributions to it are well known. On November 12, 1797, Dorothy and William and Coleridge started on a walking tour, the expenses of which they planned to earn by writing a ballad that they hoped to send to the *New Monthly Magazine*. There had been previous attempts at collaboration—"The Three Graves," which Wordsworth began and gave to Coleridge, and "The Wanderings of Cain"—and in both instances Coleridge worked enthusiastically and Wordsworth eventually withdrew.[1] As he recalled later in life,

1. The first two parts of "The Three Graves" are by Wordsworth (*WPW* 1: 308–12, 374 n). The second two parts were published in *The Friend*, Sept. 21, 1809 (2: 88–96), and reprinted in *CPW* 1: 267–84. No record of the final two projected parts exists. Reed conjectures that Wordsworth gave Coleridge the poem in June or July 1797 (*CEY* 190 n). In *The Friend*, Nov. 16, 1809, Coleridge explained his theme in "The Three Graves" as "the effect, which one painful idea vividly impressed on the mind, under unusual circumstances, might have in producing an alienation of the Understanding; and in the parts hitherto published, I have endeavoured to trace the progress to madness, step by step" (2: 172). His explanation sounds very much like Words-

Wordsworth withdrew from work on "The Ancient Mariner" because "I soon found that the style of Coleridge would not assimilate with mine." Mrs. Davy recalled that Wordsworth told a "somewhat humorous account of the rise and progress of the 'Ancient Mariner'. . . . 'We tried the poem conjointly for a day or two, but we pulled in different ways, and only a few lines of it are mine.' " Wordsworth had contributed the idea of the shooting of the albatross as a crime for which the mariner was punished, the reanimation of the dead sailors to work the ship, at least six lines of the poem, and perhaps four or five more that remain unidentified. But with these contributions his efforts stopped because "our respective manners proved so widely different that it would have been quite presumptuous in me to do anything but separate from an undertaking upon which I could only have been a clog."[2]

"The Ancient Mariner" quickly grew beyond the limitations of magazine verse. At the end of their tour, they "began to talk of a Volume, which was to consist, as Mr. Coleridge has told the world, of Poems chiefly on natural subjects taken from common life, but looked at, as much as might be, through an imaginative medium" (*WPW* 1: 361). Wordsworth thus confirms Coleridge's account of the plan of *Lyrical Ballads*, although the plan was probably not firm until late the following spring. Coleridge was to write poems in which "the incidents and agents were to be, in part at least, supernatural," and Wordsworth was to contribute poems in which "subjects were to be chosen from ordinary life" (*BL* 2: 6). While collaboration on a single poem did not work and in each instance stopped with a sometimes comic and good-hearted admission that it was impossible, a volume or collection of poems in which contrasting poems were arranged was possible. The beginnings of attempts to juxtapose and arrange their poems so that they constituted a dialogue exist in the misdirection of collaboration. They began to read their previous poems as the beginnings of such a dialogue. A crucial decision was made preserve the generative conditions of writing while at the same time preserving the possibility of claiming uniqueness for individual poems.

---

worth's explanation of his theme in writing "The Thorn" (*WPW* 2: 512–13). For "The Wanderings of Cain," see *CPW* 1: 285–92 and *CNB* 2: 2780 and note.

2. *The Reminiscences of Alexander Dyce*, ed. with a biography by Richard J. Schrader (Columbus: Ohio State University Press, 1972) 185; *The Prose Works of William Wordsworth*, ed. Alexander Grosart, 3 vols. (1876) 3: 442; and *WPW* 1: 361. Wordsworth contributed lines 17–20 and 218–19 to the poem in *Lyrical Ballads* (1798).

Wordsworth's account of their differing styles and Coleridge's explanation of the plan of *Lyrical Ballads* in the *Biographia* have indicated to many that the major irreconcilable difference between the two concerned Coleridge's use of the supernatural as subject matter and Wordsworth's contrary insistence that the proper subject matter was the common and the ordinary. But in 1797 the issue of the supernatural was a superficial one and in itself not enough to account for the failure of collaboration. Coleridge had been surfeited with the excesses of Gothic literature for well over a year and found little merit in the gratuitous presence of bloody corpses, supernatural spirits, and demons. In 1797 Wordsworth's opposition to the use of the supernatural was not as strong as it was later to become. He had used it in "Adventures on Salisbury Plain," and when he was revising the poem in preparation for having a fair copy made in late April 1799, he did not remove all the Gothic elements. He was willing to join the project of writing "The Ancient Mariner" when he knew from the outset that its source was in a "strange dream which one of Coleridge's friends had, who fancied he saw a skeleton ship with figures in it."[3] Even his own contributions to the poem, the reanimation of the dead bodies, for instance, were Gothic. His good-humored withdrawal from the project, the comic preface to "Peter Bell," and even the critical note to "The Ancient Mariner" in *Lyrical Ballads* (1800) that the poem contains passion that "is every where true to nature" suggest that he did not place serious emphasis on the presence of the supernatural in the poem. His later objections were directed to other aspects: the archaic diction, the lack of character development and the consequent figurative nature of the supernatural characters, and the emotional tone (*LB* 276–77).

The *Biographia* offers a reading of the poem in which the supernatural is used to reveal a truth or reality through the use of a fiction: "The excellence aimed at was to consist in the interesting of the affections by the dramatic truth of such emotions, as would naturally accompany such situations, supposing them real. And real in *this* sense they have been to every human being who, from whatever source of delusion, has at any time believed himself under supernatural agency." The authority for the use of the supernatural derives from "our inward nature," which provides "a human interest and a semblance of truth sufficient to procure for these

---

3. *The Reminiscences of Alexander Dyce* 185.

shadows of imagination that willing suspension of disbelief for the moment, which constitutes poetic faith" (*BL* 2: 6). During Easter week 1815 Coleridge wrote to Byron describing the contents of his projected works and echoed his comment in chapter 13 of the *Biographia* about the preface to "The Ancient Mariner" and its "critical essay on the uses of the Supernatural in poetry and the principles that regulate its introduction" (*BL* 1: 306): the works would include "a Particular Preface to the Ancient Mariner and the Ballads, on the employment of the Supernatural in Poetry and the Laws which regulate it—in answer to a note of Sir [*sic*] W. Scott's in the Lady of the Lake." E. L. Griggs identifies the note, which concludes that the supernatural "seems to be now universally abandoned to the use of poetry."[4] Coleridge's answer would have countered Scott by saying that the supernatural is the product of the seer's own mind: "The Poet of his free will and judgement does what the Believing Narrator of a Supernatural Incident, Apparition or Charm does from ignorance and weakness of mind," Coleridge wrote in a late notebook, "i.e. mistake a *Subjective* product . . . for an objective fact."[5]

As Scott admits and as Coleridge insists in the *Biographia*, the modern poet and reader are faced with particular problems with the supernatural. Coleridge's explanations can be interpreted as a distinction between a truth of "our inward nature,"—a psychological reality of truth to human emotion—and the supernatural figures by which they are represented and which they create. But Coleridge's explanation presents a more complex and involved relationship between a truth and its representation. His phrase "the willing suspension of disbelief" assumes at the outset that there is a natural and justifiable disbelief in the supernatural as Gothic and that this disbelief is a sign of the reader's sense of reality. Common sense tells us simply that ghosts do not exist objectively. The poet and intelligent reader begin with the truth of incredulity in a tale that presents a "semblance of truth." Poetic faith resides in a "semblance," itself an ambiguous word suggesting both resemblance and mere appearance. The figure that represents an emotion is disbelieved as a fiction. Reader and poet become witness to a narrator who believes himself controlled by the supernatural.

4. *STCL* 4: 561. Scott's note may be found in *The Poetical Works of Sir Walter Scott*, ed. J. Logie Robertson (1894) 278–79.

5. Notebook 43, printed in *Inquiring Spirit*, ed. Kathleen Coburn (London: Routledge, 1951) 191. The entry is dated 1830.

They willingly enact poetic faith only after disbelief is suspended. Coleridge's comment on *Osorio* could be applied with some modification to "The Ancient Mariner": "A scene of magic is introduced in which no single person . . . has the least faith" in its literal reality (*CPW* 2: 555). And that scene, in *Osorio*, generates the action. Similarly, both in the writing and in the reading of "The Ancient Mariner" the initial act is disbelief in the supernatural to realize poetic faith in its fictions.

The "semblance of truth" in "The Ancient Mariner" is further complicated by the presence of other fictions at its origin, Wordsworth's Salisbury Plain poems, from which Coleridge borrows and to which he alludes. Representation in poetic dialogue is reference, or allusion, and "The Ancient Mariner" represents those poems simply because it alludes to them. Those poems constitute a source for "The Ancient Mariner," not only in the traditional sense in which one poet borrows images and themes with little transformation, but also in the sense that Coleridge's poem is deliberately different. The allusions of "The Ancient Mariner" are also not apparent in an ordinary sense, because its appropriations are from a poem then unpublished and from canceled drafts of that poem. Wordsworth had written two versions along with unused drafts, and although he later offered them to Cottle for publication, they could not, at the time that Coleridge saw them, be considered completed poems with the authority of publication. In this part of their dialogue, the generating texts are fragments and rejected drafts, and their position as generating texts is identified by the use that "The Ancient Mariner" makes of them.

The most important of these fragments for "The Ancient Mariner" is the draft of three stanzas that Wordsworth wrote at the end of the "Salisbury Plain" manuscript that I quote at the beginning of the previous chapter to demonstrate Wordsworth's early plans for "Adventures on Salisbury Plain." The stanzas contain the basic pattern of "The Ancient Mariner." The first describes the sailor's flight from capture after he committed murder; he had "run / For years from place nor place nor known one chearful sun." The image of the sun anticipates the merciless sun of Coleridge's poem. In the second, nature restores a "second spring," a moment similar to that occurring after the blessing of the water snakes. The third opens "Yet though to softest sympathy inclined / Most trivial cause will rouse the keenest pang / Of terror." Although the sailor has his moments of joy, the return of terror will "oerwhelm . . . his mind"

(*SPP* 115–16), which is precisely what happens to the mariner when the consciousness of the curse returns to him after the blessing of the water snakes. In fact, Charles Lamb used Wordsworth's words describing the sailor to describe what happened to the mariner; the mariner's trials "overwhelm . . . all individuality or memory of what he was" (*Lamb Letters* 1: 266). As I mentioned in the previous chapter, when Wordsworth inserted these stanzas into "Adventures on Salisbury Plain," he altered some of the more optimistic phrases, changing the "second spring" to "hours of joy" and deleting references to the sailor's gaining human sympathy from his own experience of crime and guilt. "The Ancient Mariner" appropriates from both these draft stanzas and from "Adventures on Salisbury Plain," for its narrative sequence, and its conclusions resemble those of "Adventures on Salisbury Plain." The pattern is of someone whose guilt is thrust upon him, who flees persecution masquerading as justice, who has a momentary renewal of joy, but whose joy is lost at the unpredictable return of terror.[6] Crabb Robinson wrote in his diary for January 13, 1836, that Wordsworth had informed him that he had supplied Coleridge with "much of the plan," and most likely that plan came from the Salisbury Plain poems.[7] The pattern for the transformation of character that existed in "Religious Musings" is a possible paradigm for the conversion of both the sailor and the mariner. The challenge to both "Adventures on Salisbury Plain" and "The Ancient Mariner" is to enact that transformation.

Another important pre-text for "The Ancient Mariner" comes from two lines found only in "Salisbury Plain." The sailor arrives at the dead house of the plain: "Till then as if his terror dogged his

6. Charles J. Smith describes the pattern: "a man commits a crime; the crime sets in motion the machinery of justice and punishment; it also calls down a curse upon his head; the criminal suffers severe pangs of remorse; and finally, through remorse, he finds regeneration and salvation" ("Wordsworth and Coleridge: The Growth of a Theme," *Studies in Philology* 54 [1957]: 53–54). Smith's account relies on the later, revised versions of the poems, does not account for their political contexts, and thus tends to impose a traditional pattern of sin and redemption upon these poems.

7. *Diary, Reminiscences, and Correspondence of Henry Crabb Robinson*, ed. Thomas Sadler, 3 vols. (1869) 3: 85. If Robinson is correct and Wordsworth's report is accurate, Wordsworth's contributions to "The Ancient Mariner" were far greater than revealed by either Coleridge or Wordsworth in other notes and conversations. Many of the resemblances between the Salisbury Plain poems and "The Ancient Mariner" could be accounted for by their being either Wordsworth's suggestions for "much of the plan" or even Wordsworth's lines rather than Coleridge's appropriation of lines from an intimate acquaintance with the manuscripts. Nevertheless, Coleridge's poem appropriates from Wordsworth's poems and is a far superior work.

road / He fled, and often backward cast his face" (127–28). The terror in "Salisbury Plain" is that of war, for in one of the poem's most rhetorical passages the soldiers are presented as those who "dog-like wading at the heels of War / Protract a cursed existence with the brood / That lap, their very nourishment, their brother's blood" (313–15). The pursuing dogs are the hounds of hell or the furies. The Wedding Guest, perceiving the terror on the mariner's face while he tells the pleasant story of the albatross becoming a welcome visitor, sees that the mariner is pursued by demons: "God save thee, ancyent Marinere! / From the fiends that plague thee thus."[8] On the journey home, the same theme of pursuit occurs in terms that are incorporated from "Salisbury Plain":

> Like one, that on a lonely road
>   Doth walk in fear and dread,
> And having once turn'd round, walks on
>   And turns no more his head:
> Because he knows, a frightful fiend
>   Doth close behind him tread.
>
>   (451–56)

And in the 1798 version, after this spell is broken by the arrival of a springlike breeze of joy that blows him home, the fear again returns in exactly the same terms:

> A little distance from the prow
>   Those dark-red shadows were;
> But soon I saw that my own flesh
>   Was red as in a glare.
>
> I turn'd my head in fear and dread,
>   And by the holy rood,
> The bodies had advanc'd, and now
>   Before the mast they stood.
>
>   (485–492)

   In addition to the draft stanzas that set the pattern of recurrent terror and the image of the traveler pursued by fear, Coleridge appropriates the image of the dead house of the plain from the Salisbury Plain poems. The resemblances between the dead house and

---

8. Lines 77–78. Here and throughout I have quoted from the version of "The Ancient Mariner" in *Lyrical Ballads* (1798) as reprinted in *CPW* 2: 1030–48.

CHAPTER 3

the death ship of "The Ancient Mariner" as the location of fear are many. Each is surrounded by a waste, illuminated partially by a setting sun, populated by Gothic portraits of a dead man and a living woman, and in a state of ruin. The dead house of the plain is an abandoned hospital, formerly a place of refuge, which now no longer offers the community's charity to the homeless woman, who must take shelter from the storm in its ruins. The place where public charity was once available is no longer populated, and hence public charity is available only in the degrading hospital reserved for beggars, in which the woman stays upon her return from America. The isolated and outcast woman is the only source of human sympathy in the ruined hospital, and in spite of her best efforts, the sympathy has no effect. In fact her first tale of the place is that of the traveler, whose horse paws at the stones and unearths the head of a newly murdered man. The discovery of the corpse and the setting are relics of an earlier Gothicism, and their immediate affect is that of the Gothic shudder, which the sailor sees as a reminder of his guilt. The dead house images both death and the neglect of public charity and the possible return of private charity with the woman's presence, but that private charity cannot save the sailor. Wordsworth's political and social emphases require that the Gothic shudder not be mitigated, because it is intended to arouse indignation; there can be no other transformation or mitigation in poems written for such purposes. Wordsworth informed Payne Collier in 1814 that the poem was "addressed to coarse sympathies, and had little or no imagination about it . . ." (*WPW* 1: 334).

Coleridge's dead house of the plain is the death ship. Its visible content, of course, came from the "skeleton ship, with figures on it" but much of its significance preexisted in Wordsworth's dead house. In presenting it as a dream image, however, Coleridge removed it from a physical location with its particular social and political implications into the world of fiction. More important, he transformed the woman of the dead house into the leprous, vampirelike woman who casts dice for the mariner's soul. Not yet in 1798 called the "Nightmare-life-in-death," but still suggesting something of the later figure's chilling presence, she reverses the potential warm, nurturing charity of the woman in the dead house. Not presented with the same ghoulish horror as the skeleton who accompanies her, the "Nightmare-life-in-death" "is far liker Death than he; / Her flesh makes the still air cold" (189–90). Although the mariner first sees the death ship as a salvation for him and the crew, it provides no sal-

76

vation. The woman of the dead house, having completed her tale of suffering, calls the sailor's attention to the rising sun; she "saw the dawn salute the silvering east" (565) as though it were the rising of a glorious sun announcing a day of new hope, but for neither the sailor nor the mariner is the glorious sun a portent of rescue. The mate on the death ship more closely resembles the corpse of the dead house, and his presence on the ship is intended, in spite of the embarrassingly grisly detail, to reinforce the chill terror that the vampirish woman conveys. The intended effect is not the ennobling terror of the sublime, but rather the freezing shudder. Coleridge quickly realized that these "coarse" emotions were out of place in the poem and that the introduction of the popular Gothic betrayed his more serious purposes, and he deleted them later. Nevertheless, the intended effect is to reinforce the freezing terror of the death ship and to contrast it sharply with the potential warmth associated with the dead house. In the depths of his alienation, the mariner is frozen and made still.

The list of similarities between the Salisbury Plain poems and "The Ancient Mariner" could be extended: both poems draw a moral about the necessity of human sympathy and human kindness; both the sailor and the mariner are "mocked as by a hideous dream," as is the traveler in "Salisbury Plain" (101); the sailor asks to be forgiven by his wife, whom he has wronged, and the mariner asks to be shriven by the hermit; and both the sailor and the mariner are finally isolated from any human community. A search for the beginnings of Coleridge's poem comes to the paradoxical conclusion that Wordsworth's poems were present at its beginning, that Wordsworth himself wrote a significant number of lines, and that he made significant contributions to its plot. So similar are the two poems that Wordsworth used almost the same words to describe the faults of the plots of each poem. In his 1800 note to "The Ancient Mariner" he complained that "the events having no necessary connection do not produce each other" (*LB* 277), and in the Fenwick note to the early versions of "Guilt and Sorrow" he confessed that "the incidents of this attempt do only in a small degree produce each other" (*WPW* 1: 330).

On Coleridge's part, there is an act of appropriation and differentiation—a dialogic movement away from the pre-texts of his poem, which completes the fragments of its beginnings; in effect, he interleaves Wordsworth's fragments, this time not with his criticism and commentary but with his own poem, which transforms the sailor's silent nightmare into the mariner's "strange power of speech." The most important fragments that Coleridge appropriates come exactly at the transition point from one version of the Salisbury Plain poems to another; he appropriates from a work in the process of development and change, not from a work that has been completed, which in this instance underlines the importance, in their dialogue, of the moment of change and transition itself. Coleridge had used Wordsworth's incomplete texts for a number of poems— "The Three Graves," first published in *The Friend*, and "Lewti," originally intended for *Lyrical Ballads* and published in the *Morning Post* of April 13, 1798, for example. Wordsworth explained to Barron Field that he had given Coleridge "the subject of his Three Graves; but he made it too shocking and painful, and not sufficiently sweetened by any healing views. Not being able to dwell on or sanctify natural woes, he took to the supernatural and hence his Antient Mariner and Christabel."[9] This explanation of "The Three Graves" has all the marks of self-defense and special pleading; it was he, not Coleridge, who in 1797 could find no consolation for "natural woes." He said later that he was reluctant to publish the Salisbury Plain poems because "the mariner's fate appeared to me so tragical as to require a treatment more subdued and yet more strictly applicable in expression than I had at first given to it" (*WPW* 1: 330).

With these poems there is an intriguing sense of inadequacy on Wordsworth's part. He offers Coleridge incomplete poems, drafts, and fragments (or at least permits Coleridge to take them), and his comment upon the Salisbury Plain poems suggests that he thought the poem unsuited to his audience and unready for publication. What he had written did not correspond to what he thought he should have written; his poems could not become public, except through Coleridge's transformation of them. With "The Three Graves" and "Lewti" it is perhaps a matter of their collaboration being a minor and even amusing footnote to their relationship, but with "The Ancient Mariner" and the Salisbury Plain poems the case is quite different. Coleridge transformed and published what Wordsworth himself kept private. This is not the case of a derivative poet creating his own style or voice by echoing a previous text; it is the case of a poet who in 1797 is the more public and more pub-

9. Quoted by Ernest de Selincourt, "The Early Wordsworth," *Wordsworthian and Other Studies* (Oxford: Clarendon Press, 1947) 31. See also Jane Worthington Smyser, "Coleridge's Use of Wordsworth's Juvenilia," *Publications of the Modern Language Association of America* 65 (1950): 419–26.

lished writer giving life to texts that had been kept private by their author, because, in the case of the Salisbury Plain poems, he thought a public would have demanded consolation for the "natural woes," similar perhaps to those in "Religious Musings" or to those milder emotions that conclude "The Ruined Cottage" in 1798. When Wordsworth returned to "The Ruined Cottage" in the spring of 1798, he drafted a consolation that banished thoughts of vengeance and that relied strongly on Coleridge's poetry. There is the possibility that Coleridge's later problems with plagiarism and appropriation were complicated by his initial successes in efforts at collaboration.

The inadequacy that Wordsworth felt about his early poetry rests on the paradox of his having written poems that employ a public and oratorical style yet which remained completely private. His comments later in life acknowledged that the poems lack emotional maturity. They argue the unmodified presentation and unpredictable return of fear and terror, while Coleridge's speculations in "Religious Musings" had combined the terror of divine retribution with the "transfiguration of Fear into holy Awe." If the reference of the mariner's terror is the sailor's terror in "Adventures on Salisbury Plain," then one possible transformation of the sailor's terror is that of "Religious Musings," but it is not the one that Coleridge makes. Like the sailor, the mariner is pursued by recurrent fear. The transformation that Coleridge makes is that in "The Ancient Mariner" fear becomes a motive for speech, for telling a tale. In response to the Salisbury Plain poems, Coleridge turns to the difficulties involved in narration and telling a tale explored in both *The Borderers* and *Osorio*. The Jacobin origins of the Salisbury Plain poems led Wordsworth to present the sailor as an object; he is victimized by a corrupt society. He is a mute auditor of the woman's story, and his personal torment prevents him from being an adequate auditor because he cannot respond to her with full human sympathy. He has suffered, but suffering has given him no voice, no urgency of responsive confession or gesture of friendship. He is private and utters only words of bitter admonition. The closest he comes to confession is his request to his wife: "O bless me now, that thou should'st live / I do not wish or ask: forgive me, now forgive" (773–74). His final words place an ironic blessing on his executioners: "Blest be for once the stroke which ends, tho' late, / The pangs which from thy halls of terror came" (817–18).

The mariner, however, has a voice. He is the teller of his own tale, and the experience of his tale has given him the "strange power of speech." The difference in style between Coleridge and Wordsworth has been described as a theoretical disagreement over the use of the dramatic monologue.[10] Coleridge did disapprove of Wordsworth's use of the form, as did many others in the Wordsworth circle, yet "The Ancient Mariner" is also a dramatic monologue in many respects. Hazlitt's report of their individual styles of reading aloud is instructive: "Coleridge's manner is more full, animated, and varied; Wordsworth's more equable, sustained, and internal. The one might be termed more *dramatic*, the other more *lyrical*."[11]

Coleridge's major revision of Wordsworth's poem is that the mute sailor has become the mariner, who tells his own tale. In the version published in *Lyrical Ballads* (1798), the mariner has a self-awareness as a narrator that he does not have in the later, revised versions. In all versions the mariner seems to have little comprehension of the meaning of his tale. He cannot interpret its figures and grant it a context other than the orthodoxy that he and the hermit share, and he knows only that orthodoxy cannot fully explain the events. In both early and later versions the narrator says that the mariner is able to possess the Wedding Guest's will:

> He holds him with his glittering eye—
> The wedding guest stood still
> And listens like a three year's child;
> The Marinere hath his will.
>
> (17–20)

In the 1798 text the Wedding Guest interrupts the mariner as he is telling of the reanimation of the bodies of the dead sailors:

> Listen, O listen, thou Wedding-guest!
> "Marinere! thou hast thy will:
> "For that, which comes out of thine eye, doth make
> "My body and soul to be still."
>
> (362–65)

10. Stephen Parrish revised and expanded three articles on the dramatic monologue in his book *The Art of the "Lyrical Ballads"* (Cambridge, Mass.: Harvard University Press, 1973): " 'The Thorn': Wordsworth's Dramatic Monologue," *English Literary History* 24 (1957): 153–63; "The Wordsworth-Coleridge Controversy," *Publications of the Modern Language Association of America* 73 (1958): 367–74; and "Dramatic Technique in the *Lyrical Ballads*," *Publications of the Modern Language Association of America* 74 (1959): 85–97.

11. William Hazlitt, "My First Acquaintance with Poets," *The Complete Works of William Hazlitt*, ed. P. P. Howe, 21 vols. (London: J. M. Dent, 1930–34) 17: 118–19.

He interrupts the mariner's tale only to repeat the mariner's words and confirms the power of the mariner's tale, an emphasis that is not present in later versions. He is an echo of the mariner and similar to Christabel, who becomes in the second part of "Christabel" an echo of Geraldine. More important, immediately following his interruption, and in response to it, the mariner announces the effect of his tale:

> Never sadder tale was told
>   To a man of woman born:
> Sadder and wiser thou wedding-guest!
> Thou'lt rise to-morrow morn.
>
> (366–69)

The mariner utters what in the later versions is reserved for the narrator, who makes it a part of the moral at the end, where it is connected with the thought that "He prayeth best who loveth best" (647). Thus associated with the moral, the lines become a part of the wisdom of the later conclusion, but in the earlier versions they echo the mariner's own conscious knowledge of the effect of his story, where the emphasis is more heavily placed on sadness than on wisdom: "Never sadder tale was told." The narrator merely repeats what the mariner has already said, and thus his voice, like the Wedding Guest's, is subordinated to the mariner's. Both Wedding Guest and narrator double his voice. In fact, the mariner's voice subsumes or silences all the other voices in the poem. The voices of the two spirits cease their senseless chatter when the mariner comes out of his trance. The hermit, who himself is the creator of his own hymns, asks the mariner for confession and cannot exercise his spiritual authority as confessor because the mariner's tale usurps the place of the hermit's hymns. In 1798 the mariner's voice promises repetition of his experience in the voices and experiences of others, just as many of the tales in *The Borderers* are repeated in human action and as the tales in *Osorio* become true later in experience.

The mariner's consciousness of the power of his tale is reflected in his power of speech. After the killing of the albatross and after the ship is driven north into the Pacific, the mariner says "We were the first that ever burst / Into that silent Sea" (101–2). Their arrival marks the beginning of their punishment and seems itself to be almost a violation of the place: "And we did speak only to break / The silence of the Sea" (105–6). Breaking the silence is followed by a loss of speech altogether:

81

And every tongue thro' utter drouth
Was wither'd at the root;
We could not speak no more than if
We had been choked with soot.

(131–34)

The result of a violation, both in "The Ancient Mariner" and in "Adventures on Salisbury Plain," is the loss of speech. When it is restored, speech is strangely disconnected from action and event. The mariner bites his arm to moisten his mouth with blood and cries out in hopes of rescue from the death ship that appears on the horizon. But the cry is ineffective because the ship cannot be hailed as the albatross was hailed, and when it comes it does not bring the expected relief. Speech has become disconnected from action and intention.

Dominated by the overwhelming image of the ship, the mariner cannot speak or pray but utters only "wicked whispers." The blessing of the water snakes restores the mariner's power of prayer but is not in itself a verbal act. When he sees them he recognizes that "no tongue / Their beauty might declare" (274–75), and he blesses them "unaware." If the biting of his arm to call the death ship is a useless expression because its intention is frustrated, then the blessing of the water snakes disconnects the "gush of love," which is its origin, from voice. In spite of the restoration of a power of prayer, his homeward journey is plagued by an increasing awareness of the power of his own voice separated from his intention until he comes to a recognition:

The body of my brother's son
Stood by me knee to knee:
The body and I pull'd at one rope,
But he said nought to me—
And I quak'd to think of my own voice
How frightful it would be!

(333–38)

The last two lines were deleted after 1798, but they constitute the mariner's most powerful moment of self-recognition. This recognition precedes by about thirty lines his warning that "Never sadder tale was told." As an object of his thought, his voice is another and separate being, just as he himself is a being separate from the ghosts of community that surround him. And just as he would be an object of terror to them, were they present, so too is his voice frightful to him. Repressed during the voyage, it erupts in telling the tale with a consciousness of its own affect. It is a voice over which he, as a character, has no control. The voice returns to speak when the agony returns within him, the fear and dread of his voyage, but in the 1798 version the voice itself is the object of terror. Paradoxically, the suggestion that the agony is relieved by a purgative telling of the tale is countered by the presence in the telling of the tale of a voice that is and is not his and which gains a reality by becoming an object to him. It is a voice that announces its reality by speaking; in other words, the presence of the voice is prior to the mariner's recognition of it as *"my* voice." It is his curse, a curse that is upon him and which he inflicts upon others, that he possesses the voice and is possessed by it. When he returns to harbor, the mariner, finding himself in the pilot's boat, opens his mouth to speak, and immediately the pilot and the boy are seized with madness.

One of Wordsworth's criticisms of the poem in the note to it in 1800 was that "the principal person has no distinct character, either in his profession of Mariner, or as a human being who having been long under the controul of supernatural impressions might be supposed himself to partake of something supernatural" (*LB* 277). Wordsworth's observation on the defining characteristics of the poem is correct. Only his judgment of them as defects is questionable, and the reasons for this judgment are not hard to find. When Coleridge wrote in the *Biographia* that he was to use the supernatural to explore the truth of our "inward nature," most likely Wordsworth saw this as the portrayal of "character." As Wordsworth wrote in December 1798, he disliked Bürger's poetry because, "I do not perceive the presence of character in his personages. I see everywhere the character of Bürger himself . . ." (*LEY* 234). Wordsworth's attempts in the Salisbury Plain poems and *The Borderers* had been to portray the characters' moral and emotional nature, but in his reading of "The Ancient Mariner" his complaints, insofar as they are truly judgments and not self-justifications, implicitly admit the lack of connection between the character and experience of the mariner and the voice that tells the tale.[12]

Wordsworth's note to "The Ancient Mariner" and his note about "The Three Graves" that Coleridge could not sanctify "natural

12. John Jordan has written that Wordsworth's "objection is not to the supernatural in itself but to what seems to him lack of consonance between the character of the hero and his milieu" ("The Hewing of *Peter Bell,*" *Studies in English Literature* 7 [1967]: 568).

woes" indicate that he expected Coleridge to have narrated the tale of someone who underwent a transformation from fear to awe or of someone who "might be supposed himself to partake of something supernatural." He said later of his own Salisbury Plain poems that he did not publish them because "the mariner's fate appeared to me so tragical," implying that he sought for mitigation of the fear and suffering in those poems and in "The Ancient Mariner" and did not find it in either.[13] His reference to his own "mariner" instead of "sailor" is revealing. His objections to "The Ancient Mariner" are to its emotional and moral tone, and they are the very same objections he had to his own Salisbury Plain poems. It is as though he were criticizing his own work when it appeared under Coleridge's name and as though he could not see the differences between his and Coleridge's work.

Wordsworth's explicit comments on "The Ancient Mariner" criticize the lack of a transforming emotion within the mariner that would alleviate his fear and dread. There is an attempt at such a transformation that mitigates the mariner's fear, but it is not the kind of transformation that Wordsworth would initially have been led to expect from his reading of the earlier Coleridge. It is, however, one that is implicitly recognized in his own poetry, particularly "The Discharged Soldier," one of the first fragments written after he withdrew from collaboration on "The Ancient Mariner." The crucial issues in both "The Ancient Mariner" and "The Discharged Soldier" are the use of the supernatural as figurative and the meeting with the figures of the mariner and the soldier. Wordsworth's verse reads Coleridge's poem as using the supernatural, not as merely the Gothic, but as the figurative. The *Biographia*'s explanation of the supernatural is ambiguous. On the one hand, the supernatural represents the truth of human nature and human emotion; it captures the attention and provides a setting in which those extravagant human and natural emotions can work, and it reveals the

13. *WPW* 1: 330. A similar comment is recorded by J. P. Collier, who noted that on Feb. 10, 1814, he expressed admiration for "The Female Vagrant" to Wordsworth, who replied that "he was sorry for it . . . for it was one upon which he set comparatively small value; it was addressed to coarse sympathies, and had little or no imagination about it, nor invention as to story" (S. T. Coleridge, *Seven Lectures on Shakespeare and Milton*, ed. J. P. Collier [1856] li). The phrase "coarse sympathies" contrasts with his praise of "quiet sympathies" in the 1798 consolation to "The Ruined Cottage" (Butler 261). Thus Wordsworth was turning from the emotions evoked by "The Female Vagrant" before that work was published in *Lyrical Ballads* in September 1798.

truth of "our inward nature" because that is its creative source. But the *Biographia* does not have exclusive claim to interpret the supernatural as figurative language, and in fact it can be read in an entirely different way. The poem of 1798, Wordsworth and Lamb agree, has as its defining characteristic the dissociation of personality from voice, the severing of connection between authority and tale. As Lamb said, the tale buries "all individuality or memory of what he was . . . , all consciousness of personality is gone" (*Lamb Letters* 1: 266). The tale possesses its own reality, and it is difficult—even with the assistance, or perhaps one might say the hindrance, of Coleridge's own commentary on it—to know whether to read the tale as possessing the reality of human experience or the reality of fiction, whether the tale is subsumed to the reality of the terror it depicts or whether the terror is transformed by its fantastic fiction.

The *Biographia*, reread, may reinforce this puzzlement by offering an alternative way of reading the supernatural, not as representative of "our inward nature," but as an originating fiction. If "poetic faith" has its beginnings in an act of disbelief, which in turn is suspended, then its context must be a fiction or a series of fictions. It claims that "The Ancient Mariner" offers a "dramatic truth" when it invokes the supernatural and that one is able to *suppose* that the supernatural is real, and to "suppose" is to provide a ground for the real in the supernatural, which is disbelieved in the first place. The result, which Coleridge admits with almost naive candor, is the "semblance of truth." And this fiction, as Coleridge recognized, can become a powerful author. The theatrical tomfoolery in the conjuring scene of *Osorio*, which Coleridge intended to be seen as a trick by everyone who witnesses it, possesses something of the audacity of a crime, not only because it is done thoughtlessly and with mixed motives, but also because it initiates the action; it is a deception that is misinterpreted. The landscape of the supernatural becomes itself a theater of fiction similar to that which Coleridge defined as dramatic illusion:

> . . . stage presentations are to produce a sort of temporary half-faith, which the spectator encourages in himself and supports by a voluntary contribution on his own part, because he knows that it is at all times in his power to see the thing as it really is . . . which permits this sort of negative belief.[14]

14. Coleridge, *Shakespearean Criticism*, ed. Thomas Middleton Raysor, 2 vols. (London: Dent; New York: Dutton, 1960) 1: 178–79.

The difference between Coleridge's theory of the "negative belief" of dramatic illusion and the "willing suspension of disbelief" in the act of reading, both of them willed acts, and his portrait of the mariner telling his tale and the characters in *Osorio* enacting theirs is that his characters have will, purpose, and intention severed from their utterances.

When the supernatural as figurative replaces the reality of "our inward nature," the emotion generated by that reality is transformed. Wordsworth's complaint that Coleridge could not sanctify "natural woes" and so fled into the supernatural has some truth, but what Wordsworth did not openly admit was that the transformation of the supernatural altered the emotional nature of the poem. It was no longer the raw terror at which the politically sympathetic reader became indignant, such as that in the Salisbury Plain poems, but a far more subtle alleviation of terror. Terror is changed into poetic wonder. The fuller and more complete transfiguration could have taken it into the awe and wonder of the later *Prelude*. To Wordsworth it was an escape that trivialized the pain of life; to Coleridge it marked the partial alleviation of pains by placing them within the context of the literary, which raised questions of their full meaning.

Wordsworth's "The Discharged Soldier" is ample evidence that he was deeply troubled by the uncanny and unnatural figure of the mariner removed from any recognizable landscape. Above all, he was bothered by the figurative itself. Although his prose note admitted a representational quality for the figure by saying that it was "true to nature" (*LB* 277), his poetic response indicates that he knew the mariner's character was dissociated from his voice and that the alienated figure was out of place and ambiguous. "The Discharged Soldier," Wordsworth's most insightful and incisive response to the figure of the mariner, is in Book IV of *The Prelude*, written in late January or early February before "The Ancient Mariner" was completed.[15] It was the first poem of substantial length Wordsworth wrote after having withdrawn from contributing to "The Ancient Mariner" in the middle of November 1797. During December he was in London trying to arrange for the staging of *The Borderers*, and having failed, he returned the first week in January. Work began on

15. The original text was published in Beth Darlington's "Two Early Texts: *A Night-Piece* and *The Discharged Soldier*," *WBS* 425–48, from which I quote for both poems.

three poems at about that time: "The Discharged Soldier," the continuation of "The Ruined Cottage," and "A Night-Piece."

There are many obvious similarities between "The Discharged Soldier" and "The Ancient Mariner." Both present an individual who has been wasted by a long voyage or exile and who has returned as an isolated wanderer, an alienated figure who is trying to get home and who has a powerful tale to tell. More important, the soldier is described in many of the same terms in which the mariner is described:

> His legs were long,
> So long and shapeless that I looked at them
> Forgetful of the body they sustained.
> His arms were long & lean; his hands were bare;
> His visage, wasted though it seem'd, was large
> In feature; his cheeks sunken; and his mouth
> Shewed ghastly in the moonlight.
>
> (45–51)

The corresponding lines in "The Ancient Mariner" describe the mariner in the same terms:

> "I fear thee, ancyent Marinere!
> I fear thy skinny hand;
> And thou art long, and lank, and brown,
> As is the ribb'd Sea-sand."
>
> (216–19)

In *Sibylline Leaves* Coleridge acknowledged that "for the last two lines of this stanza, I am indebted to Mr. WORDSWORTH" (*CPW* 1: 196). Wordsworth is reclaiming one of his contributions to Coleridge's poem. When Wordsworth inserted these lines into *The Prelude*, he deleted the physical details of emaciation and weakness and some of the residual Gothic imagery that makes the soldier seem almost a skeleton. The man is obviously a forerunner of the leech gatherer, and Wordsworth's revisions of that character in 1802 may have influenced his revisions on "The Discharged Soldier" before it was inserted in *The Prelude* in 1804.[16] The presence of such detail in

16. Geoffrey Hartman, writing of the passage in Book IV of *The Prelude*, discussed the soldier as a border figure between life and death (*Wordsworth's Poetry, 1787–1814* [New Haven: Yale University Press, 1964] 224–25). Jonathan Wordsworth has regarded him in the same light (*William Wordsworth: The Borders of Vision* [Oxford: Clar-

CHAPTER 3

1798 is important both for the link with "The Ancient Mariner" and for the significance of the figure as a commentary on it. To see "The Discharged Soldier" as a self-generated poem or as growing, perhaps, from the figure of the sailor in "Adventures on Salisbury Plain" and as a forerunner of the leech gatherer as a border figure between life and death is to ignore its position in Coleridge's poetry.

Structurally, "The Discharged Soldier" resembles "A Night-Piece." The speaker is walking along a road at night, absorbed in the tranquillity of nature, and has a sudden encounter with a figure that takes him aback. He approaches the figure, questions him and hears his meager tale, and then leads him to shelter for the night. The emotional wonder comes, of course, from the strangeness of the soldier's appearance, his being out of place and unexpected. It is an encounter of speaker as Wedding Guest with the soldier as mariner; the speaker's struggle to accommodate the figure to his landscape implies Wordsworth's struggle to comprehend Coleridge's increasingly figurative vision and to turn it to his own. Like "Michael," the poem opens with the speaker on the "public way," yet it is a deserted road at night and ironically possesses "deeper quietness / Than pathless solitudes" (4–5). The only present voice is that of the murmur of a stream. The speaker is

> Tranquil, receiving in my own despite
> Amusement, as I slowly passed along,
> From such near objects as from time to time
> Perforce disturbed the slumber of the sense
> Quiescent, & disposed to sympathy,
> With an exhausted mind worn out by toil

endon Press, 1982] 10–14). Whether or not Wordsworth met the soldier in the summer of 1788, he did meet the figure in his childhood reading, for in the history of the Pedlar, Wordsworth described him:

> Romance of giants chronicle of fiends
> Profuse in garniture of wooden cuts
> Strange & uncouth, dire faces, figures dire
> Sharp kneed, sharp-elbowed & lean-ankled too
> With long & ghostly shanks forms which once seen
> Could never be forgotten.

(Butler 165)

Could this figure have been the origin of Wordsworth's description of the mariner or of the discharged soldier? In its early versions the discharged soldier is less of a border figure and more of an uncouth and unintelligible figure.

88

And all unworthy of the deeper joy
Which waits on distant prospect, cliff or sea,
The dark blue vault, and universe of stars.

(12–20)

If "The Discharged Soldier" is read as an individual and integral poem, these scenes could easily be mistaken for natural scenery, but regarded in the context of "A Night-Piece" they become a commentary on it. The final line refers to the vision of "A Night-Piece," of the "clear moon & the glory of the heavens. / There in a black-blue vault she sails along . . ." (10–11) to display an "interminable depth." The point made by allusion is that the mood of the poet in "The Discharged Soldier' is less that of sublime wonder than that of "peace and solitude," and "beauteous pictures" rose "in harmonious imagery—they rose / As from some distant region of my soul / And came along like dreams" (28–31). Curiously, in the midst of natural beauty, Wordsworth finds his comfort and tranquillity in the language of art, or the harmony of poetry, and the "pictures" of landscape, yet he does not seem at all troubled by the apparent conflict of art and nature. Rather, the combination of the two is a restoration to him and brings him "A consciousness of animal delight, / A self-possession felt in every pause / And every gentle movement of my frame" (33–35).

Suddenly he comes upon the figure of the soldier at the bend of the road. The shock that he receives disrupts the harmony of dream and naturalness that had subsumed the natural to his dream. His following meditations on the figure attempt to transform its strange presence into the naturalness with which the poem began, and, in the larger context of the poetic dialogue with Coleridge, constitute an attempt to come to grips with Coleridge's energetic figuration. While perhaps Wordsworth's gentle comedy of "Peter Bell" suggests that in 1797–98 he was willing to allow Coleridge the modes of the supernatural, "The Discharged Soldier" suggests that he was indeed troubled by it and the challenges that it posed to his own ability to use figurative language and remain a natural poet.

The figure that Wordsworth meets startles him because it is not a part of the landscape. It is the "uncouth" figure who is unknown, unrecognized, and not understood. Not only does it stand apart from the beauty and tranquillity in which it seems to be located, but it changes the landscape. In a strange reversal, the figure transforms the landscape into his own image; he becomes the ground for landscape. He is a "ghastly" figure whose solitude and obvious alienation replaces in the speaker's mind his own solitude amid the comforting solitudes of nature. His inarticulate murmuring of complaint and pain replaces the gentle murmur of the stream, just as the leech gatherer's words silence the "pleasant noise of waters." He, like Wordsworth, is on the public way and traveling home, yet he is a being to himself, utterly displaced. The most troublesome characteristic of the soldier is that, when questioned about his history, he is completely detached from it and his past. He possesses no self-consciousness; even his body seems at best a random collection of disconnected fragments:

> His face was turn'd
> Towards the road, yet not as if he sought
> For any living thing. He appeared
> Forlorn and desolate, a man cut off
> From all his kind, and more than half detached
> From his own nature.
>
> (55–60)

Most immediately troubling to Wordsworth is this detachment. Its inexplicable presence replaces the calm "self-possession" that he felt earlier almost as a physical pleasure.

Through the remaining lines, Wordsworth repeats the impression of the soldier's strange detachment from himself and from his tale:

> I asked his history, he in reply
> Was neither slow nor eager, but unmoved,
> And with a quiet uncomplaining voice,
> A stately air of mild indifference,
> He told a simple fact. . . .
>
> (95–99)

The "simple fact" that is his tale is reduced to four spare lines of indirect discourse, delivered without the private murmuring of pain but with a measured and public tone. When Wordsworth offers to conduct him to a cottage for the night, he acknowledges that

> He appeared
> To travel without pain, & I beheld
> With ill-suppress'd astonishment his tall
> And ghostly figure moving at my side.
>
> (122–25)

Part of the surprise is that a man who at rest murmured what the poet thought were words of painful complaint could move without physical pain, but also that the man is at his side, almost his shadow. The initial shock of seeing that "his shadow / Lay at his feet & moved not" is confirmed by the shadow's becoming his double, as though the only reference of the figure is the figure itself because it is its own image. But when the figure appears by Wordsworth's side, it becomes Wordsworth's double as well. Finally, when the soldier is questioned again on his history:

> He all the while was in demeanor calm,
> Concise in answer: solemn & sublime
> He might have seemed, but that in all he said
> There was a strange half-absence & a tone
> Of weakness & indifference, as of one
> Remembering the importance of his theme,
> But feeling it no longer.
>
> (140–46)

The separation between teller and tale is marked by the lack of feeling and understanding that the soldier displays. He no longer has any emotional motive to speak at all and only responds to questions. His is a ghostly presence, detached from a past. Even more strangely, his detachment from the sublime and solemn landscape parallels the detachment of the speaker from the sublime of the "interminable depth" of "A Night-Piece." Neither poet nor figure confronts that power.

The figure that Wordsworth meets in 1798 is not a border figure between life and death who signifies a transcendent truth beyond himself. The early poem emphasizes physical pain, and the figure does not represent sublimity; he is closer to a figure of human sympathy. The threat that he presents to the poet is the threat of the inexplicable and unnatural figure that supplants the natural landscape in many of the same ways that the vision of the towering cliff in the stolen-boat episode replaces the child's images of pastoral nature, and in ways that Geraldine dominates the familiar landscape in "Christabel." But unlike the towering cliffs, which are more clearly a projection of the child's incipient imagination, the figure seems to arise from nowhere; it is simply seen, unmoved and unmoving, resting against the stone milepost, which is its apt emblem. Wordsworth's rhetoric in such encounters is commonly that of repetition, and what is repeated, at least four times, is detachment, the lack of any enlivening motive for the soldier's tale. Exactly as in

"The Ancient Mariner," the tale is detached from the authority of the teller. Wordsworth's emphasis on this point in "The Discharged Soldier" indicates that he saw that as the characteristic of "The Ancient Mariner." The issue at this point in their poetic dialogue is, very basically, figuration itself, the issue of Coleridge's use of the supernatural as fiction and figure and the intelligibility of both. That the figure of "The Discharged Soldier" supplants the natural landscape in all of its features reveals that Coleridge's use of the supernatural as fiction and figure threatened to supplant Wordsworth's literalism, or to show him that his literalism was simply another form of figurative, artful composition, which Wordsworth partly admits in the opening lines by recording his delight in the "beauteous pictures" that "came along like dreams."

Wordsworth's varying reactions to the soldier throughout the poem describe his deepest reactions to Coleridge's vision. The figure in the landscape is pictured almost as though Wordsworth has inscribed or drawn him there: "I could mark him well, / Myself unseen" (40–41). A few lines further on he says, "I could mark / That he was clad in military garb." He possesses a distant, strange, and yet familiar presence, which evokes "fear and sorrow." The sorrow is that of pity for his state, and Wordsworth retains from his earlier poetry the impulse toward human sympathy. Shortly his fear and "specious cowardice" is subdued. He approaches the soldier, hears his narrative, and conducts him to shelter for the night, offering to pay for his bed. The only time in the poem that the soldier responds with any emotion is at the end, when Wordsworth leaves him at the cottage and "in a voice that seem'd / To speak with a reviving interest / Till then unfelt, he thanked me" (168–70). The soldier is moved, not only at charity, but also at the thought, offered by the poet, that in the future he should "demand the succor which his state required." Charity, to Wordsworth, was not something given freely and without obligation by those who could afford it; it was a matter of right that the poor, disabled, and vagrant could claim. To urge such a claim is to recognize that one has a legitimate place in society. Wordsworth not only leads the soldier to a cottage, he returns him to a social position that could not have been his in the nearby town.

There is more to Wordsworth's ushering the figure than the social theme of the rights of the poor. His reaction to the figure marks an effort to master the figure, to relocate it within the natural order, and to come to grips with the figurative as it was used in "The Ancient Mariner." To do so, he must reverse the figure's own reversal and dominance of landscape. By socializing him, he has restored what Wordsworth considered the necessary connection between character and voice in the emotion of grateful response. By presenting the soldier's tale in indirect discourse, Wordsworth can shape it to "a simple fact," as he calls it in 1798. Later, in *The Prelude*, the emphasis is lost because it is merely a "Soldier's Tale." The tension created between such an "uncouth," unearthly figure and his tale, which is "a simple fact," indicates the imperative that Wordsworth felt to return the figure to the literal. The cost of such transformation is difficult to measure. While it restores the literal and subordinates the figurative to it, that accommodation of the figurative denies the possibilities of sublimity. The poem remains one in which the greatest possible gesture is the exchange of blessings in a human context.

Wordsworth's repossession of the figure is possible in part because the emotion of his first encounter is different from that of the mariner's meeting with the figures on the death ship and from both the hermit's and the Wedding Guest's emotion on first meeting the mariner. Those encounters engender a terror that annihilates personality and past; only toward the end of the poem does the terror begin to change to wonder. Wordsworth's domestication of the figure is accompanied at first meeting with a pity that evokes, not the loss of personality, but personality's most generous impulse. The encounter that in "The Ancient Mariner" begins in terror begins in "The Discharged Soldier" in pity and wondering fear and is modified to familiar affection.

Wordsworth's response to "The Ancient Mariner" in "The Discharged Soldier" is, because of its responsive nature, one of the most important that he ever wrote in the quest for his own voice. "The Discharged Soldier" is not in any significant sense a competing poem. It does not, like the comic "Peter Bell," domesticate the plot of "The Ancient Mariner." Nor does it deal with the superficial matters of a curse and superstition, as do many of the shorter, and also partly comic, lyrical ballads, such as "Goody Blake and Harry Gill." It was not written to show Coleridge how he ought to have written his poem; there is no imperious tone about it. Although it was started before "The Ancient Mariner" was completed in March and may have been started in Wordsworth's mind at the time he withdrew from contributing to it, it incorporates very little of what critics commonly consider the essential qualities of Coleridge's poem. But it responds to "The Ancient Mariner" on a far more fundamental

93

level, by confronting and in part transforming the essential charac-
teristic of Coleridge's poem as Wordsworth saw it in January and
February 1798: the potential depersonalization of voice and discon-
nection between speaker and tale and the resulting figuration. Its
intention is to avoid becoming assimilated to the style of another
and assimilated to an uncongenial style.

Wordsworth's opinion of "The Discharged Soldier" as an inde-
pendent poem is difficult to determine. He did not publish it, and it
was embedded in Book IV of *The Prelude*, which implies that he did
not think it appropriate for earlier publication, or that it did not
have an appropriate context until it was included in *The Prelude*. It
would not fit the scheme of *Lyrical Ballads* (1798), since it was not
written in any of the varieties of ballad. It may have been revised in
1800 for the second volume, but it was excluded from it, although it
would have had an appropriate context alongside "Hart-Leap
Well," "The Brothers," "Ruth," and "Michael." Wordsworth may
have judged it to be too personal or lyric to be included there. In
Book IV of *The Prelude* it occupies an important position, preceded
by the account of the trivial festive dance that Wordsworth attends
and the dedication scene. In the context of the dedication scene, it
represents Wordsworth's relocation of the beginnings of a poetic ca-
reer from the struggle with Coleridge's poetry to an earlier stage in
his own life.

"The Ancient Mariner" and "The Discharged Soldier" present a
complex dialogue on the relation of the figures of the mariner and
the soldier to their natural settings in the landscape. These figures
and their settings mirror the position of figures of speech in their
lyric contexts and of lyric passages in the context of the dialogue.
The crucial issue is whether the figures determine the significance
of their context, or the context determines the significance of the
figures. The locations and relocations of the figure are further com-
plicated because they are appropriated and relocated from frag-
mentary texts of works in progress, poems that are in no sense
either unified or complete. Since Wordsworth's sailor becomes
Coleridge's mariner at the point of transition from "Salisbury Plain"
to "Adventures in Salisbury Plain," and since Coleridge's mariner
becomes Wordsworth's soldier before "The Ancient Mariner" is
completed, the figures reside at points of transition. The soldier re-
places Wordsworth's pleasant dreams with a ghostly presence on the
deserted public way. At first, the enigmatic figures like the mariner
and the soldier are unknown and unrecognized. Their voices are

detached from a motive to utter their narratives and to give them a clearly intended meaning. The significance of Coleridge's mariner is that he returns from his voyage with a strange tale that transforms the community of his auditors. The mariner is a figure whose narrative dominates his locations. When Wordsworth appropriates the figure from the fragments of Coleridge's poem, he transforms the strange figure into one who can utter a familiar blessing by restoring him to a human context. The implication of Coleridge's figure is that the figure can dominate and determine the context. The implication of Wordsworth's gesture of relocation is that the context can transform the figure. Neither mariner nor soldier can exist apart from their locations. Similarly, figures cannot exist apart from their contexts in the dialogue. The isolated figure is an enigmatic terror both in landscape and lyric because it has no intended meaning, no motivated narrative, and no determining context. "Christabel" is the unfinished narrative of the isolated figure.

"The Colours of our Style":

"The Ruined Cottage" and "Christabel"

WORDSWORTH'S "The Ruined Cottage," first drafted in the summer of 1797, his "The Pedlar," drafted in the late winter and early spring of 1798, and Coleridge's "Christabel," begun in April 1798, form a sequence in their dialogue that is parallel to, yet distinct from, that formed by the Salisbury Plain poems, "The Ancient Mariner," and "The Discharged Soldier." In "The Ancient Mariner" Coleridge appropriated draft stanzas that Wordsworth continued to revise before they were published as "Guilt and Sorrow" (1842). In "Christabel" he revised and reinterpreted both "The Ruined Cottage" and Wordsworth's interpretation of it in the Pedlar material and the consolation of Margaret's story. "Christabel" remained fragmentary in 1798, when he wrote the first part, and even after 1800, when he wrote the second. Wordsworth's early drafts of Margaret's and Robert's stories and Coleridge's reading of them in "Christabel" concur in identifying the central themes of "The Ruined Cottage" as the loss of hope, Margaret's and Robert's wandering, and their mutual detachment from a natural life, which forces them to create the unnatural, the novel, and the figures in landscape that landscape can neither provide nor accommodate. "The Discharged Soldier" responds directly to the figure of Coleridge's mariner, but by implication it also responds to the creation of figures by both Margaret and Robert.

Although drafted in an integral form in 1797, Margaret's story was not completed in Wordsworth's mind, because its meaning was not clear; the story told no tale in which the emotional content was settled. Looked at in the larger context of the Salisbury Plain poems and Coleridge's earlier poetry (Alhadra's final speech in *Osorio*, for example), Margaret's story could be read as similar to that of the female vagrant in "Adventures on Salisbury Plain," and the emotional reaction of the reader directed toward an honest indignation prompting vengeance. Such is clearly the intent of the final stanzas of "Adventures on Salisbury Plain." But Wordsworth said that he did not publish the Salisbury Plain poems because they appealed to the cruder emotions, and the consolation to Margaret's story drafted in 1798 specifically rejected indignation and vengeance in the name of pity and love. Thus an interpretation of Margaret's story was necessary, because the bare outlines of Margaret's despair could prompt vastly different emotional reactions. Wordsworth had to write an interpretation, not simply to characterize the Pedlar as a worthy narrator, but to determine the reader's reaction to Margaret's story. When Wordsworth attempted to compose a consolation to determine the significance of Margaret's life, he turned to Coleridge's poetry, both that which he had written earlier, "This Lime-Tree Bower," and that which he was writing, "The Ancient Mariner" and "Frost at Midnight." Canceled drafts of his consolation show that Coleridge's lines are present in each attempt.

Coleridge's response to both Margaret's story and the Pedlar material, in the first part of "Christabel," took what must have seemed to Wordsworth a strange turn. "Christabel" questions both the optimism of hope and the certainty of the meaning of signs within landscape that the Pedlar claims to be able to read. In the context of their poetic dialogue, Coleridge's response argues that the divisions occasioned by wandering, once opened, and the necessity of interpretation and figuration, once established, allow no return to the secure certainty of the literal. The mariner returns to his own country only temporarily and continues to be the enigmatic wandering figure, just as, later, Leonard in "The Brothers" remains unknown to the Priest of Ennerdale. Christabel is aware, at the end of the first part, of having been presented with the figure of Geraldine, an enigmatic figure. Both parts of the poem, the first implicitly and the second explicitly, question the Pedlar's ability to read landscape with a worthy eye.

"An Inarticulate Language": "The Ruined Cottage"

Early in October 1800 Coleridge and the Wordsworths were completing copy for the second volume of *Lyrical Ballads*. Among other projects, Coleridge had been working on "Christabel" to complete the volume. He arrived at Grasmere on October 4, and Dorothy wrote in her journal: "Coleridge came in while we were at dinner very wet.—We talked till 12 o'clock. He had sate up all the night before writing Essays for the Newspaper.—His youngest child had been very ill in convulsion fits. Exceedingly delighted with the 2nd part of Christabel" (*DWJ* 42–43). Derwent Coleridge was born September 14, and Coleridge did not expect him to live. Three days after Derwent's birth, Coleridge confessed to James Webbe Tobin the delay in completing "Christabel": "Every line has been produced by me with labor-pangs. I abandon Poetry altogether—I leave the higher & deeper Kinds to Wordsworth . . . (*STCL* 1: 623). By the beginning of October, however, "Christabel" seems to have outrun the space allotted for it in the volume and was still unfinished. On the sixth, Dorothy wrote, "after tea read The Pedlar. Determined not to print Christabel with the LB" (*DWJ* 43), and on the ninth Coleridge explained to Humphry Davy that "The Christabel was running up to 1300 lines—and was so much admired by Wordsworth, that he thought it indelicate to print two Volumes with *his name* in which so much of another man's was included—& which was of more consequence—the poem was in direct opposition to the very purpose for which the Lyrical Ballads were published—viz—an experiment to see how far those passions, which alone give any value to extraordinary Incidents, were capable of interesting, in & for themselves, in the incidents of common Life" (*STCL* 1: 631). His comment is as much a claim of independence from Wordsworth as it is an admission of failure to complete "Christabel"; it can be read to mean that he has generated a poem too great for the limited scope of *Lyrical Ballads*. The inappropriateness of "Christabel" for *Lyrical Ballads* required Wordsworth to fill the space, for which he wrote "Michael." "Christabel" never reached 1,300 lines; the first two parts, without the conclusion to Part II, which was written two years later, are only about 650 lines. "Michael," which replaced it, was 491 lines. If Coleridge had added more parts to "Christabel," it certainly would have been much longer than any other poem in the volume.

In his letter to Davy, Coleridge stated that "We mean to publish the Christabel therefore with a long Blank Verse Poem of Wordsworth's entitled the Pedlar . . ." (*STCL* 1: 631). There is some question as to precisely what poem Coleridge refers to as "The Pedlar" and what Dorothy meant when she used that title on October 9. It may refer to the Pedlar material alone, or it may refer to Margaret's story and the Pedlar material together, a total of about 900 lines.[1] Whether Dorothy and Coleridge referred to the Pedlar's history with or without Margaret's story in 1800, they may have thought for a short time in early October that one or both could replace "Christabel," because Dorothy's journal seems to link the reading of "The Pedlar" with the decision to exclude "Christabel." Furthermore, in the summer of 1800, when Wordsworth was preparing copy for the second volume of *Lyrical Ballads*, he seems to have thought, not of a collection of separate and individual poems, distinct from one another, but of a series of poems and introductory poems. His notes to "The Thorn" and "The Brothers," which I discuss in Chapter 7, suggest that he may have thought of "The Pedlar" as an introductory poem separate from, but still linked to, "The Ruined Cottage."

1. The issue of what poem, or poems, Coleridge referred to as "The Pedlar" is complicated by the history of the manuscripts. In 1799 the earlier unified manuscript of Margaret's story with the history of the Pedlar was copied into two different sections: a 538-line poem entitled "The Ruined Cottage," which told Margaret's story and included a brief consolation followed by the phrase "The End"; and an untitled collection of fragments about the Pedlar included in 1798 but removed in 1799 along with another passage immediately following "The Ruined Cottage" entitled "Fragment." These fragments, totaling about 385 lines, were published by Jonathan Wordsworth in *The Music of Humanity* (London: Nelson, 1969) with the title "The Pedlar." However, by October 1800, when both Coleridge and Dorothy referred to a poem called "The Pedlar," the earlier material had been reduced by about seventy of its most important lines on the One Life, which had been placed in *The Prelude* (1799). Does Coleridge's reference to "The Pedlar" in 1800 include both Margaret's story and the history of the Pedlar, or merely the Pedlar's history alone? In 1969 Jonathan Wordsworth observed of Coleridge's phrase "a long Blank Verse Poem" that "long may be a relative term, but in the context of *Christabel* seems more likely to describe a total *Ruined Cottage* than a poem of under 300 lines" (*Music of Humanity* 165). James Butler argued the contrary in 1977: "When Coleridge wrote Davy on 9 October 1800 of a plan to publish *Christabel* with the *Pedlar*, it is the account of the Pedlar and not the narrative of Margaret that is meant" ("The Chronology of Wordsworth's *The Ruined Cottage* after 1800," *Studies in Philology* 74 [1977]: 112); he has recently affirmed his analysis of the evidence to me.

Since a dialogic reading assumes that the boundaries of individual poems are constantly shifting and that the critical choice to read separate poems is of less importance than seeing their connections and seeing them in sequence, it is relatively unimportant whether Coleridge and the Wordsworths thought of "The Ruined Cottage" and "The Pedlar" as separate poems or one poem. What matters is that they are clearly related. They form a dialogue with "Christabel," which was begun shortly after Wordsworth completed the additions to Margaret's story in March 1798 and which provided commentary on Wordsworth's attempted resolutions and consolations for Margaret's suffering and upon Wordsworth's presentation of the figures.

"The Ruined Cottage" and "Christabel" both present a woman tied to a particular dwelling: Margaret's cottage and Christabel's castle. At least initially in each poem, the dwelling is the location of charity. Margaret offers water from her well to travelers; Christabel brings Geraldine into the castle to save her from her abductors and offers restorative wine. Each woman has been separated from her lover by war. Margaret's husband leaves home to join the army; Christabel's lover has left on the Crusades. Neither woman knows whether her lover is alive or dead, thus both are separated by distance and uncertainty. Thus, at least potentially, both present charity separated from fulfilled sexual love. They receive little comfort from others. The Pedlar visits Margaret infrequently, and Christabel's father can offer her little sympathy, because he too has lost his spouse and lives a life in death that resembles Margaret's despair. In both poems the woman wanders from the security and stability of her home. Margaret wanders over the countryside looking for her husband's return; Christabel leaves the safety of her castle at night to pray in the woods for the welfare of her lover. By brooding on their absent lovers, both women fall into passive despair, become detached from common reality, and develop severe disorientation. Margaret loses her children and no longer cares about the weeds choking her garden. Christabel, discovering her double in Geraldine, loses her individual will as Geraldine becomes "lord of thy utterance." Finally, each tale is narrated by a person whose knowledge of the events and whose interpretations of them are crucial to the individual poems and to the dialogue that the two poems constitute. The Pedlar claims to be able to see what others cannot see, to possess wisdom that he can pass on to others, yet the narrator of "Christabel," in a constant state of wonder, simply asks questions.

These two poems are further comparable in the emotions they explore and distinct from "Adventures on Salisbury Plain" and "The Ancient Mariner," which are anatomies of the effects of fear and terror. "Adventures on Salisbury Plain" and "The Ancient Mariner" present the recurrent presences of inimical external forces that control the lives of the sailor and the mariner. They are persecuted and driven to crime, led to believe that they are guilty, and finally haunted by reminders of their acts. They wander in a world that will not let them alone, in which there is an unpredictable return of the oppressive presences that determine their fate, even though they make every effort to escape, evade, or withdraw. Both poems thus present uncompleted efforts to transform the anxiety and fear into its opposite, joy. "The Ruined Cottage" and "Christabel," on the other hand, are anatomies of hope and despair. In "The Ruined Cottage" Margaret's despair comes, not from the presence of external forces and objects, but from the absence of an object of her hope. The difference between her vacancy and the hostile presences of the other poems is illustrated in passages in which both Margaret and the mariner shape images in the distance. In a verse paragraph that was written by June 1797 and that concluded the earliest version, the narrator describes his final meeting with Margaret:[2]

> On this old Bench
> For hours she sate, and evermore her eye
> Was busy in the distance, shaping things
> Which made her heart beat quick. Seest thou that path?
> (The greensward now has broken its grey line)
> There, to and fro she paced through many a day
> Of the warm summer, from a belt of flax
> That girt her waist spinning the long-drawn thread

2. The texts have been published in two important editions. The first is Jonathan Wordsworth's *Music of Humanity*, which prints MS. D (1799) of "The Ruined Cottage" and the separate Pedlar material from the same manuscript. The second is James Butler's *"The Ruined Cottage" and "The Pedlar,"* which prints "The Ruined Cottage" in parallel reading texts from MS. B (1798) and MS. D (1799) and "The Pedlar" from MS. E (1803–4). Butler has been able to reconstruct most of "The Pedlar" as it stood in 1802. For a discussion of which version should stand under the title "The Pedlar" in modern editions, see Jonathan Wordsworth's review of Butler's edition in *The Wordsworth Circle* 10 (1979): 224–25, and Butler's response to the review in the same issue. The conclusion to the work of the summer of 1797 that I quote is printed in Butler and in *STCL* 1: 327–28. Unless otherwise noted, I have quoted from MS. B, printed in the reading text of Butler's edition.

With backward steps.—Yet ever as there passed
A man whose garments shewed the Soldier's red,
Or crippled Mendicant in Sailor's garb,
The little Child who sate to turn the wheel
Ceased from his toil, and she with faltering voice,
Expecting still to learn her husband's fate,
Made many a fond inquiry; and when they
Whose presence gave no comfort were gone by,
Her heart was still more sad.

(490–506)

Margaret's eye is constantly focusing on distant figures in a vain hope that they might be her returning husband or someone who can give her information about him. Hope forms what reality cannot provide, and the failure of her hope and hope's distortions lead her to despair. Her shapings are only transient. Hope's creations vanish into the vacant landscape, leaving Margaret alone again. The mariner's shaping, in contrast, creates an image of terror that remains with him and will not rest or vanish:

I saw a something in the Sky
No bigger than my fist;
At first it seem'd a little speck
And then it seem'd a mist:
It mov'd and mov'd, and took at last
A certain shape, I wist.

A speck, a mist, a shape, I wist!
And still it ner'd and ner'd;
And, an it dodg'd a water-sprite
It plung'd and tack'd and veer'd.

(139–48)

In contrast to Margaret's hope for the return of her husband, the mariner's hope is for rescue, for relief from the terrible calm. Although the death ship unaccountably seems to shape itself before the mariner's eyes, changing from speck to mist to shape, it does not vanish into a vacant landscape as does Margaret's creation of her returning husband. In fact, the mariner's shapings become a permanent part of his landscape of fear and terror. Margaret is constantly returned to a vacancy; the mariner is dominated by the continuing presence of the death ship, its image and its curse. Although Christabel does not shape images in the distance, as do Margaret and the mariner, she, too, shapes them in her dreams to fill the void left by the absence of her lover, the death of her mother, and the indifference of her withdrawn father. Her images, like Margaret's, shift and change, and do not remain fixed in her mind. Geraldine is, to both Christabel and the narrator, an ambiguous being whose form and significance seem in perpetual change. The differences between the two sequences of poems is further indicated by the purpose of their wanderings. The sailor and the mariner are compelled to wander to avoid their past. They flee the forces that drive their fates. Margaret and Christabel wander in search of figures to fill their emptiness, even though at times it may not be clear to them that this is what they are doing.

Thus a volume that included "Christabel" along with Margaret's story with the Pedlar material would have been one in which the two poems would be complementary and rich in mutual reference. In October 1800 Coleridge and Wordsworth may have conceived a volume that would be truly one work, would respect their individual styles, and at the same time would constitute a dialogue on the themes of despair and hope as well as on the nature of poetic truth. The volume was not completed, and the circumstances of its conception in the struggle to complete the second volume of *Lyrical Ballads* led each to have ambiguous opinions on their merits. The Wordsworths' differing comments on "Christabel" reflect their uncertainty about it. Dorothy had written in her journal on October 4 that they were delighted with the second part of "Christabel." When the preface to *Lyrical Ballads* had been sent to the printer on September 27, it had contained the notice that "the long and beautiful Poem of Christabel" had been written by a friend, but the words "long and beautiful" had been deleted (*Prose* 1: 118 n). When the decision to omit "Christabel" was made on October 6, Wordsworth requested the publisher to delete from the preface the following sentence: "I should not, however, have requested this assistance, had I not believed that the poems of my Friend would in a great measure have the same tendency as my own, and that, though there would be found a difference, there would be found no discordance in the colours of our style; as our opinions on the subject of poetry do almost entirely coincide" (*Prose* 1: 120; *LEY* 304). In the light of the cancellation of "Christabel" on the grounds of style, the interesting thing is, not that Wordsworth had suddenly realized that he and Coleridge held significantly different views of poetry, but that he could have written such words for the preface in the first place, that he could have thought in the previous month that their opinions "do almost entirely coincide." Particularly interesting is Wordsworth's use of the word "colours," which refers to figures of speech. In later editions of the preface, Wordsworth said that his purpose was to select common incidents and "to throw over them a certain colouring of imagination" (*Prose* 1: 123), a later and somewhat uncertain acknowledgment of the presence of rhetoric. As their earlier dialogue suggests, one of the major issues between them was the use of figurative language. A reading of the sequence of "The Pedlar" and "Christabel" confirms the presence of the issue of the "colours of our style."

Coleridge, perhaps depressed by the difficulty he had in completing "Christabel," expressed his opinion of the poem in the same letter in which he announced the proposed joint publication: "I assure you, I think very differently of CHRISTABEL.—I would rather have written Ruth, and Nature's Lady than a million such poems / but why do I calumniate my own spirit by saying, *I* would rather— —God knows it is as delightful to me that they *are* written—I *know*, that at present (& I *hope*, that it *will* be so,) my mind has disciplined itself into a willing exertion of it's powers, without any reference to their *comparative* value."[3] Coleridge's dilemma is clear. A few lines above this wish for dissociation of his poetry from Wordsworth's, he had proposed its association. Any joint publication inevitably raises questions of relative merit and of the "direct opposition" or coincidence of their poetry. It seems that in October 1800 Coleridge feared association with Wordsworth and the dangerous amalgamation of such association more than he feared Wordsworth's discouragement and criticism. Of course, the publication of the two poems came to nothing, but the proposal itself suggests that at the time that "Christabel" was almost completed in two parts, both poets compared it to Margaret's story and the Pedlar's history.

A reading of the relationships among Wordsworth's earliest drafts of Margaret's story, "The Ruined Cottage," and Coleridge's responsive "Christabel" illuminates the conditions that gave rise to such valuations of their merits by both Wordsworth and Coleridge. The poems are best read as stages or moments in a dynamic dialogue rather than as isolated poems characteristically Coleridgean or Wordsworthian. Without the context of literary dialogue, the poems stand merely as examples of Wordsworth as the poet of the

---

3. *STCL* 1: 631–32. Griggs identifies "Nature's Lady" as "Three years she grew."

natural and quotidian, and Coleridge as the mystified poet of the supernatural. Within the context of the other poems, "Christabel" is an interpretation and criticism of "The Ruined Cottage" and "The Pedlar," and a reading of them that identifies its own beginnings in them. "Christabel" begins with Margaret's wandering and shaping figures in the distance and Robert's similar wandering and carving grotesque figures and with the Pedlar's assurance that he can see things in landscape that are real and that can be read with the worthy eye.

In this instance "Christabel" begins with the first conception or drafts of Margaret's story. Two early fragments of her story connect her plight with Wordsworth's concerns over human charity in the Salisbury Plain poems and point toward his formulation of an impulse toward figuration in a mind detached from realities. The first was written in late 1796 or the spring of 1797 and has been entitled "The Baker's Cart" by his editors.[4] A cart with its load of bread passes by a poor woman and her five children without stopping:

> While in the road I stood
> Pursuing with involuntary look
> The wain now seen no longer, to my side
> [   ] came, a pitcher in her hand
> Filled from the spring; she saw what way my eyes
> Were turn'd, and in a low and fearful voice
> She said, "That waggon does not care for us."
> The words were simple, but her look and voice
> Made up their meaning, and bespoke a mind
> Which being long neglected and denied
> The common food of hope was now become
> Sick and extravagant—by strong access
> Of momentary pangs driv'n to that state
> In which all past experience melts away
> And the rebellious heart to its own will
> Fashions the laws of nature.

>   (Butler 463)

The similarity to Wordsworth's earlier concern with charity is obvious. The woman is a victim of a society that has no charity to offer, just as the woman in the Salisbury Plain poems is victimized by a so-

---

4. The text is printed in *WPW* 1: 315–16; *Music of Humanity* 5–6, where Jonathan Wordsworth dates it in the spring of 1797; and Butler's edition, where it is similarly dated. *CEY* 27 dates it before March 1797 and gives the fragment its title.

ciety indifferent to her pains. The situation is rendered more poign-
ant because the woman is the source of as much charity as she can
offer, the pitcher of water from the well. In the earliest manuscript
Margaret, too, is a source of charity:

> many a passenger
> Has blest poor Margaret for her gentle looks
> When she upheld the cool refreshment drawn
> From that forsaken well, and no one came
> But he was welcome no one went away
> But that it seemed she loved him
>
> (Butler 81)

In the first complete version of Margaret's story, copied in March
1798, the water from the well becomes explicitly associated with Ec-
clesiastes:

> A spider's web
> Across its mouth hung to the water's edge,
> And on the wet and slimy foot-stone lay
> The useless fragment of a wooden bowl;
> It moved my very heart.
>
> (142–46)

Jonathan Wordsworth has pointed out that Wordsworth had used
the image of the broken bowl in his earlier poetry: "For hope's de-
serted well why wistful look? / Chok'd is the pathway, and the
pitcher broke," and "fair favoured region! which my soul / Shall
love, 'till Life has broke her golden bowl."[5] Also, Paul Sheats has de-
tailed throughout Wordsworth's poetry the themes of a youthful
hope inevitably disappointed by the realities of maturity and the
ambush of hope.[6] Margaret cannot survive the ambush of hope and
in her decline becomes psychically a child, unable to detach herself
from her hope or to transfer it to her "two pretty babes" who were
"their best hope next to God in Heaven" (184–85). The progress of
hope varies in her case, because hers is not a youthful fancy disap-

5. The first quotation is from *An Evening Walk* (1793) 255–56; and the second,
from *Descriptive Sketches* (1793) 740–41. Jonathan Wordsworth writes that in "The
Ruined Cottage," "the associations of *Ecclesiastes* are not less powerful for being less
obvious" (*Music of Humanity* 125).

6. Paul D. Sheats, *The Making of Wordsworth's Poetry, 1785–1798* (Cambridge, Mass.:
Harvard University Press, 1973) 32–41.

pointed by mature realities, but rather the loss of a valued posses-
sion, her family, which causes her to indulge a hope that becomes
detached from realities at the very point at which she should face
them.

In "The Baker's Cart" Wordsworth seems to associate the woman's
words with her extravagant imagination and denied hope, yet it is
difficult to understand how he could say that her words, "That wag-
gon does not care for us," bespeaks a mind that was so "sick and ex-
travagant" as to fashion "the laws of nature" and create fictions. Her
words define poignantly the attitude of her society. Her powerful
understatement embodies society's lack of charity in the familiar ob-
ject of the cart, which cannot "care" for anyone in a literal sense. In
this instance extreme distress forces her to see social practices and
political attitudes for what they really are. She does not distort the
truth; she sees it clearly. She does not "shape" the baker's cart into a
figure of fancy; she is forced to see it for what it is and for what it
represents. The contradiction between her powerful words and the
narrator's explanation of those words as spoken by a sick fancy
comes perhaps from Wordsworth's divergent purposes in 1796. He
wants to write telling social criticism, which prompts his giving her
those words, and he wants to demonstrate that the effects of injus-
tice are sicknesses that she suffers. Yet there is an aspect of the wom-
an's mind that is troublesome. It seems to concentrate on one object,
in which, as the speaker explains, "all past experience melts away."
These words are strikingly similar to those Lamb used to describe
the mariner's fate: "the Ancient Marinere undergoes such Trials, as
overwhelm and bury all individuality or memory of what he was.—
Like the state of a man in a Bad dream, one terrible peculiarity of
which is, that all consciousness of personality is gone" (*Lamb Letters*
1: 266). The woman in "The Baker's Cart" and Margaret both fix
their attention on one single object, which in "The Ruined Cottage"
becomes detached from the landscape as the only object that can sat-
isfy hope. In Wordsworth's poetry the concentration upon one sin-
gle object can either unify the scene and lead to vision, or it can ex-
clude all other objects, place the object in a vacant space, and
remove it into the figurative because it removes the object from its
natural space.

In the second fragment that contributes to "The Ruined Cot-
tage," entitled "Incipient Madness" by Wordsworth, the extrava-
gance is attributed to grief:

There is a mood,
A settled temper of the heart, when grief,
Become an instinct, fastening on all things
That promise food, doth like a suckling babe
Create it where it is not.

(Butler 468)

The speaker is drawn to a piece of broken glass within the ruins of a hut because to him it "seemed akin to life." The ruined hut, which in "Incipient Madness" surrounds and isolates the piece of glass, becomes in the earliest manuscript of "The Ruined Cottage," the "open wall / Yet dark and stained with smoke," then "these fractured walls" (Butler 85), and finally the "four clay walls / That stared upon each other" (30–31). It resembles the "dead house of the Plain" of the Salisbury Plain poems in that both are locations in which charity once resided but which, since they have fallen into ruin and their hosts have gone, are not recognizable. The "dead house of the Plain" and the death ship of "The Ancient Mariner" are both the locations of fear. The empty ruins of Margaret's cottage become the location of a failure of human hope while they testify to the absence of charity.

Along with the seminal drafts on Margaret's despair and charity in the early drafts are equally important seminal lines on her husband's mental disturbance. His hopes, too, are disappointed by two years of bad harvest and by the disruptions of the "plague of war." Although war is in part the cause of his distress, his despair results as much from natural causes. Wordsworth is less interested in emphasizing the social and political causes than he was earlier. Margaret's husband falls into an illness that drains his spirit, and when he recovers, his behavior becomes aimless. He

whistled many a snatch of merry tunes
Which had no mirth in them: for half a day
He then would leave his home and to the town
Without an errand would he turn his steps
Or wander up and down among the fields. . . .

(Butler 83)

Her husband's despair precedes Margaret's similar despair. He has no object or purpose, for to go on an errand with no object is to be errant. In one of his reminiscences about the beginnings of "The Ancient Mariner," Wordsworth said that the idea of killing the al-

batross was his and that the mariner should suffer "as a conse-
quence of that crime, and his own wanderings" (WPW 1: 361).
Wordsworth implies that in "The Ancient Mariner" wandering it-
self is errant and the cause of the mariner's nightmare vision. For
both Margaret and her husband, wandering is not an original cause
of error, but rather a symptom of despair originating in their loss.
Robert's wandering prefigures Margaret's. During one of the Ped-
lar's visits, Margaret confesses:

> It grieves me you have waited here so long,
> But in good truth I've wandered much of late
> And sometimes, to my shame I speak, have need
> Of my best prayers to bring me back again.
>
> (398–401)

Unlike her husband's wandering, Margaret's is with purpose and
conscience. She must feed the "one torturing hope" of her hus-
band's return, and her wandering is not only through the country-
side, but also a wandering in imagination as she shapes "things /
Which made her heart beat quick." Conscience tells her that she
must not permit the wandering search for her husband, which per-
petuates her hope, to turn into the aimless wandering of true de-
spair. She is keenly aware of this possibility, and the pity aroused by
her story is all the keener for her awareness.

If Margaret's wandering in the countryside is perilously close to
being aimless, and if Robert's wandering into town is without an er-
rand, their wanderings in imagination are almost imageless. Robert

> with his knife
> Carved uncouth figures on the heads of sticks,
> Then idly sought about through every nook
> Of house or garden any casual task
> Of use or ornament, and with a strange,
> Amusing but uneasy novelty
> He blended where he might the various tasks
> Of summer, autumn, winter and of spring.
>
> (216–23)

The "uncouth figures" are crude, but also strange, grotesque, un-
natural and unfamiliar. They are created for their own sake, as idle
amusement and valued only for their novelty. They reflect a mind
that creates its own images, unable to find in those images any sta-

109

bility and permanence. Robert at every turn avoids the natural. Less willing to surrender to its own creations, Margaret's imagination attempts recuperation by placing the figure of her husband in the landscape. The figures of her imagination do not reflect Robert's singularity and unnaturalness, but rather attempt to recover what memory reminds her was once natural and seemingly permament. But, like the woman in "The Baker's Cart," she must fashion "the laws of nature," and thus memory, hope, and imagination mislead her into a process of figuring the landscape, which must be endlessly repeated. Ironically, landscape is wasted by her attempt to place the figure in it. Both her cottage and garden, the former location of all her hopes, decay.

Margaret's story is narrated by the Pedlar, himself a wanderer who in the first full fair copy of "The Ruined Cottage," of March 1798, claims an insight into the significance of the familiar landscape which is obscure to the younger poet:

> I see around me [   ]
> Things which you cannot see. We die, my Friend,
> Nor we alone, but that which each man loved
> And prized in his peculiar nook of earth
> Dies with him or is changed, and very soon
> Even of the good is no memorial left.
> The waters of that spring if they could feel
> Might mourn. They are not as they were; the bond
> Of brotherhood is broken. . . .
>
> (129–37)

His purpose in retelling her story is to preserve as a sign and memorial the cottage that would otherwise be no more than the empty space that it presents to the eye. The brief introduction to the Pedlar's past contained an explanation that the Pedlar's wanderings had been an education in the reading of landscape:

> He was a chosen son:
> To him was given an ear which deeply felt
> The voice of Nature in the obscure wind,
> The sounding mountain and the running stream.
> To every natural form, rock, fruit, and flower,
> Even the loose stones that cover the highway,
> He gave a moral life; he saw them feel
> Or linked to them some feeling. In all shapes
> He found a secret and mysterious soul. . . .
>
> (76–84)

Whereas Robert carved "uncouth figures" and Margaret shapes figures in the distance, the Pedlar finds "a secret and mysterious soul" in all shapes, and he wishes to teach his knowledge to the younger poet. It is uncertain, however, what parts of wisdom the Pedlar wishes to convey. His introduction of the tale with its claim for authority, "I see around me," leaves some doubt whether his tale will be similar to the Preacher's in Ecclesiastes, where all is vanity, or whether there is a bond of brotherhood that, once broken, can be restored with hope, whether, in other words, the despair suggested by the topos of ruin can be transformed into an enduring hope that Margaret could neither sustain nor transfer to another generation. From these words it is uncertain whether Wordsworth is countering the more optimistic hope of "Religious Musings" with the tale of despair, or whether he is attempting to form a human brotherhood from Coleridge's portrayal of the human ascent to identify with God. Thus, in the spring of 1798 Wordsworth felt it necessary to add two major sections to the fair copy: one long expansion of the Pedlar's history and a second to come at the end as a conclusion.[7] Both attempt to interpret and transform the ending of Margaret's story:

> And so she sate
> Through the long winter, reckless and alone,
> Till this reft house by frost, and thaw, and rain
> Was sapped; and when she slept the nightly damps
> Did chill her breast, and in the stormy day
> Her tattered clothes were ruffled by the wind
> Even at the side of her own fire.—Yet still
> She loved this wretched spot, nor would for worlds
> Have parted hence; and still that length of road
> And this rude bench one torturing hope endeared,
> Fast rooted at her heart, and here, my friend,
> In sickness she remained, and here she died,
> Last human tenant of these ruined walls.
>
> (516–28)

7. Butler is unable to determine whether the Pedlar's history or the consolation was written first, although both were completed by March 6, 1798. He writes that there is "no certainty that the expansion of the Pedlar's history led the poet to write an addendum to agree with the Pedlar's new philosophy. The reverse could be true—perhaps composition of the reconciling addendum led to expansion of the Pedlar's history so that the sentiments he expresses can be seen to flow from his character, developed by past experiences" (21).

Wordsworth drafted three attempts at a concluding consolation at the end of the fair copy before he began a lengthy section that finally satisfied him. Each one of the three, as well as the final draft, turns to Coleridge's poetry or incorporates lines that Coleridge was also using at the same time. At no point in their careers is the correspondence between their poetry as close as it is here. It may be virtually impossible to distinguish Wordsworth's lines from Coleridge's at this point, and the worries about amalgamation that Poole mentioned must have originated at this time. Wordsworth began his revisions of Margaret's story at the end of January 1798. Coleridge had been away from Nether Stowey but returned in the middle of February, wrote "Frost at Midnight" at the end of the month, and completed "The Ancient Mariner" toward the end of March. All these texts are intimately connected.

The first canceled draft concludes:

> And waking from the silence of my grief
> I lookd around, the cottage and the elms
> The road the pathway and the garden wall
> Which old & loose & mossy oer the road
> Hung bellying, all appeared I know not how
> But to some eye within me, all appeared
> Colours & forms of a strange discipline
> The trouble which they sent into my thought
> Was sweet, I lookd and looked again, & to myself
> I seemed a better and a wiser man.
>
> (Butler 257)

Coleridge's Wedding Guest becomes a "sadder and a wiser man," as the mariner predicted. "The Ancient Mariner" was completed on March 23, after the fair copy of "The Ruined Cottage" and the Pedlar work. It is impossible to say whether Coleridge's or Wordsworth's was the first use of the phrase. There is a slight possibility that Coleridge's preceded Wordsworth's, because the phrase is used twice in the 1798 version, and substantial portions of "The Ancient Mariner" were written before Wordsworth's work on the drafts for a consolation. Coleridge told correspondents that he had finished three hundred lines on November 20 and three hundred forty lines, which he called "finished," on February 18, 1798 (*STCL* 1: 357, 387). The knowledge of strange and unfamiliar events that the Wedding Guest learns is "sad," but the knowledge gained by the young poet from the Pedlar, the "colours & forms of a strange discipline," make him a "better and a wiser man." A curious turn has occurred in their dialogue. Up to this point, Coleridge had been the optimist who could entertain millennial hopes and to whom Wordsworth turned for a more sanguine view of the social and political future and for a philosophy that would define a language of nature. But as the mariner himself says, "Never sadder tale was heard / By a man of woman born" (370–71). Wordsworth's is the more optimistic phrase, qualified only by the uncertainty of the "colours & forms of a strange discipline."

Wordsworth deleted his first attempt and drafted a second, which concludes with lines similar to the first:

> I well remember what I felt the road
> The door the pathway and the garden wall
> I turned to the old man, & said my friend
> Your words have consecrated many things
> And for the tale which you have told I think
> I am a better and a wiser man
>
> (Butler 257–59)

The perplexing "strange discipline" of the first draft has disappeared and has been replaced by a consecration, a sanctification of the cottage and its grounds. If the original "colours . . . of a strange discipline" is a vaguely worded reference to a language of nature or a divine language in nature, which Coleridge's poetry would suggest, then Wordsworth's changing it to a consecration, a blessing, hints at his uncertainty as to exactly how that language should be described, a problem both men faced in the early months of 1798. The substitution of a more traditional consecration, which contrasts with the narrative's presentation of Margaret's and Robert's acts of figuration, was only a temporarily satisfactory answer.

Wordsworth wrote a third draft, which abandons the explicit optimism of the phrase "a better and a wiser man" and the uncertainties of the language in landscape:

> How sweetly breathes the air it breathes most
> sweet
> And my heart feels it how divinely fair
> Are yon huge clouds how lovely are these elms
> That shew themselves with all their verdant leaves
> And all the myriad veins of those green leaves
> A luminous prospect [? silvered] by the sun

The very sunshine spread upon the dust
Is beautified

(Butler 259)

Wordsworth turns back to the first draft to portray the precise "colours & forms" without the abstractions of the "strange discipline." His description alludes to the language of nature in "This Lime-Tree Bower":

> I watch'd
> The sunshine of each broad transparent Leaf
> Broke by the shadows of the Leaf or Stem,
> Which hung above it: and that Wall-nut Tree
> Was richly ting'd: and a deep radiance lay
> Full on the ancient ivy which usurps
> Those fronting elms, and now with blackest mass
> Makes their dark foliage gleam a lighter hue. . . .[8]

It would seem that Wordsworth is searching for the kind of lesson that Coleridge offers in "This Lime-Tree Bower," which, considering the themes of "The Ruined Cottage," would have fit well if this third allusive beginning were completed in the spirit of "This Lime-Tree Bower":

> nature ne'er deserts the wise & pure,
> No scene so narrow, but may well employ
> Each faculty of sense, and keep the heart
> Awake to Love & Beauty

(*STCL* 1: 336)

Nature's language in "This Lime-Tree Bower" is not man's language but God's. Coleridge gazes

8. *STCL* 1: 335–36. Two versions of "This Lime-Tree Bower my Prison" originally existed from 1797. The first is printed in *STCL* 1: 334–36 from a manuscript letter to Southey. The second, described in J. D. Campbell's edition, *The Poetical Works of Samuel Taylor Coleridge* (1893) 591, is closer to the version sent to Southey than it is to the first published version in the *Annual Anthology* (1800). The second was contained in a letter to Charles Lloyd of July 1797, but E. L. Griggs comments that the letter to Lloyd "has not come to light" (*STCL* 1: 334 n). Both are considerably shorter than the later versions. I discuss some of the differences between these two shorter texts and the later ones in the next chapter. It is difficult to determine precisely when Coleridge expanded the poem to the length of the first printed version and whether Wordsworth knew an expanded version in 1798. Consequently, I will refer to the earliest version in the letter to Southey, which Griggs dates July 17, 1797.

114

till all doth seem
Less gross than bodily, a living Thing
That acts upon the mind, and with such hues
As cloathe the Almighty Spirit, when he makes
Spirits perceive His presence!

(STCL 1: 335)

The consecration that Wordsworth drafted in his second attempt would have required something similar to Coleridge's Berkeleyan meditation on the language of the spirit that speaks through nature and the visible world to man, but that supernaturalism was not completely appropriate for Wordsworth's purposes, although nature's enlivening presence in a narrow and vacant spot may have seemed enticing as a conclusion for "The Ruined Cottage," to validate the "colours . . . of a strange discipline."

Finally Wordsworth found an opening for a conclusion that satisfied him:

Not useless do I deem
These quiet sympathies with things that hold
An inarticulate language for the man
Once taught to love such objects as excite
No morbid passions no disquietude
No vengeance & no hatred needs must feel
The joy of that pure principle of love
So deeply that unsatisfied with aught
Less pure & exquisite he cannot choose
But seek for objects of a kindred love
In fellow-natures & a kindred joy
Accordingly he by degrees perceives
His feelings of aversion softened down
A holy tenderness pervade his frame
His sanity of reason not impaired
Say rather all his thoughts now flowing clear
From a clear fountain flowing he looks round
He seeks for good & finds the good he seeks

(Butler 261)

This ending proposes an emotion opposite from the anger and indignation that prompted the cry for vengeance at the end of "Salisbury Plain" when Wordsworth calls for the raising of "the herculean mace / Of Reason" against oppression. He also rejects the similar passions expressed by Alhadra at the end of *Osorio* and even, by implication, the acts of the seven angels in "Religious Musings":

> They from the MERCY-SEAT—like rosy flames,
> From God's celestial MERCY-SEAT will flash,
> And at the wells of renovating LOVE
> Fill their Seven Vials with salutary wrath,
> To sickly Nature more medicinal
> Than what soft balm the weeping good man pours
> Into the lone despoiled trav'ller's wounds!
>
> (90–96)

All three early works value wrath and vengeance over the simple act of common charity, and in 1798 Wordsworth revalues a spirit of humanity that incorporates "No morbid passions no disquietude / No vengeance." His negatives exclude both his and Coleridge's earlier themes. "Religious Musings" presented a transfiguration of fear and terror into awe, but Wordsworth's exclusion of all but "quiet sympathies" seems to turn upon the scale of transformation of emotion and to exclude the violent emotions of fear, terror, and wrath, no matter what their context or purpose. In "Religious Musings" the "wells of renovating LOVE" are the source of "salutary wrath." In "The Ruined Cottage" Margaret's well, which is deserted and no longer the source of charity, is figuratively replaced by the narrator's thoughtful sympathy "flowing clear / From a clear fountain." His purpose is to "multiply / The spiritual presences of absent things" (Butler 263).

The opening lines of the final consolation on the "quiet sympathies" have their origins, as James Butler points out, in drafts in Wordsworth's Alfoxden notebook, which he used from the end of January 1798:[9]

> Why is it we feel
> So little for each other but for this
> That we with nature have no sympathy
> Or with such idle objects as have no power to hold
> Articulate language.

9. See Butler 15, 120–23 for photographs and facing transcriptions. In private correspondence, Professor Butler has suggested dates of perhaps mid to late February, although the precise dates are very difficult to determine. Their composition thus comes almost exactly at the time that Coleridge wrote "Frost at Midnight."

A second draft plays again with the problem of defining nature's language:

> And never for each other shall we feel
> As we may feel till we have sympathy
> With nature in her forms inanimate
> With objects such as have no power to hold
> Articulate language. In all forms of things
> There is a mind.

Coleridge's meditation on Berkeley's Divine Sensible Language, elaborated in *Alciphron* (1732), is present here, as it is in the earlier canceled drafts. Coleridge had written in his letter to Southey that included "This Lime-Tree Bower" that he is "a *Berkleian*" (*STCL* 1: 335).

On March 10, 1798, Coleridge copied the opening lines of the consolation in a letter to his brother, making one revealing change. In the second line, he wrote "shadowy Sympathies" instead of "quiet sympathies," which appears in Wordsworth's draft.[10] Wordsworth's phrase may be an intentional variant of "dim sympathies" from "Frost at Midnight," which describes the relationship between Coleridge's imagination and the fluttering soot on the grate. The intelligibility and audibility of nature's language is the major theme of "Frost at Midnight." Coleridge hopes that Hartley will

> see and hear
> The lovely shapes and sounds intelligible
> Of that eternal language, which thy God
> Utters, who from eternity doth teach
> Himself in all, and all things in himself.
>
> (58–62)

These lines are similar to Wordsworth's drafts in the Alfoxden notebook and at the beginning of the consolation, but there is an important difference, which becomes more important as the Coleridge-Wordsworth dialogue progresses through the spring of 1798, as I detail in the next chapter. Coleridge speaks of the colors and forms of nature as though they were an articulate and intelligible language, similar to ordinary language. He subordinates nature to language. Wordsworth, on the other hand, seems to regard ordinary

10. Butler suggests that Coleridge may have copied from an original text that did not survive rather than making an error (21).

language and the written language of texts to be different from the language of nature and the One Life. If there is a priority to be given to one of them, it is to the language of nature. He praises, in the notebook, the "objects such as have no power to hold / Articulate language." In the consolation the "quiet sympathies" are with "things that hold / An inarticulate language." Wordsworth is careful to separate nature's language from the language of ordinary discourse. Kenneth Johnston has noted Wordsworth's reluctance to assimilate nature's language to man's language and attributes it to the inherent benevolence of nature's language and the unfortunate fact that the language of man is that of human conflict.[11] In the context of the consolation this is true, but if one relocates the consolation in the context of Coleridge's poetry and their dialogue, "Frost at Midnight" makes the intelligibility of articulate nature a complex and troublesome issue. Nature's language is not always audible, and when it is, it needs interpretation, just as human language and human texts need interpretation. Wordsworth's insistence upon an inarticulate language of nature preserves the simplicity of that language and removes it from the realm of the uncertain, where, in the fall of 1797 and the spring of 1798, Coleridge placed it.

The consolation concludes with the Pedlar's admonition to the young poet, which echoes Raphael's admonition to Adam in *Paradise Lost*, "be lowly wise" (*PL*, VIII, 173):

> The purposes of Wisdom ask no more
> Be wise & chearful, & no longer read
> The forms of things with an unworthy eye
>
> (Butler 277)

The Pedlar urges the young poet to see the spirit of charity and humanity and not to despair, but his gentle affection retains something of the limiting of inquiry from *Paradise Lost*. The Pedlar is not Raphael, who restricts even unfallen human knowledge, nor is he the Preacher of Ecclesiastes, who can see nothing of permanent value "under the sun," because the Pedlar's purpose is to counter the Preacher's lesson that "he that increaseth knowledge increaseth sorrow" (Eccles. 1: 18). Nevertheless, the Pedlar's words retain some

---

11. Johnston writes that "love of nature leads to love of man by softening down 'feelings of aversion' toward humanity that are presented as the original condition of the man who learns to love from passionless—that is, nonhuman, nonlinguistic—nature" (*Wordsworth and "The Recluse"* [New Haven: Yale University Press, 1984] 25).

of the limiting admonition of both Raphael and the Preacher; he wishes to avoid the questionings of the speaker of "Frost at Midnight," who earnestly desires that the "goings-on of life" become audible and intelligible to him. By restricting questions, the Pedlar does not explicitly limit the knowledge of providence but limits the speculations of the "unworthy eye," and warns against inquiry into the process of that eye's readings.

By early March Wordsworth had drafted not only the extended consolation but also a long section describing the Pedlar's upbringing and education in order to explain the character who could offer such wisdom and comfort. The history of the Pedlar reads almost as if it were an expansion of Coleridge's hope for Hartley in "Frost at Midnight." Or is it that Coleridge's hope is a condensation of the Pedlar's history? It may be impossible to tell, since the dialogue was so close in those months, but the major motif in Wordsworth's description of the Pedlar's education is that of his learning to read the signs of the One Life in nature. In the mountains

> Ah! then how beautiful, how bright appeared
> The written promise; he had early learned
> To reverence the volume which displays
> The mystery, the life which cannot die
> But in the mountains did he feel his faith
> There did he see the writing
>
> (Butler 159)

The Pedlar's reading is a matter of feeling, which recalls Coleridge's line in the concluding verse paragraph of "The Eolian Harp" on his "Faith that inly *feels.*" If Wordsworth's allusion is intended to include the whole structure of "The Eolian Harp," then his allusion echoes the limitations against speculation that are present in the conclusion to "The Eolian Harp."

The written promise remains for him a sign of hope, as it does not for Margaret, because her loss has led her to shape figures of false hope that efface the natural landscape. Hope was never withdrawn for him as it was for her. He suffered no crises:

> No piteous revolutions had he felt,
> No wild varieties of joy or grief.
> Unoccupied by sorrow of its own
> His heart lay open; & by nature tuned
> And constant disposition of his thoughts

119

To sympathy with man, he was alive
To all that was enjoyed where'er he went.
(Butler 183)

As a result, he sees nature as a perpetually present hope that is felt in his heart:

for in all things
He saw one life, & felt that it was joy.
One song they sang, & it was audible,
Most audible, then, when, the fleshly ear
Oer come by grosser prelude of that strain
Forgot its functions, & slept undisturbed.
(Butler 177)

Wordsworth's emphasis on the difference between ordinary articulate language and the language of nature relies strongly on Coleridge's poetry, but in the spring of 1798 it relies on poetry Coleridge had written several years before, particularly "Reflections on Having Left a Place of Retirement," with its "Unearthly minstrelsy! then only heard / When the Soul seeks to hear; when all is hush'd, / And the Heart listens!" (24–26). By the time of "Frost at Midnight" Coleridge has started to question the language of nature. While he hopes that Hartley will be able to understand the "shapes and sounds intelligible," he admits his inability to do so, and his inability leads to his listening in a silence for the evidence of the "numerous goings-on of life" that are inaudible.

"Figures Strange and Sweet": "Christabel"

"Christabel," begun shortly after Wordsworth completed his additions to Margaret's story, comments directly on the themes of wandering and the subsequent shaping of figures and on the Pedlar's confidence that he can read the landscape with a worthy eye.[12]

12. Coleridge's preface to "Christabel" (1816) states that "the first part of the following poem was written in the year 1797, at Stowey, in the county of Somerset. The second part, after my return from Germany, in the year 1800, at Keswick, Cumberland" (*CPW* 1: 213), but evidence from Dorothy's journals shows clearly that Coleridge did not begin the poem until April 1798. Coleridge used several of her observations during March for "Christabel," the last of which was for March 24: "the

There is an interesting link between Margaret's story and "Christabel" in "The Old Man of the Alps," which Coleridge published in the *Morning Post* on March 8, 1798. It was signed "Nicias Erythraeus," a signature also used for "Lewti," a Coleridgean reworking of an early Wordsworth poem published in the *Morning Post* on April 13. "The Old Man of the Alps" may be another reworking of Wordsworth's drafts.[13] In "The Old Man of the Alps" a father tells a traveler about the youthful joys and hopes of his daughter, whose lover had left for war and had been killed. She "play'd with fancies" and placed all her hopes in "promised joys," building in her imagination "a little home of joy and rest," but as the time for his return approached "her thoughts were wild." Her father describes her reactions:

> But while she look'd and listen'd, stood and ran,
> And saw him plain in every distant man,
> By treachery stabbed, on NANSY's murderous day,
> A senseless corse th' expected husband lay.
> A wounded man, who met us in the wood,
> Heavily ask'd her where *my* cottage stood,
> And told us all: she cast her eyes around
> As if his words had been but empty sound.
> Then look'd to Heav'n, like one that would deny
> That such a thing *could be* beneath the sky.
> *Again* he ask'd her if she knew my name,
> And instantly an anguish wrench'd her frame,
> And left her mind imperfect.

(63–75)

---

spring continues to advance very slowly, no green trees, the hedges leafless; nothing green but the brambles that still retain their old leaves, the evergreens, and the palms, which indeed are not absolutely green" (*DWJ* 11). The scene is that of the opening of "Christabel." Thus "Christabel" was probably started after Wordsworth had finished his major additions to Margaret's story in the beginning of March 1798. For a description of the earliest manuscript of "Christabel," see *CPW* 1: 213–14, *CEY* 322–25, and *CMY* 615–16.

13. Jane Worthington Smyser writes that "in form and style 'The Old Man of the Alps' resembles Wordsworth's *Descriptive Sketches*; its locale is, in 1798, more Wordsworth's than Coleridge's. . . . Probably only by the discovery of more Wordsworth-Coleridge MSS could one positively answer the question as to whether or not this vagrant woman is a member of Wordsworth's special gallery" ("Coleridge's Use of Wordsworth's Juvenilia," *Publications of the Modern Language Association of America* 65 (1950): 422. Eric Birdsall discovered evidence that early drafts of "The Old Man of the Alps" were Wordsworth's and printed the lines in his edition of *Descriptive Sketches* (Ithaca: Cornell University Press, 1984) 289–97.

Distracted, she wanders: "She roam'd, without a purpose, all alone, / Thro' high grey vales unknowing and unknown" (87–88), and in her wandering is caught in a storm and dies.

This public poem is explicitly an antiwar poem, similar to those written earlier by Wordsworth but not published, but the description of the daughter's distraction is remarkably similar to Wordsworth's more recent description of Margaret's shaping figures in the distance. The daughter's wandering parallels Robert's wandering with no purpose and anticipates Leonard's final wandering in the "The Brothers." The tale is told by an old man who has suffered because his hopes for his daughter paralleled hers and were crushed as were hers. He fulfills the role of Wordsworth's Pedlar, telling the tale to a stranger who is a traveler. But if Coleridge is the sole author of this poem, he has shifted the roles to anticipate those in "Christabel." The Pedlar becomes the father, who suffers along with his daughter.

"The Old Man of the Alps" indicates that what interested Coleridge was the varieties of wandering in "The Ruined Cottage." The daughter permits her youthful fancy to wander to future hopes; her mind shapes the returning form of her future husband in the distance; and then she becomes a literal wanderer, aimless and without a purpose until she dies. "Christabel" repeats these themes and is a more elaborate and more challenging revision of "The Ruined Cottage." "Christabel" finds its generating text in Margaret's confession, "in good truth I've wandered much of late / And sometimes, to my shame I speak, have need / Of my best prayers to bring me back again" (399–401) and in the lines on Robert's wandering "without an errand." Unaccountably, Christabel leaves the security of her father's castle to pray for her lover:

> She had dreams all yesternight
> Of her own betrothéd knight;
> And she in the midnight wood will pray
> For the weal of her lover that's far away.
>
> (27–30)

Unlike Margaret, she does not expect him to return and she does not shape his image in the distance, but his absence is on her mind. The absence in which she is left is total; there is neither an object upon which she can rest her eye nor a landscape in which she can form his returning figure, because the landscape outside of her father's castle is the strange land of her dream. The world of her dream has supplanted the natural landscape, and thus her imagining is more extreme than Margaret's. Figuration becomes necessary from the absence of the object as well as the vacancy of landscape. Her dream, which is perhaps involuntary, imposes upon the vacuity of landscape, not an attempted recovery of her lover, but a reflexive moment of self-doubling, which slowly becomes self-recognition of a particularly perplexing sort. The figure of Geraldine impresses upon Christabel a mark of shame and sorrow, similar to the shame that Margaret feels at her wandering.

The emptiness of landscape permits Christabel only a reflection of herself in it. The puzzling figure that Christabel finds outside the castle is introduced by a doubling of her sighs in Geraldine's moaning behind the oak tree. A canceled couplet in the first edition of "Christabel" states that her dreams before she left the castle "made her moan" (*CPW* 1: 216, app. crit.). In the earliest manuscript, which probably dates from 1800, the doubling is apparent in the briefer description of Geraldine's first appearance. Christabel sees

> A damsel bright
> Clad in a silken robe of white,
> Her neck, her feet, her arms were bare,
> And the jewels were tumbled in her hair.
>
> (*CPW* 1: 217, app. crit.)

There is here certainly nothing of the terrifying and deathly white of the woman on the death ship in the early version of "The Ancient Mariner," and there is also nothing of the ghostly white of Geraldine as she appears in later versions:

> Drest in a silken robe of white,
> That shadowy in the moonlight shown:
> The neck that made that white robe wan,
> Her stately neck, and arms were bare;
> Her blue-veined feet unsandal'd were,
> And wildly glittered here and there
> The gems entangled in her hair.
>
> (59–65)

The first version presents a virgin and bride, a doubling of Christabel's image of her own wedding. The only unsettling note in the portrait at first is, like that in "The Discharged Soldier," the figure's location. The narrator, perhaps echoing Christabel's thoughts, says, "I guess, 'twas frightful there to see / A lady so richly clad as she—." The mystery of the poem's opening is Geraldine's presence in such a location.

At first sight Geraldine is not frightening, but rather an object of pity. Because she is in a landscape or context in which she cannot reasonably belong, she becomes an enigmatic figure. Christabel cannot interpret this figure because it does not belong where it is, and it thus becomes unintelligible. In the land of dream, which reflects an almost pagan and druidical darkness, the figure has no clearly intended meaning. Geraldine explains her presence in words that only hint at the supernatural:

> Five ruffians seized me yestermorn,
> Me, even me, a maid forlorn;
> They chok'd my cries with wicked might.
> And tied me on a palfrey white
> The palfrey was as fleet as wind,
> And they rode furiously behind.
> They spurred amain, their steeds were white:
> And once we crossed the shade of night.
> (CPW 1: 218, app. crit.)

The first three lines are from the earliest manuscript and emphasize, as the later lines do to a lesser degree, the force of violent sexual abduction. The "five ruffians" used "wicked might." Since in the early version Geraldine herself has few supernatural attributes, Coleridge emphasizes the theme of innocence being violated by evil. Even though Geraldine is so clearly a double of Christabel, Christabel does not seem to respond to Geraldine's experience as though it were possibly her own. Geraldine's presence in the forest as the abducted bride is unexpected, and as the enigmatic figure she is unintended. Her figure is gratuitous and by implication suggests a failure in Christabel's intention, a disjunction between the dreamer or shaper and the figure created. Christabel cannot see Geraldine's location as her own; she cannot see herself, at this moment, as the abducted bride, yet violent abduction is the possible risk of sexual initiation. Her dreams do not recover the image of her lover; they prefigure an uncertain possibility for herself.

The figure that Margaret shapes in the distance is that of her husband or someone who can inform her of her husband. She places the intended figure in the familiar landscape. Coleridge, however, created a person whose figure is unintelligible because of its context. Christabel cannot recognize or interpret Geraldine. Geraldine vaguely hints of some unearthly doings when she mentions that "five ruffians" took her beyond the "shade of night." Christabel's only possible reaction to her story is to extend hospitality and charity, to bring Geraldine back to her father's castle, to accommodate Geraldine, and to make her familiar by placing her in an intelligible place, a gesture similar to Wordsworth's in "The Discharged Soldier." Contrary to her intentions, her conventional charity does not succeed in placing Geraldine within a context in which she belongs. Rather, Geraldine's movement from the nocturnal landscape into the castle brings with it the landscape in which she was first found. As she enters the castle, numerous signs of the supernatural suggest that her presence transforms the castle into an unfamiliar space. Geraldine repeatedly asks Christabel to touch her, and Christabel must carry her over the threshold and lead her into her chamber:

> The moon shines dim in the open air,
> And not a moonbeam enters here.
> But they without its light can see
> The chamber carved so curiously,
> Carved with figures strange and sweet,
> All made out of the carver's brain,
> For a lady's chamber meet:
> The lamp with twofold silver chain
> Is fastened to an angel's feet.
>
> (175–83)

These carvings resemble the "uncouth figures" that Robert carved on the "heads of sticks," and, with the exception of the figure of the angel, they appear now strange and curious, artful, elaborate, and singular.

The final scene of Part I intensifies to the point of utter confusion the uncertainty of intention that surrounds Geraldine. The narrative exploits, not simply the initiation of innocence into evil or the intrusion of evil, but the duplicity and uncertainty surrounding Geraldine's presence. In one simple sense, Geraldine is a duplicitous figure because to the reader she appears to be a stock figure of evil appearing under the guise of good, whose evil nature will later be revealed, or to be a spirit with good intentions whose purpose is to test or tempt Christabel for good purposes, as some conventional accounts would have it.[14] Christabel's initiation is not into the reality of sexuality, nor even the reality of evil, but into the unintelligibility of a figure that creates its own landscape in the image of its own unfathomable nature.

The confusion that immobilizes Christabel extends to the contest over the unstable roles of guardianship. She has promised a hospitality to "guide and guard" Geraldine, according to the tale she has been told, but when she provides shelter in her chamber, that enclosed space is presided over by the curious figures "strange and sweet," which have appeared angelic but which are now unfamiliar and correspond to nothing previously known. Christabel's charity in offering restorative wine made by her mother implies the protection of her mother as a guardian spirit. Christabel cries "O mother dear! that thou wert here!" She invokes a familiar spirit and comfort to give meaning in a spot suddenly become unknown territory. Geraldine then begins a series of transformations that startle Christabel, not because they unveil a terrible evil, but because they display opposite and contrary signals. At first she echoes Christabel's invocation of her guardian spirit: "I would, said Geraldine, she were!" (203). Her echo is a comforting doubling of Christabel's wish for a benevolent and loving familiar presence, yet immediately her invocation abruptly alters to its opposite, a banishment:

> 'Off, wandering mother! Peak and pine!
> I have power to bid thee flee.'
> Alas! what ails poor Geraldine?
> Why stares she with unsettled eye?
> Can she the bodiless dead espy?
>
> (205–9)

She abruptly changes from an echoing to an initiating voice, rejecting a conventional guardian presence that had taken its supernatural authority from the corresponding image of the angel in Christabel's chamber. Her initiating voice, however, echoes the witches in *Macbeth*, whose songs invoke a competing supernaturalism. With

14. James Gillman, for instance, reported that Coleridge told him that "the story of the Christabel is partly founded on the notion, that the virtuous of this world save the wicked. The pious and good Christabel suffers . . . and thus she defeats the power of evil represented in the person of Geraldine" (*The Life of Samuel Taylor Coleridge* [1838] 301–2). Derwent Coleridge denied that Geraldine was a "witch or goblin, or malignant being of any kind" (E. H. Coleridge, ed., *Christabel* [London: Frowde, 1907] 52).

the voice of Shakespeare's figures, she regards Geraldine's mother as a "wandering mother," literally a spirit condemned to wander upon earth like Hamlet's father. The banishment of the spirit of Christabel's mother questions her angelic nature and interprets her wandering as a purgatorial quest, not as a purposeful guardianship. Geraldine's subversive voice interprets the mother's wandering to be similar to Christabel's in that both indicate, not a clearly determined purpose, but confusion and uncertainty. And Christabel's and her mother's imaginative and supernatural wandering parallels Margaret's and Robert's natural wandering.

Geraldine's purpose is not to supplant or negate Christabel's guardian spirit, for a second abrupt transition occurs in which she seems to return to her previous confirmation of Christabel's wish for divine protection:

> 'All they who live in the upper sky,
> Do love you, holy Christabel!
> And you love them, and for their sake
> And for the good which me befel,
> Even I in my degree will try,
> Fair maiden, to requite you well.—'
>
> (227–32)

At this point Geraldine invokes an entire supernatural and angelic cosmology in which Christabel's charity is repeated on the heavenly scale with reciprocal charity between heaven and earth, in which Christabel is both receiver and granter of charity. Each successive transformation of Geraldine's voice does not negate the previous utterance, and her banishments are ineffective gestures. If her utterances were mere negation, then no confusion would result in Christabel's mind and no uncertainty of intention would be present. Geraldine's successive voices coexist in Christabel's mind:

> But through her brain of weal and woe
> So many thoughts moved to and fro,
> That vain it were her lids to close:
>
> (239–41)

The confusion brought by Geraldine's altering voice is confirmed by Christabel's vision of her disrobing, which in the earliest version is more explicitly evocative of Geraldine's duplicity:

127

Behold! her bosom and half her side—
Are lean and old and foul of hue.
And she is to sleep with Christabel
(*CPW* 1: 224, app. crit.)

The later text then includes seven lines reflecting Geraldine's reluctance to lie beside Christabel, indicating that Geraldine is a possessed spirit, but these lines are not in the earliest manuscript, which moves directly from the view of Geraldine's side to her going to bed:

She took two paces and a stride,
And lay down by the maiden's side,
　　Ah wel-a-day!
And with low voice and doleful look
These words did say:
'In the touch of this bosom there worketh a spell,
Which is lord of thy utterance, Christabel!
Thou knowest to-night, and wilt know to-morrow
This mark of my shame, this seal of my sorrow.'
(*CPW* 1: 224–25, app. crit.)

Geraldine is a figure that comes to dominate Christabel in a way utterly different from that in which Margaret's figure of hope dominates her consciousness. Geraldine is the figure of duplicity and unintelligibility, the figure that in successive moments seems to affirm and then deny, to invoke a supernatural blessing and then to usurp the place of the guardian spirit. She appears to be a mere reflexive fiction of a dreamlike imagination and at the same time, through the sense of touch, a substantial reality in a recognizable landscape. The conclusion to Part I emphasizes the uncertainty:

With open eyes (ah woe is me!)
Asleep, and dreaming fearfully,
Fearfully dreaming, yet, I wis,
Dreaming that alone, which is—
O sorrow and shame! Can this be she,
The lady, who knelt at the old oak tree?
(292–97)

Either asleep or awake, or in that twilight state in between in which the realities of the waking world are mixed with the images of dreams, Christabel doubles the fits from which Geraldine has suffered. There is a telling reversal in which formerly Geraldine had been a reflected image of Christabel projecting herself as a bride, but now, as Geraldine had predicted, she becomes a mere echo of Geraldine. She knows "that alone, which is." As an echo is always a fragment of its original, Christabel in her fit of imitation has become a mere fragment, an echo of the curse that has been impressed upon her. Christabel, once the originator, has become the fragmentary echo, because the figure to which she gave existence has mastered her. Yet, still, this is a momentary recognition because it occurs in a dreamlike state. Soon Christabel relaxes, and the conclusion to Part I finishes on the more optimistic note that Christabel knows that her guardian spirit is near and "That saints will aid if men will call: / For the blue sky bends over all!" (330–31), which is a distant semblance of the "secret spirit of humanity" that Wordsworth's Pedlar finds amid the ruins of Margaret's cottage. Both embody the idea of a permanent charity.

Part I of "Christabel" questions a number of confident claims that Wordsworth makes in the Pedlar manuscripts, particularly those of the intelligibility of nature's language. Christabel finds a figure that demands interpretation yet at the same time resists intelligibility. Coleridge thus questions Wordsworth's claim that nature's language is communicative although not articulate in the way that ordinary human language is communicative, Coleridge's counterrecognition is that to demand intelligibility is inevitably to raise possibilities of interpretation, because nature and figure questioned by interpretation become figurative and forsake the realm of the Wordsworthian literal and natural. Christabel becomes an embodiment, like many others in this poetic dialogue of the incipient poet and reader. By selecting the poetics of the supernatural, Coleridge introduced the possibility of superstition that both Wordsworth and Coleridge associated with incipient imagination. Wordsworth's "Goody Blake and Harry Gill" and "The Thorn" present superstition as the beginnings of imagination, but unlike Christabel's imagination, those of Harry Gill and the narrator of "The Thorn" project their fancies upon a familiar landscape. Their projected images are simply mistakes, errors in seeing in familiar landscape what is not there. In "Christabel," however, there is no familiar landscape in which Christabel can place the figure of Geraldine and test her validity; Geraldine makes her own ambiguous context. And because she belongs nowhere she cannot be relocated, or even doubled. Although she is Christabel's double, she herself cannot be reflected; she refers to nothing. Christabel's perceptions of this figure are confused; her gestures, without confidence; and her voice, a fragmentary echo.

"Christabel" also challenges Wordsworth's assurance that things can be read with a "worthy eye." In "Christabel" the eyes are occluded, as when Geraldine stares with "unsettled eye" and when Christabel's eyes become small and dim like those of a snake. In Wordsworth's Pedlar drafts the simplest objects of nature, perceived correctly, guarantee the permanence of charity and humanity. Coleridge's counterstatement is that if the spirit of charity and humanity resides within these objects and their inarticulate language, then these objects must nevertheless be interpreted and the language become articulate. There cannot be, in other words, such a thing as an inarticulate language. That which is interpreted becomes figurative and no longer possesses the assurance of the literal. For Wordsworth, Margaret's shaping of figures in the distance is a fanciful error, that she cannot overcome, and the Pedlar's interpretation of the ruined cottage is the reality. For Coleridge no such certainty remains, because it is difficult to distinguish the figure from the landscape, the figurative from the literal, and the prior voice from the responding echo. Yet Coleridge's counterstatement is not simply a negation of Wordsworth's claims for naturalism; it opens the field of writing and reading in their dialogue to many new possibilities.

Coleridge's choice of a narrator for "Christabel" contrasts with Wordsworth's use of a similar form of narration. In Chapter 14 of the Biographia Coleridge stated that "The Ancient Mariner" had been written to illustrate the "willing suspension of disbelief . . . which constitutes poetic faith," and that he was "preparing among other poems, the 'Dark Ladie,' and the 'Christabel,' in which I should have more nearly realized my ideal, than I had done in my first attempt" (*BL* 2: 6–7). But "Christabel" is no mere reiteration of "The Ancient Mariner." It discards the role of a confessing voice and substitutes a variation of a Wordsworthian narrator to tell the tale. "Christabel" experiments with a narrator who asks interpretive questions, as did the narrator of "Goody Blake and Harry Gill," written at approximately the same time:

> Oh! what's the matter? what's the matter?
> What is't that ails young Harry Gill?

That evermore his teeth they chatter,
Chatter, chatter, chatter still.

(*LB* 54)

Wordsworth's narrator is difficult to characterize. He may or may not be a literalist. He may believe that Harry Gill actually suffers from a curse placed on him by Goody Blake and believes in such superstition. Whatever his credulity, he nevertheless manages to convey an unequivocal meaning: Harry Gill suffers physical cold because he has denied physical warmth and human comfort to Goody Blake. We are certain that Harry Gill believes that he has been cursed. The poem's moral judgment is clear.

When Coleridge uses the question-and-answer form of narration, he does so with an entirely different purpose. The narrator's questions probe beyond the literal without any clear answers. When he asks about Christabel's leaving the castle to pray in the woods, he inquires about motive. Although there is the faint suggestion that leaving the castle is an act of disobedience to her father, her motives are not clear. His next question, "Is it the wind that moaneth bleak?" (44) is answered by a denial—Geraldine moans. When Christabel goes to the other side of the oak, the narrator asks "What sees she there?" (57). The question might be asked by Christabel herself. Many of the narrator's questions sound exactly as though they were paraphrases of Christabel's own doubts and fears. The narrator asks no questions that could not have been asked by Christabel. When she guides Geraldine across the courtyard of the castle, the mastiff utters an "angry moan" in her sleep. The narrator then asks:

> And what can ail the mastiff bitch?
> Never till now she uttered yell
> Beneath the eye of Christabel.
> Perhaps it is the owlet's scritch:
> For what can ail the mastiff bitch?

(149–53)

These are questions that Christabel might ask herself, and they sound similar to those that the narrator asks after Geraldine has usurped the place of Christabel's mother as a guardian spirit, "what ails poor Geraldine? / Why stares she with unsettled eye?" (208–9). There is no clear answer, as there is to the question "What is't that ails young Harry Gill?" At one point Christabel echoes directly the narrator's words "Jesu, Maria, shield her well!" by praying "Mary

131

mother, save me now." The narrator is an echo of her own doubts, but his voice is presented in such a way that Christabel does not hear that echo, and it is no help to her self-awareness.

The narrator's question "What sees she there?" is echoed by Christabel's questions "And who art thou?" (70) and "How camest thou here?" (76). These in turn echo the question of the hermit to the mariner: "What manner of man art thou?" His questions to the mariner inquire whether the mysterious mariner, who has arrived amid unaccountable events, is a mortal or a spirit at the same time that they ask about the state of his soul. So, too, Christabel's questions imply that she is uncertain of the figure before her, who seems to represent an experience that her knowledge cannot comprehend. Their questioning of the strange figure is remarkably different from Margaret's "fond inquiry" and "sad question," because Margaret has come to learn that she asks for a known impossibility, the return of her husband. The answer is implied in the tone of her question. Christabel's and the narrator's questions ask an unknown possibility. The doubling of awareness in Christabel and the narrator, and the echoing of the hermit's voice in Christabel's indicate a fragmented awareness that reflects the mysterious, usurping figure that it contemplates. Christabel becomes only a fragmentary echo of what she sees, while, later, the awareness that could have been hers to articulate is reserved for the narrator and Bracy.

The second part of Christabel was written in the Lake Country in the summer and early fall of 1800. The second part echoes and reverses the first part. The second part begins with the death knell at morning, whereas the first had begun with the cock's crow at midnight. Although Coleridge continues the threads of his narrative, there are significantly altered emphases. At the time he was finishing the second part, Wordsworth was completing copy for the second volume of *Lyrical Ballads*, had composed large sections of what was to become "Home at Grasmere," and had completed *The Prelude* (1799), specifically addressed to Coleridge. Perhaps some of the sections of the additions to "Christabel" reflect Coleridge's knowledge of Wordsworth's recent work. The account of the relationship of Christabel's father with Lord Roland de Vaux may play on the themes of "The Brothers." As Coleridge undoubtedly realized, however, Wordsworth's most important work in the intervening years was his writing of *The Prelude* (1799), to which he transferred major passages from the history of the Pedlar. Thus the issues that were raised in 1798 were still immediately relevant in the summer of 1800, particularly those associated with the Pedlar's history.

As a youth the Pedlar gained

> An <u>active</u> power to fasten images
> Upon his brain, & on their pictured lines
> Intensely brooded, even till they attained
> The liveliness of dreams.
>
> (Butler 153)

The second part of "Christabel" finds Christabel awakening after her night with Geraldine to find that the spell Geraldine had uttered has taken affect and has become "lord of thy utterance." She is completely the reflection and can only passively imitate Geraldine's look and gesture. She greets Geraldine "with such perplexity of mind / As dreams too lively leave behind" (385–86). "Too lively" dreams, in "Christabel," become a burden. By her wandering, Christabel has exercised an "<u>active</u> power" to shape, as Margaret has shaped, that which is a reflection of dream and desire, not an image in nature's language. Christabel's lively dreams bring her, not the idealizations of the Pedlar's youth, but confusion. The relocation of the mysterious landscape outside the castle to the interior of Christabel's familiar shelter and into the previously assured innocence of her dreams criticizes the similar movement in the Pedlar's imagination. That movement from external to internal constitutes the movement from form or image to a language that must be interpreted in perplexity.

In Part II, Christabel's perplexity seems to be sinful, whereas in the first part it had been merely "shame and sorrow." Margaret, too, is ashamed to confess to the Pedlar that her wandering is wrong. Christabel says, "Sure I have sinn'd"; she prays that "He, who on the cross did groan, / Might wash away her sins unknown" (389–90). Her confusion extends to an inarticulate intuition of her sinfulness. In a similar situation, the mariner acquires a "strange power of speech," but Christabel loses her voice:

> all her features were resigned
> To this sole image in her mind:
> And passively did imitate
> That look of dull and treacherous hate!
> And thus she stood, in dizzy trance,
> Still picturing that look askance
> With forced unconscious sympathy
>
> (603–9)

The curse on the mariner gave him a voice; the spell cast on Christabel reduces her voice to an echo.

Her father's reaction to Christabel's request that he send Geraldine away demonstrates that he interprets her request as an offense against the laws of hospitality. Part II consists of a dialogue between her father, a hot-tempered literalist, and Bracy the Bard, who is aware of the complexities, and perhaps the perplexities, of the literal tale that Geraldine tells. Bracy replaces, as an interpreter, the narrator of the first part, who questioned appearances. The narrator still remains in Part II, but most of his questions concern, not Christabel, but her father and her father's anger. Bracy now probes, from a more skeptical and knowing mind, what the narrator of Part I had been able only to guess.

Bracy is introduced in Part II as someone familiar with the implications of echo. Half comically, half seriously, he explains the echo of the matin bell as the devil's mocking "the doleful tale / With a merry peal from Borodale" (358–59). His explanation of Geraldine's presence contradicts her own tale and derives, he claims, from the liveliness of his own dreams:

> I saw that dove,
> That gentle bird, whom thou dost love,
> And call'st by thy own daughter's name—
> Sir Leoline! I saw the same
> Fluttering, and uttering fearful moan
> Among the green herbs in the forest alone.
> . . . .
> I went and peered, and could descry
> No cause for her distressful cry;
> But yet for her dear lady's sake,
> I stooped, methought, the dove to take
> When lo! I saw a bright green snake
> Coiled around its wings and neck.
>
> (531–36, 545–50)

He tells Sir Leoline that "But though my slumber was gone by, / This dream it would not pass away— / It seems to live upon my eye!" (557–59). It is difficult to decide whether Bracy is recounting his actual dream, which would claim for his dream a perception of truth, or whether he has witnessed the relationship between Geraldine and Christabel and heard Sir Leoline's boastful remark that he would dislodge the "reptile souls" of the ruffians and then con-

structed an interpretation of that relationship using the fiction of
the dream. In the first case he would have special access to the land-
scape of Christabel's mind and her own dreams, and in the second
he would be playing the part of the responding echo himself, inter-
preting what he sees and hears before him at present. The second is
perhaps the more likely, considering his claim that the dream
"seems to live upon my eye!" His voice is thus the responding echo
in contrast to Christabel's responding silence.

The Pedlar teaches the young poet not to read things with "an un-
worthy eye," but Sir Leoline cannot credit Bracy's identification of
his dream's meaning. He misinterprets it to mean that Geraldine is
the dove and that her abductors are the snake. His rage at their
enormity so offends his sense of chivalry that he is blinded by his
passion. He reacts with precisely those passions that Wordsworth's
consolation for Margaret's story had rejected: indignation and the
rage for vengeance. He is so taken by Geraldine, so deceived by her
beauty, that he gives her a place that Christabel's mother might have
occupied. He cannot imagine her as the serpent. He may be a liter-
alist, but his literalism precedes Bracy's dream with a fiction of his
own, his judgment upon the "reptile souls" of the abductors. That
"sole object" upon his mind is his determining utterance. The figu-
rative identification that he has already made cannot be altered by a
new appropriation of his own utterance. Bracy, alert to the possibil-
ities of echo and response, finds that a self-assured clinging to a fig-
ure that is taken to be fact halts dialogue. Not only does Sir Leoline
persist in thinking of Geraldine as "Lord Roland's beauteous dove,"
he also senses Christabel's imitation of Geraldine's hissing but fails
to see it in Geraldine, and he thus connects the repitilian souls of the
ruffians with the discourtesy of his daughter. At the end of Part I
Christabel is left perplexed, and at the end of Part II Sir Leoline is
similarly perplexed and blinded:

> Within the Baron's heart and brain
> If thoughts, like these, had any share,
> They only swelled his rage and pain,
> And did but work confusion there.
> His heart was cleft with pain and rage.
>
> (636–40)

Thus Part II implies that even though things are read with a literal
eye, the tales that are told may go unheeded, perhaps because they

must be couched in the figure of a dream. Bracy's worthy eye is not that eye that can see simple humanity in the signs that it has inscribed on the landscape but that can see the complexity and perplexity in figures that the mind creates to fill the void left by the absence of landscape and a proper context for its figures. The Bard's tale and its interpretation are not understood, because contrary interpretations are established before the tale is told. Consequently, the teller of the tale is banished on a fruitless mission to inform Lord Roland de Vaux that his daughter is safe, but Coleridge's narrative suggests that Bracy is sent to chase the fiction of another tale, and one far less reliable than his own.

Since "The Pedlar" was read aloud on the day that the decision was made to exclude "Christabel" from the second volume of *Lyrical Ballads*, it most likely had some influence on that decision. Undoubtedly there was an incompatibility of style between "Christabel" and the rest of the volume. Part of the incompatibility came from what Wordsworth considered crude emotions in the references to violence, abduction, and ghastly ugliness. The poet of "Hart-Leap Well," the first poem in the second volume, announced his role in that volume: "The moving accident is not my trade." But "Christabel" is not only incompatible with the other poems, "The Ruined Cottage" and "The Pedlar," it questions the premises upon which such poems are written. Wordsworth's response to that questioning in 1800 was to organize a second volume of *Lyrical Ballads* with his own poems to exclude Coleridge's discordant note. The Pedlar of "The Ruined Cottage" might well be the narrator of the second volume. Coleridge's contrasting figure for the poet is the narrator of "Christabel" in the spring of 1798 and Bracy the Bard in the early fall of 1800. The narrator is a questioning voice. In the second part, Christabel is rendered passive, as though she were an ancient mariner silently contemplating her own voyage and tale. Bracy's is the significant voice. Coleridge shifted his emphasis from the mind that shapes to the poet who interprets. The irony of Coleridge's creation of Bracy is that he is the Bard whose tale is misunderstood and who is dismissed on a wandering errand in pursuit of a fiction.

The questioning of the literal in "Christabel" is a genuine questioning, not an insistence on the absolute necessity of acknowledging the complexities of the figurative. In April 1798, about the time that Coleridge began "Christabel," he wrote "The Nightingale," one of his most Wordsworthian poems and one that seems to confirm

Wordsworth's view of nature's language. It begins with a rejection of the conventional association of melancholy with the bird's song:

> 'Most musical, most melancholy' bird!
> A melancholy bird? Oh! idle thought!
> In Nature there is nothing melancholy.
> But some night-wandering man whose heart was pierced
> With the remembrance of a grievous wrong,
> Or slow distemper, or neglected love,
> (And so, poor wretch! filled all things with himself,
> And made all gentle sounds tell back the tale
> Of his own sorrow) . . .
>
> (13–21)

Coleridge rejects the fictions of "many a poet" who "echoes the conceit" for the quiet receptivity of one who is alive to the "influxes / Of shapes and sounds and shifting elements" of nature. He is alert to the trap of making the landscape a void by replacing it with his own fictions and finds, curiously, the perfect ideal of the poet's response to nature in the nightingale's song and in Hartley's "imitative lisp."[15] The questioning and probing of appearances conducted by the narrator in "Christabel" seem to be cast out when Coleridge speaks in his own voice. "The Nightingale" seems to contradict "Christabel" and to confirm Wordsworth's allegiance in the spring of 1798 to a language of nature that is prelinguistic and inarticulate. The ideals of expression are those of a bird's song and an infant's imitation. "The Nightingale" offers the alternatives of the conceits of poetry or the silent, or merely imitative, response to nature's activity. The absent perplexity of "The Nightingale," which is explicitly faced in "Frost at Midnight," is the relationship between the conceits of poetic language, Coleridge's toying with thought, and the inarticulate joy of the bird and the infant; they are separated, rather than being joined on any continuum of personal development or growth, and the ideal of poetic response appears more regressive than progressive.

If "The Nightingale" appears to ventriloquize Wordsworth's voice but subtly subverts it by seeing it as regressive, one of Wordsworth's responses to "The Nightingale" criticizes its Wordsworthianism. It is contained in a short passage in the drafts toward the end

15. For an analysis of "The Nightingale" as a poem about the inescapability of figuration, see Jean-Pierre Mileur's *Vision and Revision: Coleridge's Art of Immanence* (Berkeley: University of California Press, 1982) 45–52.

of Wordsworth's additions to the history of the Pedlar and was probably written after "The Nightingale" and before the fair copy of "The Ruined Cottage" was made before the fall of 1799.[16] In the context of "The Pedlar" and Wordsworth's Alfoxden notebook drafts, its justification of poetic conceits seems out of place:

> The Poets in their elegies and songs
> Lamenting the departed call the groves
> They call upon the hills & streams to mourn
> And senseless rocks, nor idly; for, inspired
> By no fallacious oracle they speak
> Obedient to the strong creative power
> Of human passion. Sympathies there are
> More mild, yet haply of a kindred birth
> That steal upon the meditative mind
> And grow with thought.
>
> (Butler 195)

The phrase "nor idly" refers to Coleridge's phrase "idle thought" in "The Nightingale" (14) and in the 1978 quarto edition of "Frost at Midnight" (20). Wordsworth's response justifies poetry's fictions on the grounds that they are prompted by the human passion of the sympathetic poet responding to nature. While Coleridge emphasizes the fictive quality of conceits, Wordsworth, only a little embarrassed by the fallacy, considers them as integral to the influence of nature. Wordsworth's lines admit that Coleridge may be correct. Their tone, which is both assertive and apologetic at the same time, reveals that Coleridge's questioning of the poetic voice and figures was unsettling to Wordsworth, who in the spring of 1798 was attempting to affirm a nature whose voice was inarticulate. The dialogue of their narrative poems is interwoven with those lyrics in the spring of 1798.

16. Butler 195. Professor Butler has informed me that it is possible that the passage was written earlier rather than later within the probable dates of its composition, March 1798 to December 1799, which would place it close to the time of the composition of "The Nightingale."

"My Genial Spirits":

The Conversation Poems and "Tintern Abbey"

T HE DIALOGUE in narrative poetry of the Salisbury Plain poems, "The Ancient Mariner," "The Ruined Cottage," and "Christabel" moves from social concerns with the causes of poverty and suffering to psychological explanations of evil and guilt. The recurrent interest in the transformation of character from good to evil or from evil to good and the transformation of emotion from fear and terror to hope and joy leads to a poetry that explores the mind and, in the spring of 1798, to a poetry that explores the personal development of a poet. Poetic dialogue is conscious of its own procedures and progress, and that awareness led Coleridge and Wordsworth to investigate the claims of poetic language to literal and figurative truth. Each succeeding poem or draft is, of course, a commentary on a preceding one, and each poet struggles to find a unique voice and persona. In narrative, Wordsworth develops the persona of the Pedlar, who can read landscape's human meaning sympathetically, the *spectator ab extra*, who loves those whose stories he narrates, the poet who will later write "Ruth," "The Brothers," and "Michael." Even the most personal of Wordsworth's early experiences are incorporated into objective third-person narrative for the Pedlar. Coleridge becomes the poet of intense fiction and figuration. His narratives take place at the meeting point of dream and the supernatural, but unlike the dream, the narratives are aware of their own uncertainty, with poetic figures that try to retain a representational quality with accurate depiction of psychological states. As Coleridge well knew, the individual within a dream does not judge whether the dream is true or false,[1] but the poet of the dream must judge.

In these distinct voices there is some fear of amalgamation or assimilation. The dialogue of the spring of 1798, however, generated lyric voices that posed a more serious threat of amalgamation that worried Coleridge and Thomas Poole the following fall. Wordsworth's turn to nature for the wisdom to alleviate despair permits him to expand the role of the Pedlar and to make the young narrator who hears his tale "a better and a wiser man." Just as Wordsworth had turned to Coleridge's optimism in "Religious Musings," he turned to Coleridge's poetry for a consolation to Margaret's story. The pattern of turning to Coleridge is repeated again and again in the next few years, complicated always by the poetics of those poems to which he turned. The philosophy and optimism that he needed were often qualified by their status as poetic utterance.

Wordsworth's use of Coleridge's poetry is manifestly evident in his quotations from it or in his echoes of it or allusions to it, and most often they are found in his earliest drafts of poems or in the beginnings of his drafts, as they are in his attempts at a consolation for "The Ruined Cottage." In his hopes for humanity Wordsworth turned, not to nature itself, which in his narratives was for the most part merely the ground upon which human life had left its traces, but to Coleridge's poetry, particularly "The Eolian Harp" (1795), "Reflections on Having Left a Place of Retirement" (1796), and "This Lime-Tree Bower" (1797). The Pedlar additions to Margaret's story raise the issue of the reading of nature and its proper interpretations, but it is sometimes hard to know whether Wordsworth is reading landscape or Coleridge's poems and difficult to know whether nature or Coleridge's poetry is primary. The threat of amalgamation comes just at the point at which Wordsworth's appropriation of Coleridge's poems and figures as beginnings for his own becomes his domination of Coleridge.

In January, February, and March 1798 Wordsworth's reading of Coleridge's poetry is selective, primary, and untroubled by the

1. *Shakespearean Criticism*, ed. Thomas Middleton Raysor, 2 vols. (London: Dent; New York: Dutton, 1960) 1: 116.

speculative nature of the poems. He selects Coleridge's repeated use of the image of the Eolian harp and the Berkeleyan idea of nature as the language of spirit to guarantee the permanence of the "secret spirit of humanity," but he does not meditate upon the contexts within Coleridge's poetry that place the image in the realm of mere possibility. He seems to evade, rather than face, the bothering implications of Coleridge's poetry, which is, at the very least, always searching for new possibilities in language. Within some of his poetry, Coleridge qualifies the metaphysics that his speculations have created, as he does in "The Eolian Harp." The problems that Coleridge saw in these speculations were, among others, that their poetic language was highly figurative and that, as in the case of "Religious Musings," the very lyric structure required that speculations must be altered by contrary movements of thought and emotion.

A further problem was that the poems that Wordsworth appropriated were located within a context of Coleridge's published volumes that underlined both their fictional, and even playful, nature and formed a sequence in which individual poems with apparent closure were revised and altered by following poems. A sequence of this kind found in Coleridge's early volumes that progresses on the basis of repetition and turn creates a set of utterances that are necessarily transitory and bound by their position in a sequence. A criticism or reading that removes either a figure from a poem or a poem from a sequence attempts to unbind both the figure and the poem and usually results in the creation of lyric fragments. If the removal is to be a seminal act, it must be followed by a replacement within another context, and in either previous or subsequent contexts, poems lose their individual boundaries while being bound. Wordsworth's reading and appropriation from Coleridge's poetry removes sections of poems and their figures and replaces them within his own context.

At first Wordsworth avoids the troubling aspects of Coleridge's poems by reading them as though they were a set of isolated fragments and by reading them with the same inattention to their figurative nature as he tried to read nature itself. The Pedlar's upbringing is characterized, not by the sounds or voices of nature, but by its silence and silent thought; if nature were to possess a voice, it would need a poetic or prophetic language. Questions of interpretation would inevitably arise. Their relationship in the spring of 1798 is less an instance of Wordsworth's subscribing to a

Coleridgean philosophy than it is an instance of Wordsworth's selective and fragmentary reading of Coleridge's poems and his appropriation of Coleridge's fragments for his own poetry. One result of his borrowing is that the incorporation of Coleridge's figures within Wordsworth's poetry has, ironically, placed a Wordsworthian stamp on Coleridge's poems that succeeding generations have continued to read with Wordsworth's interpretive stamp on them. Coleridge's fears of amalgamation were well founded, because his lines became Wordsworth's, and even his full poems continue to be read as Wordsworth read them.

Their poetic dialogue in 1798 debates issues of nature's language: whether it is articulate or inarticulate, similar or dissimilar to human language, and whether it can be read with a "worthy eye." The reticulated structure of a philosophy of the One Life is important, but so too is the evidence by which such a life is known, its presence in the movements of wind and clouds, in the patterns of light and shade, and in the activity of frost. Nature, in 1798, is a palimpsest of animated nature and the marks that humanity has written on landscape. Before 1798, in *An Evening Walk* (1793) and in his revisions of it in 1794, nature's life was conveyed in the play of light on landscape, in the vibrations that run from nature to man, and in Gothic voices of terror in the winds.[2] Coleridge's "The Eolian Harp," written approximately at the same time that he met Wordsworth, pointed a way in which Wordsworth seemed to be moving at a much slower pace:

> And what if all of animated nature
> Be but organic Harps diversly fram'd,

2. Wordsworth's early views of nature in the Windy Brow revisions of *An Evening Walk* have often been discussed. See especially the expanded version of 1794, lines 125–32, 191–96, and 548–51 in *EW*, also printed in *WPW* 1: 10, 12, 29 app. crit. G. W. Meyer saw in these sections Wordsworth's mature nature myth (*Wordsworth's Formative Years*, University of Michigan Publications in Language and Literature, vol. 20 [Ann Arbor: University of Michigan Press, 1943] 167–68). H. W. Piper sees Wordsworth's revisions connected with materialism and pantheism (*The Active Universe* [London: Athelone, 1962] 72–74). Jonathan Wordsworth suggests that the materialism of the earlier revisions is not the same as the later idea of the One Life, which Wordsworth picked up from Coleridge (*The Music of Humanity* [London: Nelson, 1969] 186). Paul Sheats discusses the language by which Wordsworth conveys his philosophical notions in 1794 (*The Making of Wordsworth's Poetry, 1785–1798* [Cambridge, Mass.: Harvard University Press, 1973] 95–104).

That tremble into thought, as o'er them sweeps,
Plastic and vast, one intellectual Breeze,
At once the Soul of each, and God of all?

(36–40)

Wordsworth had used the idea of sympathetic vibrations to conceive of man and nature in a social relationship and to apply that sympathy to social issues. Coleridge's figure emphasizes, not a material secret power, such as that in *An Evening Walk* (*EW* 135) that is perhaps similar to the power in Shelley's "Mont Blanc," but an intellectual force that animates man and nature, moves a mind to a more perfect consciousness of its individuality and place in the world, and provides a metaphysical, rather than a material and social, ground for consciousness. Coleridge's is an intellectual breeze, not a natural one, and its product is a tune that implies a universal harmony.[3]

In the spring of 1798 Wordsworth turned to Coleridge's use of the figure of the breeze that is a source of a language of nature and a voice of the One Life. In his Alfoxden notebook he drafted two passages, both later incorporated into *The Prelude*:[4]

There would he wander in the storm and there
He felt whateer there is of power in sounds
To breathe an elevated mood—by form
Or image unprofaned of sounds that are
The ghostly language of the antient earth
Or make their dim abode in distant winds.

(Parrish 153)

3. For a discussion of "The Eolian Harp" and "Reflections on Having Left a Place of Retirement" in their early contexts in the volumes of 1796 and 1797 and in his letters, see my " 'The Eolian Harp' in Context," *Studies in Romanticism* 24 (1985): 3–20. For "The Eolian Harp" and other poems from the 1796 volume, I have quoted from that volume. On the contents page of *Poems* (1797) "Reflections on Having Left a Place of Retirement" is called "Reflections on Leaving a Place of Residence," although the title on the poem itself is "Reflections on Having Left a Place of Retirement." I will use the title on the contents page to refer to the poem in 1797 to distinguish it from the later version.

4. I have simplified the transcriptions of these two fragments in Parrish 153. See also Michael C. Jaye's "William Wordsworth's Alfoxden Notebook: 1798," *The Evidence of the Imagination: Studies of Interactions between Life and Art in English Romantic Literature*, ed. Donald H. Reiman, Michael C. Jaye, and Betty T. Bennett (New York: New York University Press, 1978) 62–63. The first fragment was copied with "The Pedlar" fragments in MS. D (1799) and later used in *The Prelude* (1799) II, 352–59, and (1805) II, 322–29. The second was used in *The Prelude*, MS. JJ (Parrish 83).

Its language is pure, "unprofaned" by association with "form" or "image." It is associated with nothing outside of itself, even, Wordsworth seems to imply, human language. In a second passage, a breeze that floats over and animates the lake in which landscape is reflected becomes a light that is a "strain of music" and sinks into the heart:

> There would he stand
> In the still covert of some [? lonesome] rock
> Or gaze upon the moon untill its light
> Fell like a strain of music on his soul
> And seem'd to sink into his very heart.

(Parrish 153)

Wordsworth's natural sound and natural music are not truly equivalent to Coleridge's "intellectual Breeze." In the early months of 1798 Wordsworth was careful to avoid the implications of an "intellectual" force in nature and did his best to naturalize it, just as in "The Eolian Harp" Coleridge himself kept speculation at arm's length. Wordsworth isolated and appropriated Coleridge's figure, thus fragmenting his original context.

It would be more accurate to say that Wordsworth appropriated the figure of the breeze from Coleridge's contexts and that those contexts determined the significance of the figure. When "The Eolian Harp" was presented in the 1796 volume *Poems on Various Subjects*, it was titled "Effusion XXXV. Composed August 20th, 1795, At Clevedon, Somerset," and in *Poems* (1797) the title was reduced to "Composed at Clevedon." It did not get its familiar title until 1817. The early titles indicate the personal content of the poem, and the preface to the 1796 volume justifies the poems' egotism by saying that they were "written at different times and prompted by very different feelings" (*CPW* 2: 1135). Most were playful expressions of the feelings of the moment. A contemporary reader would have looked on them as such rather than as statements of a considered body of thought. In the same preface Coleridge remarked on his choice of "effusion" as a title: "I could recollect no title more descriptive of the manner and matter of the Poems—I might indeed have called the majority of them Sonnets—but they do not possess that *oneness* of thought which I deem indispensible [*sic*] in a Sonnet . . ." (*CPW* 2: 1137). In 1796 "Effusion XXXV" was preceded by the previous effusion, "To an Infant," an emblem poem of a child who is "Man's breathing Miniature" because in frustration he reaches for his mother as man reaches for God. It was followed by another effusion, later called "Lines on an Autumnal Evening," some drafts of which were completed as early as 1793. In 1797 "Composed at Clevedon" was followed by "Reflections on Having Left a Place of Retirement" (then titled "Reflections on Leaving a Place of Residence"), a more familiar context for the modern reader. Finally, in 1817 "The Eolian Harp" was included in its familiar context in a group of poems under the title "Meditative Poems in Blank Verse" along with other Conversation Poems, "This Lime-Tree Bower my Prison," "The Nightingale: A Conversation Poem," and "Frost at Midnight." In 1796 and 1797 it would have been difficult to have seen "Effusion XXXV" as anything other than a set of private associations. There was no special attention to the image of the harp, later singled out by its title after Wordsworth's extensive use of it. The contexts of 1796 and 1797 almost preclude the reading of the figure as Wordsworth read it. In isolation from its surrounding contexts, Coleridge's figure of the breeze and the harp provided Wordsworth with a far more philosophical view of the relationship of the mind to nature's activity than Wordsworth had formulated in the Windy Brow revisions of *An Evening Walk*. But to read its figurative implications without question, Wordsworth had to separate it from its context. To remove a fragment from its context, in this instance their dialogue, is to remove the figure from another figure, the figure of form in which the context qualifies the significance of any figure that it contains. Placing a fragment within a context is an act of formal figuration.

"Effusion XXXV"[5] opens with an apostrophe to "pensive Sara," which seems to introduce a meditative poem, but the poem becomes a meditation upon the ways in which nature's images convey meaning and consequently a poem about the style of its expression and about the playful shifts of style throughout. At first, images appear as emblems: the "white-flower'd Jasmin, and the broad-leav'd Myrtle, / (Meet emblems they of Innocence and Love!)" (4–5). The second line troubled Coleridge. He left it out of the 1803 text and then reinserted it in 1817. It recalls the seventeenth-century emblem poetry of Wither and Quarles, the latter of whom defined an emblem

5. John Beer reprints the 1796 volume without the later revisions and states that Coleridge is "still very much the provincial poet with an enthusiasm for effects of sublimity and pathos. His later revisions tend to destroy the fullness of this impression" (Beer xxx).

as a "silent parable,"[6] but in "Effusion XXXV" the emblems have lost the simple morality of earlier emblems and have become playfully erotic. The reader of 1796 would have turned from "Effusion XXXV" to the following effusion, "Lines on an Autumnal Evening," and seen a similar use of the emblem of myrtle:

> SPIRITS of LOVE! ye heard her name! Obey
> The powerful spell, and to my haunt repair,
> Whether on clust'ring pinions ye are there,
> Where rich snows blossom on the Myrtle trees,
> Or with fond languishment around my fair
> Sigh in the loose luxuriance of her hair. . . .
>
> (37–42)

Further on in the same poem Coleridge becomes more extravagant:

> A flower-entangled ARBOUR I would seem
> To shield my Love from Noontide's sultry beam:
> Or bloom a MYRTLE, from whose od'rous boughs
> My Love might weave gay garlands for her brows.
>
> (61–64)

In "Effusion XXXV" the "star of eve" becomes an emblem of wisdom that shines "serenely brilliant," a phrase Coleridge borrowed from one of his earlier, unpublished poems, "To the Evening Star," in which the lover, like the star, inspires *"Pure* joy and *calm* Delight" (*CPW* 1: 17). Commonly associated with erotic and generative love, the evening star is here an emblem of the wisdom gained only by a parenthetical denial of the erotic and by an affirmation of purity and innocence. The emblems exist in a "world *so* hush'd" that nature "tells us of Silence." There is no discordant sound, no interruption of the calm and harmony. The purity of the moment resides in its innocence and simplicity, but unlike Wordsworth's images unprofaned by meaning, Coleridge's emblems have a decipherable meaning. Here, as later in their poetry, meaning is intended for images by a denial or limitation of previous associations, not primarily through original and natural perception.

The associations of these emblems come, not from their inherent nature, but from the signatures borrowed from tradition that the poet places on them: the whiteness of innocence, the myrtle's con-

6. *The Complete Works in Prose and Verse of Francis Quarles*, ed. Rev. Alexander Grosart, 3 vols. (1880–81; New York, AMS Press, 1967) 3: 45.

nection with Venus, and the eroticism of the evening star. Similarly, the allusions to music in "Effusion XXXV" contain a medley of various styles dissociated as far as possible from individual poetic voices and reminiscent of historical or period styles in English and classical literature. The harp and the breeze are linked by simile to seduction; the harp is

> Like some coy Maid half-yielding to her Lover,
> It pours such sweet upbraidings, as must needs
> Tempt to repeat the wrong!
>
> (15–17)

The following "Lines on an Autumnal Evening" repeats the sentiment:

> To fan my Love I'd be the EVENING GALE;
> Mourn in the soft folds of her swelling vest,
> And flutter my faint pinions on her breast!
> On Seraph wing I'd float a DREAM, by night,
> To soothe my Love with shadows of delight:—
>
> (66–70)

In "Effusion XXXV" the "sweet upbraidings" becomes

> Such a soft floating witchery of sound
> As twilight Elfins make, when they at eve
> Voyage on gentle gales from Faery Land,
> Where *Melodies* round honey-dropping flowers,
> Footless and wild, like birds of Paradise,
> Nor pause nor pearch, hov'ring on untam'd wing.
>
> (20–25)

Again, the following "Lines on an Autumnal Evening" boldly (or perhaps carelessly) repeats the sentiment. The "Spirits of Love" are invoked to "heed the spell, and hither wing your way, / Like far-off music, voyaging the breeze."

These repetitions and echoes in a poem that immediately follows "Effusion XXXV" in 1796 reinforce the reader's tendency to follow the implications of the preface and to take the emblems and similes to be merely playful associations. They invoke, not Spenser's voice, but Spenserianism; the Faery Land of "Effusion XXXV" is nearer to that of the "Song of the Pixies" than it is to Spenser's Faeryland. As Lowes pointed out many years ago, the sources for the footless birds of paradise are articles in contemporary travel literature.[7] Coleridge's note to "Lines on an Autumnal Evening" disavows any originality in his similes: "I entreat the Public's pardon for having carelessly suffered to be printed such intolerable stuff as this and the thirteen following lines [including 'To fan my love I'd be the EVENING GALE']. They have not the merit even of originality: as every thought is to be found in the Greek Epigrams" (*CPW* 1: 52). Coleridge simply accumulates figures of speech from the vast reservoir of anonymous and traditional literature.

The following eight lines of "The Eolian Harp," beginning with "O! the one Life within us and abroad," were added in their final form in the errata of *Sibylline Leaves* (1817) and were not in the original "Effusion XXXV." Wordsworth had first used the phrase "one Life" in the Pedlar material, and Coleridge first used it in an 1802 letter to William Sotheby. It is familiar to readers of Coleridge criticism, and it is followed by a discussion of rhetoric that dismisses, by implication, the fanciful play of 1796:

> It must occur to every Reader that the Greeks in their religious poems address always the Numina Loci, the Genii, the Dryads, the Naiads, &c &c—All natural Objects were *dead*—mere hollow Statues—but there was a Godkin or Goddessling *included* in each—In the Hebrew Poetry you find nothing of this poor Stuff—as poor in genuine Imagination, as it is mean in Intellect— / At best, it is but Fancy, or the aggregating Faculty of the mind—not *Imagination*, or the *modifying*, and *co-adunating* Faculty. (*STCL* 2: 865–66)

The closest Coleridge comes in 1796 to the idea of the One Life is the passage on the "intellectual Breeze." To introduce such a thought in "Effusion XXXV," Coleridge had to alter radically the rhetoric of the poem. Philosophical speculation on the breeze as a ground for nature and man requires that the emblems and similes in the first part of the poem be disregarded as at best capricious moods that have no relation to the metaphysical speculation, even though their themes of love would seem to lead to thoughts of a purified universal spiritual love. The apparent progress in theme is disrupted by the inconsistencies in style and figuration. The speculation does not grow from the earlier fanciful similes. Coleridge has

---

7. John Livingston Lowes, *The Road to Xanadu: A Study in the Ways of the Imagination* (Boston: Houghton Mifflin, 1927) 458. See also *CNB* 1: 51 and note. Coleridge tried to have these lines deleted from *Poems* (1797) (*STCL* 1: 331).

a Keatsian suspicion of his appropriated rhetoric. If speculation has any claim on truth, the lyric must turn from the preceding sections.

Even though Wordsworth read Coleridge's speculations as providing a philosophical framework for his intuition of nature's animation, Coleridge's placement of the lines suggests, rather, that they are one in a succession of associations concluding in a rejection and introduced with a description of the process of association itself:

> Full many a thought uncall'd and undetain'd,
> And many idle flitting phantasies,
> Traverse my indolent and passive brain
> As wild and various, as the random gales
> That swell or flutter on this subject Lute!
>
> (31–35)

Introduced as a phantasy of association, the "intellectual Breeze" is dismissed in lines that follow in 1796 without a break for a new verse paragraph:

> But thy more serious eye a mild reproof
> Darts, O beloved Woman! nor such thoughts
> Dim and unhallow'd dost thou not reject,
> And biddest me walk humbly with my God.
>
> (41–44)

The "shapings of the unregenerate mind," the mind clouded by ignorance, are rejected for a "Faith that inly *feels*."

"Effusion XXXV" is a poem of explicit and implicit rejections that works through a medley of styles that has only the appearance of a progress. Coleridge's faith at the end of "Effusion XXXV" is the faith of an admonished Adam, and Wordsworth transformed it into the faith of his natural Adam, the Pedlar: "in the mountains did he feel his faith" (Butler 159). The implicit rejection of the similes and emblems is followed by the explicit rejection of the "intellectual Breeze" as an "idle flitting" fantasy. All are forms of a language that is necessarily provisional and temporary, bordering on the fictional, not simply because its figure of speech is fanciful, but because in the context of the poem and of the volume its stylistic turns classify it as one figure among many. The image of the harp has no special privilege. Its surrounding contexts locate the image in the field of their

149

own references. As Coleridge made quite clear in the 1796 preface, an effusion does "not possess that *oneness* of thought."

Wordsworth would have known the poem, of course, not only in its 1796 context, but in that of 1797 as well, where it is followed by "Reflections on Leaving a Place of Residence." While this poem does not influence a reading of "Effusion XXXV," now titled "Composed at Clevedon," as "Lines on an Autumnal Evening" influenced the reading of "Effusion XXXV," it still places it in a sequence in which its calm domestic and rural tranquillity is viewed from another perspective and seen as a severely limiting restriction. The close correspondence between the title of the first poem, "Composed at Clevedon," and the following one present the two as a sequence. The second begins where the first ends. "Composed at Clevedon" ends with a prayer of thanks for "PEACE, and this COT, and THEE, heart-honour'd Maid," and "Reflections on Leaving a Place of Residence" begins "Low was our pretty Cot." The opening verse paragraph duplicates and elaborates the final scene of "Composed at Clevedon." The "Faith that inly *feels*" is present at the end of the verse paragraph in the hearing of the skylark's song "when all is hush'd,/ And the Heart listens!" The "little landscape" of the cottage and its grounds, however, is presented as a natural place, not a landscape of emblems and similes. In the sequence of the two poems, it is a natural place only by virtue of the deletion of its previous literary associations, by the deletion of its figurative value. Myrtle and jasmine bloom as part of the "green and woody" beauty of landscape and have lost their emblematic associations. It continues to be a "Blesséd Place," but just as there was a strong revisionary impulse in "Effusion XXXV," there is here a similar impulse. The blessed spot that Coleridge praises in the final line of "Effusion XXXV" he here regards as a "Valley of Seclusion," which introduces the enclosed or limited space in which many of Coleridge's later poems begin.

The cottage is a blessed place because there is nothing to desire; it appears to be a place of fullness. The "little landscape" of the cottage is reflected in the larger world of the prospect from the hill over the Bristol Channel in the second verse paragraph:

> It seem'd like Omnipresence! God, methought,
> Had built him there a Temple: the whole World
> Seem'd *imag'd* in its vast circumference:
> No *wish* profan'd my overwhelmed Heart.
> Blest hour! It was a luxury—to be!
>
> (38–42)

Coleridge quickly turns from the praise of a literal paradise, because it is a secluded place where only the heart listens in indulgent complacency and where political and social activity is excluded. The rejection of seclusion is a rejection as well of the tranquillity of the concluding lines of "Composed at Clevedon." However valuable the "Faith that inly *feels*," and however thankful Coleridge is for the blessings he has received, he cannot rest with them, because they are associated, ironically, with a luxury. The citizen of Bristol intrudes to remind Coleridge of a world more real than the delightful spot in which he lives, listening only to the "inobtrusive song of Happiness." At first the citizen's intrusion is covered by the song of the skylark, but it cannot be ignored. It must be accommodated, and in the spring of 1800, when Wordsworth began work on "Home at Grasmere," he was troubled by a similar intrusion from the active life.

Coleridge's rejection of the place of retirement is a rejection only of its literal presence. He cannot live there and fulfill his Christian duty to mankind. He cannot pamper his heart. The spot remains only as an image:

> Yet oft when after honourable toil
> Rests the tir'd mind, and waking loves to dream,
> My spirit shall revisit thee, dear Cot!
> Thy Jasmin and thy window-peeping Rose,
> And Myrtles fearless of the mild sea-air.
> And I shall sigh fond wishes—sweet Abode!
> Ah!—had none greater! And that all had such!
> It might be so—but the time is not yet.
> Speed it, O FATHER! Let thy Kingdom come!
>
> (63–71)

Having rejected the literal spot, the poem turns it into an image, a promise of a paradise to come, a millennium that exists in the dreams of the poet who has left the natural paradise. The myrtle and jasmine of "Composed at Clevedon," which were stripped of their emblematic significance in the opening verse paragraph to be naturalized into the landscape, have been returned to the status of an image that prefigures a later paradise. The "Blessèd Place" is reflected or imaged in the larger prospect of the channel, and the prospect itself images the "whole world." The word "reflections" in Coleridge's title refers as much to the mirror imaging that is the necessary and saving substitute for literalism as it does to the meditations that produce images.

Wordsworth rewrote these final lines in "Tintern Abbey":

> If this
> Be but a vain belief, yet, oh! how oft,
> In darkness, and amid the many shapes
> Of joyless day-light; when the fretful stir
> Unprofitable, and the fever of the world,
> Have hung upon the beatings of my heart,
> How oft, in spirit, have I turned to thee
> O sylvan Wye! Thou wanderer through the woods,
> How often has my spirit turned to thee!
>
> (50–58)

The final line is an appropriation of Coleridge's "My spirit shall re-visit thee, dear Cot!" Wordsworth's context for the line, however, determines that his appropriation gives the line a different significance. While Coleridge seeks the active life, Wordsworth wishes to avoid the "fretful stir / Unprofitable," and his return in imagination to the Wye is to restore the literal presence of a landscape that he fears will become mere imagery and to escape the turmoil that tends to efface the memory of that image. Coleridge wishes to retain only the image, not the literal presence, to assure himself that there is a promised good in a millennial future. Wordsworth's borrowing in this instance is an intepretation of Coleridge's lines, because it does not accept all of their contextual implications. His echo of "Reflections on Leaving a Place of Residence" fragments Coleridge's sequences and thus suppresses, for a time, Coleridge's insistence that the image is the only permissible human reality.

There is one further early Coleridge poem that influenced Wordsworth's work in the late winter and early spring of 1798 and that he read to fit his emerging nature myth as he did "The Eolian Harp" and "Reflections on Leaving a Place of Residence." "This Lime-Tree Bower" was drafted in July 1797 and sent to Southey less than a month after Coleridge had transcribed the final lines of Margaret's story for a letter to John Prior Estlin. Two versions survive from 1797, and both are considerably shorter than the published poem,[8] so that it is difficult to conclude anything about Wordsworth's reading in 1798 from the later printed versions. For instance, in the version sent to Southey the first twenty-eight lines of the later version are sketched in about ten lines. The particular ob-

---

8. See Chapter 4, note 8.

servations of nature in the dell and in the prospect of the "many-steepled tract magnificent / Of hilly fields and meadows" is almost entirely missing. The poem moves quickly from the opening state of deprivation to contemplate a natural scene in the process of losing its material presence and becoming an image similar to those images in "Reflections on Leaving a Place of Residence":

> Ah slowly sink
> Behind the western ridge; thou glorious Sun!
> Shine in the slant beams of the sinking orb,
> Ye purple Heath-flowers! Richlier burn, ye Clouds!
> Live in the yellow Light, ye distant Groves!
> And kindle, thou blue Ocean! So my friend
> Struck with joy's deepest calm, and gazing round
> On the wide view, may gaze till all doth seem
> Less gross than bodily, a living Thing
> That acts upon the mind, and with such hues
> As cloathe the Almighty Spirit, when he makes
> Spirits perceive His presence!
>
> (*STCL* 1: 335)

Without the later ballast of Wordsworthian observation of physical landscape, the poem presents a movement of light over landscape that makes objects "shine," "burn," "live," and "kindle." Nature appears to be both a reflection of light and a source of light itself, not palpable objects. They are the images of a language of spirit. As Coleridge said in a note to his letter to Southey, "You remember, I am a *Berkleian*." The version published in 1800 in the *Annual Anthology*, with its detailed description of the dell and the prospect, changes Coleridge's earlier version by making the language of spirit into a more concrete, literal, and Wordsworthian instrument of communication than it had been originally.

Coleridge is able to view nature as a spiritual language because he is distant from it. The "Blessèd Place" can be an effective image only when one has rejected its literal reality. Similarly, in the early drafts of "This Lime-Tree Bower" the language of nature can be understood only at a distance from nature:

> Henceforth I shall know
> That nature ne'er deserts the wise & pure,
> No scene so narrow, but may well employ
> Each faculty of sense, and keep the heart
> Awake to Love & Beauty: and sometimes

'Tis well to be bereav'd of promis'd good
That we may lift the soul, & contemplate
With lively joy the joys, we cannot share.

(*STCL* 1: 336)

Wordsworth appropriated these lines, as well, for "Tintern Abbey": "Nature never did betray / The heart that loved her." Coleridge's "hues" that "cloathe the Almighty Spirit" resemble Wordsworth's "nature and the language of the sense." The presence of these languages assures that vacancy or loss will not diminish their ability to communicate joy. But Wordsworth's assurance rests in his ability to return to the natural; and Coleridge's, in a movement away from it. Coleridge's 1797 word "bereav'd," later changed to "bereft," associates the distance from nature with a loss or death. "This Lime-Tree Bower" may have been prompted by Coleridge's hearing Wordsworth read the early version of "The Ruined Cottage." Coleridge's moral for Margaret's suffering is that one should keep "the heart / Awake to Love & Beauty." The Pedlar must teach the young poet to see human hope where only loss and despair claim their dwelling.

The consolation to Margaret's story draws on the affirmation of "This Lime-Tree Bower." The sympathetic heart in "This Lime-Tree Bower" is the same that retains "quiet sympathies with things that hold / An inarticulate language" for the heart of man (Butler 261). In the first few months of 1798 the One Life was of value primarily as a guarantor of the spirit of humanity to Wordsworth and only secondarily as an active principle that supported and nourished individual growth. The sense of unity that Wordsworth derived from Coleridge's poetry assured the continuance of human joy and charity. When Wordsworth praised Coleridge in *The Prelude* (1799) as someone to whom "the unity of all has been revealed" (II, 256) the phrase in context refers to the social order as well as to the location of an individual within a benevolent natural order. Only later in the spring of 1798, again under the pressure of Coleridge's poetry, did the most challenging questions arise about the relationship of an individual mind to nature and its own past. The emphasis on the nature myth shifted from nature as the dwelling place of the "secret spirit of humanity" to the providential activity that nourished human imagination. The change is clearly indicated in the shift from the construction of the Pedlar's history in the third person, with strict chronology to the point at which he is able to see that spirit in all things, to "Tintern Abbey" in which individual history becomes retrospective, personalized, and even somewhat reclusive, a history of the growth not mainly of humanitarianism but of the genial spirits of individual imagination.

Wordsworth's poetry in these months responds to and interprets Coleridge's and follows Coleridge's lead. His responses echo only portions of Coleridge's poetic sequence constructed in the 1797 volume of "Composed at Clevedon" and "Reflections on Leaving a Place of Residence" and by "This Lime-Tree Bower," itself perhaps a reply to Margaret's story. The portions of Coleridge's poetry that were available as consoling were bits and fragments of Coleridge's sequence. The sequence itself, the corpus of Coleridge's poetry, was unavailable, because the form of sequence argued against the certainty of unity that individual fragments and passages affirmed. The sequence itself, with its speculations, turns, rejections, and qualifications, presents a continually shifting view of nature and poetic language. To find a unifying ground for his nature myth, Wordsworth had to divest the borrowed fragments of any suggestion that they were tentative and mere images, and criticism has followed his lead. Coleridge's sequences are read with highly selective eyes that find statements of belief that Wordsworth sought and disregard their full context. For Wordsworth it became typical to speak as though images were things with substantial weight. The Pedlar

> perceived the presence & the power
> Of greatness, and deep feelings had impressed
> Great objects on his mind, with portraiture
> And colour so distinct [that on his mind]
> They lay like substances, & almost seemed
> To haunt the bodily sense.[9]

The images that haunt the Pedlar have little resemblance to those of Clevedon that remain in memory and to the images, "less gross than bodily," of "This Lime-Tree Bower."

In an earlier portion of their dialogue, Coleridge responded to Wordsworth's fragments to create "The Ancient Mariner," a reading of the drafts of the Salisbury Plain poems. Wordsworth's turn to Coleridge's poetry in early 1798 reversed the process. He responded to Coleridge's poems that had been published and thereby

9. See Butler (150–51) for photographs and transcriptions from MS. B (1798). The words in brackets are supplied from MS. D (1799) (Butler 341). The lines are 29–34 in Jonathan Wordsworth's text (*Music of Humanity* 173–74).

placed in a context of a volume that determined, to a large extent, the significance of individual poems. Wordsworth's selective use of Coleridge's poems reduced them to fragments so that they could be generative for his poetry. By removing the generative fragments from a sequence that argued an artfulness in language and form, Wordsworth attempted to relieve the figurative language in those fragments of the burden of their artfulness and to restore them to an almost literal, at times even a physical, naturalness. His intention is not to add to Coleridge's sequence, or medley of styles, or succession of figures, but to deny the figurative implications of sequence altogether. He is unwilling to acknowledge that his response to these figures and these sequences is itself a figure. His tactic is to strip off the figurative. Yet through 1798 and 1799, when he turns to autobiographical writing, the specific problems of the arbitrariness of the literal, of the figurative, and of poetic order and sequence become urgent to him.

From the early months of 1798 to the fall of that year, Wordsworth's poetry underwent a radical transformation. From the objective narration that used autobiographical elements in the Pedlar's history to the probing, private meditations that began *The Prelude*, Wordsworth's subject matter shifted from humanitarianism to a questioning of the sources of his own poetry within himself and nature. The change is partly the result of the dialogue that his work on "The Ruined Cottage" conducts with Coleridge's earlier poetry, and to a greater degree it is the result of Coleridge's writing, in late February 1798, "Frost at Midnight,"[10] the most important poem Wordsworth ever rewrote. In the context of their poetic dialogue, "Tintern Abbey" is not an isolated moment of Wordsworth's individual achievement, his first great poem and a fit conclusion to his own efforts in the spring of 1798. It is, rather, an interpretation by revision of "Frost at Midnight." A worry about the loss of genial spirits and the distance of the present moment from its source is not exclusively Wordsworth's private concern; it is a shared one. The presence of them in "Tintern Abbey" identifies their similar presence in "Frost at Midnight." It is, at first, an astute recognition of the problems that Coleridge raised by placing the issues of the intelligibility of nature and its language in the context of personal growth. "This Lime-Tree Bower" confronted the problem of an absence of nature's im-

10. In my discussion of "Frost at Midnight" I have used the 1798 quarto edition. See *CPW* 1: 240–42 app. crit.

mediate language, but it was a separation of a present speaker from a present joy that others shared and that the speaker had shared, but "Frost at Midnight" separated a past in which there was an audibility and intelligibility from a present in which there was silence and unintelligibility. In the recognition of the essential dimension of time, change, and personal growth in their poetics and in the invocation of genius, which is always individual, there is an implicit recognition of the threat of amalgamation. As a consequence, Wordsworth must insist, as he does in "Tintern Abbey," that his genius must be preserved, not only from decay but also from amalgamation with Coleridge's poetry. As a result, the history of his genius must be an individual story. It must take place in isolation.

"Frost at Midnight" is dated February 1798, and the poem was probably written in the second half of the month. He was away from Nether Stowey until February 9, and the weather for the next five or six days was mild. On the evening of the sixteenth, a light snow began to fall and fell through the night. February 17 dawned with a heavy snow on the ground:

> A deep stillness in the thickest part of the wood, undisturbed except by the occasional dropping of the snow from the holly boughs; no other sound but that of the water, and the slender notes of a redbreast, which sang at intervals on the outskirts of the southern side of the wood. There the bright green moss was bare at the roots of the trees, and the little birds were upon it. The whole appearance of the wood was enchanting; and each tree, taken singly, was beautiful. The branches of the hollies pendent with their white burden, but still showing their bright red berries, and their glossy green leaves. The bare branches of the oaks thickened by the snow. (*DWJ* 7)

Coleridge borrowed much of this entry for the final images of "Frost at Midnight": the "deep stillness," the "dropping of snow," the "slender notes of a redbreast," "the bright green moss," and the "bare branches." Dorothy's entry dates the poem, then, very close to the time that Wordsworth was completing his additions to "The Ruined Cottage" and close to the time that the consolation was developed from drafts in the Alfoxden notebook.

These images of natural beauty conclude the poem, but the poem opens, not with natural description, but with a typically Coleridgean description of a calm and vacuity, the initial image of which Cole-

157

ridge borrowed from Cowper's *The Task*.[11] Coleridge is troubled by
vacuity, mystery, and calm, all of which vex him into thought.
Throughout "Frost at Midnight" the significant theme is neither de-
tailed natural description nor the mystery of nature's activity, but
the audibility and intelligibility of the "numberless goings on of
life." Alone at night, Coleridge can hear only the owl's cry and his
son's breathing and see the movement of the sooty film, the "sole
unquiet thing," with which he, also "unquiet" and restless, feels
companionship. From his seat by the fire he cannot see the activity
of the frost, or the "sea, hill, and wood" and the "populous village."
They are beyond his sight or hearing, yet he wonders about their
activity and their life. They are silent and do not speak to him; they
are "inaudible as dreams," and their inaudibility causes Coleridge's
unquiet.

Their inaudibility contrasts with the articulate sounds that the
church bells brought to Coleridge when he was a child. The bells
were "most like articulate sounds of things to come" because they
were associated with the fairday and with the joyous company of
family and friends. Removed from school and sent to Christ's Hos-
pital in London, Coleridge dreams of the articulate sounds, which
to him had been real, but while it brings back the image of his for-
mer festive company, dreaming prevents the arrival of the promise
that it articulates, because it requires a separation from it. His school
dreams resemble the inaudibility of the world from which he is sep-
arated as an adult. When he awakens from the dream at school, he
finds only a dispiriting absence of friends and family.

The transition to the next verse paragraph, which begins with the
apostrophe "Dear babe," has the tone of another awakening from a
dream, the dream of recollection, and again he awakens to a place
and time that bring him no change from the vacuity in which he be-
gan his meditation. He hears only what he has heard before, Hart-
ley's breathing in the "dead calm." The phrase, "dead calm," was
later changed to "deep calm," totally altering the original text.
Doubtless, Hartley's presence somewhat relieves Coleridge's vexa-
tion in the "dead calm." Coleridge is moved and his heart is "filled."
He becomes "unquiet" in another sense, because some vitality re-
turns to him. Yet the returning vitality at the sight of Hartley, the

11. *The Task*, IV, "The Winter Evening," in *Cowper: The Poetical Works*, ed. H. S. Mil-
ford, 4th ed. (London: Oxford University Press, 1967) 286–310. Humphry House
discusses the relationship of Cowper's lines to "Frost at Midnight" (*Coleridge: The
Clark Lectures, 1951–52* [London: Rupert Hart-Davis, 1967] 78–83).

stranger whom he has been expecting, comes from the hope that
Hartley will grow up in an environment different from that which,
at this moment, seems to Coleridge as the prison of his childhood.
He makes a sharp distinction between himself and Hartley:

> I was rear'd
> In the great city, pent mid cloisters dim,
> And saw nought lovely but the sky and stars.
> But *thou*, my babe! Shalt wander, like a breeze
> . . . .
> Therefore all seasons shall be sweet to thee . . .
>
> (56–59, 70)

While he is filled with the thought of all seasons being sweet to Hart-
ley, he is not relieved totally from the void of unintelligibility in
which he, as an adult, finds himself. He hopes that Hartley will be
able to "see and hear / The lovely shapes and sounds intelligible / Of
that eternal language, which thy God / Utters." Hartley's future ap-
pears remarkably close to the Pedlar's childhood, which Words-
worth was composing at the same time. As the Pedlar matured, he
compared all his impressions with "all his ideal stores, his shapes &
forms":

> Nor did he fail
> While yet a child, with a child's eagerness
> Incessantly to turn his ear & eye
> On all things which the rolling seasons brought
> To feed such appetite. . . .
>
> (Butler 153)

It is impossible to determine whether Coleridge's "all seasons shall
be sweet to thee" or Wordsworth's "rolling seasons brought" was the
first written, but Coleridge's context is significantly different. The
"goings on of life," which are to Coleridge still unintelligible at the
end of the poem, will be comprehensible to Hartley. He will be able
to receive the season's gifts, even in the dead of winter, when the
frost freezes the icicles and when there is no sound to interrupt the
"strange / And extreme silentness" of a winter's evening. The si-
lence that continually vexes Coleridge will be intelligible to Hartley
and the Pedlar, who reads "unutterable love" in the "silent faces" of
the clouds and who can read the "<u>silent</u> stars" and

some peak
Familiar with forgotten years, which shews,
Inscrib'd as with the silence of the thought,
Upon its bleak and visionary sides,
The history of many a winter storm,
Or obscure records of the path of fire.[12]

If the "secret ministry of cold" is Coleridge's phrase for nature's language as Wordsworth conceives of it, Coleridge suggests that it may be silent and incomprehensible. And when he hopes that it will be intelligible to Hartley, he imposes his own criteria for language on what is essentially a Wordsworthian description of the growth of a mind under nature's tutelage. Hartley will be like the Pedlar except, Coleridge implies, his understanding of nature will be, not a matter of the intuition of beauty and love unmediated by language, but rather a matter of hearing "articulate sounds" and seeing "lovely shapes and sounds intelligible / Of that eternal language, which thy God / Utters."[13]

Coleridge regards his own inability to comprehend nature's activity and the "secret ministry of cold" as a result of his separation from the natural world in childhood and of the necessity of self-conscious thought as an adult. His excursion into his own past reminds him of his distance from it. In the 1798 quarto version of "Frost at Midnight," he reposes by the fire and plays with the image of the film:

But still the living spirit in our frame,
That loves not to behold a lifeless thing,
Transfuses into all it's own delights
It's own volition, sometimes with deep faith,
And sometimes with fantastic playfulness.

12. These quotations are from MS. B (1798). The first is from page 157 in Butler's edition, and the second two are from page 169, where the word "silent" is underlined in the manuscript.

13. Coleridge's use of Berkeley's idea of the divine language in nature in "This Lime-Tree Bower" and "Frost at Midnight" may resemble, in general, his lines in "The Destiny of Nations," "For all that meets the bodily sense I deem / Symbolical, one mighty alphabet / For infant minds" (18–20) and the contemplation of the "Great Invisible (by symbols seen)" in "Religious Musings" (1796), but the lines from "The Destiny of Nations" are followed by the statement that "Fancy is the power / That first unsensualizes the dark mind" (80–81), and the entire section introduces "Wild phantasies" (121) of allegorical visions. The differences between the poetics of the earlier poems and those of "This Lime-Tree Bower" are great. The earlier abandons the reliance on the senses and the later embraces it.

Ah me! amus'd by no such curious toys
Of the self-watching subtilizing mind,
How often in my early school-boy days,
With most believing superstitious wish
Presageful have I gaz'd upon the bars. . . .

(21–30)

Vexed at the silence around him, Coleridge lapses into childhood dreams, willfully transferring his own fancies and feelings into things. Coleridge no sooner expresses his idle toying than he recognizes, as soon as he pairs "deep faith" with "fantastic playfulness," a phrase on which the poem turns, that the playfulness appropriate to childhood has overcome his meditation. He is not brought back to the reality of the storm from his own dreams, but he is brought to consciousness by his own fancy, which fills a vacancy left by the failure of his more serious meditations on the "secret ministry of cold." It is as though Coleridge reverted to the fanciful play of the early "Effusion XXXV," but the reversion is functional because he is able to recapture, through a distorted lens, a view of childhood. It is distorted because the superstitions and dreams of childhood, which were "like articulate sounds of things to come," are to the adult mere "curious toys / Of the self-watching subtilizing mind." The comforting promise of childhood "prolong'd my dreams" at school and encouraged his brooding on joys to come, but the dreams of childhood became the adult's inaudible dreams.

The attraction that the drafts of the Pedlar's history had for Coleridge is evident in a letter he sent to his brother, the Reverend George Coleridge, about March 10, 1798. He is eager to justify himself before his brother, who held his radical brother in high suspicion. The lengthy passage is important, not only for what Coleridge says about himself, but also for his use of Wordsworth's poetry to explain his own feelings and aspirations. He explains that he has "snapped my squeaking baby-trumpet of Sedition & the fragments lie scattered in the lumber-room of Penitence." He then continues in Wordsworth's style, quoting Wordsworth's poetry:

I devote myself to such works as encroach not on the antisocial passions—in poetry, to elevate the imagination & set the affections in right tune by the beauty of the inanimate impregnated, as with a living soul, by the presence of Life. . . . I love fields & woods & mounta[ins] with almost a visionary fondness—and because I have found benevolence & quietness growing within me as that fondness [has] increased, there-

161

fore I should wish to be the means of implanting it in others—& to destroy the bad passions not by combating them, but by keeping them in inaction.

> Not useless do I deem
> These shadowy Sympathies with things that hold
> An inarticulate Language: for the Man
> Once taught to love such objects, as excite
> No morbid passions, no disquietude,
> No vengeance & no hatred, needs must feel
> The Joy of that pure principle of Love
> So deeply, that, unsatisfied with aught
> Less pure & exquisite, he cannot chuse
> But seek for objects of a kindred Love
> In fellow-natures, & a kindred Joy.
> Accordingly, he by degrees perceives
> His feelings of aversion softened down,
> A holy tenderness pervade his frame!
> His sanity of reason not impair'd,
> Say rather that his thoughts now flowing clear
> From a clear fountain flowing, he looks round—
> He seeks for Good & finds the Good he seeks.
> Wordsworth.—
> (*STCL* 1: 397–98)

Coleridge explains himself to his conventionally religious brother by using Wordsworth's recently drafted opening for the consolation of Margaret's story. He is not offering Wordsworth's poetry here as a fine sample of the work of his friend but as verse that speaks for and of himself, although he identifies Wordsworth as the author. He wants to be understood as a Wordsworth, and it is a bit surprising to see him select Wordsworth's poetry rather than a poem of his own—"Frost at Midnight," for example—when Wordsworth's secularized version of the presence of love and joy in nature is far less conventional than Coleridge's own references to the "Almighty Spirit" of "This Lime-Tree Bower my Prison" and "God" and "Great universal Teacher" of "Frost at Midnight." But it is even more surprising to find echoes of "Frost at Midnight" in the very passages in Wordsworth that Coleridge is quoting to explain himself. I have already noted the similarities of "shadowy Sympathies" and the "dim sympathies" of "Frost at Midnight," and in Coleridge's prose there is the phrase "the beauty of the inanimate impregnated, as with a living soul, by the presence of Life," which parallels three lines of "Frost at Midnight" in the quarto version of 1798: "But still the living spirit in our frame, / That loves not to behold a lifeless thing, / Transfuses into all its own delights." The surprise is that the lines from "Frost at Midnight" refer to a capricious granting of life to things in which Coleridge can see no life or in which he cannot experience life directly through its language, and that Wordsworth's lines refer to a joy and love that has its life in nature.

The relationship between "Frost at Midnight" and Wordsworth's work on "The Ruined Cottage" and the history of the Pedlar is complex. It may be that the concluding lines of "Frost at Midnight" are the source that Wordsworth elaborated for the Pedlar, or it may be that "Frost at Midnight" is a condensation of the Pedlar's history. If "Frost at Midnight" is a source of the consolation that Coleridge quoted in his letter, then Coleridge's letter quotes Wordsworth's poetry, which differs from his own yet may be derived from it, to explain and justify his own state of mind. Coleridge writes to give Wordsworth a voice, so that Wordsworth can echo Coleridge's. It may simply be that Coleridge wishes "Frost at Midnight" and his other poetry to be read as though it were written by Wordsworth, or as though it were read by Wordsworth and contained Wordsworth's creed as elaborated in the history of the Pedlar. As appealing as this explanation is to common sense, especially to those who have learned to read Coleridge with Wordsworth's eyes, it is difficult to imagine that Coleridge would so soon suppress his recognitions in "Frost at Midnight." In these weeks he was completing "The Ancient Mariner," certainly no nature poem about "fields & woods & mountains," and he is about to write "The Nightingale" and "Christabel," both of which question the articulation of nature. Whatever the case may be, Coleridge's and Thomas Poole's shared "fears of amalgamation" have their beginnings here.

Coleridge provided a hint of the connection between Wordsworth's work on "The Ruined Cottage" and "Frost at Midnight" that Wordsworth's drafts confirm by echo and allusion. Wordsworth's later, and more thoughtful, response is "Tintern Abbey," in which he returns to the theme of the "language of the sense" to affirm its intelligibility at all seasons of life. Seen in the continuing dialogue about poetic language, "Tintern Abbey" has another, more important, preoccupation, that of the temporal continuity and development of poetic imagination. With a newly introduced temporal dimension to the discussion of the "language of the sense," the issues of language's ability to represent and its tendency to be self-referential become far more complex. Coleridge's poem challenges the assumption of Wordsworth's drafts of the Pedlar's history that growth is a steady, uninterrupted progress that assures that the continuity of earlier experience and its later transformations. Insofar as "Frost at Midnight" questions simple linear development, it is not a condensation of the Pedlar's history; only in its summary hope for Hartley's future does it appear Wordsworthian.

There can be no doubt that in the Pedlar's history Wordsworth was composing his own life, for many of the lines he used were later transferred to *The Prelude*, but one major difference between the Pedlar's history and *The Prelude* is that the Pedlar has suffered no personal crises, no "piteous revolutions" (Butler 183). Wordsworth claims that the Pedlar is a man sympathetic to the pains of others because he has not been separated from his own past. These disruptions can come, Wordsworth notes in an anticipation of "Resolution and Independence," through "wild varieties of joy or grief." Why should "wild varieties of joy" be disruptive? The Pedlar's strengths are calmness and tranquillity, and strong emotion of any kind would disturb the tranquillity. The Pedlar does not suffer, as do the sailor and Coleridge's mariner, from "wild varieties of joy or grief"; the onset of strong emotion of any kind is, in part, the beginning of the lyric impulse. Wordsworth's addition to the Pedlar's history that recognizes that "The poets in their elegies and songs / Lamenting the departed call the groves . . . nor idly" (Butler 195) tacitly acknowledges the connection between strong, disruptive emotion and the lyrical impulse's infusion of its own fictions into the landscape. Coleridge's "The Nightingale" acknowledges the same insight throughout the entire poem. Wordsworth wished to present the Pedlar as one whose life had never been affected by revolutions. To preserve the Pedlar's strength of sympathy and to assure the continuities of narrative chronology, Wordsworth isolated him from the lyrical impulse, whether of joy or grief, that interrupts the steady logic of chronology and narrative. The questions raised by "Frost at Midnight," those of the relation of a personal past to the present as a source for imagination, the problem of a lyric form that threatens to be disruptive, and the problem of figuration, persisted in Wordsworth's poetry at least until he completed *The Prelude* (1799). If narrative is disrupted, then a longer work becomes a series of lyric moments dissociated from each other. If the lyric moments are dissociated from one another, Wordsworth came to understand, they have little meaning in themselves and in a pattern that constitutes a life. As a response to "Frost at Midnight," "Tintern Abbey" faces these questions, poses a tentative answer, and leads to the deeper pondering of the issues in the early work on *The Prelude*.

Wordsworth implies that he reads "Frost at Midnight" as a challenge to his construction of an uninterrupted personal development by duplicating its structure and by relying so heavily on "Frost at Midnight" to affirm by denying its implications. Both poems possess a circular form based on the workings of memory. Wordsworth's earlier dialogic and highly selective reading of Coleridge's poems fragmented them to remove figures, but in "Tintern Abbey" he had to appropriate and transform a poetic structure to recompose the fragments from Coleridge's poetry. Coleridge had crafted his earlier Conversation Poems on the basis of a return, at the end of the poem, to the images with which it began, but none used the model of memory so centrally. "Tintern Abbey" opens with the scene of the valley and closes with the same images of the "steep woods and lofty cliffs, / And this green pastoral landscape"; "Frost at Midnight" begins and ends with the "secret ministry of cold," although the 1798 quarto version contains an additional six lines at the end that Coleridge later removed because, as he said, "they destroy the rondo, and return upon itself of the Poem. Poems of this kind of length ought to be coiled with its' tail round its' head."[14] Both poems begin their meditations in a silent and solitary present, recollect childhood or early youth, and return to the present with renewed hopes for the future. Both refer to three distinct periods of life. Wordsworth tries to integrate the present with his first visit

14. B. Ifor Evans, "Coleridge's Copy of 'Fears in Solitude,'" *Times Literary Supplement*, April 18, 1935: 255. Evans records unpublished notes by Coleridge in the Beaumont Trust copy of the quarto edition of "Fears in Solitude," "France: An Ode," and "Frost at Midnight." For the development of the Conversation Poems, see G. M. Harper, "Coleridge's Conversation Poems," *Spirit of Delight* (New York: Holt, 1928), rpt. in *English Romantic Poets*, ed. M. H. Abrams (New York: Oxford University Press, 1960) 144–57; Max F. Schulz, *The Poetic Voices of Coleridge: A Study of His Desire for Spontaneity and Passion for Order* (Detroit: Wayne State University Press, 1963) 82; and M. H. Abrams, "Structure and Style in the Greater Romantic Lyric," *From Sensibility to Romanticism*, ed. Frederick W. Hilles and Harold Bloom (London: Oxford University Press, 1965) 527–60. For a questioning of the order implied by the paradigm of the Conversation Poems, see my *Coleridge's Nightmare Poetry* (Charlottesville: University Press of Virginia, 1974) 18–38. H. M. Margoliouth has noted that Wordsworth "could not have written ['Tintern Abbey'] a year before. Coleridge taught him introspection and provided him with a technique, here flawlessly used" (*Wordsworth and Coleridge, 1795–1834* [London: Oxford University Press, 1953] 35). I have quoted from the 1798 version of "Tintern Abbey" in *LB*.

to the Wye valley in 1793 and with some indefinite time before 1793 in the parenthetical comment, "The coarser pleasures of my boyish days, / And their glad animal movements all gone by" (74–75). He follows "Frost at Midnight," which describes the present evening in the cottage, a youth in Christ's Hospital in London, and a childhood at Ottery Saint Mary.

Both poems are addressed to another person, a practice Coleridge developed in "Effusion XXXV." While "Frost at Midnight" hopes that the child, Hartley, will grow up in an environment different from that of the adult speaker and will be able to understand the nature that vexes the speaker, the younger Dorothy in "Tintern Abbey" becomes integrated into Wordsworth's own personal development: "May I behold in thee what I was once" (121). Coleridge's auditor in the Conversation Poems is always kept distinct from Coleridge himself, while in "Tintern Abbey" Dorothy becomes an earlier self. Coleridge's generous willingness to permit his auditors to remain their individual selves and his prayerful blessing on Hartley divert attention from his knowledge that he is separate from Hartley. His son will live as the Pedlar has lived, but Coleridge cannot. Conversely, Wordsworth's incorporation of Dorothy into an earlier, thoughtless stage of his own life argues for an integration that "Frost at Midnight" could not completely affirm and implies a continuance from stage to stage that "Frost at Midnight" presented as difficult and that the dialogue between the Pedlar and the young poet implied was possible.

The opening verse paragraphs in each poem are remarkably similar in their initial, brief statements and in their syntactical expansion and repetition. Each begins with a short line-and-a-half statement:

> The Frost performs it's secret ministry,
> Unhelp'd by any wind.
>
> (1–2)

> Five years have passed; five summers, with the length
> Of five long winters!
>
> (1–2)

Each poem progresses by expansion of the opening short statements accomplished by repetition emphasized by the word "again":

166

> The owlet's cry
> Came loud—and hark, again! loud as before
>
> (2–3)

> and again I hear
> These waters, rolling from their mountain-springs
> With a sweet inland murmur.
>
> (2–4)

Coleridge's meditation expands to four lines as he thinks in the pervasive silence:

> The inmates of my cottage, all at rest,
> Have left me to that solitude, which suits
> Abstruser musings: save that at my side
> My cradled infant slumbers peacefully.
>
> (4–7)

His opening statement claims the presence of a "ministry" that is both "secret" and "unhelped by any wind." He is puzzled by a presence that provides no signs of its presence and by an activity that is divorced from other sources of natural energy. The lack of such signs leaves Coleridge with the necessity of repeating his own thought in an effort to comprehend the mystery, and his repetition becomes a reverberation, a repetition in his own words that substitutes for the absent signs of the frost's ministry:

> Sea, hill, and wood,
> This populous village! Sea, and hill, and wood,
> With all the numberless goings on of life,
> Inaudible as dreams!
>
> (10–13)

The necessity of reverberation, the compelling need to repeat what he cannot sense, leads inevitably to the fanciful toying with the soot to fill the vacancy. In the absence of intelligible signs of the frost's ministry, he must supply his own inadequate ones.

Wordsworth's expansion of his opening statement proceeds in similar stages, with a sentence of just over four lines:

> Once again
> Do I behold these steep and lofty cliffs,

Which on a wild secluded scene impress
Thoughts of more deep seclusion; and connect
The landscape with the quiet of the sky.

(4–8)

Coleridge's "sea, and hill, and wood, . . . all the numberless goings
on of life" are distant and "inaudible," but the cliffs, landscape, and
sky are presently visible to Wordsworth, although the sky, like the
clouds and stars in the history of the Pedlar, is silent. Wordsworth is
not isolated as Coleridge is. Yet, although nature is before his eyes,
he reads it, surprisingly, as containing signs of seclusion when the
total prospect offers evidence of the contrary. The cliffs that unify
landscape and sky impress thoughts of seclusion. Wordsworth sees
unity and thinks of seclusion. His poem proceeds, not by a Coleridg-
ean reverberation, but by reiteration of the things that he actually
sees:

The day is come when I again repose
Here, under this dark sycamore, and view
These plots of cottage-ground, these orchard-tufts,
Which, at this season, with their unripe fruits,
Among the woods and copses lose themselves.

(9–13)

Wordsworth's answer to Coleridge's vexed meditation is to enumer-
ate the images of nature that need no mediation because they are
immediately present, both in their individuality and in their visual
connection with one another.

In addition to the similarities in the rhythms of expansion, there
are a number of clear verbal parallels, which indicate that Words-
worth was incorporating Coleridge's Conversation Poems in "Tin-
tern Abbey." The landscape of the Wye valley had not been to
Wordsworth "as is a landscape to a blind man's eye" (25), which re-
sembles Coleridge's fear in "This Lime-Tree Bower" of being una-
ble to accompany Lamb and the Wordsworths on their walk
through the hills: "I have lost / Beauties and feelings, such as would
have been / Most sweet to my remembrance even when age / Had
dimm'd my eyes to blindness" (2–5). One must be cautious in assign-
ing priority for this image to Coleridge, because the two versions of
"This Lime-Tree Bower" that survive from before 1798 do not in-
clude these lines. They may have been added to the two manuscripts
shortly after Coleridge sent them to friends in 1797; if not, then the

expansion of "This Lime-Tree Bower" is a result of Wordsworth's lines, another instance of an amalgamation so close that it may be impossible to determine priority. But lines that were in the earliest version of "This Lime-Tree Bower" did find their way into "Tintern Abbey": Coleridge learns that "nature ne'er deserts the wise & pure," while it keeps the heart "Awake to Love & Beauty" (*STCL* 1: 336). Wordsworth contemplates the valley "not only with the sense / Of present pleasure, but with pleasing thoughts / That in this moment there is life and food / For future years" (63–66). With Coleridge's lines in mind, Wordsworth raises his song of thanks and praise

> to recognize
> In nature and the language of the sense,
> The anchor of my purest thoughts, the nurse,
> The guide, the guardian of my heart, and soul
> Of all my moral being.
>
> (108–12)

Wordsworth duplicates even the form of argument and the invocation of the moon's blessing in the final stanza of "Frost at Midnight." At the end of "Tintern Abbey" Wordsworth turns to Dorothy and prays that the moon will "shine on thee in thy solitary walk" (136). His blessing repeats Coleridge's upon Hartley, when the "secret ministry of cold" freezes the eaves drops "in silent icicles, / Quietly shining to the quiet moon." Wordsworth repeats, not only the moon's blessing, but the underlying form of Coleridge's argument that leads to that blessing. Coleridge proceeds from "I was rear'd / In the great city . . ." (56–57) to "But *thou* . . ." (59) to "Therefore all seasons shall be sweet" (70). Wordsworth's argument, purged of its tortured syntax and double negatives, proceeds in a similar manner: I fear a loss of my genial spirits, but my sister will possess "the language of my former heart . . ." (118), "Therefore let the moon / Shine on thee" (135–36).

These parallels and repetitions demand that we read "Tintern Abbey" as a response to "Frost at Midnight." They are two further parts of the poetic sequence that begins with "Effusion XXXV." Coleridge suggested as much when he wrote to Cottle on May 28, 1798, shortly before "Tintern Abbey" was written, that "our different poems are as stanzas, good relatively rather than absolutely" (*STCL* 1: 412). Coleridge's comment is more than merely a humble attempt to find value in his own poetry by its association with Wordsworth's. "Tintern Abbey" was not inspired primarily by Wordsworth's visit to the Wye, or Dorothy's presence, or even his own anxiety about his ability to continue to write. It originates in the poetic dialogue with Coleridge. That Wordsworth would have written *a* poem inspired by the joy he felt while visiting the Wye is understandable without the Coleridgean context, but that the poem should have taken the form that it did cannot be accounted for except by the assumption that he wanted to respond to "Frost at Midnight."

In spite of the vicarious joy that Coleridge experienced in contemplating Hartley's future joy, there is in "Frost at Midnight" an unresolved seclusion. Coleridge is not fully reunited with the expected company and does not form for himself a fully satisfying comprehension of the "ministry of cold," because separation and self-awareness have removed him from his childhood, whose dreams he can no longer view innocently. "Tintern Abbey" identifies its generating text in "Frost at Midnight" as a poem about seclusion. Wordsworth recognized that the seclusion of "Frost at Midnight" could become his own. The only thought or emotion that Wordsworth mentions explicitly in the first verse paragraph is seclusion. Wordsworth's seeing seclusion comes as a surprise only if one ignores the context of "Frost at Midnight." Wordsworth sees harmony and unity yet continually returns to haunting images of seclusion: the hermit before his lonely fire, the city's lonely rooms, his own flight from society, and the fear of his future separation from Dorothy and nature.

A fear of society's absence is typically Coleridgean. When he tries to escape an enclosed space that imprisons him at the beginning of several of the Conversation Poems, he moves toward society. Wordsworth's affirmation of the landscape's presence during his absence in the city points to concern over a similar seclusion—that of the landscape's permanent distance from comprehension, his own seclusion from his past, and the decay of his genial spirits. The worry over the loss of "genial spirits" makes explicit what the play of language in "Frost at Midnight" implies: the loss in "Tintern Abbey" is the fear of the loss of poetic individuality, because, as De Quincey and Wordsworth agreed, genius is always individual. Wordsworth ventriloquizes Coleridge's voice, yet his identification of the source of his imagination in his own past instead of in Coleridge's poetry attempts to avoid the possible recognition of influence and fosters the myth of his own self-generation. As he was to discover in work on *The Prelude*, the location of his imagination in his own past was difficult to sustain, because if the past slips from memory, it is clouded by interpretation and devoid of context, it cannot provide the ground in reality that it requires. And if his and Coleridge's fears about the connection of past and present were true, the past is merely a disconnected succession of individual moments. These fears underlie "Tintern Abbey" and persist in the fall of 1798 and the spring of 1799. Early work on *The Prelude* demonstrates that Wordsworth was deeply concerned, not only with the careful expression of his recollections of childhood, but also with the appropriate form for expressing his new self-presentation as a self-generated poet whose origins are solely in his own childhood.

Since he, like Coleridge, felt the possible consequences of seclusion, he had to respond to them in the form in which they were originally expressed. "Tintern Abbey" is the only poem that Wordsworth wrote in this conversational mode. *The Prelude* grew from it, but it grew to take epic form very quickly. There are no other Wordsworth conversation poems. To a poet who in 1798 was beginning to locate the origin of his imaginative vitality and individual genius in childhood experience, the isolation that Coleridge expressed provided a particular challenge that Wordsworth could overcome only by employing the same form to assert that Coleridge's isolation was not his. The problem in the summer of 1798 and for well over a year later was one of poetic form, which could not be solved by a particular doctrine of philosophy, which had nothing to say about the problem of personal growth expressed in the conflicting modes of lyric and narrative. Nor could the problem be solved by objective narration of the joy and tranquillity of the Pedlar, who is only half a poet, a man who can tell a tale sympathetically but who is spared the "wild varieties of joy and grief" that generate lyric. He has a poetic temperament and he has been touched by human life, but not by writing.

When Wordsworth chose to answer "Frost at Midnight" in "Tintern Abbey," he could not adopt Coleridge's form and expression by mere imitation, for to do so would continue the fears of amalgamation and admit that Coleridge's seclusion was his own. Wordsworth had to alter Coleridge's poem to assure himself of his own individuality. The joy that Coleridge feels is vicarious; he hopes that he will be able to see and hear through Hartley. Wordsworth could not gain poetic confidence in himself through vicarious experience; he could not preserve his individual "genial spirits" through the joy of others. Consequently, he varied the paradigm of the Conversation Poems to make that form his own. He places himself at the poetic center. He is the one who experiences the "sense sublime / Of something far more deeply interfused." He thus borrows, not only from "Frost at Midnight," but also from "The Eolian Harp," in which Coleridge is centered and open to the influence of the "intellectual Breeze." Thus Wordsworth runs great risks. To preserve his individuality and "genial spirits" and to avoid amalgamation, he had to avoid locating his own beginnings as a poet in Coleridge's poetry and to locate them in his own childhood, but to do that he faced the problem of seclusion, which is precisely the problem that Coleridge himself faced.

To alter Coleridge's poem and make it his own, Wordsworth begins "Tintern Abbey" with the substantives of actual presence, where Coleridge had begun in a reverie broken occasionally by external sounds. A prospect is open to Wordsworth, and he concentrates on its particular details. Wordsworth's is a summer poem and a poem of day; Coleridge's is of the winter night. Each has beauty in its setting, but the "general earth" to which Coleridge refers in the final verse paragraph is something he hopes will minister to Hartley; the generating summer landscape is before Wordsworth's eyes. The frost performs its ministry secretly, silently, and spontaneously, "unhelp'd by any wind." Its language is unintelligible. Wordsworth sees the totality of landscape; he hears and sees its unity. His response to hearing the "sweet inland murmur" and to seeing the "quiet of the sky" and the smoke that rises in "silence" recalls the silence of Coleridge's winter midnight, when all is "inaudible as dreams," yet, while he echoes Coleridge, he uses verbs of direct sensation: "hear," "behold," "view," and "see."

Coleridge's childhood is in direct contrast to his adult, solitary midnight reverie. At his "sweet birth-place," in company with friends and family at the "hot fair-day," he heard the church bells' music as "articulate sounds of things to come." He returns to childhood to find what he does not have in the present. Wordsworth's brief reference to a time before his first visit to the Wye, to before 1793, is often referred to as a time of childhood sensation when he was unconsciously nourished by the permanent and grand forms of nature.[15] But in "Tintern Abbey" the glance is to adolescence, not

15. See, for example, the schemes in Arthur Beatty *William Wordsworth: His Doctrine*

earlier childhood, and is a brief, parenthetical reference to his "glad animal movements." If the reference places his spontaneity in childhood, then in "Tintern Abbey" it begins, not in the remembered beauty and sublimity of nature, but in physical energy and exuberant activity. His "genial spirits," the deities of individual energy, sport in childhood's physical activity. By avoiding characterizing childhood as an age of sensation, Wordsworth avoids the problem that confronted Coleridge, the interpretation of childhood's sensations and their promise.

Coleridge's youth in "Frost at Midnight" completely reverses the situation of his childhood in festive summer company. Separated from home and sitting by the fire at school, his habitual action is reverie—dreams of the past and hopes that the future will restore the company that the past has promised. Without the adult's self-conscious dreaming and toying with thought, the youth entertains the superstition that the fluttering soot predicts the arrival of a friend. Thus these moments were times of anticipation, not fulfillment. Wordsworth's youth is different. It is both a time of fulfillment and a time that contains a promise. In spite of his claim that his "glad animal movements" were past, he says that when he first came to the Wye "like a roe / I bounded o'er the mountains, by the sides / Of the deep rivers, and the lonely streams." If these actions are different from his earlier exuberance, they are so only in that they are prompted by strong feelings. They still preserve the physical energy of childhood and tie it to the affections for nature. Wordsworth experiences emotion without the intrusion of thought, which at that time would have annexed only "remoter" charms to nature. That time contained its continuity with the past and important anticipations for the future. Its passions include fear and dread, for the woods' gloom fit well his passionate love of nature. The discordant and unassimilated emotion is the dread from which he flies to the woods and to nature and which is later transformed into sympathy with the sufferers in war, into the "still, sad music of humanity" that he hears as an adult.

In the present moment, Coleridge is detached from his earlier life and from "that eternal language" by the "self-watching subtilizing mind." Wordsworth sees and hears directly and holds productive

---

and Art in Their Historical Relations, 3d ed. (Madison: University of Wisconsin Press, 1960) 127, and Melvin M. Rader, *Wordsworth: A Philosophical Approach* (Oxford: Clarendon Press, 1967) 81–118.

dialogue with nature's "language of the sense." He rejoices in the "elevated thoughts" that create and are created. His knowledge of the "sense sublime / Of something far more deeply interfused" and of a "motion and a spirit, that impels / All thinking things, all objects of all thought, / And rolls through all things" alludes directly to Coleridge's "The Eolian Harp":

> And what if All of animated Life
> Be but as Instruments diversly fram'd,
> That tremble into thought, while thro' them breathes
> One infinite and intellectual Breeze,
> And all in diff'rent Heights so aptly hung,
> That Murmurs indistinct and Bursts sublime,
> Shrill Discords and most soothing Melodies,
> Harmonious from Creation's vast concent—
> Thus *God* would be the universal Soul,
> Mechaniz'd matter as th' organic harps
> And each one's Tunes be that, which each calls I.[16]

Coleridge's draft, which attempts to account for self-consciousness as the product of the breeze's impulse, was never printed in "The Eolian Harp." Yet Wordsworth makes that breeze the "motion" and "spirit" that informs "all thinking things" and alters Coleridge's notion of the "self-watching" mind that separates consciousness from its objects to a mind that regards its objects with a sympathy. Wordsworth's consciousness is a product of the chastening power of human sympathy that quiets youth's energetic exuberance.

Thought separates the adult from the youth in both poems, but Coleridge's breaks the continuity of the dream and contradicts it. The dream's language is regarded from the perspective of the adult's thought as the language of promise, in which meaning is not present but is yet to be. The adult understands that what was understood by the child as unequivocal signs of joy was merely a fictional dream; he is reminded of those formerly unequivocal forms by his own toying with thought. To Wordsworth, thought proves continuity because it transforms childhood emotions into the emotions of the adult and because it confronts, for the first time in his career, nature as a language. In the earlier paragraphs of "Tintern Abbey"

---

16. *CPW* 2: 1022–23. The manuscripts of these drafts are now in the Miriam Lutcher Stark Library, University of Texas, Austin. The similarity in wording of this revision to Coleridge's letter to John Thelwall of December 31, 1796, suggests a date of late 1796 or early 1797 (*STCL* 1: 294–95).

nature did not point to any meaning or to any promise beyond itself. Wordsworth had earlier written of the Pedlar's growth in nature as though the youth were able to understand a language of nature, but it was also a pure language, free of extraneous association. He seems cautious in "Tintern Abbey" of attributing any conscious understanding to his earlier self except for that which is pure emotion. His caution in "Tintern Abbey" comes from Coleridge's questioning in "Frost at Midnight."

The transition from one moment or period of life to another in "Frost at Midnight" is either a reversal or a repetition. His imprisoned school days reverse entirely his free childhood, and his adult reveries merely repeat his school dreams by the fire. His life is parceled out in lyric form. Wordsworth portrays his maturing as a continuous growth, a process in which the activities of childhood are transformed into the adult's power of insight and sympathy; his life, too, is parceled out in a transformation of lyric form. His poetry is "spontaneous," not in the sense that it is unpremeditated or thoughtless, but in the sense that he has created a myth of self-generation.[17] In the preface to *Lyrical Ballads* (1800) he explains that the poetic process is one that transforms one emotion into another: poetry takes "its origin from emotion recollected in tranquillity" and a "kindred" emotion is produced, the mood in which the poet begins to write. The emotion that is recollected and the emotion in which a poet begins to write are significantly different. The recollected emotion is the raw material of experience, the events of childhood with the attending fears, anxieties, and haunting memories. The second emotion is produced by contemplation of the original and "by a species of re-action." The second, the emotion that produces poetry, is "similar" to the original one. In the revised preface of 1802 Wordsworth changed the word "similar" to "kindred" to emphasize the genetic relationship between the two emotions (*Prose* 1: 148–49). In "Tintern Abbey" the emotions that provide continuity are the fear and dread that combined with his earlier love of nature and the subsequent sublimity that lifted "the burthen of the mystery" and the secret spirit of humanity that transformed dread into sympathy. The same relationship between emotions informs Wordsworth's early work on *The Prelude*, where the child's fear and terror are transformed into the adult's religious awe.

17. For further discussion of this issue, see my "Wordsworth and Spontaneity," *The Evidence of the Imagination* 101–18.

Wordsworth offers an account of creativity in self-generation that may begin in any stage of life and that preserves his "genial spirits." Memory, in "Tintern Abbey," is neither simple repetition of childhood experience nor a recapturing of it. To recapture childhood experience would be to regress and surrender his matured genius. Wordsworth's answer to Coleridge's seclusion is his formulation of a development, a steady growth of self-generation and self-sufficient energy, which, as poetic power, resides in himself. The tone of "Tintern Abbey" is generally optimistic if it is read in the context of Coleridge's Conversation Poems. It betrays little overt worry about its debts to Coleridge's poems. In the spring of 1798 Wordsworth seems content to rest his identity as a poet in relation to Coleridge and to locate his poetry in a dialogue with Coleridge's poetry. "Tintern Abbey" overcomes the seclusion in which it begins and makes of that seclusion a strength, yet its solutions were not completely satisfactory, because as soon as Wordsworth settled in Goslar in the fall of 1798, he began to write more detailed, extended retrospective poetry in the early drafts of *The Prelude*. The drafts undo the assured hope of "Tintern Abbey" and question its affirmations at the same time that they raise again the relationship of his poetry to Coleridge's.

The Search for "Perfect Form"

The Goslar Poetry and *The Prelude* (1799)

R EAD IN THE CONTEXT of "Frost at Midnight" and the
Conversation Poems, "Tintern Abbey" is an optimistic
affirmation of a continuity of personal growth grounded in
nature's continuous ministry and in the "language of the sense"
that is direct and unambiguous. Wordsworth can see "into the
life of things." The seclusion that Coleridge could not com-
pletely overcome in "Frost at Midnight" Wordsworth confident-
ly affirms he can overcome by the retention of the natural
images associated with his feelings. But read closely in the con-
text of his early work on *The Prelude* and the Lucy poems, the
calm assurances of "Tintern Abbey" seem to be achieved by an
evasion of the challenges of "Frost at Midnight." A dialogic
reading of the sequence of Conversation Poems, "Tintern Abbey,"
and *The Prelude* (1799) reveals that each utterance is a mo-
mentary one, generative and valuable if it provides a turning
point for further utterances. "Tintern Abbey" is a conclusive
affirmation only if it is regarded as a concluding poem, a ter-
mination. But it is clearly not, because the drafts and frag-
ments that constitute the early *Prelude* work probe more deep-
ly the confidence of "Tintern Abbey." The Goslar drafts are
a turbulent effusion of fragmentary recollection, and Words-
worth's reflections on those fragments lead him to realize that

the recollections and fragments do not, as he had earlier assumed, bring their clear significance with them. Rather, as fragments they have little meaning, because they have no literary order, no context, and no "perfect form," as he later called it.

Wordsworth's deepest response to Coleridge's poetry comes in *The Prelude* drafts of 1798. "Tintern Abbey" was one earlier response, but its inadequacy is revealed by Wordsworth's returning to the Conversation Poems. There are no new Coleridgean contributions to the dialogue; Wordsworth is still responding to what Coleridge had written earlier. Wordsworth's fragmentary drafts rely on the form that Coleridge developed for the Conversation Poems. His longest continuous draft begins with a quotation from "Frost at Midnight," and many of its lines address Coleridge directly. His discontinuous drafts accumulated toward an understanding of his past discompose the form of the Conversation Poems upon which they are based. Without the context that Coleridge's form provides, the fragments are adrift and isolated. They confirm the seclusion and loss that "Tintern Abbey" confidently overcame. The episodes that were later composed into Book I of *The Prelude* proclaim that recollection of potential sublimity is possible, but other poetry written at exactly the same time argues the contrary. The Lucy poems lament the loss of a past, a past so finally lost that recollection is no longer generative and the poet becomes mute. The presence of fragments and poems that present exactly contrary views of memory must seem strange to readers who seek for a single mood of a poet's mind that motivates writing. How is it that Wordsworth can affirm at one moment that recollection can recover moments of joy and strength and at the next grieve over their loss? The answer is not to be found within the mood of a poet's mind but within the texts themselves. Wordsworth came to realize that it is not a matter of recollection's failure, or even interpretation's distortion of individual events, but of the dissociation of individual fragments. Wordsworth's approach to the problem of dissociation was, not simply to generate more lyric fragments to increase the collection that he had already accumulated, but to try to recompose them into an order and form that would give them life and meaning. In themselves they were meaningless; in an ordered form they received significance from their context.

"A Storm Not Terrible but Strong": The Prelude *Drafts*

On March 5, 1798, Dorothy wrote to Mary Hutchinson that "The Ruined Cottage" had grown to nine hundred lines and that "The Pedlar's character now makes a very, certainly the *most*, considerable part of the poem" (*LEY* 199). The following day Wordsworth, writing to James Tobin, announced that he was at work on a major poem "in which I contrive to convey most of the knowledge of which I am possessed. My object is to give pictures of Nature, Man, and Society. Indeed I know not any thing which will not come within the scope of my plan" (*LEY* 212). A few days later he informed James Losh that "its title will be *The Recluse or views of Nature, Man, and Society*" (*LEY* 214). During these days Wordsworth was adding the history of the Pedlar to "The Ruined Cottage," composing a consolation for Margaret's story, and incorporating some of Coleridge's texts in his consolation. *The Recluse* was never completed in any form that Wordsworth then contemplated, and *The Prelude* was not completed as a separate poem until years afterward, yet the first thoughts of such a poem were present in the optimism of the spring of 1798.

In the same letter in which Dorothy told Mary Hutchinson of the growth of "The Ruined Cottage," she also said cryptically, "It is decided that we quit Allfoxden—The house is lett. It is most probable that we shall go back again to Racedown, as there is little chance of our getting a place in this neighbourhood" (*LEY* 199). Throughout the spring, numerous different plans were made for a move and for a place to live. It appeared essential that the Wordsworths and Coleridge live close to one another. Finally, during the middle of July the Wordsworths decided to accompany Coleridge to Germany, "for the purpose of learning the language, and for the common advantages to be acquired by seeing different people and different manners" (*LEY* 220). In the middle of September the Wordsworths, Coleridge, and John Chester sailed for Germany, but within ten days it was decided that the Wordsworths would "travel on into Saxony, to seek cheaper places" (*STCL* 1: 419).

At Goslar, Wordsworth began the first drafts toward an independent poem that was to become *The Prelude*. The optimism that had predominated in the spring had become tempered. The exhilaration in nature, the warmth of human sympathy, and the glee of writing jocular poems were replaced by a more sober questioning of vocation and aptitude. Among Wordsworth's writing that winter were the Lucy poems, the Matthew poems, and a substantial draft of almost three hundred lines which was to become Book I of *The Prelude*. In December Wordsworth and Dorothy wrote to Coleridge and included copies of two Lucy poems, "Strange Fits of Passion" and "She Dwelt among the Untrodden Ways," and the skating and stolen-boat episodes from the drafts along with "Nutting."[1] In the same letter Wordsworth apologized for not having completed more work: "As I have had no books I have been obliged to write in self-defence. I should have written five times as much as I have done but that I am prevented by an uneasiness at my stomach and side, with a dull pain about my heart" (*LEY* 236).

The troublesome thought that he ought to have done more, that he ought to have been more productive, caused his nervous disorder and prompted his confessions to Coleridge, whose continued enthusiasm for *The Recluse* must have increased Wordsworth's anxiety. Coleridge's response to Wordsworth's concern is expressed in a letter to Thomas Poole written in early May 1799 after the Wordsworths had spent a day with him before leaving for England at the end of April:

> W. was affected to tears at the thought of not being near me, wished me, of course, to live in the North of England near the Sir Frederic Vane's great Library . . . It is painful to me too to think of not living near him; for he is a *good* and *kind* man, & the only one whom in *all* things I feel my Superior—& you will believe me, when I say, that I have few feelings more pleasurable than to find myself in intellectual Faculties an Inferior. . . . My many weaknesses are of some advantage to me; they unite me more with the great mass of my fellow-beings— but dear Wordsworth appears to me to have hurtfully segregated & isolated his Being / Doubtless, his delights are more deep and sublime; / but he has likewise more hours, that prey on his flesh & blood. (*STCL* 1: 490–91)

1. *The Prelude* (1799) was first published in the third edition of the *Norton Anthology of English Literature*, ed. M. H. Abrams et al. (New York: W. W. Norton, 1974) and has become available in the Cornell Wordsworth series, edited by Stephen Parrish (1977), and in a Norton Critical Edition, *The Prelude: 1799, 1805, 1850*, ed. Jonathan Wordsworth, M. H. Abrams, and Stephen Gill (New York: W. W. Norton, 1979). I quote from Parrish's edition for MS. JJ of *The Prelude*. I quote from the Lucy poems sent to Coleridge in December from *LEY*.

Coleridge diagnoses Wordsworth's personal and practical problems of where and how to live in terms of the political and social issues of withdrawal from public concerns, but his analysis turns quickly from a reading of Wordsworth's character to a reading of Wordsworth's texts and the problems of creativity. Coleridge attributes Wordsworth's anxiety to his isolation, yet at the same time he acknowledges that it is intricately involved with his "more deep and sublime" delights; his understanding of Wordsworth is formed as much on Wordsworth's poetry, the "thoughts of more deep seclusion" of "Tintern Abbey" and the drafts of *The Prelude*, as they are on Wordsworth's private expressions of anxiety in letters and conversation. In the fall of 1799 there coexists in Wordsworth's writing the exultation in nature's ministry and a recognition of the "grandeur in the beatings of the heart" with the somber reflections of "A Slumber Did my Spirit Seal," which Coleridge interpreted to Thomas Poole as a poem in which he had "fancied the moment in which his Sister might die" (*STCL* 1: 479). Whether or not Coleridge is correct in the identification of Lucy with Dorothy, his identification reinforces his understanding that the fears of isolation are embodied in Wordsworth's poetry. In Coleridge's interpretation, the sister who was present at the end of "Tintern Abbey," who guaranteed the continuance of nature's presence, and who became incorporated into Wordsworth's own personal development might no longer be present and might leave him disconnected from nature and his own past self. The themes of the Goslar poems and the drafts of *The Prelude* indicate that the full confidence of "Tintern Abbey" was a temporary mood, one which would return to Wordsworth in the moments of his greatest creative achievement. At other times doubts arose at the very moment in which there was true exultation.

Stephen Parrish has written that the drafts of *The Prelude* written in 1799 "represented for Wordsworth an extension of a mode of verse he had already adopted, a mode based upon Coleridge's conversation poems" (Parrish 7). Parrish presents those drafts in three sections: the first consisted of fragmentary drafts of about twenty lines on the "mild creative breeze" that becomes a "redundant energy"; the second, a continuous section of about 150 lines beginning with the question "was it for this"; and the third, a collection of passages that followed the longer draft, including the stolen-boat and skating episodes, which were not clearly woven into the longer sequence. The 150-line draft includes, near its beginning, a quotation from "Frost at Midnight": "my sweet birth-place." And toward the end of the drafts Wordsworth added an apostrophe to Dorothy similar to that in "Tintern Abbey": "Then dearest maiden on whose lap I rest / My head do not deem that these / Are idle sympathies" (Parrish 79), a phrase associated with "Nutting" and with the *Prelude* drafts. The final phrase recalls the "quiet sympathies" of the consolation to Margaret's story and the "shadowy Sympathies" of Coleridge's transcription of that passage.

The 150-line passage opens with the half-line question "was it for this," and Parrish is correct to see it as referring to the fragmentary drafts on the breeze as the "tempest" and the "redundant energy," although it is difficult to know whether in 1799 Wordsworth intended those lines to precede the question in a more complete version: " 'This' seems here to have been the powerful disturbance of mind occasioned by a superabundant flow of inspiration—not incapacity, or guilt, or self-reproach of the type that later entered the 'post-preamble.' The tone of 'was it for this' may not, in fact, be ironic, or regretful, but wondering, perhaps confused, even perhaps quietly exultant" (Parrish 6). These drafts do not show evidence of a deep anxiety that leads to a creative blockage or a failure to write; the problem, and a problem that is very real, is the opposite. There is an excess of energy and imagination whose activity is momentary and not sustained, and if it is momentary, it is fragmentary and disconnected. The uncertainty of early fragmentary work on a major literary project would ordinarily be a matter of little anxiety to a writer. Most beginnings are tentative and uncertain, but in Wordsworth's case the uncertainty becomes the theme of the work.

The drafts on the "mild creative breeze" describe Wordsworth's reflection upon his present state of mind and his experience in writing:

> a mild creative breeze
> a vital breeze that passes gently on
> Oer things which it has made and soon becomes
> A tempest a redundant energy
> Creating not but as it may
> disturbing things created.—
>
> a storm not terrible but strong
> with lights and shades and with a rushing power

trances of thought
And mountings of the mind compared to which
The wind that drives along th[']autumnal [? leaf]
Is meekness

(Parrish 123)

It is difficult to make sense of these lines without another substantial text. The most obvious choice would be their later context in Book I, where they appear in 1804, but as Jonathan Wordsworth points out, it is doubtful that Wordsworth thought of them as beginning the poem in 1798–99 because they do not form a part of the *Prelude* that was copied in the fall of 1799.[2]

Whether or not Wordsworth intended these drafts for one integral poem or another poem later, these fragments are related in a dialogic reading that cannot assign formal intention to fragments, especially as in this instance, when the fragments are so clearly dialogically related to the other drafts. A few generalizations can be made about the fragments as they stand. Above the first line Wordsworth wrote "inspiration" and above the second he wrote "a gentle inspiration."[3] The breeze is internal, and creativity is poetic. Inspiration begins and is creative, but it quickly becomes a "tempest" almost with a will of its own "disturbing things created," presumably its own beginnings. These drafts and his later effusions show that Wordsworth is concerned with the presence of brief lyrical moments that cannot be sustained. It is not simply that the lyrical moments exhaust themselves but that they turn upon their own creation.

The particular significance of the passage, however, is best understood, not in itself or in what it was to become six years later, but in comparison with earlier uses of the figure in the previous year and with the drafts that follow. The syntax suggests, by its negatives, that Wordsworth's purpose is to limit and define his use of the figure in relation to earlier texts. The breeze here is not the "intellectual

2. In his reading text of MS. JJ (1798), Stephen Parrish places these lines before the longer 150-line fragment beginning "was it for this" (Parrish 123). Jonathan Wordsworth places them at the end of the series of fragments and argues that there was no connection between the lines and the opening question of the longer fragment (*Prel.* 486).

3. Parrish 117. Professor Parrish has informed me that the words were probably written above the lines at approximately the same time as the lines themselves and are not later additions, because the notebook was not used for revisions at a later date.

Breeze" of "The Eolian Harp," because although the "intellectual Breeze" is "plastic and vast," in 1796 it is a figure for a force external to and independent of the individual mind, which it shapes. The language of the *Prelude* drafts also points to several important passages by both Wordsworth and Coleridge, all written in the early months of 1798. The first was drafted in Wordsworth's Alfoxden notebook, was later associated with "The Pedlar," and was placed in the second part of *The Prelude* (1799). It is not a source for the "creative breeze" passage in any usual sense; the verbal parallels are slight. The differences in the use of the figure of the breeze and tempest, however, indicate Wordsworth's attempt in the fall of 1798 to define and limit its significance:

> In storm and tempest and beneath the beam
> Of quiet moons he wandered there—and there
> Would feel whateer there is of power in sound,
> To breathe an elevated mood, by form
> Or image unprofaned—there would he stand
> Beneath some rock, listening to sounds that are
> The ghostly language of the antient earth.
>
> (Parrish 155)

In the early months of 1798 Wordsworth and Coleridge contemplate the language of nature and engage in a dialogue on its intelligibility. The drafts of the fall shift the context of the figure of "storm and tempest" from nature as a timeless and imageless language to a momentary personal utterance. The autumnal wind that blows the leaves has become "meekness" compared to the "creative breeze" that brings "trances of thought" that are his own possession. The two passages together not only mark a shift from Wordsworth's allegiance to an inarticulate and natural language to a recognition of a creative and projecting mind; they also indicate Wordsworth's recognition of the inadequate response, in the fall of 1798, to a language that he had formerly thought reached him in clear communication.

A second passage that seems to be indicated by the negatives of the drafts is from "The Ancient Mariner," a passage on the storm that drives the ship to the pole and one that was revised out of the later versions:

> Listen, Stranger! Storm and Wind,
> A Wind and Tempest strong!

184

For days and weeks it play'd us freaks—
Like Chaff we drove along.

(45–48)

Written at approximately the same time as Wordsworth's fragment on "storm and tempest" or earlier, it portrays a natural storm that is hostile to the fate of the ship. Its unexpected ferocity leads the mariner to see it as irrational, unjust, and inexplicable. It plays "freaks" and consequently is interpreted as being grotesque and unnatural. Thus a reversal occurs from the natural to the unnatural within the mariner's mind that is similar to the reversal of the "creative breeze" in the drafts, which began as mild and formative but which quickly turned to its opposite. But Wordsworth's tempest is "a storm not terrible but strong" and distinct from the mariner's. At the same time that he recognizes the possibility of terror, he denies it, and in comparison to the storm in "The Ancient Mariner," his storm is not characterized by the antinaturalism that the mariner's is, and hence, perhaps, can be redeemed or recaptured.

A more important context is the poem that Wordsworth quoted at the beginning of the 150-line sequence, "Frost at Midnight," which was on Wordsworth's mind when he was writing in the fall of 1798. Both "Frost at Midnight" and Wordsworth's drafts establish their individual understanding of the context in which creativity can occur and their experiences with it. The silence of "Frost at Midnight" "disturbs / And vexes" meditation, and Coleridge remains in that vacancy throughout the poem. His condition enables him only fanciful toying with thought and the vicarious joy of his hope for Hartley. While his meditations begin in the vacancy "unhelp'd by any wind," Wordsworth's begin in a plenitude, an excess that is the opposite of the "dead calm" in "Frost at Midnight." Yet a similar disturbance occurs. The "redundant energy" disturbs its creation, and "disturbs" suggests both an agitation of calm and tranquillity and a breaking apart and fragmentation, a discomposition and disarrangement.[4] The difference between "Frost at Midnight" and these drafts is measured in the difference between Coleridge's phrase "trances of the blast" and Wordsworth's quite different "trances of thought." Coleridge's, occurring at the end of the poem, duplicates the setting of its opening. The "trance" is a quiet vacancy. Wordsworth's trance is the opposite—an excess, not an absence—but

4. The OED defines "to disturb" as "to discompose" and defines "to discompose" as "to disturb the order or arrangement of."

Wordsworth's phrase intimates also a transition and an accompanying transience of utterance.

Wordsworth's tentative efforts to explain his creative experience are expressed in reference to other texts, his own and Coleridge's. He seems to have determined to distinguish his texts from Coleridge's by arguing that his creative condition is the opposite of Coleridge's. The dialogue here anticipates the dialogue of 1802, in which Coleridge responds to Wordsworth's dejection by defining his own in opposition. Both in 1802 and in 1798 the dialogue turns from the text, or context, of nature to the texts of writing. The *Prelude* drafts on the "mild creative breeze" are not about nature or its intelligibility. Finally, they have little to do with the recollection of childhood experiences, but they have a great deal to do with the recollection of poetry written before. The present tense of the drafts and their references to creating and breaking apart clearly indicate that the drafts are a reflection upon what has been written. It may be impossible to determine whether the drafts on the "mild creative breeze" were written before, after, or during the composition of the other work in the fall of 1798. If they were written after, they refer to the experience of writing in the fall of 1798; if they were written before, they may well refer to the work on "The Pedlar" in the spring of the year, when many fragments were drafted in the Alfoxden notebook.

Although the order of composition of the "creative breeze" drafts and the longer 150-line section cannot be determined, there is a clear relationship between them in the opening lines of the longer draft:

> was it for this
> That one, the fairest of all rivers, loved
> To blend his murmurs with my nurse's song
> And from his alder shades and rocky falls
> And from his fords and shallows sent a voice
> To intertwine my dreams, for this didst thou
> O Derwent—travelling over the green plains
> Near my sweet birth-place didst thou beauteous stream
> Give ceaseless music to the night & day
> Which with its steady cadence tempering
> Our human waywardness compose[d] my thought
> To more than infant softness . . .

> (Parrish 123–24)

The antecedent of "this" is not in *The Prelude* until 1804, when the "glad preamble" provided the reference. Nevertheless, the connection between the opening question and the drafts is implied. The "storm not terrible but strong," the disturbance that discomposes beginnings, is the critical generating text of the longer drafts. Wordsworth does not use childhood memories to recapture the sources of his creative energy or originating emotion in the "glad animal movements" of "Tintern Abbey." His confusion comes from having too much imaginative and emotional energy. He begins with a collection of fragmentary drafts, the trances of his thought, and turns from them to a recollection of childhood to calm his tempestuous energy. He turns to childhood, not for a memory of inchoate sublimities, but to compose his thoughts. He invokes childhood to be quieted, to be tempered, to be steadied, and to find "a dim earnest of the calm / That Nature breathes." The final lines of the 150-line draft emphasize this purpose:

> these primordial feelings[s] how serene
> How calm those seem amid the swell
> Of human passion even yet I feel
> Their tranquillizing power
>
> (Parrish 127)

The tranquillity that he finds in writing the longer draft is not clearly defined except in the context of the "creative breeze" passage and the fragments that it, in turn, implies.

If Wordsworth's childhood experiences of sublimity are not the origin of these meditations, then what kind of childhood is he talking about? And whose childhood is he talking about? The presence of Coleridge's phrase "my sweet birth-place" is a bit unsettling in what claims to be personal reminiscences. Wordsworth's portrait of childhood and the purposes of its invocation recall the rhythm of early life: the nurse's song, the murmur of the river, its "ceaseless music" with a "steady cadence." Coleridge's prior recollection of childhood in "Frost at Midnight" is also represented as strains of music:

> I dreamt
> Of my sweet birthplace, and the old church-tower,
> Whose bells, the poor man's only music, rang
> From morn to evening, all the hot fair-day,
> So sweetly, that they stirr'd and haunted me

187

With a wild pleasure, falling on mine ear
Most like articulate sounds of things to come!

(32–38)

Not only does his childhood live within the presence of common music, but Coleridge's childhood also hears the promise of "articulate sounds of things to come," a promise that precedes Wordsworth's "dim earnest of the calm." Both turn to childhood for what is absent at present: Wordsworth to temper his imagination, and Coleridge to attempt to recover the audibility of a natural language. That Wordsworth's association of his birthplace with music may come from Coleridge's poem is suggested by a very early blank-verse fragment in which Wordsworth returns to his birthplace near the river Derwent and in which the river is given a voice that is characterized in no precise way and without music:

> YET once again do I behold the forms
> Of these huge mountains, and yet once again,
> Standing beneath these elms, I hear thy voice,
> Beloved Derwent, that peculiar voice
> Heard in the stillness of the evening air,
> Half-heard and half-created.[5]

This fragment was obviously incorporated into "Tintern Abbey," but here there is no emphasis, as there is in that poem, on the language of the sense.

In the *Prelude* drafts a curious reflection intrudes upon memory's attempts to recapture the tranquillizing cadences of childhood. The transcription of the photographs of MS. JJ in the Cornell Wordsworth edition shows the following:

> I speak of things
> ~~That have been & that are no gentle dreams~~
> Complacent fashioned fondly to adorn
> The time of unrememberable being

(Parrish 115)

Both the reading text of the Cornell Wordsworth edition and the transcription in the Norton edition restore the second line as though it had not been crossed out. As the passage was originally

---

5. *WPW* 5: 340. Reed dates this fragment "between the latter half of 1796 and the early June 1797 reading of *The Borderers*" (*CEY* 27, 346).

written, Wordsworth seems to be certain that, in opposition to other texts depicting childhood, his recollections are not merely fashionable fictions, but his deletion of the second line proves that, in fact, at some time he feared that his recollections were possibly fictional coverings of a time that memory cannot recover. There seems genuine doubt in his mind that is finally overcome by a determination that he has captured a real past. The problem is, of course, that if his recollections are not derived from accurate memory, then they have their origin in other texts of childhood and claim an awareness of their position in a dialogue of texts.

Whether or not Wordsworth seriously doubted memory, these lines reveal that recollection and self-reflection are accompanied by reflection on other texts. His memories of childhood are never so pure that they do not bring with them recollections of other descriptions of childhood. This intrusion suggests that Wordsworth shapes his own recollections in comparison to others already written. He argues that his are true and really individual. His negative "no gentle dreams" appears to deny its connection with "Frost at Midnight" and Coleridge's recollection of his school days, when he recalled his birthplace: "So gaz'd I, till the soothing things, I dreamt, / Lull'd me to sleep, and sleep prolong'd my dreams." At the same time, Wordsworth acknowledges the division between the adult's mind and childhood in Coleridge's poem and denies that the fictions that inevitably result from such division are present in his own. Toward the end of the 150-line fragment he turns to the problem of the return of other texts when he tries to construct his own childhood:

> I have stood to images like this
> A stranger li[n]king with the spectacle
> No body of associated forms
>
> (Parrish 127)

The phrases that precede this statement, his thanks for the "pure motions of the sense," and the "pure organic pleasure," recall his efforts in the spring of 1798 to divest nature of associated meanings and emphasize within these drafts his effort to rid his lines of the very texts that preceded them and to a large extent gave them their beginning.

The following episode, the "one long bathing of a summers day" and the standing "alone / A naked savage in the thunder shower," shifts attention in the previous lines from the thinly veiled allusion to Coleridge's poem to a more obvious textual opposite, Gray's "Ode on a Distant Prospect of Eton College." The third and fourth stanzas provide many of the activities contained in the early *Prelude* drafts:

> Say, Father Thames, for thou hast seen
> Full many a sprightly race
> Disporting on thy margent green
> The paths of pleasure trace,
> Who foremost now delight to cleave
> With pliant arm thy glassy wave?
> The captive linnet which enthrall?
> What idle progeny succeed
> To chase the rolling circle's speed,
> Or urge the flying ball?
>
> While some on earnest business bent
> Their murmuring labours ply
> 'Gainst graver hours, that bring constraint
> To sweeten liberty:
> Some bold adventurers disdain
> The limits of their little reign,
> And unknown regions dare descry:
> Still as they run they look behind,
> They hear a voice in every wind,
> And snatch a fearful joy.[6]

Paul Sheats has called attention to the importance of Gray's poem for Wordsworth's theme of the ambush of hope, and the poem is no less important for the recollections in the early *Prelude*.[7] The childhood activities that both Gray and Wordsworth choose to remember are surprisingly similar: swimming, capturing birds, crossing boundaries in the quest for adventure, and the delightful terror of being pursued by voices in "every wind." Wordsworth did not "cleave / With pliant arm thy glassy wave," but "made one long bathing of a summers day." There is more at stake here than the simple matter of a shift away from Gray's poetic diction. The intrusive reflection upon the dreams that are "fashioned fondly" alludes to Gray's fictions, or fictions similar to Gray's. Wordsworth rejects

6. 11. 21–40 in *The Poems of Thomas Gray, William Collins, and Oliver Goldsmith*, ed. Roger Lonsdale (London: Longman; New York: W. W. Norton, 1969).

7. Paul Sheats, *The Making of Wordsworth's Poetry, 1785–1798* (Cambridge, Mass.: Harvard University Press, 1973) 34.

them as fictions for the reasons that make them fictional. Gray's children are merely innocent and surrounded by simple joy; Wordsworth's experience a real terror and fear. Gray's children suffer an ambush of hope later in life that produces an abrupt break with childhood innocence; Wordsworth wishes above all to preserve the continuity of childhood and adulthood, to bridge the chasm between the two, a division that is created in "Frost at Midnight," not by an ambush of hope, but by the poet's acts of self-reflection. In the context of the swimming episode, the preceding reflection on the "gentle dreams" deflects its allusions from "Frost at Midnight" to Gray's poem, yet both are present and have a large share in determining Wordsworth's recollections. In fact, it might be argued that when Wordsworth claims to return to his own childhood for the steady cadence of his nurse's song and is also turning to the steady cadences of composition, he is also turning to the tempering cadences of other poems.

Any abrupt break from childhood would challenge the truth of recollection and raise the possibility of recollection's being merely fanciful, but, more dangerously, it could separate Wordsworth from the tranquilizing effect of childhood. The question "was it for this" implies that the steadying cadences may not be present. The question is repeated at least five times in the opening thirty lines of the 150-line segment, after which there is an abrupt turn to "Ah not in vain ye beings of the hills" repeated shortly after in "Ah not in vain ye spirits of the springs." His denial that the events of childhood were in vain suggests that he feared that they might be and that he might be unable to articulate their influence on his adult imagination. The first denial expresses his understanding of the effect of recollection:

> Ah not in vain ye beings of the hills
> And ye that walk the woods and open heaths
> By moon or starlight thus from my first day
> Of childhood did ye love to interweave
> The passions [   ]
> Not with the mean & vullgar works of man
> But with high objects with eternal things
> With life & nature, purifying thus
> The elements of feiling & of thought
> And sanctifying by such disc[i]pline
> Both pain & fear untill we recognize
> A grandeur in the beatings of the heart

(Parrish 125)

191

In the *Prelude* of 1799 and subsequent versions, this section follows the stolen-boat episode. There its function is to explain the shift from the child's incipient sublime experiences in the raw fear and terror of actual events to the adult's internalized and sublimated emotion, which proves, not the grandeur of nature, but the grandeur of the human imagination. Here, however, the context is different, and the emphasis and the urgency are also different. The connection between past and present permits him to draw upon, not only the sources of great emotion, but also the tempering influence from childhood. The emphasis falls on the "discipline" of fear and terror, not the energy. The change in tense from "did . . . intertwine" to "we recognize" transforms past into present, and fear and terror into grandeur, the "mountings of the mind." Wordsworth here drafted his own preliminary statement of what Coleridge had written in the note to "Religious Musings": ". . . we had allegorically narrated the transfiguration of Fear into holy Awe."

The second denial that childhood was in vain again turns to Coleridge's poem, his prayer for Hartley at the end that "all seasons shall be sweet to thee":

> ah not for trivial ends
> Through snow & sunshine & the sparkling plains
> Of moonlight frost and through the stormy [? day]
> Did ye with such assiduous love pursue
> Your favorite and your joy
>
> (Parrish 125)

Hartley will be blessed by the "secret ministry of frost," and Wordsworth says that "I may not think / A vulgar hope was your's when ye employed / Such ministry . . ." (Parrish 125).

Yet, having drafted the transformation of childhood fear into adult grandeur and having claimed the presence of a universal language in childhood similar to that which in "Frost at Midnight" Coleridge called the "eternal language," Wordsworth permits further intrusive doubt to interrupt a draft that has become a hymn of thanksgiving:

> Nor while, thou[gh] doubting yet not lost, I tread
> The mazes of this argument, and paint
> How Nature by collateral interest
> And by extrinsic passion peopled first
> My mind with beauteous objects may I well

Forget what might demand a loftier song
How oft the eternal spirit, he that has
His life in unimaginable things
And he who painting what he is in all
The visible imagery of all the worlds
Is yet apparent chiefly as the soul
Of our first sympathies . . .

(Parrish 126)

When this passage was transferred to the end of Part One of *The Prelude* (1799), it signaled a transition from the presentation of emotions associated with boyhood sports to "other pleasures" and "joys of subtler origin" in the "pure motions of the sense" (380–83). But here its context is different and its emphasis is not on the experiences that are represented but on writing and representation. The "joys of subtler origin," which resemble the "gift / Of aspect more sublime" in "Tintern Abbey," are here not defined as natural emotions but are merely identified as those that "demand a loftier song." The phrase translates Virgil's opening of the Fourth Eclogue, *paulo majora canamus*, used as the first motto for "The Immortality Ode" (1807). It invites the reader to ask, Loftier than what? After all, he has just drafted some of the most powerful and essentially Wordsworthian passages for Book I of *The Prelude*. What does Wordsworth intend to write? One possible answer is *The Recluse*, the subject of which obviously contrasts with the subjective pondering of his own imagination and past. Wordsworth assures himself that although he doubts, he is not lost; he knows that his goal is to write that "loftier song."[8] But it is doubtful that the "loftier song" is *The Recluse*, because the lines that follow sound very much like the subjectivity of "Frost at Midnight." When he defines the "loftier song" as the poetry of "the eternal spirit" who paints "what he is in all / The visible imagery of all the worlds," he gives voice, not to *The Recluse* or even to his own recollections and the beatings of his heart, but to Coleridge's "Frost at Midnight":

so shalt thou see and hear
The lovely shapes and sounds intelligible
Of that eternal language, which thy God

8. Paul Sheats has explicated the tension between the attraction of retrogression and the duty of narrative progression in *The Prelude* ("Wordsworth's 'Retrogrades' and the Shaping of *The Prelude*," *Journal of English and Germanic Philology* 71 [1972]: 473–90).

Utters, who from eternity doth teach
Himself in all, and all things in himself.

(63–67)

Wordsworth's lines are closer to Coleridge's poem than they are to anything in the history of the Pedlar, which "Frost at Midnight" resembles. It comes closer than anything Wordsworth wrote in the previous spring to adopting Coleridge's view of nature's language. When he uses Virgil's original for "The Immortality Ode," his "loftier song" is another personalized recollection on the fugitive origins of his poetic genius.

As he did earlier in the drafts, and as he did earlier in 1798 when he was at work on "The Pedlar," Wordsworth has turned to the precedent of Coleridge's poetry as a prop in the recollection of his childhood affections. When he seems to be the most personal and individual, he comes close to ventriloquizing Coleridge's voice and appropriating his texts. When he claims to be turning to childhood for the steadying cadences of nature's calm and the discipline of fear and terror, he recalls poetry that has already been composed. These drafts argue that his poetry is self-generated, yet in his turning to Coleridge it is clear to him that what ought to be is not yet. At the moments when he reflects upon his own writing of these drafts, he finds that he must allude to other writing either to pay or deny his debts. The recognition of the inevitability of a context for his poetry is perhaps the greatest recognition that Wordsworth makes in these drafts, because he learns, through work in composing *The Prelude* (1799), that his urge for a myth of self-generation can be supplied only by his poetry's becoming its own context. At this point in their dialogue, the burden of amalgamation falls on Wordsworth as much as it does on Coleridge.

When Wordsworth reached the point at which he began the reflection on the "loftier song," he added up the lines he had written in continuous sequence and wrote "94" in the margin. The remaining drafts in the manuscript, which include the stolen-boat episode and a later one known as the Winander Boy passage, are not as clearly attached to the main sequence. They exist, as presented by recent editors, as separate drafts. There is little indication as to their precise significance for Wordsworth. The collection of these episodes ends, in the Cornell Wordsworth edition, with a passage that refers to all his recollections in the drafts and that, in the reading text of the Cornell edition, is not printed in its complete form. In the transcription of the photographs the passage reads

> Those hours that cannot die those lovely forms
> And sweet sensations which throw back our life
> And make our infancy a visible scene
> On which the sun is shining
> Those recollect hours that have the charm
> Of visionary [? thoughts]
>   islands in the unnavigable depth
> Of our departed time
>
> (Parrish 80–81)

The final two fragmentary lines were not incorporated into the later *Prelude*, but they do indicate what concerned Wordsworth in 1798. The moments recollected in lyric effusions are not, in this particular draft, qualified by doubt in any way in themselves. They are genuine seminal episodes, but the final two lines suggest that Wordsworth is worried that they are isolated moments, that they are both moments of time not clearly connected to the chronology of his personal development and, perhaps more important, that the "recollect hours" are separate lyric effusions with no intelligible context through which they would possess their place and hence their significance.

Jonathan Wordsworth includes in his edition of the *Prelude* texts two sections from another manuscript, which he dates from February 1799, a few months after Wordsworth's work on the first drafts of *The Prelude*:

> nor had my voice
> Been silent—oftentimes had I burst forth
> In verse which with a strong and random light
> Touching an object in its prominent parts
> Created a memorial which to me
> Was all sufficient, and, to my own mind
> Recalling the whole picture, seemed to speak
> An universal language. Scattering thus
> In passion many a desultory sound,
> I deemed that I had adequately cloathed
> Meanings at which I hardly hinted, thoughts
> And forms of which I scarcely had produced
> A monument and arbitrary sign

195

A second fragment comments on the first:

> In that considerate and laborious work,
> That patience which, admitting no neglect,
> [? By] slow creation doth impart to speach
> Outline and substance, even till it has given
> A function kindred to organic power—
> The vital spirit of a perfect form
>
> *(Prel.* 495)

Jonathan Wordsworth has taken the first of these two fragments to indicate Wordsworth's desire to make his personal experience a universal language, which is certainly true.[9] There is, as well, an honest meditation upon his present writing. The "strong and random light" is the light that he described in the fragmentary drafts of the "mild creative breeze," which is a "storm not terrible but strong / with lights and shades." Both allude to creation that begins with promise but which ends, not just in silence, but in discomposition. The fragment of memory cannot reconstruct a whole, and the implied synecdoche becomes arbitrary association. To have produced merely arbitrary associations was to have failed, for the moment, to live up to Coleridge's expectations for "perfect form." Wordsworth addressed him in Part II as one to whom "the unity of all has been revealed." On September 30 Coleridge wrote Southey that he was "sunk in Spinoza'" and remained "as undisturbed as a Toad in a Rock," and in November he entered in his notebook the following plan for a poem:

9. See also Parrish 163. Jonathan Wordsworth comments that the first fragment probably reflects a "failure to begin work on Part II, and may, conceivably represent an early attempt to write an introductory section for 1799 in the manner of 1805, I, 238–71" *(Prel.* 495). More recently he has written of this first fragment that "there is the failure to achieve universality, but this time it is a universal language. . . . If it were not that the mood is placed firmly in the past, it would be among the most despairing passages that Wordsworth ever wrote" *(William Wordsworth: The Borders of Vision* [Oxford: Clarendon Press, 1982] 220). In the context of the second fragment, it reflects Wordsworth's concern with form and with appropriate context. Hazlitt commented on this problem: Wordsworth "cannot form a whole. He has not the constructive faculty. He can give only the fine tones of thought, drawn from his mind by accident or nature, like the sounds drawn from the Æolian harp by the wandering gale.—He is totally deficient in all the machinery of poetry" ("On the Living Poets," *Lectures on the English Poets, The Complete Works of William Hazlitt*, ed. P. P. Howe, 21 vols. (London: J. M. Dent, 1930–34) 5: 156.

If I began a poem of Spinoza, thus it should begin/ I would make a pilgrimage to the burning sands of Arabia, or &c &c to find the Man who could explain to me there can be *oneness*, there being infinite Perceptions—yet there must be a *one*ness, not an intense Union but an Absolute Unity, for &c.[10]

Without the order of "perfect form," the memorial that seemed sufficient proves meaningless and provides a dead language. What Wordsworth does not say here is as significant as what he does say. The loss—the abrupt rupture of present from past, of the fragment from its whole—does not lead him to suspect that his meditations and lyric effusions produced fictions. That possibility was rejected in the opening drafts. He fears that his lyrics have no meaning, even a personal meaning to him, that his fragments bear no intelligible whole, and he is beginning to suspect that personal experience cannot in itself give meaning to his writing and that he must find the context that would impart meaning elsewhere than in personal experience. The fears that he expressed in "Tintern Abbey" over the loss of his "genial spirits," his individuality, are revived in his awakening knowledge that his lyric fragments must have a context in his own poetry, not in a dialogue with Coleridge's. Thus while the discomposition that is implied in the creative breeze's exuberance is a trouble to him, it serves a useful purpose in discomposing the contexts of his poetry.

The second fragment suggests that a possible context of a "perfect form" may be produced by conscious and deliberate art. Without that form, fragments are merely the unintelligible ruins of the past or irretrievably dispersed emotions and thoughts. By realizing that he is at the point of a beginning and not an ending, trying to piece together what has been lost, Wordsworth begins to recognize that the lyric fragments are tentative efforts at finding a "perfect form." His emphases have shifted from the spring of 1798, when he located the vital language in an inarticulate nature, to the spring of 1799, when he located the source of "organic power" and the "vital spirit" in his own patient, "considerate and laborious work." This recognition promises that the fragments are not the relics of a dead life but may possibly be the beginnings of a living text that is about to be. As in other instances of creative innovation in their dialogue,

10. *STCL* 1: 534; *CNB* 1: 556. See also *CNB* 1: 1561.

beginnings are marked by nothing as much as uncertainty and confusion, particularly confusion about a context to provide meaning.

Wordsworth's "universal language" echoes Coleridge's "eternal language" of "Frost at Midnight," where the colors and forms of nature constitute a Berkeleyan divine sensible language by which spirit manifests itself to man. This universal language remains intelligible, for both Wordsworth and Coleridge, only in the "vital spirit of a perfect form." Wordsworth here makes a distinction between the spontaneous "strong and random light" that flashes forth and the "considerate and laborious work" that creates a "function kindred to organic power," a phrase which places poetic creation somehow parallel to, but not the same as, organic energy in nature. The emphasis in this second fragment on the deliberate effort of shaping and ordering is particularly Coleridgean; imagination, in the words of the *Biographia*, must be kept under the "irremissive, though gentle and unnoticed, controul" of the will (*BL* 2: 16). Wordsworth's emphasis on diligent attention to "perfect form" and the shaping spirit that alone confers vitality qualifies his more usual emphasis on spontaneity and relies on the art of composition, hinting that an artistic order is perhaps parallel to, but surely distinct from, any natural order. Wordsworth is moving toward a recognition that significance resides in the ordering of a text.

If his insistence upon a universal language, which speaks through symbols of spirit in nature, and upon organic form created by deliberate craft reflects prime Coleridgean principles, his analysis of his own difficulties in constructing that ideal language reflects Coleridgean anxieties. The spontaneous light that imperfectly illuminates is both "strong," a word that alludes to the power of the storm to disturb its own creation, and "random," a word that recalls the "random gales" of "The Eolian Harp." Wordsworth learned that "random" fragments become scattered: "Scattering thus / In passion many a desultory sound," a shift of the figure from that of light to the Coleridgean one of the harp, in which the harp is by the "desultory breeze caress'd." However joyous the overflow of initial creativity, the results are fragments floating without substance, foundation, or outline. The 1805 *Prelude* states explicitly that the purpose of writing was to "fix the wavering balance of my mind" (I, 650), an image and theme that he was to use throughout *The Prelude* to indicate his indifference, detachment, and random purposelessness, particularly in the days at Cambridge, London, and Paris.

The irony of Wordsworth's appropriation is that while he began with and relied upon Coleridge's poetry, he found within that context and its lyrical form the same discontinuities between past and present and between mind and nature. The tempest that "disturbs" Wordsworth's creation also discomposes the lyric context, which, at the beginning, the effusions assume as their context. In other words, while the *Prelude* drafts seem intended to be placed in a poem or series of poems like "Frost at Midnight" or "Tintern Abbey" and could have been written in continuous order only under that assumption, the drafts themselves fragment and disperse that order. Appropriation precedes fragmentation, and dispersion occurs only after Wordsworth has tried to make the form his own. The drafts constitute a moment in Wordsworth's writing in which one context is no longer complete enough to supply a ground for meaning and in which another "perfect form" has not yet been created. The result is indecision, uncertainty, and confusion, with an awareness of the possibility that individual fragments would remain isolated and therefore arbitrary memorials of what cannot be recomposed. The issue of isolation, which seemed in "Tintern Abbey" and in individual lyric moments of recollection in the drafts to be overcome by the forging of a psychic connection to childhood as the source of order, became in the early work on *The Prelude* a question of the arrangement of the text itself and not at all a matter of memory—a contextual, not a psychological, problem.

"The Silence and the Calm": The Lucy Poems

A month before Coleridge sent Poole his comments on Wordsworth's having "hurtfully segregated & isolated his Being" he had sent Poole a copy of "A Slumber Did my Spirit Seal" with his brief interpretation: "Wordsworth transmitted to me a most sublime Epitaph / whether it had any reality, I cannot say,—Most probably, in some gloomier moment he had fancied the moment in which his Sister might die" (*STCL* 1: 479). Coleridge had received copies of some other Lucy poems before, "She Dwelt among the Untrodden Ways" and "Strange Fits of Passion." The moods of these "gloomier" moments contrast sharply with the exultation of some of the *Prelude* drafts. The *Prelude* drafts joyously proclaim moments "that have the charm of / visionary" thoughts (Parrish 81), and "She Dwelt among the Untrodden Ways" concludes, "But now she's in her grave, and Oh! / The difference to me!" (*LEY* 237). The first affirms the clarity and presence of memory; the second acknowledges an irretrievable past. Whether or not Coleridge's interpretation of Lucy as Dorothy is biographically accurate, it is an imaginative realization that Wordsworth's melancholy originated in a fear of being separated from his past and from the source in which he had located his imaginative beginnings.[11] As a figure of poetry rather than as a figure of biography, Dorothy usually represented Wordsworth's own past. In "Tintern Abbey" he incorporated her as a stage in his growth:

> in thy voice I catch
> The language of my former heart, and read
> My former pleasures in the shooting lights
> Of thy wild eyes. Oh! yet a little while
> May I behold in thee what I was once . . .
>
> (117–21)

In his poetry she is a figure to be read, and the poignancy of her death in "Slumber Did my Spirit Seal," "She neither hears nor sees," is sharper in comparison to these lines from "Tintern Abbey." As a figure in the later, revised Lucy poems, Lucy is not individualized or humanized. She dies before she becomes a woman, as many critics have noted. The poems are not primarily poems that cherish the memory of a lost lover but elegies over an internal loss that cannot be compensated, just as Matthew cannot find and does not desire a surrogate for his lost child. The drafts of *The Prelude*, on the one hand, and the Lucy and Matthew poems, on the other, seem to argue contrary views. The second mourn the passing of what the first claimed to have recovered. The contradictions in the two confirm Wordsworth's worries about writing and composing a text in the fall and winter of 1798–99.

An intriguing connection between the *Prelude* drafts and the Lucy poems is the section in the drafts published as "There was a Boy" in

11. David Ferry has written of the Lucy poems that "in one way or another, the speaker is uncertain of his vision of these girls; or rather, he is certain of the instability and perishability of his vision of them. He knows he is making up a fiction and that his fiction will not be able to sustain itself forever" (*The Limits of Mortality: An Essay on Wordsworth's Major Poems* [Middletown, Conn.: Wesleyan University Press, 1959] 79). Ferry's observations could be extended to Wordsworth's early work on *The Prelude* in the fall of 1798. Frances Ferguson discusses the Lucy poems in their final printed sequence as a succession of echoings in which "through the course of these poems, Lucy is repeatedly and ever more decisively traced out of existence . . ." (*Wordsworth: Language as Counter-Spirit* [New Haven: Yale University Press, 1977] 174).

Lyrical Ballads (1800) immediately before "The Brothers." The draft contains only the lines on the boy's calling to the owls and concludes:

> And when it chanced
> That pauses of deep silence mockd my skill
> Then, often, in that silence while I hung
> Listening a sudden shock of mild surprize
> Would carry far into my heart the voice
> Of mountain torrents: or the visible scene
> Would enter unawares into my mind
> With all its solemn imagery its rocks
> Its woods & that uncertain heaven rece[i]ved
> Into the bosom of the steady lake
>
> (Parrish 128)

The seven lines that follow in *Lyrical Ballads* (1800) on the poet musing at the child's grave do not appear in the earliest drafts, although stubs in the Christabel notebook suggest that they were written very shortly after the earliest drafts.[12] On December 10, 1798, Coleridge wrote to Wordsworth praising the lines as uniquely Wordsworthian: "had I met these lines running wild in the deserts of Arabia, I should have instantly screamed out 'Wordsworth!'" (*STCL* 1: 453). The *Prelude* draft makes it clear that Wordsworth is describing his own childhood, since it is in the first person. Without the elegiac conclusion and the third-person narrative, it takes its meaning from the surrounding drafts. In that context, the episode illustrates the joyous moment in which he "held unconscious intercourse / With the eternal beauty drinking in / A pure organic pleasure" (Parrish 127) and the patterns of a tumult subsiding into a calm that he sought as an adult. In addition, it echoes the ending of "Frost at Midnight," in which the silence that was punctuated by the owlet's cry becomes a moment of complete silence and inactivity in which Hartley will be able to comprehend nature's language.

12. Professor Butler has informed me that the probable dates of "There was a Boy" are late 1798 to early 1799 in the Christabel notebook (DC MS. 15), where the concluding elegiac lines were drafted. A later version appears in notebook 18A (DC MS. 16), which Professor Butler dates from late 1798 to early 1799. The version in 18A is preceded by a long draft (*Wordsworth's Prelude*, ed. Ernest de Selincourt, 2d ed., rev. Helen Darbishire [Oxford: Clarendon Press, 1959] 545–46) later placed in Book V (1805), where it contrasts with Wordsworth's satire upon modern systems of education. See also *CEY* 258–59, *Prel.* 170 n, Parrish 16–17, and *Prose* 3: 35, where a canceled portion of the 1815 preface places the poem within the context of the classification of "Poems of the Imagination."

The elegiac concluding lines printed in 1800 change the meaning of the preceding lines from the joyous celebration of childhood's influence to a melancholy recollection of what has been lost:

> Fair are the woods, and beauteous is the spot,
> The vale where he was born: the Church-yard hangs
> Upon a slope above the village school,
> And there along that bank when I have pass'd
> At evening, I believe, that near his grave
> A full half-hour together I have stood,
> Mute—for he died when he was ten years old.
>
> (*LB* 135)

The child delights in the echoes that are redoubled in response to his call, and when the echoes subside, a compensating vision enters his mind. The adult, however, is a poet without an echoing response; he must stand "mute," just as Leonard in "The Brothers" stands at his brother's grave for half an hour and can say nothing to the Priest of Ennerdale. The child's tranquillity is a plenitude of beauty; the adult's calm is an empty silence with no initiating or responding utterance, similar to that at the end of "Three Years She Grew":

> She died and left to me
> This heath, this calm and quiet scene,
> The memory of what has been,
> And never more will be.
>
> (*LB* 199)

The adult of the elegy resides in the "silence and the calm / Of mute insensate things," that Nature predicts for Lucy. The shifting contexts of the Winander-boy fragment reflect Wordsworth's uncertainty and what Coleridge might have called a "gloomier moment." The original fragment in the *Prelude* drafts resides with the other work, almost all of which has Coleridgean overtones and a Coleridgean context. It then becomes a separated fragment in which Coleridge recognizes a uniquely Wordsworthian voice of joy and promise, and it finally becomes a lament for the loss of that promise and ends in silence. The fate of the child becomes the fate of the text itself. It is not merely that the child, or childhood, has been lost; it is also that the significance and the generative potential of the text itself has been lost. Wordsworth's "segregation of his Being" is also the segregation of his texts.

The melancholy traced by the shifting contexts of "There was a Boy" was not a permanent gloom, nor was it an admission of failure. It was, rather, a fear of what might happen, of how significance and generative energy could be lost without the "vital spirit of a perfect form." The drafts led Wordsworth to a continuous language evermore about to be. The Lucy poems, the Matthew poems, and "There was a Boy" in its 1800 version are not similarly prelusive. They are, however, directly related to the drafts of *The Prelude* and do reflect Wordsworth's fear of what might happen if his major project did not become fulfilled.

The two Lucy poems that Wordsworth sent to Coleridge in December 1798, "She Dwelt among the Untrodden Ways" and "'Strange Fits of Passion," were quite different from those published in 1800. "She Dwelt among the Untrodden Ways" is a poem of five, not three, stanzas. Although the published poem is aesthetically superior, the earlier version reveals interesting connections with Wordsworth's earlier poetry and with the poetry that he was writing at the same time. The final two stanzas portray Lucy, not as the depersonalized object of the later poems, but as someone who has suffered and died an untimely death:

> And she was graceful as the broom
>   That flowers by Carron's side;
> But slow distemper checked her bloom,
>   And on the Heath she died.
>
> Long time before her head lay low
>   Dead to the world was she:
> But now she's in her grave, and Oh!
>   The difference to me!

(LEY 237)

The cause of her "slow distemper" is unspecified, but it is an affliction shared by Hamlet, Betty Foy, and Robert in "The Ruined Cottage," whose malaise became a "petted mood / And a sore temper" (232–33). The phrase describes a general anxiety, and in "She Dwelt among the Untrodden Ways" it hints at the loss of a loved one and the loss of hope, since the first line calls Lucy "my hope." Lucy is nature's child and lives in the isolation of uninhabited nature. The speaker hints that he was her lover and that his absence caused her derangement. The Lucy of this version shares with Margaret of "The Ruined Cottage" a mood of unsettled mind and despair. Like Margaret, Lucy is "dead to the world" long before she actually dies. The Lucy of this poem is another version of Margaret.

The shifting contexts of "There was a Boy" describe a movement from tumult and redoubled echoes to silence in which there is an ample recompense of natural beauty and finally to a silence in which the poet is mute. "She Dwelt among the Untrodden Ways" traces a similar decline from a presence of Lucy in a natural order to a disorder that disturbs her hope and that leads to her death. The second Lucy poem that Wordsworth sent Coleridge in December reflects a similar disturbance, but in "Strange Fits of Passion" the disturbance is the speaker's, not Lucy's. This early version included a final stanza deleted from the later versions:

> I told her this; her laughter light
> Is ringing in my ears;
> And when I think upon that night
> My eyes are dim with tears.
>
> (*LEY* 238)

Like the Lucy of "She Dwelt among the Untrodden Ways," she expresses emotion and human feeling and is not the depersonalized being of the later poems. Hers is laughter and not despair. The speaker's fixation upon the moon becomes nature's "sweet dream" of fancy and blindness in which, in a vague and unconscious way, he allegorizes Lucy as the moon until its traditional mythological associations with idealized chastity become transformed into a token of mortality. The strangeness of the poet's fanciful dream is that while his eye is fixed on the moon, his mind is in constant motion, playing over the half-understood and barely expressed meanings:

> My horse moved on; hoof after hoof
> He raised and never stopped,
> When down behind the cottage roof
> At once the planet dropp'd.
>
> (*LEY* 238)

The shift from "moon" to "planet," even if it were for no other reason than to fill the need for a word of two syllables, suggests that the speaker associates the moon with the planet Venus, the evening star and guardian deity of lovers. At first he interprets the descent of the

204

moon-Venus emblem to Lucy's cottage as the mark of favor granted to Lucy and as an emblem of its identification with her, but simultaneously he sees the contrary association: mutability. The irony of this poem is that the capricious associations of fancy have a truth when they contradict one another, and when they disturb their own creation, because in an inexplicable way they lead to a death.

A further irony of the Lucy poems in their context of 1798 is that they end in a calm that is the opposite of the tranquillity that the *Prelude* drafts claimed to have composed. Those drafts present a tranquillity that tempers the "redundant energy" and promises future creativity. The silence and calm of "mute insensate things" and of the poet who stands mute beside the grave offer no possibility of the recovery of what has been lost and no possibility of future creativity. A final irony of the Lucy poems is that, while the *Prelude* drafts attempted to escape the implications of the calm in "Frost at Midnight," the Lucy poems reproduce that calm with even direr consequences. The "dead calm" that Coleridge experiences when he returns from his imaginative excursion into his past repeats the calm of the opening of the poem:

> 'Tis calm indeed! so calm, that it disturbs
> And vexes meditation with it's strange
> And extreme silentness
>
> (8–10)

Coleridge's calm vexes him into toying with thought, but the calm of the elegiac Lucy poems admits only silence. When he tried to assure himself that Coleridge's calm was not his, when he tried to deny that the separation between childhood and the adult poet that Coleridge lamented was his also, he found, in the "gloomier" moments, that Coleridge's calm was his. Thus in both the optimistic moments of 1799, when Wordsworth joyously recovers movements of great intensity, and the "gloomier" moments, when his loss ends in silence, Wordsworth reproduces Coleridge's themes and some of his language. The problem of amalgamation is still his.

Milestones on the Bridgewater Road: The Spots of Time

By October 12, 1799, Coleridge had heard from Wordsworth that *The Prelude* was to be addressed to him: "I long to see what you have been doing. O let it be the tail-piece of 'The Recluse!' for of nothing but 'The Recluse' can I hear patiently. That it is to be addressed to me makes me more desirous that it should not be a poem of itself" (*STCL* 1: 538). Although the Goslar drafts of *The Prelude* contain an apostrophe to Dorothy, "dearest maiden," they incorporate so much of Coleridge's verse and spirit that they assume Coleridge as their best reader. In fact, there is good evidence that Coleridge is considered to be the auditor of the poem in some of the earliest drafts, in which Wordsworth says that one purpose of his writing is for "thou to know / With better knowledge how the heart was framed / Of him thou lovest" and that he need not "dread from thee / Harsh judgements if I am so loth to quit / Those recollected hours that have the charm / Of visionary things . . ." (Parrish 12–13). Addressing the poem to Coleridge made explicit what the early manuscripts had assumed, that Coleridge was always Wordsworth's best reader. It was not merely Coleridge's sympathetic presence as reader or auditor that shaped the work, it was also the presence of Coleridge's poetry at the beginning of the work. In the early drafts, Wordsworth raises his song of thanks and praise for the spirits of nature that nourished him in youth, but the most important nourishment came from Coleridge's poetry. While Wordsworth labored under the burden of thinking of himself as a chosen being, he had Coleridge as much as nature to thank for the election.

Having heard in about the middle of September that Wordsworth was ill, Coleridge took the opportunity of traveling north with Joseph Cottle to see Wordsworth, who with his sister was then staying at Sockburn with the Hutchinsons. They arrived on October 25 or 26. Within a day Wordsworth, Coleridge, and Cottle had set out on a walking tour of the Lake District, the first visit Wordsworth had made to Hawkshead since his school days. In the weeks before Coleridge's arrival, Wordsworth had been at work on the second part of *The Prelude*. Manuscript evidence shows that Dorothy and he had transcribed 292 lines before Coleridge's arrival interrupted their work (Parrish 30). Cottle left Wordsworth and Coleridge about October 30. The two continued by themselves until they were joined by Wordsworth's brother John a few days later (*CEY* 275). Early in November they visited Hawkshead, where Wordsworth found the town greatly changed, which he described in lines later added to the beginning of the second part of *The Prelude*. Coleridge left Wordsworth about November 18, after Wordsworth had made preliminary inquiries about obtaining a house in Grasmere, and passed through Sockburn on his way to work for Daniel Stuart and the *Morning Post* in London. Wordsworth remained in the Lake District, apparently to make final arrangements to lease Dove Cottage, to which Dorothy and he moved at the end of December. After years of homeless wandering, the prospect of permanence and freedom elated him, and the opening lines of the "glad preamble," which formed the first fifty-four lines of Book I of the 1805 *Prelude* reflect that joy. When Wordsworth arrived back at Sockburn on November 25, he returned to work on *The Prelude*, adding lines taken from his observations at Hawkshead and expanding earlier lines into a book of over five hundred lines.

The "glad preamble" was most likely written after Coleridge had left for London and when Wordsworth was completing the second part of *The Prelude* (1799).[13] Before the walking tour he had copied the lines on the difficulty of identifying an origin for poetic emotion, the blessed-babe passage on the first poetic spirit of life, and the description of the removal of the "props of my affections," commonly taken to refer to the death of his mother. After the tour and the conversation with Coleridge, Wordsworth not only wrote the "glad preamble" but also completed Book II by returning to the lines he had written for "The Pedlar" in the spring of 1798 and including the famous lines on the "sentiment of being" and "the one life." The "glad preamble" was not included in the fair copy of *The Prelude* compiled and copied in the last months of 1799, and Wordsworth probably thought of it as a separate work.

While the preamble celebrates liberation and a prospective joyous effusion of optimism, it also incorporates the Goslar drafts on the "mild creative breeze" and thus repeats the uncertainties of his writing. The "sweet breath of heaven" that greets Wordsworth is met by a "corresponding mild creative breeze, / A vital breeze," but the internal breeze "is become / A tempest, a redundant energy, / Vexing its own creation" (*Prel.* [1805] I, 41–47). The last phrase is a revision of the earlier line "disturbing things created," and the substitution of "vexing" for "disturbing" echoes Coleridge's phrase in "Frost at Midnight" that the silence "disturbs / And vexes meditation." Wordsworth contrasts his creative situation with Coleridge's. Coleridge is vexed by silence and the absence of a creative breeze; the

13. For the dates of the "glad preamble," see Parrish 34–35; *CMY* 628–29; and John Alban Finch, "Wordsworth's Two-Handed Engine," *WBS* 1–13.

frost conducts its ministry without any wind. Wordsworth is vexed by the excess of creative energy that discomposes its own creation.

When the preamble was placed into Book I in 1804, the figure of the creative breeze was elaborated in Coleridgean terms:

> It was a splendid evening, and my soul
> Did once again make trial of the strength
> Restored to her afresh; nor did she want
> Eolian visitations—but the harp
> Was soon defrauded, and the banded host
> Of harmony dispersed in straggling sounds,
> And lastly utter silence.
>
> (*Prel.* [1805] I, 101–7)

The impediments he found from "day to day renewed" were his own "unmanageable thoughts." There was no lack of "vital soul." He possessed "general truths" as well as "external things, / Forms, images." He lacked, however, "time, place, and manners," a structure, a form or fable for a great work; he had accumulated fragments toward a great poem but could not see it as a total structure. Consequently the later opening lines of *The Prelude* record his search for a fable: "vanquished Mithridates," Oden, and the "followers of Sertorious," and so on. Ordinary fable, legend, and narrative would not do, because no single theme or legend seemed any more compelling than any other. Even some more common history nearer "to my own heart" would not do: "the whole beauteous fabric seems to lack / Foundation, and withal appears throughout / Shadowy and unsubstantial" (*Prel.* [1805] I, 226–28).

The "mild creative breeze" drafts in the earliest *Prelude* manuscripts and the fragment of February 1799 on "perfect form" identify two related problems raised in the process of dialogue: the existence of fragments that do not unite into a whole and the representative memorials that are inadequate to evoke a living unity. Both prevent the "universal language"; the absence of form creates a vacancy in which representation is only distortion. The fragments discompose the whole. Instead of total representations, the fragments are merely meaningless parts. The failure to articulate full meaning threw doubt on the origin and location of what he later called in *The Prelude* the "hiding-places of my power" (*Prel.* [1805] XI, 335), his unique generating spirit.

Wordsworth's response to these impediments was, not to return to the point of origin, but to turn to what he understood as the intrusive element of time and memory that separated past from present and the memorial from the departed presence. The problem of form became the problem of narrative in which the spatial relations of part to whole became the temporal string of the succession of events to the present moment. The problem of unity was evident to Wordsworth from the presence of these fragments. It was also presented to him in another form by Coleridge when he visited Coleridge on his way back to England at the end of April (*LEY* 23). On April 6 Coleridge had written Poole about the death of Berkeley Coleridge:

> My Baby has not lived in vain—this life has been to him what it is to all of us, education & developement! Fling yourself forward into your immortality only a few thousand years, & how small will not the difference between one year old & sixty years appear!—Consciousness—! it is no otherwise necessary to our conceptions of future Continuance than as connecting the *present link* of our Being with the one *immediately* preceding it; & *that* degree of Consciousness, *that* small portion of *memory*, it would not only be arrogant, but in the highest degree absurd, to deny even to a much younger Infant.—'Tis a strange assertion, that the Essence of Identity lies in *recollective* Consciousness—'twere scarcely less ridiculous to affirm, that the 8 miles from Stowey to Bridgewater consist in the 8 mile stones. (*STCL* 1: 479)

The death of his son brought to Coleridge the same puzzle that writing childhood recollections brought to Wordsworth: the difficulty of conceiving of self or self-in-text as a succession of moments and the difficulty of locating a text with a "perfect form." How is it possible to give them a unity and life? And can the life or the testimony of *"recollective* Consciousness" stand as a ground for the composition of a text?

Wordsworth's work on the later sections of Part I addresses just these issues. It does not attempt to fix the source of his effusions in singular and isolated moments but attempts to describe a process of emotional genesis that sustains present creative energy. He makes the point emphatically that the impressive moments of childhood are neither complete in themselves, a totality that authorizes his poetic aspiration, nor the ultimate source of his creativity. While at times he refers to them as the "hiding-places of my power," more often he refers to them as flashes of promise, indications of "something evermore about to be" (*Prel.* [1805] VI, 542)—moments that become significant only by being redeemed by the present. He had heard, as a child, nature speak

> sometimes, 'tis true,
> By quaint associations, yet not vain
> Nor profitless, if haply they impressed
> Collateral objects and appearances,
> Albeit lifeless then, and doomed to sleep
> Until maturer seasons called them forth
> To impregnate and to elevate the mind.
>
> (*Prel.* [1799] I, 420–26)

Even when the exuberant joys of childhood were past and when he sought nature for its own sake in moments of "shadowy exultation"

> the soul—
> Remembering how she felt, but what she felt
> Remembering not—retains an obscure sense
> Of possible sublimity, to which
> With growing faculties she doth aspire,
> With faculties still growing, feeling still
> That whatsoever point they gain they still
> Have something to pursue.
>
> (*Prel.* [1799] II, 364–71)

These declarations, combined with the "glad preamble," indicate that while the ostensible subject of *The Prelude* is retrospection, the end is clearly prospective.

Nature in the earliest experiences was "intervenient" and "secondary" (*Prel.* [1799] II, 240–41). In these scenes the emotion engendered is that of "vulgar joy," a joy that must, if imagination is to live, be forgotten:

> And if the vulgar joy by its own weight
> Wearied itself out of the memory,
> The scenes which were a witness of that joy
> Remained, in their substantial lineaments
> Depicted on the brain, and to the eye
> Were visible, a daily sight. And thus
> By the impressive agency of fear,
> By pleasure and repeated happiness—
> So frequently repeated—and by force
> Of obscure feelings representative
> Of joys that were forgotten, these same scenes,

So beauteous and majestic in themselves,
Though yet the day was distant, did at length
Become habitually dear. . . .

(*Prel.* [1799] I, 427–40)

The final lesson of Part I provides the only extended explanation of the way in which recollection feeds imagination and in which feelings follow feelings. The child's "vulgar joy" and "giddy bliss" pass into oblivion and are forgotten, but the accidental associations and scenes that accompany those joys are unconsciously impressed upon his mind to be recognized much later. If anything remains of the "vulgar joys" and the accidental emotions that accompany early experiences, they are "obscure feelings representative / Of joys that were forgotten," a phrase that recurs in the preface to *Lyrical Ballads* when Wordsworth introduces the idea that "thoughts . . . are indeed the representatives of all our past feelings" (*Prose* 1: 127). Earlier in Part I he gives thanks to nature: "from my first dawn / Of childhood, did ye love to intertwine / The passions that build up our human soul / . . . until we recognize / A grandeur in the beatings of the heart." The recognition of grandeur is the act of the mature poet in the present.

The frequent abrupt transitions between the presentation of the child's terror and the adult's thanks and praise in the later versions of the first books of *The Prelude* indicate that the value of experience is known by its expression in verse. The "whole picture" and the "universal language" do not reside in individual spots of time or in their origins. The whole is the completed text, perhaps even in an imaginary total text impossible to realize. If fragments cannot stand alone because they lack the significance of form, Wordsworth's purpose in constructing *The Prelude* is to redeem the spontaneous fragments, to give spots of time significance, not only by expostulating on their meaning, but also by placing them in a context. The context gives meaning to the fragments rather than the fragments giving meaning to the whole. In themselves, the spots of time are merely milestones on the Bridgewater road. Although his whole seemed to be grounded in the naturalness of time and personal past, physical growth, and the emotional progression of the natural man, the projected goal of the generation of texts themselves requires the context of writing itself. Like the sounds of the bells in "Frost at Midnight," the spots of time in the early *Prelude* indicate only promise; they locate fulfillment in a time yet to be. In an irony that Wordsworth well understood, the lyric fragments are not memorials of something hidden in the "unnavigable depth / Of our departed time," of something lost, but are promises of something yet to be, something that resided, not in the "pictures" of his past, but in the depictions of his verse. Finally, it is not a matter of self-depiction or self-representation in individual lyric moments, but a matter of locating depiction within a continuing process of composition. His form was to be ordered by the process of dialogue and its turns. As his work on *The Prelude* grew through 1805, the dialogue became more a dialogue with his own earlier work and less a dialogue with Coleridge's poetry.

Wordsworth's later work on *The Prelude* is a continuous arrangement and rearrangement of his lyric fragments, the most famous of which are perhaps the spots of time. In 1799 the episodes are preceded by the narrative of the drowned man, which in turn is preceded by a statement about the uncertainty of the progress of his poem:

> I perceive
> That much is overlooked, and we should ill
> Attain our object if, from delicate fears
> Of breaking in upon the unity
> Of this my argument, I should omit
> To speak of such effects as cannot here
> Be regularly classed, yet tend no less
> To the same point, the growth of mental power
> And love of Nature's works.
>
> (*Prel.* [1799] I, 250–58)

This transition implies that what is to follow, the episodes of the drowned man and the spots of time, cannot be "classed." It invites the reader to ponder which of the previous episodes could be "classed" and in what categories. Are these later experiences really anomalous? Without the apology, it would be easy to see many similarities between these episodes and those that came before. The sudden rising of the dead man from the water provokes fear and wonder, just as the animated cliff does in the stolen-boat episode. Like the other spots of time, it consists of the child's sudden confrontation with death. All these episodes foretell a separation of the child from its accustomed home in pastoral nature and its increasing self-sufficiency.

Without Wordsworth's comments about the unity of his argument, there would be much less of a temptation to question that unity and the episodes that do not seem to fit perfectly. The language of the drowned-man episode is starkly literal and avoids any explicit identification of either mood or emotion in the child. The episode could be placed into a context in which the terror is emphasized or one in which the traumatic confrontation with death brings no such terror. Instead of elaborating on the terror in the image of the "ghastly face," Wordsworth turns abruptly from the scene to allude to other "accidents in flood or field," whose images were later to become associated with "other feelings," although he does not specify them, their occasions, or their effects. In the commentary surrounding this episode, Wordsworth reveals an urge for the unity of argument and the classification of his experiences and at the same time offers the episode as one that he says does not fit well into the sequence that he is composing. He includes an episode that a sympathetic reader could construe as similar to the others, yet with his commentary he prevents such construction.

The spots of time are preceded by an interpretation that expands upon the introduction to the drowned-man episode. Wordsworth singles out particular moments in childhood that possess

> A fructifying virtue, whence, depressed
> By trivial occupations and the round
> Of ordinary intercourse, our minds—
> Especially the imaginative power—
> Are nourished and invisibly repaired.
>
> (*Prel.* [1799] I, 290–94)

This introduces a new turn in his meditations upon the relationship of past to present. Elsewhere in Part I he had emphasized that the recognition of the "grandeur in the beatings of the heart" was the adult's and that the "vulgar joy" of childhood was forgotten, but these lines argue that the strength of childhood is retained and is efficacious enough to renew the adult depressed by the loss of imagination. The emphasis on preservation anticipates Wordsworth's later use of these episodes in Book XI of 1805, but they seem a bit out of place here among episodes that become significant only to the adult.

The first spot of time duplicates the previous episode's confrontation with death, but actually the child's fear comes, not from that meeting, but from the loss of his guide. Separated from his guide, he stumbles on a place where a murderer had been hanged and sees "the long green ridge of turf . . . / Whose shape was like a grave" (*Prel.* [1799] I, 312–13). Having lost his guide, the child imperfectly understands death, not as a loss of something that once was present, but as an uncertain sight of what is to be. Again the problem is prospective, not retrospective. The child suffers a loss of sight of the future for which death is the ultimate uncertainty. But having descended to that darkness, the child reascends. He resumes the search for an identifiable way and guide. He gazes upon the "naked pool," the "girl who bore a pitcher on her head," and the "beacon on the summit."

At this moment in the narrative a strange thing happens. Wordsworth interrupts stark narration to admit the poverty of language to convey the feelings of the child: "I should need / Colours and words that are unknown to man. . . ." The natural time of narration is thus changed to the present, not as natural time, but as grammatical tense, which then is interrupted so that the tense of narration becomes present and conditional. Interruption admits the impossibility of description of the "visionary dreariness / Which, while I looked all round for my lost guide, / Did at that time invest" the landscape (*Prel.* [1799] I, 322–24), and such an admission recalls Wordsworth's fragmentary recognition that what he "deemed that I had adequately cloathed / . . . scarcely had produced / A monument and arbitrary sign" (*Prel.* 495). Interruption, however, has permitted the shift of tense to describe an emotion different from his initial fear. "Visionary dreariness" replaces the unmodified fear and is a mood that cannot be painted and cannot exist in landscape; it can only exist in imagination. Landscape cannot contain, nor can poetry paint, an emotion in the landscape; it is removed from nature, just as Wordsworth has removed it from natural time and placed it in the rhetorical dimension of tense and mood. Interruption then signals a shift from naturalism in time and image to the literary and figurative. It destroys the illusion of realism and the accuracy of narrative and suggests that the narrative itself is a construction of the present.[14]

14. The phrase "visionary dreariness" echoes lines from "The Pedlar" in which the Pedlar measures

> the crag
> Which is the eagle's birth-place; or some peak
> Familiar with forgotten years, which shews,
> Inscrib'd as with the silence of the thought,

The process Wordsworth describes is that of the transformation from the raw fear of the child, who has lost his guide and who comes upon the grave of the murderer, into the "visionary dreariness" that is projected upon the landscape. He repeats the triad of images— the beacon, the girl with the pitcher, and the pool—both before the interruption and after. The first appears in apparent naturalism; the second, invested with the "visionary dreariness" of what Wordsworth claims is the child's search for his guide, detaches the narrative from the specific images and places it in the paradoxical realm of imageless images, in which the emotion is neither blind fear nor melancholy, but the perplexity of strangeness and disorientation. To search for a lost guide and to find instead, at first, ordinary things—a mountain tarn, the Penrith beacon, and a woman—is inexplicably dislocating. These objects are removed from their local habitation and impress the child with vague uncertainty that replaces a fear that has not yet matured into awe.

While Wordsworth struggles to construct an intelligible explanation of the workings of the spots of time, his words imply the struggle he has in composing his texts. The problem is not only one of representation, of the difficulty in finding language to paint what once he was. It is also a problem of being lost in his texts, uncertain of his way, and being faced with the prospect of differing possibilities in constructing a text and investing it with meaning. To invest is, of course, to single out and to confer significance, but here investiture implies two contrary acts: it is a clothing, a granting of meaning, special privilege, and intelligibility, but to associate the moment with special meaning is to dissociate it from the ordinary, to remove it from familiarity and its context within a whole. The first is a process of adding to, and the second is a process of discomposing and disconnecting, a stripping of associations. The images themselves, particularly the "naked pool," seem divested of ordinary meaning and connection one with another, and the child sees them as he sees later sights in Book I, "linking with the spectacle / No body of associated forms" (*Prel.* [1799] I, 405–6). Paradoxically, the investing is a stripping and a paring down, presenting the images in their stark-

---

Upon its bleak and visionary sides,
The history of many a winter storm.

(Butler 169)

"The Pedlar" passage identifies an intelligible sign in a measurable landscape, but *The Prelude*'s phrase turns upon the former one to measure an uncertainty and a dislocation.

est form. Even singling out suggests isolating them from their poetic environment. Yet, too, they are invested with a "visionary dreariness" that promises a reinvestment that must come if they are to possess value. It is as though Wordsworth were, in this episode, interrupting his narrative to push aside the problem of representation to reflect upon his own creative process in establishing a text, a "perfect form."

The following spot of time, the death of his father, repeats the pattern of an obscured prospect and an uncertain way. The child, "feverish, and tired, and restless," waiting impatiently for the horses to take him home for the Christmas holiday, climbs a crag to peer through the mist to try to see the guide coming to meet his brothers and him. At a moment of expectation and search the scene is again etched in his mind, as it was when he saw the Penrith beacon. Again the scene is composed of a triad of images: the "naked wall," "a single sheep," and a hawthorn through which the wind whistled. Landscape foreshadows the solitude to come when he returns home to find his father dying. Before his father's death, the landscape impresses him with its strangeness and seclusion. It almost predicts his father's death and his isolation. An early version of this episode in "The Vale of Esthwaite" juggles actual chronology so that it appears that the child knew of his father's death while he was waiting for the guide to take him home:

> One Evening when the wintry blast
> Through the sharp Hawthorn whistling pass'd
> And the poor flocks, all pinch'd with cold
> Sad-drooping sought the mountain fold
> Long, long, upon yon naked rock
> Alone, I bore the bitter shock;
> Long, long, my swimming eyes did roam
> For little Horse to bear me home,
> To bear me—what avails my tear?
> To sorrow o'er a Father's bier.[15]

The version in *The Prelude* (1799) is as much a revision of the earlier text as it is a childhood recollection. The process of composition is

15. *WPW* 1: 279–80. Mary Moorman has commented on this passage that "it is curious that in his account of the incident in this poem, Wordsworth implies that while waiting for the ponies he already knew of his father's death. . . . This, however, must be inaccurate for the boys always returned home before Christmas. *Prel.* XII, ll. 287–399, gives the correct version" (Moorman, 1: 68 n).

not simply one of recovering the sensations and emotions of childhood but of revising texts by dissociating them from their earlier contexts and of singling out that particular text and stripping it of its previous conventional associations. The "poor flocks, all pinch'd with cold / Sad-drooping," become a "single sheep," "yon naked rock" becomes the "naked wall," and the "sharp Hawthorn" becomes the "one blasted tree." When, about forty lines later, Wordsworth says that as a child he stood viewing nature's beauty with "no body of associated forms," he is being a bit disingenuous. The process of memory in 1799 is not one of trying to recapture the naked simplicity of nature's images but one of stripping away the encrusted associations. Revision as investiture dissociates the scene from the sentimental melancholy of the first version:

> For much it gives my heart relief
> To pay the mighty debt of grief,
> With sighs repeated o'er and o'er,
> I mourn because I mourned no more.
>
> (*WPW* 1: 280)

The contrary act of investiture relocates the passage in the context of the work of 1798–99. While the chronology is more accurate in the second version, and his father died after he returned home, not before, and while this seems to be a return to naked fact and historical accuracy, Wordsworth has made unusual claims for the prescience of landscape in predicting the death. The new significance of landscape as an emblem is that of a "chastisement" and an admonition to temper the "anxiety of hope." His father's death, logically dissociated from the landscape yet placed into it, tempers emotion and humbles hope. Its tempering completes the calming and tranquilizing Wordsworth sought in the earlier episodes by adding a stern moral message. Its tempering also contrasts with the implied liberation of fear and its transformation into "visionary dreariness" of the previous episode; it tempers hope, but importantly does not hold the promise of transformation. His way remains clouded and he is tutored in patience. Spots of time that cloud perspective as these do, that hold imperfectly realized promise, imply a whole or unity that is to be. The obscured prospect of childhood anticipates the obscured prospect of Wordsworth's future poetry. The spots of time point toward a unity that has its foundation in its own writing.

In Part I Wordsworth brought together a number of fragmentary episodes that collectively had indicated to him the difficulty of representing the past as a whole. At first the question seemed to be whether the figures of speech and words, colors, and forms were accurate representations, or whether language could find words to correspond to the life he remembered. As he worked on Part I, however, the texts and their organization demonstrated that the issue of representation became subordinated to the rhetorical problem of repetition, doubling, and revision. In both spots of time, images are repeated, with the narrator's interruption separating them. The differences within the repetitions argue that Wordsworth's doublings do not repeat, and thus they do not attempt simple representation. The text becomes self-generating, and the second term of the repetition often becomes the point of origin for the later text.

Wordsworth's 1800 note to "The Thorn" offers an astute comment on representation and repetition:

> the Reader cannot be too often reminded that Poetry is passion: it is the history or science of feelings; now every man must know that an attempt is rarely made to communicate impassioned feelings without something of an accompanying consciousness of the inadequateness of our own powers, or the deficiencies of language. During such efforts there will be a craving in the mind, and as long as it is unsatisfied the speaker will cling to the same words, or words of the same character. There are also various other reasons why repetition and apparent tautology are frequently beauties of the highest kind. Among the chief of these reasons is the interest which the mind attaches to words, not only as symbols of the passion, but as *things*, active and efficient, which are of themselves the part of the passion. And, further, from a spirit of fondness, exultation, and gratitude, the mind luxuriates in the repetition of words which appear successfully to communicate its feelings. (*WPW* 2: 513)

Repetition, or tautology, is one answer to the deficiencies of language in conveying emotion. The "craving in the mind," the emotion searching for expression, clings "to the same words, or words of the same character." Wordsworth assigns priority to the emotion that is separate from words; the motive for poetry is the emotion forced by the inadequacy of language to search language for expression and to rest in tautology to cover the failure of language itself, a Coleridgean reverberation. Once having realized a rhetoric for emotion, Wordsworth shifts his argument to say that words are not only representative—or as he says, "symbols" of the passion, but *"things."* They are not things in the simple mechanist sense that they are vivid and clear images, transparencies in which both empirical reality and word correspond with perfect symmetry. They are things in themselves independent of the empirical reality and are "active and efficient" in the generation of passion and text. Wordsworth's struggles with his own texts led him to the idea that words not only represent events or incidents that occasion passion but also to the more troublesome idea that words themselves are the motives for poetry because they possess the generating passion. Words usurp the priority of events and themselves embody the passion. The repetition of words and images in the spots of time signals a turn that disrupts the narrative continuity and shifts the origin from events to words themselves.

New Beginnings: Book II of The Prelude *(1799)*

Part I has, in its early drafts, two different moods in its conclusion. With the first, Wordsworth apologizes to Coleridge for dwelling on childhood experiences and assures himself that he will pardon him

> if I am so loth to quit
> Those recollected hours that have the charm
> Of visionary things, and lovely forms
> And sweet sensations, that throw back our life
> And make our infancy a visible scene
> On which the sun is shining.
>
> (*Prel.* [1799] I, 459–64)

He asks pardon for dwelling so long on childhood when he felt Coleridge would have urged him on to work on *The Recluse* and fears that the desire to complete that is a mere "impotent desire." His doubt is expressed more directly in a canceled ending for Part l, which in an intermediate version followed immediately upon the apology to Coleridge:

> Here we pause
> Doubtful; or lingering with a truant heart
> Rarely adventurous studious more of peace
> And soothing quiet which we here have found.—
>
> (Parrish 145)

The doubt as to the future course of the poem is momentarily sub-
dued into inactivity with the absence of a powerful motive for going
on. The "visible scene" of childhood offers tranquillity and excludes
the disturbing or vexing energy. A canceled opening of Part II con-
firms an almost pastoral calm:

> Friend of my heart & Genius we had reach'd
> A small green island which I was well pleased
> To pass not lightly by for though I felt
> Strength unabated yet I seem'd to need
> Thy cheering voice or ere I could pursue
> My voyage, resting else for ever there
>
> (Parrish 145)

However pleasant the imagery of these canceled fragments that
seek repose in the "green island," and however genial the apos-
trophe to Coleridge, Wordsworth rests on the island only to avoid
the "unnavigable depth" in which, in the first part, he had difficulty
locating himself. The canceled beginning of the second part ac-
knowledges the obligation to compose the "loftier song" that Cole-
ridge expected of him. His desire to extend the poem came from his
knowledge, documented in the associated fragments collected in
Part I, that he had not yet constructed a perfect form of the "unnav-
igable depth" of his poem. Insofar as the fragments stood most
clearly as indices of promise, of something about to be, more of the
chronological journey had to be traced. Part II begins with further
examples of episodes of late adolescence, which tend to duplicate
those of childhood. It repeats the characteristics of his youth, exu-
berant physical activity conveyed in three separate episodes of rac-
ing: rowing on Windermere, riding through Furness Abbey, and
racing along the sands, episodes that are introduced in an early
manuscript as the "boisterous race" of youth[16] and in the fair copy
of 1799 as a "round of tumult." These dizzying physical games are
contrasted to the tempering influence of nature and its moral affect.
In the rowing episode, for example:

> our selfishness
> Was mellowed down, and thus the pride of strength
> And the vainglory of superior skill
> Were interfused with objects which subdued

16. Parrish 171. The phrase is in MS. RV (DC MS. 21), which precedes the fair cop-
ies of *The Prelude* (1799).

And tempered them, and gradually produced
A quiet independence of the heart.

(*Prel.* [1799] II, 67–72)

The result here, which is not attained in Part I, is the "self-sufficing power of solitude." To express the calm of adolescence, Wordsworth must revise the portrait of early childhood, characterized in Part I by the child's openness to powerful, haunting impressions and inchoate sublimities. In Part II adolescence is the time of physical activity, similar to that of the time of the first visit to Tintern Abbey, but in Part II he finds the tranquillity he sought before.

As Wordsworth progresses through Part II, the revisions of his view of childhood continue so strikingly that it is as though he were creating a new beginning for the poem. He starts to introduce a new chronological stage of growth in which nature is sought for her own sake and not as the accidental accompaniment of sports or pranks. Then he abruptly discards the strategy of classification for a further revision of the origins of poetic energy. The significant experiences of childhood are now not those high-spirited games of the beginning of Part II or the haunting experiences of Part I—which come, as he says there, at the dawn "of rememberable life"—but moments even earlier, those in which the infant receives the love of its mother. Each successive attempt to characterize childhood is accompanied by an abrupt transition that denies the previous characterization or category by turning from it and so reinforces the fragmentary nature of each new start. Underlying the increasingly fragile narrative fiction of personal growth is a succession of beginnings, moments of great promise and postponed fulfillment, of imperfectly united fragments. Whatever each beginning and each individual lyric effusion may signify about creativity by itself, it takes a wider significance in relation to those other beginnings that it replaces.

Accompanying his misgivings about the very system of chronological classification on which, in part, he has been structuring his poem is his admission that recapturing precise origins in his own life is impossible:

Hard task to analyse a soul, in which
Not only general habits and desires,
But each most obvious and particular thought—
Not in a mystical and idle sense,
But in the words of reason deeply weighed—
Hath no beginning.

(*Prel.* [1799] II, 262–67)

Yet immediately he returns to analyze the relation of the mother to the "infant Babe" to discover a unifying strength in the love that the mother awakens in the child. Her love passes "into his torpid life / Like an awakening breeze." Wordsworth has replaced the natural and correspondent breeze of the "glad preamble" with the breeze of maternal love, and in doing so he revises, not only the "glad preamble," but also "The Eolian Harp." The figure of the breeze indicates that the mother exercises the same providential influence on the child that nature and its intellectual breeze did before. Now the mother, not nature, has priority. Her love, and not nature, provides the ground for a unity in which all objects coalesce. Her influence is returned by the child's affection, which becomes "a virtue which irradiates and exalts / All objects through all intercourse of sense," not a breeze that could become a tempest, but a glory that illuminates nature.

It is curious that Wordsworth's identification of "the first / Poetic spirit of our human life," a few lines further on, is preceded by an admission that the soul has "no beginning." The construction of an origin in the child's relationship to its mother rests on a different order of truth than the episodes supported by individual memory in Part I. In comparison to the more literal portraits of childhood in Part I, the blessed-babe passage is mythical and fictional, and predates memory. Wordsworth's claim to the contrary, "Emphatically such a being lives" ironically raises doubts that it exists in the same way that memory verifies the actuality of the events of childhood. Further, the description of the blessed babe is interrupted by the intrusive negative, which begins "No outcast he, bewildered and depressed." Why, at the very moment when Wordsworth locates the "virtue which irradiates and exalts" does he suddenly turn to the negative to deny a possibility that occurs to him at the very moment of exultation? At first it seems that he denies only to turn to an even more exalted description:

> Along his infant veins are interfused
> The gravitation and the filial bond
> Of Nature that connect him with the world.
> Emphatically such a being lives,
> An inmate of this *active* universe;
> From Nature largely he receives, nor so
> Is satisfied, but largely gives again;
> For feeling has to him imparted strength,
> And—powerful in all sentiments of grief,
> Of exultation, fear and joy—his mind,

Even as an agent of the one great mind,
Creates, creator and receiver both.

(Prel. [1799] II, 292–303)

This passage does not, as Wordsworth himself suggests, offer a strictly literal recovery of the origins of poetic power, but rather it is designed to revise an earlier view of childhood in Part I. The intrusive negative points toward an earlier text. Why would such a doubt arise? Where did it come from? When has the child been viewed as an outcast, "bewildered and depressed?" The phrase refers to the episodes in Part I in which the child is an outcast who is bewildered and depressed. The words are common Wordsworthian terms for stages in life (and in writing) in which the poet has lost his way and is confused. At the soul's "last and lowest ebb" during the French Revolution, when moral questions were unanswerable, he was "Depressed, bewildered thus" *(Prel.* [1850] XI, 321). The winds in the Simplon Pass were "bewildered and forlorn." Wordsworth uses the words to convey a confused and blinded sight. The child haunted by recollection of the mountain striding after him, the child who hears voices in the wind, and the child who flees the site of the gibbet feels that he is an outcast. The pleasant, pastoral nature that surrounded him is replaced by a "blank desertion."

The blessed-babe passage relocates origins in the mother, makes nature secondary, replaces the child's blindness and confusion with irradiated light, and insists that the child is fully at home and accommodated in an *"active* universe." Although Wordsworth now "emphatically" states that the child is an inmate of a sympathetic world and exemplifies our "first / Poetic spirit," this child is a new inhabitant of *The Prelude.* He resides there as much to revise the first portraits of the child in the previous book as to establish a new beginning for the poem. Often in *The Prelude,* to revise is not to delete or cancel but to amplify. Wordsworth attempts to reach his ideal loftier song by a succession of new fragmentary beginnings, which by the nature of his poetic project and by the nature of their placement within a larger context, imply that they too will be revised. A common practice of reading sections of the poem as individual lyric effusions that imply the whole structure or theme or that stand as clear milestones in the progress of his song is inadequate. Wordsworth feared that the part did not imply the whole, and fragmentary beginning revises fragmentary beginning by turning from it, not by incorporating it.

The affirmation of the presence of initiating love concludes with a transition as surprising and intrusive as earlier transitions. Having stated that this virtue that flowed from his mother remains "preeminent till death," he states that

> a trouble came into my mind
> From obscure causes: I was left alone
> Seeking this visible world, nor knowing why.
> The props of my affections were removed,
> And yet the building stood, as if sustained
> By its own spirit. All that I beheld
> Was dear to me, and from this cause it came
> That now to Nature's finer influxes
> My mind lay open. . . .
>
> (*Prel.* [1799] II, 321–29)

Having just offered an alternative to the explanations in Part I of the origins of imagination, Wordsworth circles back to pick up a transition based on the scheme that he had just superceded. Earlier in the book, he had intended to mark a change from boyhood to adolescence. He returns to that distinction and reformulates the transition but links it to the death of his mother. The loss of the "props of my affections" is usually taken to be the death of his mother. If that identification is correct, the crisis of separation is decidedly nontraumatic. He is troubled that it was not traumatic. The crises of separation as presented in Book I were nothing but traumatic. The loss of a guide and father, the eclipse of pastoral nature by the haunting form of the admonishing cliff, were abrupt ruptures that left a terrified child. But the loss of the mother in Part II leads to nature's quickly filling the void and the youth's self-sufficiency and independence.

To fill out the final lines of Part II, Wordsworth included two extended passages from "The Pedlar." The first describes his listening

> to sounds that are
> The ghostly language of the ancient earth
> Or make their dim abode in distant winds.
> Thence did I drink the visionary power.
> I deem not profitless these fleeting moods
> Of shadowy exaltation; not for this,
> That they are kindred to our purer mind
> And intellectual life, but that the soul—
> Remembering how she felt, but what she felt

> Remembering not—retains an obscure sense
> Of possible sublimity. . . .
>
> (*Prel.* [1799] II, 357–67)

This passage deftly translates Wordsworth's earlier concern with the language of nature into the *Prelude* context, in which it supplements his explanation of the workings of memory. Those moments of childhood that are singled out by memory are ones in which a promise of something about to be was inscribed. The second, an even more famous passage, imports a pantheistic notion into the conclusion of *The Prelude* (1799):

> I felt the sentiment of being spread
> O'er all that moves, and all that seemeth still,
> O'er all that, lost beyond the reach of thought
> And human knowledge, to the human eye
> Invisible, yet liveth to the heart
> O'er all that leaps, and runs, and shouts and sings,
> Or beats the gladsome air, o'er all that glides
> Beneath the wave, yea, in the wave itself
> And mighty depth of waters. Wonder not
> If such my transports were, for in all things
> I saw one life and felt that it was joy.
>
> *Prel.* [1799] II, 450–60)

The idea of the One Life attracted Wordsworth in the spring of 1798. Then his best work seemed to express such a philosophy, but here it follows the blessed-babe passage and is placed in Part II, the theme of which is independence and self-sufficiency and which acknowledges

> A plastic power
> Abode with me, a forming hand, at times
> Rebellious, acting in a devious mood,
> A local spirit of its own, at war
> With general tendency, but for the most
> Subservient strictly to the external things
> With which it communed.
>
> (*Prel.* [1799] II, 411–17)

The necessity to incorporate fragments written in 1798 for "The Pedlar" may be a sign of failing inspiration, an inability to generate more lyrics, and a confirmation of the problems with composition that he had acknowledged in the earliest *Prelude* drafts. A more accurate description, however, would see that by importing earlier drafts, Wordsworth is concerned, not only with generating more lyric effusions, but also with composition, the attempt to create an integral text from his fragments. Thus his return to fragments written earlier is not a sign of failing inspiration, but an effort to integrate texts that contribute to an understanding of his growth of imagination, even though the various fragments tend to give a somewhat confused and inconsistent picture of that growth.

The second passage that he incorporated from "The Pedlar" was originally written in the third person and surrounded by no commentary or transitions that would signal its place in the rest of the Pedlar's history. In *The Prelude* it is prefaced by commentary that qualifies its significance:

> My seventeenth year was come,
> And, whether from this habit rooted now
> So deeply in my mind, or from excess
> Of the great social principle of life
> Coercing all things into sympathy,
> To unorganic natures I transferred
> My own enjoyments, or, the power of truth
> Coming in revelation, I conversed
> With things that really are.
>
> (*Prel.* [1799] II, 435–43)

Before he presents the "sentiment of being," he offers doubts about its origin, and, more surprisingly, when he does so, he echoes the earliest version of "Frost at Midnight":

> But still the living spirit in our frame,
> That loves not to behold a lifeless thing,
> Transfuses into all it's own delights
> It's own volition, sometimes with deep faith,
> And sometimes with fantastic playfulness.
>
> (21–25)

In a poem addressed to Coleridge and which begins with a quotation from "Frost at Midnight," Wordsworth concludes with telling allusions to that same poem, which struggles to resolve the "great social principle of life." Wordsworth relies on Coleridge's doubts about the intelligibility of nature's activity, and when he tries to integrate his texts into a poem on his life, he alludes to Coleridge's poem.

Wordsworth's response to Coleridge's encouragement to complete *The Recluse*, the great philosophical poem, was to compose his own life. His first effort, "Tintern Abbey," was formed on the model of Coleridge's "Frost at Midnight," but Coleridge's use of that form argued a discontinuity between the adult's consciousness and the child's reveries. Wordsworth's early *Prelude* drafts confirm the discontinuities by their fragmentary nature. In Germany, Coleridge rested the ground of a life and education on the principle of "*recollective* Consciousness." Yet Wordsworth came to realize that his drafts produced only "memorials," arbitrary signs of a past that cannot be represented. Wordsworth's appropriation of Coleridge's lyric form resulted in the discomposition of that form.

Wordsworth's answer to the problem of the dispersion of fragments was the patient labor on a poem, a text, that he hoped would produce "a function kindred to organic power— / The vital spirit of a perfect form." It is not entirely clear whether he intended to ground the poem of his life on an organic form with its basis in nature, or on a "vital spirit" of his own consciousness, or in the ordering of fragments in "outline and substance" that are the properties of the text. Where does the substance of his poem lie? Ideally, of course, it would be in a unity of nature, consciousness, and poem, but the fragmentary state of recollection, its arbitrary nature, and the collaborative efforts in its production imply that perhaps Wordsworth thought the ground may be the text itself. His fragments state explicitly that the creative inspiration vexes and discomposes his poem and that his scattered fragments hardly hinted at meaning. The implication is that consciousness could not provide the ground for his poem. Since imagination and memory disperse his text, there may be a fundamental incompatibility between consciousness and the text itself. The ground for his text became an ordering of the fragments, a textual, not a psychological or phenomenological, principle. The form that the text of *The Prelude* finally took was lyric and dialogic, reflecting the condition of its generation.

CHAPTER 7

A Farewell to Coleridge:

Grasmere, 1800

THE FINAL LINES of *The Prelude* (1799) bid farewell to Coleridge and allude to "Frost at Midnight":

> Thou, my friend, wast reared
> In the great city, 'mid far other scenes,
> But we by different roads at length have gained
> The self-same bourne. . . .
> . . . .
>   For thou hast sought
> The truth in solitude, and thou art one
> The most intense of Nature's worshippers,
> In many things my brother, chiefly here
> In this my deep devotion. Fare thee well:
> Health and the quiet of a healthful mind
> Attend thee, seeking oft the haunts of men—
> But yet more often living with thyself,
> And for thyself—so haply shall thy days
> Be many, and a blessing to mankind.
>   (*Prel.* [1799] II, 495–98, 505–14)

Coleridge left the Lake Country in November for London to write for Daniel Stuart and the *Morning Post*, where on December 7, 1799, he began a series of articles on the proposed new French constitution in which he examined the apparent enfranchisement of French citizens (*EOT* 1: 31). There is in Wordsworth's farewell and in a letter he wrote to Coleridge shortly after moving into Dove Cottage no hint of any conflict, personal or literary, between the two: "I arrived at Sockburn the day after you quitted it, I scarcely knew whether to be sorry or no that you were no longer there, as it would have been a great pain to me to have parted from you" (*LEY* 274). Coleridge returned to the Lake Country on April 6 and stayed for about a month and again toward the end of June before moving his family into Greta Hall at the end of July. During that summer Coleridge was hard at work preparing copy for the second edition of *Lyrical Ballads*, writing letters, and making fair copies of Wordsworth's poems for the printer. His contributions for the volume faltered. Finally in October it was decided that the second volume would not conclude with "Christabel," which Coleridge had difficulty finishing. Literary disagreements then proliferated. Wordsworth composed his ungenerous note to "The Ancient Mariner" and canceled complimentary lines on Coleridge's poetry that were intended for the preface.[1] In the fall of 1800 Coleridge's visits to Dove Cottage became less and less frequent as he became ill and his friendship with Wordsworth cooled.

Wordsworth's blessing and farewell to Coleridge and his move to Dove Cottage signal a poetic turning away from the poetry that he had been writing under Coleridge's influence. In 1798 Wordsworth was content to publish his poetry with Coleridge's. "Tintern Abbey" relies upon a context of Coleridge's Conversation Poems. *The Prelude* (1799) discomposes that dialogue and the structures that it generated and also seems uncertain of its direction and final form; Wordsworth's prospect is not at all clear. In 1800, settled in Grasmere, he tries to establish a context for his poetry within his own work and to exclude Coleridge's poetry. His work in the past two years had been personal, retrospective, and lyric. With the exception of fragmentary work on "Home at Grasmere," his writing in

1. Marilyn Katz has explained that "there was sharp private disagreement concerning theory from the very beginning, and that this disagreement surfaced in 1800" ("Early Dissent between Wordsworth and Coleridge: The Preface Deletion of October, 1800," *The Wordsworth Circle* 9 [1978]: 50). As I suggest later in this chapter, the second volume of *Lyrical Ballads* may never have been intended as a joint publication or as a book of "lyrical ballads." As early as April 1800, Wordsworth seems to have thought of the volume as his alone. See also John Edwin Wells, "*Lyrical Ballads*, 1800 Cancel Leaves," *Publications of the Modern Language Association of America* 53 (1938): 207–29.

1800 is prospective and narrative. "Hart-Leap Well," "The Broth-
ers," and "Michael" all employ objective narrative. "Home at Gras-
mere" celebrates his return to the Lake Country as though the re-
turn were a fitting conclusion to *The Prelude* (1799), which ended
with a description of his growth to the age of seventeen. The second
part of *The Prelude* (1799) presents the calming of turbulent boy-
hood energy and the exchange of the "boisterous race" of child-
hood for the "calmer pleasures" of adolescence and for the self-suf-
ficiency in the presence of "objects which subdued / And tempered
them, and gradually produced / A quiet independence of the heart"
(70–72). Similarly, the "glad preamble" to *The Prelude* rejoices in a
new-found exaltation of freedom and enfranchisement: "Now I am
free, enfranchised." And he repeats the phrase: "Enough that I am
free, for months to come / May dedicate myself to chosen tasks"
(*Prel.* [1805] I, 9, 33–34). The sequence of work on *The Prelude*, the
"glad preamble," and "Home at Grasmere" presents a pattern from
a separation from nature in childhood to isolation and solitude, to
self-sufficiency, and finally to enfranchisement, freedom, and ma-
turity. Although there is no reason to believe that Wordsworth
thought of his work on "Home at Grasmere" in 1800 as a continua-
tion of his work on *The Prelude*—as drafts for a third book—the
work does form a continuous meditation on his growth and position
as a poet. It attempts to create a ground for his poetry elsewhere
than in his dialogue with Coleridge.

"A Whole without Dependence": "Home at Grasmere"

The earliest manuscripts of "Home at Grasmere" survive from
1806, but Beth Darlington, their editor, identifies almost five
hundred lines that she dates from 1800.[2] Textual evidence indicates

2. Of the dates of composition and the state of the manuscripts, Darlington writes
that manuscripts from 1800 "now lost, must have carried versions of most of lines 1
to 457 of MS. B [1806] . . . and lines 859 to 874 of MS. B. The degree to which this
composition was linked in sequence cannot be determined. Additionally these man-
uscripts may have contained odd fragments later incorporated in MS. B, lines 875 to
958. . . . It is conceivable but unlikely . . . that lines 469 to 859 of MS. B were drafted
in MS. R [1806] at this time" (Darlington 13). Following John Alban Finch ("On the
Dating of *Home at Grasmere*: A New Approach," *WBS* 14–28), Darlington dates the
remainder of MS. B in 1806. Mark Reed concludes that "no occasion can be fixed
prior to mid-1806, on present evidence, when W can have composed the poem in its
basic present form" (*CMY* 659). Jonathan Wordsworth's review of *CMY* argues that

that the sections written in 1800 were probably not composed in a coherent sequence. Like the earlier beginnings of *The Prelude*, the beginnings of "Home at Grasmere" were fragmentary, and in them, as in the "glad preamble," Wordsworth celebrates an enfranchisement grounded in solitude and possession:

> This solitude is mine; the distant thought
> Is fetched out of the heaven in which it was.
> The unappropriated bliss hath found
> An owner, and that owner I am he.
> The Lord of this enjoyment is on Earth
> And in my breast. What wonder if I speak
> With fervour, am exalted with the thought
> Of my possessions, of my genuine wealth
> Inward and outward?

(83–91)

Grasmere, the "majestic, self-sufficing world" (204), this "blissful Eden" (124), is

> A Centre, come from whereso'er you will,
> A Whole without dependence or defect,
> Made for itself and happy in itself,
> Perfect Contentment, Unity entire.

(167–70)

Free and located in Eden, Wordsworth anticipates the poetry to be written, the joy to be experienced. He roams the valley as a new Adam, familiarizing himself with it and, later, writing poems on the "Naming of Places." He portrays himself as the first inhabitant of the valley in possession of "unappropriated bliss." His figure of Eden announces a new beginning rather than an arrival or return from the end of a journey. It fervently proclaims an originality with no source elsewhere and a self-sufficiency that promises to lead to self-generation. The boldness of speculation in the figure of Eden, however, masks an abrupt turn in his mood. The figure of Eden intends to isolate "Home at Grasmere" from association with the dia-

---

much of "Home at Grasmere" has the tone of celebration of 1800, not the more sober and stern tones of the poetry of 1806 ("Secession at Grasmere," *Times Literary Supplement* Mar. 26, 1976: 354–55). Since no manuscript survives from before 1806, I have followed Darlington's more cautious dating and have referred to the 1800 work as fragmentary because of her reluctance to say that the first 457 lines of MS. B were arranged in their present order in 1800. Throughout I have quoted from her reading text of MS. B.

231

logue. The self-reproach of Goslar is behind him. At the end of the first part of *The Prelude* (1799) he admits that "my hope has been that I might fetch / Reproaches from my former years, whose power / May spur me on, in manhood now mature / To honourable toil" (450–53). In Grasmere confidence is seated in his soul, and the fragments that he wrote at the time were, as he said, his "prelusive songs" (273). He now needs no reproaches as he did earlier:

> What if I floated down a pleasant stream
> And now am landed and the motion gone—
> Shall I reprove myself? Ah no, the stream
> Is flowing and will never cease to flow,
> And I shall float upon that stream again.
> By such forgetfulness the soul becomes—
> Words cannot say how beautiful.

(381–87)

"Home at Grasmere" rejoices in the perfection and completeness of the valley, and Wordsworth implies that what is characteristic of the valley will also be characteristic of his poetry, that it will be a "Whole without dependence or defect" and a self-sufficient unity. The "perfect form" that he anticipated in the spring of 1799 now seems to imply that each work is a new beginning without dependence on Coleridge's earlier work. "Home at Grasmere" may almost be read as Wordsworth's declaration of independence from Coleridge. But in several places within "Home at Grasmere" unexpected and intrusive doubts arise which have their origin in previous writing.[3] One instance of self-reproach comes initially from the ungenerous thought that others in the valley have killed the swans that he and Dorothy admired so much. That unworthy thought is dismissed by a continuation of the fiction of Eden and the idea that "they who are dwellers in this holy place / Must needs themselves be hallowed" (366–67). The question "Shall I reprove myself?" (383) refers to his thoughts on the death of the swans, but his answer changes the con-

3. Kenneth R. Johnston has written of "Home at Grasmere" that Wordsworth "fears being 'home at Grasmere' might not be the kind of being, the kind of home, or even the kind of Grasmere he says it is—that it might not be, in short, a glorious return to the one place where Nature and Imagination live together in harmony. But—and this is the force of the argument—that it is all of these things, nevertheless, and triumphantly so." Then in commenting upon the missing swans, Johnston asks, "Who is this man arguing with?" (" 'Home at Grasmere': Reclusive Song," *Studies in Romanticism* 14 [1975]: 5, 7). Johnston's question, rephrased to read, What texts is "Home at Grasmere" arguing with? could be answered, His own and Coleridge's "Reflections on Having Left a Place of Retirement."

text of the question so that it seems to have less to do with the swans and more to do with his meditations on writing. The image of the stream continuing to flow is a confident denial of the failure of inspiration. By such denial the lines call to mind just what they seem to exclude, the doubt and self-reproach of his earlier *Prelude* drafts. Wordsworth's emphatic "Ah, no" (383) functions here as negatives often do in his poetry. It marks a sharp turn away from something that he has earlier written, or Coleridge has written; it carries a heavy intertextual burden.

His troubled retrospective poetry, which earlier had sailed on the "unnavigable depth / Of our departed time" (Parrish 81), turns in 1800 to the confident knowledge that the streams of inspiration will continue to flow. There could hardly be a more dramatic shift from the earlier work than is contained in the lines "By such forgetfulness the soul becomes— / Words cannot say how beautiful." Forgetfulness, which later he calls a "placid sleep," is a forgetting of earlier work. When in 1804 Wordsworth completed "The Immortality Ode," he resumed work on it with the same strategy: "Our birth is but a sleep and a forgetting." As in the blessed-babe passage in Part II of *The Prelude* (1799), Wordsworth in "Home at Grasmere" tries a new beginning, one that is not dependent on other texts, and he hopes that this independence will bring its own perfection, but his optimism is betrayed by the allusiveness of his texts.

Since the mood of "Home at Grasmere" is mainly exalting and his view is prospective, recollection has a smaller role to play than it did when he was trying to write on the Coleridgean model of "Frost at Midnight" and to compose his "loftier song." One of the fragments of 1800, which he later used to begin "Home at Grasmere," records his first visit to the valley in childhood. The lines are remarkable as much for what seems to be missing as for what they say. They are not presented as a spot of time and are not invested with the significance of the childhood passages that he had been composing in the previous two years. They come closer to the portrait of childhood in "Tintern Abbey," which is characterized simply by "glad animal movements." He first saw Grasmere as a spot placed in constant motion by the breeze and clouds and by the play of light on the water, a place of liberty and freedom. He felt at home there "To flit from field to rock, from rock to field, / From shore to island, and from isle to shore . . ." (37–38). Life at Grasmere appeared to him a prospect, an endless joy. There is no extended meditation on a particular moment, no singling out of one episode or scene, and no emotional turn leading to sudden recognition. The recollection is in this instance a forgetting, in the interests of prospective poetry, the greater passions of his earlier lyric effusions. His birth here is truly a forgetting for the purposes of the hope for liberty emparadised in Grasmere.

Much of the work on "Home at Grasmere" in 1800 is similar to the opening recollection of his first visit in that it avoids the intense moments of lyric exaltation. The verse is still deeply personal, but Wordsworth chooses to suppress the lyric episodes that had motivated his early work on *The Prelude*. The visit to Hart-Leap Well is too emblematic and studied to resemble the spontaneous lyric moments of the early *Prelude* drafts, and the birds wheeling over the lake circumscribe, rather than liberate, imagination. It is as though the lyric moments have been left behind or turned from. What remains are meditations upon possible meanings. The meditation that represses former lyric moments nevertheless alludes to them. The valley of Grasmere may be a perfect whole with no dependencies, but the poetry that describes it is not entirely independent of its poetic surroundings. The memory of moments of exaltation is neglected, but the memory of earlier moments of the poetic dialogue is not so easily excluded.

Wordsworth's exaltation is modified by a calculation of a possible loss incurred by his move to Grasmere's solitude, which invokes the poetic texts that it revises:

> And did it cost so much, and did it ask
> Such length of discipline, and could it seem
> An act of courage, and the thing itself
> A conquest?
> . . . .
> But I am safe; yes, one at least is safe;
> What once was deemed so difficult is now
> Smooth, easy, without obstacle; what once
> Did to my blindness seem a sacrifice,
> The same is now a choice of the whole heart.
> If e'er the acceptance of such dower was deemed
> A condescension or a weak indulgence
> To a sick fancy, it is now an act
> Of reason that exultingly aspires.

$$(64-67, 74-82)$$

The banishment of doubt about the values of retirement functions the way his denial of self-reproach functions in his dialogue with his earlier poetry. The dialogue at first seems to refer to his vacillation over the relative values of political involvement and social concern, on the one hand, and the strength of solitude and depth of sublimity on the other. The references seem to be biographical, but they are also importantly textual, referential to earlier attitudes expressed in "Lines Left upon a Seat in a Yew-Tree," written in early 1797 and published in the first volume of *Lyrical Ballads*. It is somewhat curious that at this time, when he had started to compose poems that would appear in the second volume of *Lyrical Ballads*, Wordsworth was writing fragments of "Home at Grasmere" that contained thoughts to contradict or qualify those in the first volume. Solitude is repudiated as an indulgence in "Lines Left upon a Seat in a Yew-Tree," in which youthful vanity, disappointed by the world's neglect of its talents, retires to nurse wounded pride: "On visionary views would fancy feed, / Till his eye streamed with tears" (40–42). To Wordsworth in 1800, retirement was not retreat, not the exchange of worldly expectation for the protective security of self-indulgence; it was the hope that the "noblest Temple" of Grasmere nurtured the best of human nature.

In their dialogic turns and negations, these fragments do not merely refer to his own poetry, as these allusions might suggest. They also allude to Coleridge's poetry and at the same time try to exclude it. The farewell to Coleridge at the end of *The Prelude* (1799) was uttered on the occasion of Coleridge's return to political writing. The isolation of Grasmere must have been obvious. Wordsworth's doubts about retirement were shaped by Coleridge's "Reflections on Having Left a Place of Retirement," written in 1796 on a parallel occasion when Coleridge left a comfortable private paradise for involvement in public affairs. In Coleridge's poem, that paradise is the "Valley of Seclusion," which is the term Wordsworth uses first to describe Grasmere, "this seclusion" (6). Coleridge's is a luxurious, "delicious solitude," where he can indulge "feelings all too delicate for use." Although the Coleridge who resides in this paradise is not the character described in "Lines Left upon a Seat in a Yew-Tree," an example of selfish pride, but rather simply someone passively delighting in nature's abundance, the value of seclusion is similar in the two poems. Wordsworth tries to create a Grasmere that evokes the seclusion of "Tintern Abbey" and the cliffs of the opening verse paragraph which impress thoughts of "more deep seclusion."

Grasmere is the "noblest Temple" (194), and Coleridge sees, across the Bristol Channel, a vision of

Omnipresence! God, methought,
Had built him there a Temple: the whole World
Seem'd *imag'd* in its vast circumference:
No *wish* profan'd my overwhelméd heart.
Blest hour! It was a luxury,—to be!

(37–42)

While Coleridge's landscape mirrors the whole world, Wordsworth's valley is merely self-sufficient. It is exclusionary, almost womblike, a "concave," which he asks to "embrace me then, ye Hills, and close me in" (129). Its solitude is as important for what it excludes as for what it includes. Coleridge's omnipresence includes "seats, and lawns, the Abbey and the wood, / And cots, and hamlets, and faint city-spire." Addressing Grasmere, Wordsworth proclaims:

Thou art pleased,
Pleased with thy crags and woody steeps, thy Lake,
Its one green Island and its winding shores,
The multitude of little rocky hills,
Thy Church and Cottages of mountain stone—
Clustered like stars, some few, but single most,
And lurking dimly in their shy retreats,
Or glancing at each other cheerful looks,
Like separated stars with clouds between.
What want we?

(136–45)

Within Wordsworth's fragments, the answer to his rhetorical question is that nothing is wanted, because everything is present, but in Coleridge's context the question is not rhetorical. What is left out of Wordsworth's inventory is supplied by Coleridge's.

Besides opening to a social world and community that Wordsworth's valley excludes, Coleridge's "Valley of Seclusion" opens away from itself. The skylark in "Reflections on Having Left a Place of Retirement" unites the "Valley of Seclusion" and the mountain from which Coleridge views omnipresence. In flying from the valley to the viewless sky, it shows a way out of seclusion. Bristol's citizen intrudes, but the skylark is "inobtrusive"; the bird is part of the natural scene, yet it points beyond its own naturalism. Wordsworth's waterfowl in the "Home at Grasmere" fragments skirt the limits of the natural world in ever-ascending, intricate flight. They "shape, / Orb after orb, their course, still round and round, / Above the area of the Lake . . ." (292–94), but their flight always returns. Their circling encloses the valley. Coleridge's valley is of primary value only when it has been left behind and remains as an image or reflection of what is to be, not as an enclosing reality. From the time of Wordsworth's first childhood visit to Grasmere, the valley "was the place to me / As beautiful in thought as it had been / When present to my bodily eyes" (44–46), just as the Wye valley remained present in his mind's eye after his first visit. His return to Grasmere, however, makes it a literal paradise, which Coleridge's "Valley of Seclusion" could never be, because to locate it in one particular place would be to regress to its original limitations and to efface the ideal value of reflection.

The sometimes apologetic and doubting and sometimes assured tone of "Home at Grasmere" is determined by Wordsworth's awareness that the fragments would rival Coleridge's poem. The difficulty of his task was that he had to re-form what Coleridge and he had previously rejected. The description of Grasmere argues that the valley is a total world and unique; it mirrors nothing outside itself. The writing about it reveals the opposite. Wordsworth's Grasmere is shaped and defined in comparison to Coleridge's Clevedon and to the Wye valley. If in the early drafts of *The Prelude* one is tempted to wonder whose childhood Wordsworth has in mind, here one is tempted to wonder which valley he is thinking of. The two instances of intertextual reference are different, however. In the *Prelude* drafts Wordsworth borrows from Coleridge in hopes of composing his "loftier song." In "Home at Grasmere" Wordsworth turns from Coleridge's reflection on the valley by negation. But in spite of his denials, the earlier text returns persistently to shape Wordsworth's dialogue with Coleridge and himself.

Perhaps the most telling moment at which Coleridge's valuation of his retirement interrupts Wordsworth's meditations is the point at which he dismisses the thought that the swans were shot:

> I should say unto myself,
> They who are dwellers in this holy place
> Must needs themselves be hallowed. They require
> No benediction from the Stranger's lips,
> For they are blessed already.
>
> (365–69)

Grasmere contains its own blessing and has no need of one from elsewhere. Its present blessing precludes the monitory intrusion

that comes in "Reflections on Having Left a Place of Retirement."
Coleridge's cottage at Clevedon suffers a necessary intrusion from
"Bristowa's citizen":

> he paus'd and look'd
> With a pleased sadness and gaz'd all around,
> Then eye'd our cottage and gaz'd round again,
> And sigh'd, and said, *it was a blessed place.*
> And we *were* bless'd.[4]

The visitor to Clevedon is himself blessed to have his lust for "idle
gold" calmed, but Coleridge himself, ironically, is also blessed by the
intrusion of a citizen of a larger world to remind him of that world.

Again Wordsworth's negatives reveal an intertextual reference.
His "They require / No benediction" points to Coleridge's poem, in
which there is a need for an exchange of blessings. In Grasmere,
Wordsworth occupies the position of both the stranger and the
dweller in the valley and its possessor. Earlier he had compared
himself and Dorothy to the swans: "They strangers, and we stran-
gers; they a pair, / And we a solitary pair like them" (340–41). As a
stranger he is momentarily tempted to bless the inhabitants because
he thinks they need a blessing, but he rejects that role for the role of
the dweller who knows that no blessing is needed. The shift of role
is embodied in the lines following the rejection of the blessing:

> None would give
> The greeting "peace be with you" unto them,
> For peace they have; it cannot but be theirs.
> And mercy and forbearance—nay, not these;
> There is no call for these; that office Love
> Performs and charity beyond the bounds
> Of charity—an overflowing love,
> Not for the creature only, but for all
> Which is around them, love for every thing
> Which in this happy Valley we behold!
>
> (369–78)

With the "we" in the final line, Wordsworth has ceased to speak of
the inhabitants of the valley as "they," because he has rejected the

4. 1797 text with Coleridge's italics (*CPW* 1: 106, app. crit.). Coleridge's lines may
be a borrowing from *An Evening Walk* (1793): "Haply some wretch has ey'd, and call'd
thee bless'd" (242). In *An Evening Walk*, as in "Home at Grasmere," the lines are con-
nected with a portrait of the swans.

role of the stranger himself and has become an inhabitant. In later editions of the final line, he recognized the confusion of roles and changed the "we" to "they."

When Wordsworth plays the role of the inhabitant, the stranger—whose blessing he claims is unnecessary—becomes the voice of Coleridge's citizen and Coleridge's text, the unaccommodated intruder in "Home at Grasmere." Wordsworth dismisses the stranger in his text, not only because his blessing is unnecessary, but also because it brings an admonition that leads Wordsworth to doubt the choice that he has made. The stranger in his text violates the serenity of Grasmere as surely as the child in the *Prelude* drafts troubles the peace around him, and Wordsworth has chosen the position of inhabitant, not intruder. He would prefer that the citizen remain in a world that is to him merely a confusion of ambition and vanity. But the world that the stranger represents and the challenges to the values of seclusion that he brings remain in Wordsworth's drafts of "Home at Grasmere" as persistent doubts that shape his argument.

Even if Wordsworth did not compose a sequence of these fragments in 1800, there is an important relationship among the fragments implied in their rhetoric and their juxtaposition. The continued presence of intrusive doubt is countered by strong affirmation and optimism. The defense against the doubt is an act of enclosure by denial, negation, and abrupt turn. Lines used to begin "Home at Grasmere" imagine the child's first thoughts at entering the valley:

> "What happy fortune were it here to live!
> And if I thought of dying, if a thought
> Of mortal separation could come in
> With paradise before me, here to die."
>
> (9–12)

The stark opposition of paradise and death is unexpected yet characteristic of much of the work on "Home at Grasmere." At first it seems a repetition of "that sweet mood when pleasant thoughts / Bring sad thoughts to the mind" from "Lines written in early spring," written two years before, but the context is quite different. "Home at Grasmere" does not lament, as the earlier poem does, the violation of man by man, with the sanctity of nature remaining unviolated. They rejoice that the greatest happiness is a permanent and unchanging life in Grasmere until death, yet the unavoidable intrusive thought is that the static life is a kind of death. A similar

surprising association of opposites follows shortly after the opening
lines:

> I seemed to feel such liberty was mine,
> Such power and joy; but only for this end:
> To flit from field to rock, from rock to field,
> From shore to island, and from isle to shore. . . .
>
> (35–38)

Childhood liberty, which might well have been a promise of a
greater liberty to come, is quickly limited by Wordsworth's "but only
for this end," the freedom to explore the valley. The association of
death and paradise, and of liberty and limitation, offer strange par-
adoxes. They do not, as they often do, indicate an inclusiveness and
a plenitude, nor do they indicate a set of irreconcilable oppositions
that cancel one another. Their function is to circumscribe and limit
the valley to a "termination and a last retreat" (165). Paradise is re-
duced to pastoral, which contains the tomb inscribed "Et Ego in Ar-
cadia," and the enthusiasm that figured the valley as an Eden is tem-
pered. As in "Religious Musings," lyric exultation must turn toward
its opposite.

A further instance of the oppositions that limit Grasmere's para-
dise comes when the "gates of Spring" open and the water birds'
ceaseless vitality brings to mind the swan's absence. Wordsworth
blames only himself for the intrusive thoughts of death:

> I cannot look upon this favoured Vale
> But that I seem, by harbouring this thought,
> To wrong it, such unworthy recompence
> Imagining, of confidence so pure.
>
> (358–61)

Wordsworth's phrase "unworthy recompence" turns upon the
"abundant recompence" of "Tintern Abbey," which comes with the
sensitivity to hear the "still, sad music of humanity." His thoughts of
death, however, are "unworthy recompence" for the grace and gift
of Grasmere. His reaction is an odd one. In "Tintern Abbey" the
recompense is a substitute of a greater gift for the loss of childhood
exuberance, the natural progression toward maturity and sublim-
ity. The recompense of the "Home at Grasmere" fragments, on the
other hand, is not a process of natural growth, except in the inap-
propriately ironic sense of an ending. Wordsworth's thought of

death is the inappropriate response to a natural scene that presents abundance, an anticipation, perhaps, of the wrongful echo that he will utter two years later in his first writing on "The Immortality Ode," in which his dejection violates the joy of the spring.

Yet it is not altogether inappropriate. Grasmere's abundance limits the omnipresence of "Reflections on Having Left a Place of Retirement," where, as Coleridge gazes over the landscape, "No *wish* profan'd my overwhelméd heart. / Blest hour! It was a luxury,—to be!" (41–42). Coleridge's view at this point in the poem is not of something that will be in the future, a kingdom that will come, but a luxury of the moment. The limitations of abundance in his view over the Bristol Channel are that they stifle desire. When, at the end of his poem, Coleridge rejects solitude, desire is again generated in contemplation of the image of an omnipresence to be. Although Wordsworth's portrait of Grasmere is itself a reduction of Coleridge's landscape of omnipresence, it has the same effect of limiting desire:

> Delightful Valley, habitation fair!
> And to whatever else of outward form
> Can give us inward help, can purify
> And elevate and harmonize and soothe,
> And steal away and for a while deceive
> And lap in pleasing rest, and bear us on
> Without desire in full complacency,
> Contemplating perfection absolute
> And entertained as in a placid sleep.
>
> (389–97)

If desire rests in a "placid sleep," imagination and passion must also rest. Later in *The Prelude* (1805) Wordsworth rejoiced in "something evermore about to be" (VI, 542). When he claims here that all is present and he carries the burden of abundance, it is hard to imagine him singing, as he says here, his "prelusive songs" (273).

A possible exception to omnipresence is contained in the lines about the visit to Hart-Leap Well. There he found "the intimation of the milder day / Which is to come, the fairer world than this" (238–39). The promise of the "fairer world" is granted to him on his way to Grasmere. It is difficult to determine whether the "fairer world" is equivalent to the kingdom that Coleridge hopes will come or whether it refers primarily and literally to Grasmere itself, whether the "this" refers to the "doleful place" of Hart-Leap Well or to this whole world:

> we found
> A promise and an earnest that we twain,
> A pair seceding from the common world,
> Might in that hallowed spot to which our steps
> Were tending, in that individual nook,
> Might even thus early for ourselves secure,
> And in the midst of these unhappy times,
> A portion of the blessedness which love
> And knowledge will, we trust, hereafter give
> To all the Vales of earth and all mankind.
>
> (247–56)

If Grasmere is a portion of a blessedness that the world will later share, a spot that needs no blessing now, it has nothing more to gain. And the irony is that desire may fail, not from despair, but from the embarrassments of abundance.

The description of "full complacency" and the "placid sleep" is immediately preceded by the lines that present the soul's beauty as a creation of forgetfulness. In "Home at Grasmere" forgetfulness is a deliberate strategy of exclusion. The "dreamless sleep" of the skating episode, a tranquillity that follows the frenzied activity of racing, is a promise of tranquillity to come, but when "all was tranquil as a dreamless sleep" (*Prel.* [1805] I, 489), the tranquillity is neither willed nor tendentious. The "placid sleep" brought by nature in Grasmere is of an entirely different nature. It is the sleep of a deception, the acknowledgment of a forgetting that still remembers, not a promise of something to be, but a present that wishes to disown memory but cannot. Although the more optimistic moments in these fragments celebrate an abundance, it is often an abundance circumscribed by exclusion, a security obtained by reduction.

The strong oppositions that arise in the dialogue of "Home at Grasmere" with previous poems and that result in a continuous revision of those poems by exclusion and reduction also operate in the relationships of fragment to fragment or section to section in "Home at Grasmere." The enthusiasm that allows Wordsworth to portray Grasmere as a paradise is tempered. At first the valley seems literally a paradise, but as his enthusiasms increase, so too does his awareness that his description is too hopeful. Nature's purifying and elevating of the soul is at the same time a desired deception that will protect him in a "pleasing rest." The more explicit he becomes about the influence of the valley, the more intrusive doubt leads him to qualify his enthusiasms, but at times even the strategy of reduction is insufficient. He turns upon his own text to question his own defenses, not by reduction or exclusion, but by direct negation:

> But not betrayed by tenderness of mind
> That feared or wholly overlooked the truth
> Did we come hither, with romantic hope
> To find in midst of so much loveliness
> Love, perfect love, of so much majesty
> A like majestic frame of mind in those
> Who here abide, the persons like the place.
>
> (398–404)

Another negative, indicating a revisionary turn, introduces a long section in which he admits the evil of the valley's inhabitants:

> I look for man,
> The common creature of the brotherhood,
> But little differing from the man elsewhere
> For selfishness and envy and revenge,
> Ill neighbourhood—folly that this should be—
> Flattery and double-dealing, strife and wrong.
>
> (433–38)

Acknowledging the inaccuracy of his fictions, he denies at this point that he has been deceived by them, but he said in another section that the comforting presence of nature does deceive. Similarly, if his more realistic view of the inhabitants is correct, they do need the blessing that he had dismissed as unnecessary in another context. Coleridge's stranger resides in Grasmere after all.

The turns within "Home at Grasmere" do not attempt to repress the sections that they turn upon. There is no effort to exclude them, as there is to exclude the previous poems upon which "Home at Grasmere" itself turns. The tempering of enthusiasm that is implied in his collection of fragments is itself a principle of poetic order, and one that Wordsworth used when he structured them, probably in 1806. The principle of structure that he used is remarkably similar to that which Coleridge used in "Religious Musings": an initial enthusiasm that permits extravagant speculation, which must be corrected by a return to the facts of historical and social realities. Coleridge's "But first offences needs must come" in "Religious Musings" is paralleled by Wordsworth's "But not betrayed. . . ." And if Darlington's dating of the writing of "Home at Grasmere" is correct, the 1800 work stops precisely at the point at which Coleridge turned to the historical moment and its realities in "Religious Musings."

"A Simple Song to Thinking Hearts": "Hart-Leap Well"

If the farewell to Coleridge at the end of Part II of *The Prelude* (1799) marks Wordsworth's turning away from the retrospective poetry inspired by Coleridge's poetry, particularly "Frost at Midnight," it also indicates a temporary turning away from personalized lyrics. In the winter of 1799–1800 Wordsworth returned to the narratives of suffering and loss, like "The Ruined Cottage." Over half of the poems published in the second volume of *Lyrical Ballads* were written in Grasmere, and almost all of these describe local settings. The subtitle that he used to categorize some, "Poems on the Naming of Places," might equally well fit all the Grasmere poems in the second volume. A theme that runs through all of them is that of a poet taking stock of his new possessions, a public calculation of the gains that he claimed in the "Home at Grasmere" fragments. Although the second volume includes some of the most famous of Wordsworth's poems, including the Goslar lyrics and the Lucy poems, its organization demonstrates that its primary theme is the record of a poet's finding a home. It opens with "Hart-Leap Well," which records a visit that the Wordsworths made on their way to Grasmere. In fact, there was some indecision as to whether the volume ought to be called *Lyrical Ballads* at all. Coleridge wrote to Southey on about April 10, 1800, that Wordsworth "publishes a second Volume of Lyrical Ballads, & Pastorals" (*STCL* 1: 585), as though the pastoral were a genre as important as the lyrical ballad. The first volume had been published anonymously, but the second was to be published with Wordsworth's name. In the first week of September, Coleridge wrote to William Godwin that "Wordsworth is publishing a second Volume of the Lyrical Ballads—which title is to be dropt, & his 'Poems' substituted (*STCL* 1: 620–21). A few days later, Dorothy confirmed Coleridge's report: "My Brother William is going to publish a second Edition of the Lyrical Ballads with a second volume. He intends to give them the title of 'Poems by W. Wordsworth' . . ." (*LEY* 297). The printer was instructed on October 2 to set up the title page to read "Poems / in two Volumes / By W. Wordsworth" (*LEY* 303). The second volume might well have been entitled "Home at Grasmere," and its Grasmere poems are written with a public voice, rather than a private and lyrical one.

In the Grasmere poems, nature and landscape become significant to Wordsworth because he can attach human meanings and human feelings to Michael's sheepfold, Hart-Leap Well, Emma's Dell, Joanna's Rock, Point Rash-Judgment, and other locations memorialized by his inscriptions. The "Poems on the Naming of Places" give names to locations by associating them with recent events within the Wordsworth circle; the other narratives relate tales or traditions connected with local spots. None of the Grasmere poems is important because it embodies a personal association from his childhood, none is a spot of time, and none is a source of imagination. Locations are important now, not because they reveal the One Life or the "sentiment of being," but because human life has inscribed its record upon the landscape. When Leonard returns to the country graveyard in "The Brothers," he finds the graves unmarked; he has become a stranger to whom the graveyard has no more significance than the neighboring fields. He must be tutored by the priest to read the landscape. Similarly, Wordsworth must become accustomed to reading the otherwise unintelligible signs of human life in Grasmere. Just as Margaret's story in "The Ruined Cottage" renders the roofless cottage a memorial of human life, so the Grasmere poems create a set of narratives that give meaning to the locations in landscape. Shortly after Wordsworth wrote Coleridge in December 1799 telling him that he had begun work on "The Brothers," Coleridge wrote back, "I grieve that 'The Recluse' sleeps" (*STCL* 1: 575).

The first two poems that Wordsworth wrote after moving into Dove Cottage on about December 20, 1799, were "Hart-Leap Well" and "The Brothers." His letter to Coleridge about beginning "The Brothers" was written on December 24, and the Fenwick note to "Hart-Leap Well" recalls that it was written at the same time:

> The first eight stanzas were composed extempore one winter evening in the cottage; when, after having tired myself with labouring at an awkward passage in 'The Brothers', I started with a sudden impulse to this to get rid of the other, and finished it in a day or two. (*WPW* 2: 514)

The "first eight stanzas" simply recount the events of the hunt, the daylong chase that exhausted all horses, dogs, and huntsmen but one, who finds the hart dead after it lept three long bounds down a cliff to a well. The brief narrative contains no commentary on the significance of the event. There is just the vaguest suggestion that at first Wordsworth may have thought of it as a supernatural ballad, because the hunt is described as "not like an earthly race." Within "a day or two" he returned to complete the poem. The huntsman builds a pleasure dome on the spot, and when the Wordsworths arrived at the spot on their trip to Grasmere, nothing remains but several trees and some stone pillars. The shepherd who tells the tale entertains the local superstition that the place is cursed, because none of the animals will drink at the well:

> Some say that here a murder had been done,
> And blood cries out for blood; but, for my part,
> I've guess'd, when I've been sitting in the sun,
> That it was all for that unhappy Hart.[5]

The sequence of composition illustrates Wordsworth's common practice. The first impulse is to write brief narratives or emotionally charged events and then to ponder their significance. The importance of the hart's history, in itself, is not at all clear, so that multiple interpretations must be placed on it. "The Ruined Cottage" and *The Prelude* progress similarly. The shepherd who relates the tale to Wordsworth has his interpretation. Like the narrator of "The Thorn," he dismisses the more sensationalist themes of revenge but still is superstitious about the spot:

> But now here's neither grass nor pleasant shade;
> The sun on drearier hollow never shone:
> So will it be, as I have often said,
> Till trees, and stones, and fountain all are gone.
>
> (157–60)

Wordsworth acknowledges that the location is a waste, but says, "Nature, in due course of time, once more / Shall here put on her beauty and her bloom" (171–72). If nature is granted intentionality, it is so because nature can heal the wounds that man has recorded in it. It restores by forgetfulness that which cannot preserve the memorial of human folly as an admonition to men. In time, time's ruins will pass. Poetry, as written emblems, thus must supply the memorial that would otherwise be obscured by nature's conspiracy with

5. For "Hart-Leap Well" and other poems in *Lyrical Ballads* (1800), I have quoted from the earliest printed texts in *LB*.

time. The permanent memorial resides in verse, not nature, a discordant thought to a reader who has completed the first volume of *Lyrical Ballads* with the sublime notion that nature possesses a permanent language of the sense. The motive for "Hart-Leap Well" as a public poem is the same as that for "The Ruined Cottage" and "Michael": to preserve in a more permanent and human form what nature's generous restoration would efface.

The context for the hart's death and its narrative is, of course, not restricted to "Hart-Leap Well." It is not restricted to the boundaries of the single poem or closed by the last line. Its position as the opening poem in the second volume provides a larger context in both volumes. When the first volume was reprinted in 1800, the final two Poems were "The Ancient Mariner" and "Tintern Abbey." The reader who turned from the reprinted first volume to the second found a new direction in Wordsworth's poetry and a new poetic voice. The visionary who "saw into the life of things" presents himself in "Hart-Leap Well" in a far more modest role:

> The moving accident is not my trade,
> To freeze the blood I have no ready arts;
> 'Tis my delight, alone in summer shade,
> To pipe a simple song to thinking hearts.
>
> (97–100)

James Averill has taken the phrase "moving accident" to refer to fiction and sensationalism that in 1800 Wordsworth wishes to avoid, but it may also refer to his avoidance of the supernatural in Coleridge's "The Ancient Mariner."[6] The line to which Wordsworth ap-

---

6. James Averill discusses the importance of the phrase "moving accident" in *Wordsworth and the Poetry of Human Suffering* (Ithaca: Cornell University Press, 1980). The phrase is present in an early manuscript (MS. B) of "The Ruined Cottage" (1798):

> 'Tis a common tale,
> By moving accidents uncharactered,
> A tale of silent suffering, hardly clothed
> In bodily form, and to the grosser sense
> But ill adapted, scarcely palpable
> To him who does not think.
>
> (290–95)

The repetition of the phrase in the first poem in *Lyrical Ballads* (1800) demonstrates that in 1800, settled in Grasmere, Wordsworth turned his attention back to the narrative poetry of 1797 and 1798.

247

pears to allude, "The Night-mare LIFE-IN-DEATH was she, / Who thicks man's blood with cold," was a later addition; its earlier version stands as Wordsworth's reference: "And she is far liker Death than he; / Her flesh makes the still air cold" (189–90). "Hart-Leap Well" may be read as one of Wordsworth's notes on "The Ancient Mariner," but it is not only one in which he asserts his naturalism in the presence of Coleridge's supernaturalism. Nor is it merely a sign of Wordsworth's amused detachment from the splendid confusion of "The Ancient Mariner," as is much of "Peter Bell." Like the Pedlar, the narrator reposes in "summer shade" to awaken "thinking hearts" to the human history written around them.

The moral of 'Hart-Leap Well" is that suffering will not be allowed to pass unnoticed:

> This beast not unobserv'd by Nature fell,
> His death was mourn'd by sympathy divine.
>
> The Being, that is in the clouds and air,
> That is in the green leaves among the groves,
> Maintains a deep and reverential care
> For them the quiet creatures whom he loves.
> . . . .
> One lesson, Shepherd, let us two divide,
> Taught both by what she shews, and what conceals,
> Never to blend our pleasure or our pride
> With sorrow of the meanest thing that feels.
>
> (163–68, 177–80)

As the narrator's explanation of his modest role alludes to "The Ancient Mariner," so too does the moral point to that of "The Ancient Mariner": "He prayeth well who loveth well, / Both man and bird and beast." The allusion, however, is a little too obvious, a little too carefully placed, to mark either a generous modesty or an incipient egotistical exclusion of the supernatural. While it domesticates "The Ancient Mariner" and recalls the simple faith of an earlier lyrical ballad, "Lines written in early spring," "And 'tis my faith that every flower / Enjoys the air it breathes," it also chooses the simple pieties of conventional consolation over the perplexed sublimities of "Tintern Abbey."

The contrast between the context of the two morals in "Hart-Leap Well" and "The Ancient Mariner" measures the distance between the two narrators and Wordsworth's new, public presentation of himself as a poet. The mariner's moral is powerful because it is totally inadequate to the horrors and trials that he has undergone. He has earned the right to utter a platitude by his personal suffering, and the moral is emotionally significant because it is the one comprehensible message that he can utter, the one statement that he can make to an uncomprehending community that will lessen his alienation. Otherwise he would remain locked within his own nightmare. The moral of "Hart-Leap Well," on the other hand, possesses no such authority. It is an emblem detachable from its illustration, and it is spoken by a kindly but casual observer, not the suffering participant. It recalls "Lines Left upon a Seat in a Yew-Tree," in which the narrator moralized:

> know, that pride,
> Howe'er disguised in its own majesty,
> Is littleness; that he, who feels contempt
> For any living thing, hath faculties
> Which he has never used; that thought with him
> Is in its infancy.
>
> (46–51)

These lines were most likely written before "The Ancient Mariner" (*CEY* 192), and "The Ancient Mariner" is a comment upon them. The mariner's moral and the tale that gives rise to it together argue that ordinary pieties are not sufficient to comprehend the complexities of human life. The moral of "Hart-Leap Well" appears more of a return to "Lines Left upon a Seat in a Yew-Tree" than an answer to "The Ancient Mariner." In their poetic dialogue it is a reverberation of an earlier mode that uses moral emblems similar to those of other poems in the second volume, "The Oak and the Broom" and "The Waterfall and the Eglantine."

In addition to its context in the volumes of *Lyrical Ballads*, "Hart-Leap Well" has another context, the section of "Home at Grasmere" that describes the visit to the well. The suppression of the personalized lyrical and meditative poetry in the second volume is evident in a comparison of the two. The first is the objective, moralized narrative delivered in a public voice. The second is the private and unpublished fragment of the individual promise of tranquillity:

> And when the trance
> Came to us, as we stood by Hart-leap Well—
> The intimation of the milder day

Which is to come, the fairer world than this—
And raised us up, dejected as we were
Among the records of that doleful place
By sorrow for the hunted beast who there
Had yielded up his breath, the awful trance—
The Vision of humanity and of God
The Mourner, God the Sufferer, when the heart
Of his poor Creatures suffers wrongfully—
Both in the sadness and the joy we found
A promise and an earnest that we twain,
A pair seceding from the common world,
Might in that hallowed spot to which our steps
Were tending, in that individual nook,
Might even thus early for ourselves secure,
And in the midst of these unhappy times,
A portion of the blessedness which love
And knowledge will, we trust, hereafter give
To all the Vales of earth and all mankind.

(236–56)

This section of "Home at Grasmere" adds another interpretation of the well to those in "Hart-Leap Well," one that differs significantly from the published poem and which draws more directly upon the poetic dialogue with Coleridge. The trance that comes upon the Wordsworths at the well is a moment of calm in the turbulence of their December journey to Dove Cottage, when trees, showers, and "all things were moved; they round us as we went, / We in the midst of them." This trance is similar to the "trances of the blast" at the end of "Frost at Midnight," which holds such promise for Hartley. Its tranquillity recalls the calm that follows turbulence in many of the *Prelude* episodes. It becomes an "awful trance" because, instead of being merely a moment of calm, it offers a sight of the "Vision of humanity," of suffering that promises blessedness through sympathy. Their dejection "in the midst of these unhappy times" permits them to be fellow sufferers with the hart. Their vision is generated from their own experience, whereas the moral that the narrator of "Hart-Leap Well" offers is derived from no such personal involvement. He is the detached stranger who listens to the shepherd's tale and rejects his superstitious account. He is deliberately dispassionate and resembles the Pedlar who sympathizes with others because he has not suffered himself. The "Home at Grasmere" fragment promotes the more positive moral that "in the sadness and the joy" can be found the promise of a "milder day." Yet, ironically, their trance justifies their separation from "these unhappy times" and their escape to an enclosed paradise. They are a "pair seceding from the common world," to an individual and self-sufficient spot.

Because "Hart-Leap Well" turns so abruptly from "Tintern Abbey" by changing the "language of the sense" into a moral emblem and transforming the role of the speaker from someone who can see "into the life of things" to someone who is a detached moralist, the unfinished and private "Home at Grasmere" fragments are a more natural sequel to "Tintern Abbey." The "Vision of humanity" echoes the "still, sad music of humanity" in "Tintern Abbey," and its promise of a "milder day" echoes Wordsworth's earlier hope for the preservation of his genial spirits. In 1798 Wordsworth's memory of war with France combined with the sublime gloom of landscape to compose his youthful emotion and remove the immediate terrors of war. In 1799 the Wordsworths are at the end of a more determined journey to secede from the "common world." These two similar statements of human sympathy, although they appear in similar sequences of flight and hope and seem to repeat one another, are actually transformed by their contexts. Their uses and their affects vary from context to context. In "Tintern Abbey" the "music of humanity" chastens and subdues youth's exuberance and leads to an imaginative thoughtfulness and to the "sense sublime / Of something far more deeply interfused." The consciousness it brings renders nature's language intelligible. A similar phrase from "The Ruined Cottage," "the secret spirit of humanity" (Butler 75), links pity for Margaret to a spirit that dwells in nature itself. The "Vision of humanity" in "Home at Grasmere" guarantees something quite different, an escape to a sanctuary that excludes suffering and loss by forgetfulness. In "Tintern Abbey" the "music of humanity" mediates the transformation from youth to poetic maturity which will continue to be generative. The "Vision of humanity" announces a perfect repose at the end of a quest, a consolation for the trials of the journey.

Although "Home at Grasmere" makes important changes in the context—and consequently the significance—of phrases from "Tintern Abbey," it is still closer to that poem than is "Hart-Leap Well." The fragment remained unpublished as a part of a longer autobiographical and philosophical poem whose boundaries were highly uncertain in 1800. "Hart-Leap Well" introduces a volume of public poetry, less dependent on Coleridge's encouragement and support and less dependent upon their poetic dialogue. "Hart-Leap Well" and the "Home at Grasmere" fragments are complementary versions of the same episode, but the private, autobiographical, and visionary version is excluded from the volume. "Hart-Leap Well" is thus only apparently independent. The cost of the apparent independence is the temporary suspension of his role as the visionary poet and the assumption of the more modest role of the wise moralist. Wordsworth's calculation of the cost of moving to Grasmere avoids the implications of his changing role as a public poet in 1800.

The dates of composition of "Hart-Leap Well" and the "Home at Grasmere" fragment illustrate further the turn that Wordsworth's poetry took in the winter of 1799–1800. "Hart-Leap Well" was written at the end of December 1799, and the "Home at Grasmere" fragment was probably written in March or April 1800, when Wordsworth began work on the other fragments associated with it. The narrative and its accompanying moral thus preceded the writing of the personal lyric, which accounts in part for the narrative's emblematic quality. The sequence of writing on "Hart-Leap Well" began as simple narrative, perhaps on the model of a German ballad with supernatural overtones, and quickly became a poem that turned away from the thrilling tale and the "moving accident" toward a "simple song to thinking hearts." Finally, months later, when there was a possible context for it in the fragments about his move to Grasmere, he wrote the personal lyric, with its "Vision of humanity."

Although there is, in 1800, a determined effort on Wordsworth's part to create a context in Grasmere which will generate poetry and support his theme of enfranchisement and self-sufficiency, the echoes of his previous dialogue with Coleridge's poetry remain. The isolation and solitude of Grasmere are interrupted by recollections of "Reflections on Having Left a Place of Retirement." To compensate, Wordsworth turns to writing poems of human sympathy, which stand as his answer to the intrusion of a social world. He became both the poet who lived in splendid isolation, sufficient to himself, and a public poet, whose themes were those of human sympathy and love. His task as a poet is both to take possession of the valley, to make its history part of his own by his ability to read the signs of its humanity in landscape, and to make them public, to make them the possessions of all mankind. Both of these tasks were set by their poetic dialogue's having raised the issues before, and both struggle with the issues of the efficacy of human sympathy and

endurance in the face of loss of the significance of signs in land-
scape. Wordsworth's struggle is to become a public poet, confident
of his own possession of individual genius, free from all dependen-
cies, and fully capable of presenting an organized volume of poems
to the public.

"Names and Epitaphs": "The Brothers"

Wordsworth rested his hopes for the second volume of *Lyrical Bal-
lads* on the public themes contained in "The Brothers" and "Mi-
chael." The presentation copy sent to Charles James Fox was accom-
panied by a letter, actually composed by Coleridge but signed by
Wordsworth, in which he assumes the public role as a poet and de-
fines his public utterance: ". . . were I assured that I myself had a
just claim to the title of a Poet, all the dignity being attached to the
word which belongs to it, I do not think that I should have ventured
for that reason to offer these volumes to you: at present it is solely
on account of two poems in the second volume, the one entitled
'The Brothers,' and the other 'Michael,' that I have been embold-
ened to take this liberty." Coleridge states Wordsworth's public and
political purpose in these poems: "In the two Poems, 'The Brothers'
and 'Michael' I have attempted to draw a picture of the domestic af-
fections as I know they exist amongst a class of men who are now
almost confined to the North of England. They are small independ-
ent *proprietors* of land here called statesmen, men of respectable ed-
ucation who daily labour on their own little properties. . . . Their lit-
tle tract of land serves as a kind of permanent rallying point for
their domestic feelings, as a tablet upon which they are written
which makes them objects of memory in a thousand instances when
they would otherwise be forgotten" (*LEY* 313–15). Throughout
John Wordsworth's letters from London from January to April
1801, he reported that "The Brothers" and "Michael" were the most
popular poems among those to whom he showed the volume: "I
cannot express how much everyone that I have seen appears to be
delighted with some *one* of your poems & more particularly the
Brothers."[7]

7. *The Letters of John Wordsworth*, ed. Carl H. Ketcham (Ithaca: Cornell University
Press, 1969) 82. For further reactions to "The Brothers," see 115–16 in the same
work and *LEY* 316.

When Wordsworth turned from the *Prelude* work of 1798 and 1799, the same problems in composition that he had found there were present in composing the 1800 volume. They are reflected in the shifting contexts of individual poems. There was evident uncertainty as to where to place poems and how to weave them into a single volume, as well as problems with the purpose and function of narrative. A note to "The Brothers" explains: "This Poem was intended to be the concluding poem of a series of pastorals, the scene of which was laid among the mountains of Cumberland and Westmoreland. I mention this to apologise for the abruptness with which the poem begins" (*LB* 135). His apology echoes his note to "The Thorn" added in 1800 to the first volume: "This Poem ought to have been preceded by an introductory Poem, which I have been prevented from writing by never having felt myself in a mood when it was probable that I should write it well." If his note was intended to supply the lack of that introductory poem, the poem would have described the narrator's state of mind. Wordsworth then apologizes again: "The Reader will have the kindness to excuse this note as I am sensible that an introductory Poem is necessary to give this Poem its full effect" (*LB* 288). Wordsworth thought of the introductory poem as similar to his description of the Pedlar's character and education, which was written to precede Margaret's story. But it is not certain what Wordsworth may have had in mind, because if "The Brothers" were to conclude a series of pastorals, presumably there would have been other narratives that preceded it to provide a context for it.

The note to "The Brothers" contradicts the decision, made toward the end of July, to have the second volume begin with "The Brothers." The first copy that was sent to the printers had the poems in the following order: "Hart-Leap Well," "There was a Boy," "Ellen Irwin," and the first part of "The Brothers" (*STCL* 1: 611; *LEY* 289). Dorothy requested that "The Brothers" have a separate title page, as though it were to be singled out from those that preceded it. She had mailed her instructions on July 29, although the letter containing the poem could have been copied before that day. Four days before, Coleridge had written to Humphry Davy that "that beautiful Poem, the Brothers . . . must begin the Volume" (*STCL* 1: 611). About August 1, Dorothy, sending the next collection of poems to the printer, repeated Coleridge's instructions: "If the Printing of the second Volume have not commenced, let 'The Brothers' *begin* the Volume—and then the Hart-leap-well, etc. as stated in a former letter. But if the Printing should have commenced follow the old or-der" (*LEY* 290). Evidently there was some uncertainty as to exactly where it was to go; it was to conclude a series of pastorals, to be sin-gled out as a separate poem within a collection, and then it was to begin the volume. Amid all this uncertainty, one thing is clear. Their indecision reflects an awareness that where a poem appears in a vol-ume or collection is significant. Individual narratives, like individual lyric poems, must have a context to make them fully intelligible.

Wordsworth's note to "The Brothers" apologizes for the "abrupt-ness" with which the poem opens and it provided the reviewer in the *Monthly Mirror* the occasion to remark that "there is a studied abruptness in the commencement and termination of several pieces, which makes them assume an appearance of mere frag-ments. Where we meet with a complete poem, like that entitled 'The Brothers,' our gratification is proportionately complete."[8] Appar-ently the abruptness of the opening of "The Brothers" was obvious only to Wordsworth, but the fragmentary nature of other poems, which the reviewer did not name, gave the impression that the vol-ume was composed of fragments. One poem, "The Danish Boy," was titled "A Fragment," and many others, including three of the Lucy poems, carried no titles at all and were separated from the pre-ceding poems only by a double ruled line. Wordsworth's note sug-gests an indifference to the conventional settings of poems in titles, generic groupings, and introductory poems. His more serious con-cern and bafflement with the order of poems reflects, perhaps, Coleridge's thinking in the spring of 1798 on the relationship of the poems in a volume. Coleridge's contribution to the second volume may have been to remind Wordsworth of their earlier idea that in-dividual poems resemble stanzas of a lyric poem, and Wordsworth and his reviewer both suggest this idea by their notice of the poems' abrupt openings. The common and conventional narrative or di-dactic setting for a poem or set of poems was excluded, leaving a space to indicate not only a shift in theme but a change in emotional tonality as well. In this sense, individual poems do not need to be complete integral units but may be fragmentary. A full reading of a poem as a stanza must take into account the poem's placement in its

8. *Monthly Mirror* 11 (June 1801) reprinted in *The Romantics Reviewed: Contemporary Reviews of British Romantic Writers*, Part A: *The Lake Poets*, ed. Donald H. Reiman (New York: Garland, 1972) 2: 687.

context in the volume and must be alert to those unexpected turns in mood and theme.

Organized into a single volume, individual lyrics—or poems of any kind—receive their context from the surrounding poems, of whatever genre. They are not fragments in that they are incomplete, unfinished, or partial representations of a reality outside the texts themselves. They are fragments in that they are parts of a whole that is the sequence itself, the volume, the total canon, and the poetic dialogue with Coleridge. If one common idea of a fragment is that it is the relic of a ruin, fragments mark a creative condition that forever fails to reach a final unity.[9] The opposite idea, that they are parts of a continuing sequence, conceives of them as generative, as beginnings in a continuous process of creativity, even though a goal of final unity may be as unreachable as when they mark failure.

If "The Brothers" is read in comparison with the poems in the second volume that precede it and those written at the same time, its significance becomes clearer by the comparison. It shares with "Hart-Leap Well," the "Home at Grasmere" fragments, and *The Prelude* a pondering of the values of a figurative or literal return to a birthplace. The shepherd who relates the story of the hart thinks that "this water was perhaps the first he drank / When he had wander'd from his mother's side" (151–52). Leonard returns to his birthplace to discover whether his brother is still alive. Their early life is reflected in the twin springs that flow from the mountainside. The blocking of one by the fallen crag parallels the death of Leonard's brother. In both poems the return to a birthplace is accompanied with a death, a theme that is echoed in the "Home at Grasmere" fragments with the disappearance of the swans. Both "Hart-Leap Well" and "The Brothers" commemorate suffering and despair by their association with particular locations, and both evoke sympathy with suffering. In "The Brothers" the reader is poignantly reminded of the power of what Wordsworth called the "domestic affections," the primary ties of family and brotherhood. Read in such a way, the two poems, along with many others in the second volume, constitute variations on the themes of elementary human joy and suffering in rural life.

The concern about the ordering of the poems, however, along

9. Two recent works treat romanticism and ruins: Laurence Goldstein, *Ruins and Empire: The Evolution of a Theme in Augustan and Romantic Literature* (Pittsburgh: University of Pittsburgh Press, 1977), and Thomas McFarland, *Romanticism and the Forms of Ruin* (Princeton: Princeton University Press, 1981).

with the circumstances of composition, suggest that the relationship among them is more involved than their offering separate variations upon common themes. "Hart-Leap Well" and "The Brothers" may be read as one text, one poem standing as a counterstatement to the other. It is impossible to know which sections of "The Brothers" gave Wordsworth the most difficulty and prompted him to turn with a "sudden impulse" to "Hart-Leap Well," but a reading of "Hart-Leap Well" may shed some light on the matter. The motive for "Hart-Leap Well" is to preserve a memorial that time and nature will efface. "The Brothers," on the other hand, leads to an opposite conclusion. When Leonard's worst fears about his brother's death are confirmed, he cannot identify himself to the Priest of Ennerdale. Leonard's only articulate response to the knowledge of James's death is the whispered "My Brother," which the Priest does not hear. Leonard continues conversing with the Priest, refusing his invitation to dinner, but the dialogue between them has come to an end. He cannot articulate his grief, nor identify himself. His final communication with the Priest is a letter that Leonard sends him explaining that "it was from the weakness of his heart, / He had not dared to tell him, who he was" (446–47). Unlike "Hart-Leap Well," in which suffering finally finds a sympathetic voice, "The Brothers" ends in silence. "There was a Boy," untitled as a separate poem in the second volume, was placed between the two poems and anticipates the silence of "The Brothers." The narrator, having related the death of the child, states simply, "I believe, that near his grave / A full half-hour together I have stood, / Mute—for he died when he was ten years old." When Leonard arrives at the unmarked graves in Ennerdale, "He had found / Another grave, near which a full half hour / He had remain'd . . ." (82–84). The final words of the narrator of "The Brothers" offer neither consolation nor hope: "This done, he went on shipboard, and is now / A Seaman, a grey headed Mariner." He implies that human relationships decay. It could be that Wordsworth turned from "The Brothers" to "Hart-Leap Well" because he wanted to turn from that troubling theme.

Most of "The Brothers" is in the form of a dialogue. The narrator offers little interpretation of events; he merely sets the scene. The dialogue does not realize Leonard's hopes in his homecoming, because there is no mutual understanding between the Priest and him. On the contrary, at the moment when Leonard should be recognized, at the point at which he could become a part of that community once again, the bonds of humanity and community are broken because their dialogue fails. In "Hart-Leap Well," dialogue is a progressive refinement of the significance of the spot. In "The Brothers," however, dialogue is a continuing confirmation of the rupture of human relationships. When the Priest first sees Leonard at a distance, he sees only an idle, melancholy sentimentalist indulging his emotion and neglecting his own and the world's business. The Priest sees him as a harmless and somewhat comic intruder, a stranger.

In the Grasmere poems in the second volume, the signs in the landscape are the relics of the human life lived there. In "The Brothers," dialogue fails because Leonard cannot read those signs. From the very outset of the volume, Wordsworth identifies the problem in his accommodation to the valley as the decay of the signs in landscape. Other questions of the proper interpretation of landscape's signs and of their adequacy as memorials of human life are subordinated to the issue of their inevitable decay. Although landscape is the background for human life, it is not the ground of human life; it is merely the setting. The signs are unintelligible to a stranger, and they will be so to future generations of the valley's inhabitants as well. Even the public signs will be lost. They are read as a text by both stranger and inhabitant alike, but their texts are essentially different from, and inferior to, poetic texts. The fragments that are the individual poems attempt to recreate the human passions and hopes for which landscape's signs are inadequate memorials. The poet of "Michael" writes for "the sake / Of youthful Poets, who among these Hills / Will be my second self when I am gone" (37–39).

When Leonard returns after twenty years at sea, rather than making his return public and inquiring after his brother, he goes to the graveyard to find whether there is a grave that could be his brother's. His attempt to read the graves leads him only to confusion, because most are unmarked. His memory fails. He cannot remember whether the grave he contemplates is new or old, just as he could not remember the correct path into the village. When he finds a new grave in the family plot,

> there grew
> Such a confusion in his memory,
> That he began to doubt, and he had hopes
> That he had seen this heap of turf before,
> That it was not another grave, but one
> He had forgotten.[10]

10. Lines 84–89. Frances Ferguson suggests that Leonard's seeking "from the nat-

Nature had altered the landscape:

> He had lost his path,
> As up the vale he came that afternoon,
> Through fields which once had been well known to him.
> And Oh! what joy the recollection now
> Sent to his heart! he lifted up his eyes,
> And looking round he thought that he perceiv'd
> Strange alteration wrought on every side
> Among the woods and fields, and that the rocks,
> And the eternal hills, themselves were chang'd.
>
> (89–97)

The Priest remarks that although changes take place in the valley and in the community, and although the graves are not marked, their memory is preserved in the minds of those who remain. They have no need of memorials or epitaphs; the Priest explains why the "natural graves," as he calls them, are not marked:

> We have no need of names and epitaphs,
> We talk about the dead by our fire-sides.
> And then for our immortal part, *we* want
> No symbols, Sir, to tell us that plain tale:
> The thought of death sits easy on the man
> Who has been born and dies among the mountains.
>
> (179–84)

Leonard recognizes that those who have lived and died in the valley are no less present to the Priest, for he says, "Your dalesmen, then, do in each other's thoughts / Possess a kind of second life" (185–86), which precludes the need for symbols. The Priest is an integral and articulate member of the community. He is the literal presence of its humanity and its past. He claims that they have no need of symbols or epitaphs written on the natural world, that no figuration is necessary, because the community exists as a presence unbroken by departure or death. Since all are present, no writing is necessary. But although he knows the history of the Ewbanks, he cannot recognize Leonard, who has been separated from that community. Leonard is the unrecognized figure, a cypher whom the Priest must categorize as a stranger and tourist. The Leonard he remembers is almost a St.

---

ural landscape an ostensible sign which would quell his fears that his brother is, in fact, dead" is prompted by his associations of his affections with landscape (*Wordsworth: Language as Counter-Spirit* [New Haven: Yale University Press, 1977] 46).

Christopher, "staggering through the fords / Bearing his Brother on his back" (262–63), but his memory blinds him to Leonard's presence. Eventually he has the sensitivity to revise his initial judgment of Leonard as frivolous and insensitive, but even his final judgment is that he is still a stranger.

If the Priest embodies both humanity and simple literalism that has no need of a figurative representation, Leonard embodies a literal knowledge of his past, but his grief over the loss of his brother issues in no self-identification to the Priest. He refuses the Priest's invitation for a meal and continues to be a wanderer. He chooses to be an unintelligible presence because that unintelligibility serves to suppress his grief. He is content to remain a stranger because the valley has become strange to him. Because he has been separated from local and public knowledge by an absence of many years, his knowledge of the community and the landscape has been frozen in a past time, and he cannot be a literalist. When he returns home, he does not seek his brother or any living person; he searches for a symbol or a sign:

> not venturing to inquire
> Tidings of one whom he so dearly lov'd,
> Towards the church-yard he had turn'd aside,
> That, as he knew in what particular spot
> His family were laid, he thence might learn
> If still his Brother liv'd, or to the file
> Another grave was added.
>
> (76–82)

The tragedy of "The Brothers" is, not only that James has died and that Leonard gives up all hope, but also that Leonard cannot rejoin the community and must remain private and unrecognized because he has been separated from it. As a result, Leonard and the Priest cannot conduct a dialogue, because they are forced to use language in different ways. The Priest, only at home as a literalist, consistently mistakes Leonard, and Leonard, who must read the landscape as though it were composed of signs, commonly fails to understand the signs. The Priest mistakes Leonard for a summer tourist who could, like the butterfly, "rapid and gay" (3) fly from spot to spot, or who could, like a picturesque tourist, spend time idly sitting with pencil and notebook. Leonard to him is "that moping son of Idleness" (11) who follows "his fancies by the hour" (107).

Speaking with Leonard before him, the Priest says that if Leonard were to return

> The day would be a very festival,
> And those two bells of ours, which there you see
> Hanging in the open air—but, O good Sir!
> This is sad talk—they'll never sound for him
> Living or dead. . . .
>
> (319–23)

Since the last report about Leonard was that he was made a slave in the East, the Priest assumes that Leonard is dead. Ironically, Leonard is not recognized and is dead to the community before he learns of James's death.

Whenever the Priest speaks figuratively, he mistakes Leonard. Leonard is to him someone who "needs must leave the path / Of the world's business, to go wild alone: / His arms have a perpetual holiday . . ." (103–5). The poignancy of these lines resides in their irony. The Priest sees Leonard as having left the path of profitable business to venture on perpetual holiday, which is literally false. Leonard has not left that path; he has returned "with some small wealth / Acquir'd by traffic in the Indian Isles" (63–64). He has perhaps gone "wild alone," as the Priest says, but not in the sense intended by the Priest. He has not turned from sober industry to careless amusement but has gone into the wild alone on his voyage. The Priest modifies his view of Leonard when Leonard shows genuine emotion at James's grave, and he quickly apologizes for his callous judgment: "Forgive me, Sir: before I spoke to you, / I judg'd you most unkindly" (364–65). But since Leonard gives no indication of his identity, he remains a stranger who cannot receive the blessings of his home.

It is not surprising that the writing of "Hart-Leap Well" should have come with a "sudden impulse" to Wordsworth while he was working on a difficult Passage in "The Brothers." In opposition to "The Brothers," "Hart-Leap Well" offers the consolation that suffering will find a voice; its conclusion is antithetical to that of "The Brothers." In the order of composition, it follows "The Brothers" in conception. It is, in other words, the antistrophe to "The Brothers." In the order of the second volume of *Lyrical Ballads*, however, "The Brothers" becomes the qualifying antistrophe to the final optimism and promise of "Hart-Leap Well." Wordsworth's placing "There was a Boy" between the two poems only makes the turn from "Hart-Leap Well" to the silence that exists at the end of "The Brothers" more obvious. More important, "The Brothers" challenges the assurance of "Hart-Leap Well" that intelligible signs and memorials can create a community of sympathetic hearts. In the statements and counterstatements of the poem printed in 1800, the themes of the volume are established: speaking and silence, the public and the private voices, the articulate and the inarticulate, the literal and the figurative. Can the private voice become public and find a sympathetic audience? Can landscape be read literally or figuratively? Can landscape preserve the traces of humanity? To discuss poems in isolation from their contexts or surrounding poems is to ignore the location that Wordsworth gave them.

In addition, these questions revive within the dialogue of the texts in the 1800 volume the poetic dialogue with Coleridge in the previous years. It is as though Wordsworth's desire to be a self-sufficient poet recognizes that his poetry has its origin in the dialogue with Coleridge and that to lessen his dependence, he must reproduce that dialogue within his own poetry. Leonard's return echoes the mariner's dialogue with the hermit, just as the mariner's return plays upon the sailor's in "Adventures on Salisbury Plain."

"The Public Symbol": "Michael"

"Michael" occupies a unique position among Wordsworth's most famous poems; it was written to fill a specific gap at the end of the second volume of *Lyrical Ballads* created by Coleridge and Wordsworth's decision not to print "Christabel" as the final poem. When they made the decision to omit "Christabel," they began to send copy for the second volume to Biggs and Cottle, the printers, in July. A space in the publication existed for "Michael" before it was written. "Michael" is determined by the definitions of poetry in the preface, the exclusion of "Christabel," and, most important, its relationship to the poems that precede it in the second volume. The Wordsworth circle had consistently linked it with "The Brothers." Wordsworth began work on "Michael" about October 11 and considered it complete by December 9. Dorothy notes that composition was difficult, but work on it generated a great number of lines of poetry. Aside from the 491 lines in the 1800 edition, including the fifteen omitted by the "shameful negligence" of the printer (*LEY* 323), there are over two hundred lines that Ernest de Selincourt printed as notes to the poem (*WPW* 2: 479–84) and another ninety that were finally included in *The Prelude*, Book VIII, commonly called "The Matron's Tale" ([1805] VIII, 222–311). Before "Michael," Wordsworth's creative problem had been to find an intelligible context for his lyric effusions, to give them a meaning by providing a context. Here the situation was the opposite. He had to select, focus, and prune. The standards by which he chose reveal the generation of the poem, not only in the vacant spaces that it was to occupy, but also in the volume that it was to conclude and in the poem that it was to replace.[11]

Some of the blank-verse fragments, that Wordsworth composed for "Michael" identify his views on nature and landscape in 1800:

> For me,
> When it has chanced that having wandered long
> Among the mountains, I have waked at last
> From dream of motion in some spot like this,
> Shut out from man, some region—one of those
> That hold by an inalienable right
> An independent Life, and seem the whole
> Of nature and of unrecorded time;
> If, looking round, I have perchance perceived
> Some vestiges of human hands, some stir
> Of human passion, they to me are sweet
> As lightest sunbreak, or the sudden sound
> Of music to a blind man's ear who sits
> Alone and silent in the summer shade.
> They are as a creation in my heart;
> I look into past times as prophets look
> Into futurity, a [?] of life runs back
> Into dead years, the [?] of thought
> The [   ] spirit of philosophy
> Leads me through moods of sadness to delight.
>
> (*WPW* 2: 479–80)

11. See Parrish, *WBS* 50–69. For a discussion of the composition of "Michael," see Robert S. Woof, "John Stoddart, 'Michael,' and Lyrical Ballads," *Ariel* 1 (April 1970): 7–22; Jonathan Wordsworth, "A Note on the Ballad Version of 'Michael,' " *Ariel* 2 (April 1971): 66–71; Mark Reed, "On the Development of Wordsworth's 'Michael,' " *Ariel* 3 (April 1972): 70–79; and Stephen Parrish, " 'Michael,' Mr Woof, and Mr Wordsworth," *Ariel* 3 (April 1972): 80–83.

Ernest de Selincourt commented that "these lines may have been intended as part of an Introduction to *Michael* . . . or they may be merely an 'Extempore Effusion' on a theme dear to W." (*WPW* 2: 480). Whether or not they were intended to form a part of "Michael," they express Wordsworth's way of looking at landscape at the time that he was writing it. One should not disregard this fragment on the grounds of uncertainty about the author's intention, which is impossible to recover, or on the grounds of concern with determinate boundaries of poems.

The passage begins as though it were going to introduce a visionary or sublime moment for a poet who is isolated from merely human concerns. Wordsworth reposes, after the exertion of thoughtless wandering, in a spot that possesses "by an inalienable right / An independent Life, and seem the whole / Of nature and of unrecorded time." The spot resembles the Grasmere of the "Home at Grasmere" fragments, in which spots of nature are perfect unities in themselves. But the fragment turns from nature's perfection to human imperfection before Wordsworth's mind can be usurped by nature's ministry and influence. His attention is caught, not by nature itself, but by "vestiges of human hands" and "some stir / Of human passion." The signs of human life that remain in the landscape, not the motion of the clouds or the sound of the winds, arrest him and are "as a creation in my heart." His immediate recognition of the meaning of the signs of human life changes what, one or two years before, might have been a nature animated by providential intention to mere landscape, as a background or repository of the signs that human activity has placed there. His prophetic role is, not to celebrate nature devoid of human life, but to find traces of humanity. In the fall of 1800 his prophetic task is to recover, not his own past, but the humanity of those who lived and suffered. With the same purpose, the poet who in the previous spring seceded from the "common world" looked at Hart-Leap Well, the graveyard in Ennerdale, and other signs in the landscape.

The urgency of preserving these signs in the landscape is also as clear in these fragments associated with "Michael" as Wordsworth's choice of a poetic role and use of language. In one, the sheepfold is presented differently than in "Michael":

There is a shapeless crowd of unhewn stones
That lie together, some in heaps, and some
In lines,that seem to keep themselves alive

In the last dotage of a dying form.
At least so seems it to a man who stands
In such a lonely place.

(WPW 2: 482)

The sheepfold possesses a life, to the speaker's eye, but that life is dying. The sign cannot survive in landscape. The signs in landscape are the works, not the words, of mankind, and when they are placed in landscape they perish in nature's destructive renewal. Humanity's traces are almost an alien intrusion upon nature, and although the sheepfold, in this version, seems to have an organic life of its own, it will decay as human life decays, while nature and landscape renew themselves.

A second fragment addresses the same concerns with the presence of signs in landscape with a different hope and a different conclusion. Two travelers, perhaps Michael and Luke or perhaps the father and son of "The Matron's Tale," travel over the fells:

> Thence journeying on a second time they pass'd
> Those small flat stones which, rang'd by
>   Travellers' hands
> In cyphers on Helvellyn's highest ridge,
> Lie loose on the bare turf, some half o'ergrown
> By the grey moss, but not a single stone
> Unsettled by a wanton blow from foot
> Of Shepherd, man or Boy. They have respect
> For strangers who have travell'd far perhaps
> For men who in such places feeling there
> The grandeur of the earth have left inscrib'd
> Their epitaph which rain and snow
> And the strong wind have reverenced.

(WPW 2: 484)

Wordsworth's attraction to humanity's signs in the landscape is as strong here as it is elsewhere in his poetry of 1800, but the tone is somewhat different. The stones formed into cyphers are "half o'ergrown," and one might infer that they are soon to be forgotten, yet at the same time he plays with the fiction that the elements have not disturbed them. He hopes for their persistence, which parallels his hope that his poetry will preserve the significance of the cyphers. The cypher itself is a perfect definition of these signs. The cypher is a sign left by strangers and respected by a local community, although its significance is unknown to them. It raises the question, which is raised in "Michael," of the adequacy of any local community to perpetuate the meanings of signs. As a result, there are in the 1800 volume important distinctions between the public and the private and between that which is immediately known to a community and that which is known to strangers. The cyphers are epitaphs, but only in a particular and unusual sense. The strangers who left them have departed, leaving the cyphers as testimony of their visit, but they are neither dead nor speaking from the grave. The cyphers point, not to the absence of the individuals they represent, but, ironically, to the presence of the natural beauty and grandeur that surrounds the cyphers themselves, and they are reverenced for that reason. These epitaphs point to what is immediately present.

"Michael" opens with Wordsworth's invitation to turn from the "public way" up Green-head Gill to a "hidden valley," an "utter solitude." The object of the turn from the common path is a "straggling heap of unhewn stones," which an ordinary traveler "might see and notice not." The human meaning of the sheepfold has been almost lost, and Wordsworth's purpose is to revitalize it in poetry by telling its tale and to preserve for others the sympathy that nature taught him to feel for "the heart of man and human life." Since the preservation can occur only in verse, the purpose quickly becomes one in which Wordsworth wishes to perpetuate the kind of tales that attach themselves to such objects:

> Therefore, although it be a history
> Homely and rude, I will relate the same
> For the delight of a few natural hearts,
> And with yet fonder feeling, for the sake
> Of youthful Poets, who among these Hills
> Will be my second self when I am gone.

(34–39)

Michael's sheepfold is a private covenant, but other more public signs in the poem have a significance to the entire community. Michael's cottage is the Evening Star, the "public Symbol of the life, / The thrifty Pair had liv'd." Near the cottage is the Clipping Tree, under which the sheep are shorn. But at the end of the poem, Wordsworth remarks that the cottage has disappeared: "the ploughshare has been through the ground / On which it stood" (486–87). The public symbol remains only as long as its living inhabitants are present to make it intelligible. When they are gone, their symbols vanish with them. The recognition of the value and permanence of the signs in landscape is the same as that in "The Brothers," in which Leonard, having been separated from his birthplace, cannot remember their meanings. And it is the same in "The Ruined Cottage," in which the young poet is ignorant of the significance of the cottage, whose meaning is preserved only in the Pedlar's memory. The significance of the Clipping Tree remains only because it is in constant use.

The commonly visible signs in landscape persist only when they point to what is commonly present and when, ironically, they are not needed. They decay when their significance has departed, because nature and landscape do not sustain them. Wordsworth's descriptions of nature's ministry to Michael seem at points to be totally in accord with his treatment of nature in 1798–99. Michael "heard the South / Make subterraneous music, like the noise / Of Bagpipers on distant Highland hills" (50–52). These lines sound almost like a paraphrase of some he drafted in the Alfoxden notebook and later used in Book II of *The Prelude* (1799), in which he describes himself "listening to sounds that are / The ghostly language of the ancient earth" (357–58). The similarities between these two extracts would suggest that Michael himself is similar to the Pedlar, a figure gifted with the ability to read landscape because he has heard nature's ancient language. But the context in "Michael" determines another meaning, one more suited to Michael's character and more in accord with Wordsworth's presentation of landscape in 1800. Nature is not here as a speaking presence but simply as the set of natural conditions under which Michael must labor. Its signs dignify Michael, not itself. The "subterraneous music" is, not a sign of benevolent ministry or a subject of contemplation, but a sign of danger:

> The Shepherd, at such warning, of his flock
> Bethought him, and he to himself would say
> The winds are now devising work for me!
> And truly at all times the storm, that drives
> The Traveller to a shelter, summon'd him
> Up to the mountains. . . .
>
> (53–58)

The ground of the sign's truth does not exist permanently in nature or nature's articulation but in the generative hope of the poems themselves. "Hart-Leap Well," "The Brothers," and "Michael" all begin with the idea that the landscape will change and will not continue to be the dwelling place of human value. Yet "Michael" stands as an epode to the strophe of "Hart-Leap Well" and to the antistrophe of "The Brothers." While it shares the themes of the decay of signs, it offers the positive hope that verse will be the permanent memorial. In "Hart-Leap Well" the narrator's "simple song to thinking hearts" memorializes suffering. "The Brothers" questions both the possibility of a comforting voice issuing from suffering and the simplicity of song. In contrast to the dejection of "The Brothers," "Michael" turns to the strength of love that persists in the face of loss:

> There is a comfort in the strength of love;
> 'Twill make a thing endurable, which else
> Would break the heart:—Old Michael found it so.
>
> (457–59)

Michael's actions express, not melancholy or elegiac despair, but an heroic and stoic constancy. When the decision is made to send Luke to the city to redeem the debt and keep the patrimony secure, Michael has initial doubts that parallel precisely Leonard's reaction to the knowledge of his brother's death. Isabel could see "that all his hopes were gone," and she tells Luke that he must not leave, because "if thou leave thy Father he will die" (308). But Isabel is wrong; when the plans are completed, Michael recovers his optimism. He is able to overcome the loss of his hopes, whereas Leonard is not. After Luke's departure, Michael "as before / Perform'd all kinds of labour for his Sheep, / And for the land his small inheritance" (466–68).

In both "Hart-Leap Well" and "Michael" suffering finds expression in hope, but "Michael" acknowledges what "The Brothers" implicitly suggests: there can be no such thing as a "simple song," and the language of both song and landscape can be a complex matter. "Hart-Leap Well" argued that ultimately a just memorial to the hart's death will be perpetuated. In the context of its own narration, the memorial is appropriate and an important moral insight: "Never to blend our pleasure or our pride / With sorrow of the meanest thing that feels" (179–80). From the perspective of "The Brothers" and "Michael," the moral is naive, because it insists that emotion can be only simple and unmixed. In "Hart-Leap Well" the narrator properly divides sorrow at the hart's death from the pride of the hunter. But "The Brothers" implies that emotions are as complex as the language in which they are expressed, and in "Michael" we miss Wordsworth's point if we do not mix sorrow and pride. We sympathize with Michael's loss at the same time that we take pride in his humanity and strength of love.

At the end of the poem, we view Michael through public eyes:

> 'Tis not forgotten yet
> The pity which was then in every heart
> For the Old Man—and 'tis believ'd by all
> That many and many a day he thither went,
> And never lifted up a single stone.
>
> (471–75)

The final line, the most affecting in the poem and often cited as an example of Wordsworth's adherence to the program of the preface, has been justly praised since Arnold's singling it out: "There is nothing subtle in it, no heightening, no study of poetic style, strictly so called, at all; yet it is expression of the highest and most truly expressive kind."[12] Of course, Arnold is right on the simplicity of its style, but the line in its context has its subtle complexities. Its precise meaning remains unclear. If it means that whenever Michael went to the sheepfold he "never lifted up a single stone," it is wrong, and the public who witness Michael's actions misinterpret them:

> The length of full seven years from time to time
> He at the building of this Sheep-fold wrought,
> And left the work unfinished when he died.
>
> (479–81)

If, on the other hand, it means that although Michael may have worked at the sheepfold occasionally, he often went there and did no work, it is figuratively wrong, because it evokes pity, and Michael is anything but a pitiable man. To the public, the pile of stones indicates his dead hope and dead emotion; to Wordsworth, it indicates his stoic endurance and strength. Wordsworth admires him for his courage certainly as much as he pities his loss. Michael kept the covenant. At best the public has a partial grasp on the private symbol of the sheepfold. Their shortcomings as readers of signs cast doubt on their ability to read either character or landscape. Like the shepherd in "Hart-Leap Well," they have some, but not all, the truth, and like the Priest of Ennerdale, they can read signs when

12. *The Complete Prose Works of Matthew Arnold*, vol. 9, *English Literature and Irish Politics*, ed. R. H. Super (Ann Arbor: University of Michigan Press, 1973) 53.

signs are least needed because their significance is present to them. But their shared symbols cannot endure.

Even to Michael, the sheepfold is a complex sign. It is not a sheepfold but a pile of stones that Michael intended to be a sheepfold. Significantly, Wordsworth defines the sheepfold in negatives. When Michael brings Luke to the pile of stones before he leaves, he asks him to start the building:

> Now, fare thee well—
> When thou return'st, thou in this place wilt see
> A work which is not here, a covenant
> 'Twill be between us. . . .
>
> (422–25)

Michael's words mean that the sheepfold is not complete but that Luke will see it literally complete when he returns. The meaning of this sign, the covenant between Michael and Luke, precedes its literal construction. When Luke departs, the sheepfold is incomplete, a pile of rough stones. Michael's words could also mean that when Luke returns, the covenant will be fulfilled even though the sheepfold may not be literally complete and present. The sheepfold as an intended object is an anchor for Michael's hope. He indicates to Luke that it should be so to him also. In the published version of "Michael," Luke's departure from home separates him, and like Leonard he is lost. Wordsworth spends little time in explaining Luke's fate; it is the mere fact of separation that leads to his loss. When Luke leaves, he takes the "public Way" and is lost. In a short passage originally intended for "Michael" that was used in Book VII of *The Prelude* to describe St. Bartholomew's Fair (*CMY* 90), Wordsworth describes the kind of life in the city that Luke found:

> The slaves unrespited of low pursuits,
> Living amid the same perpetual flow
> Of trivial objects, melted and reduced
> To one identity by differences
> That have no law, no meaning, and no end—
>
> (*Prel.* [1805] VII, 701–5)

Wordsworth's original conception was to contrast the unique and private possession of Michael and Luke that they derived from their patrimony with Luke's being lost amid the utterly meaningless public "flow / Of trivial objects," where there is no significance for him at all. Luke is lost amid a world of signs with no value whatever, but to Michael, signs should be more than bearers of meaning; they are sacred bonds between individuals. Although the literal sign is in fragments and may remain so, Michael vows to fulfill the covenant and continues to love even though Luke breaks the covenant. At its beginning the covenant implied that the fragments of the sheepfold indicate something that was to be, something to be built from the pieces, but when Luke is lost amid a multitude of objects the fragments of the sheepfold are the ruins of a sheepfold that never was, yet they still possess a vitality and strength for Michael.

In "Michael," as in much of the 1800 volume, signs are unstable. The public can neither read them accurately nor preserve them. They are kept in the private passions of their creators. When Michael dies, the public symbols lose their meanings, and the private sign of the pile of stones becomes the fragments of ruin rather than the materials from which the sheepfold is to be created. Private passions are lost with the private life that created and sustained them. Wordsworth's motive is thus to make public and preserve these passions. He tells Michael's story to make it accessible to "a few natural hearts" and to "youthful Poets, who among these Hills / Will be my second self when I am gone," those who can see the figurative and among whom the significance can be published. He writes with a "fonder feeling" for future poets because they are the more competent readers. Although "Michael" is the concluding poem in the volume and although it alludes to the poems that precede it, it is one of Wordsworth's most prospective poems, and it attempts to create its future public.

If "Michael" preserves the intelligibility of natural objects for future generations, it also bequeaths to them the problem of signs. Literally, the sheepfold is a fragment, and its covenant is broken when Luke takes the "public Way" and is "driven at last / To seek a hiding-place beyond the seas," ironically the place of ultimate privacy because it has no meaning. The implied parallel between Michael's covenant and that between Wordsworth and future poets suggests that Wordsworth's might also be broken.[13] The 1800 volume pre-

---

13. Two recent articles have noted the parallel between Michael's covenant and that implied between Wordsworth and future poets. Sydney Lea argues that Wordsworth feared his attempts to transmit the English pastoral to future poets might fail ("Wordsworth and his 'Michael': The Pastor Passes," *English Literary History* 45 [1978]: 55–68). Peter Manning shows that the breaking of the covenant between Michael and Luke implies Wordsworth's fear of discontinuity between youth and maturity and that the purposes of the narrator of "Michael" are to repair that discontinuity (" 'Michael,' Luke, and Wordsworth," *Criticism* 19 [1977]: 195–211).

sents a paradox of language. Public, literal, and natural language is, contrary to the preface, insufficient; it requires the figurative language of poetry to make signs fully intelligible. Yet the passion that sustains the figurative, in "Michael" is private, and Wordsworth implicitly fears that it may not be communicated. His covenant may also be broken. The paradox does not inhibit Wordsworth's creativity; rather, it generates much of the second volume. The fragment and the fragmentary in Wordsworth's poetry and in the poetic dialogue between Wordsworth and Coleridge is often generating rather than inhibiting. Poems do not end in silence but in continuing thought.

1802:

The Dejection Dialogue

SOME of Wordsworth's most optimistic and exulting poetry had been written in the spring of 1800, shortly after he moved into Dove Cottage, but when the gates of spring opened in 1802, the enthusiasm of 1800 had been severely tempered by the struggle he had during the winter of 1801–2 to fulfill the promise of 1800. Perhaps the lyric forms in which he wrote the "Home at Grasmere" fragments permitted or required wild speculation and perhaps his extravagant enthusiasm was more of an expression of his hopes than a sober assessment of his possibilities. At any rate, his prelusive songs ended in silence. The result was a strong disappointment after an intense effort to get on with the major projects of *The Prelude* and *The Recluse*. At the end of December 1801 he attempted to recast the Pedlar material into a coherent whole, and a few days later he took up *The Prelude* with the idea of adding a third book. December saw little accomplished, and during January the Wordsworths were on a visit to the Clarksons in which Wordsworth wrote little, if anything. At the end of January, when they returned, Wordsworth worked on "The Pedlar." Dorothy's journals record the daily difficulty and stress that the work brought. For example, on February 11 she wrote, "William sadly tired and working still at the Pedlar" (*DWJ* 88). James Butler has reconstructed the work that Wordsworth did in February to produce "The Pedlar" (1802), which was presumably completed about mid-February.[1] Later in February Wordsworth turned to "Peter Bell" to produce a version that Dorothy copied, and on March 10 they considered publishing "The Pedlar" with "Peter Bell," as though they were companion poems (*DWJ* 99). When spring arrived in March Wordsworth wrote a number of short poems with a variety of subjects and tones: poems of human sympathy, such as "The Sailor's Mother" and "Alice Fell" along with those of simple fanciful joy, such as "To a Butterfly" and "To a Cuckoo."

Coleridge, who had been in London and Stowey since November, arrived back at Dove Cottage on March 19. The next day Wordsworth read him the most recent version of "The Pedlar." For several years Coleridge had been urging Wordsworth to work on his great philosophical poem, and his arrival must have reminded Wordsworth of the great distance that he still had to travel before that approached completion. Coleridge's reaction to hearing "The Pedlar" on March 20 is not known, but later in the summer he was openly disappointed with Wordsworth's writing shorter poems and neglecting what Coleridge considered his more important project. On July 29 he wrote to Southey that Wordsworth "has written lately a number of Poems (32 in all) some of them of considerable Length / (the longest 160 Lines) the greater number of these to my feelings very excellent Compositions / but here & there a daring Humbleness of Language & Versification, and a strict adherence to matter of fact, even to prolixity, that startled me . . ." (*STCL* 2: 830). The seeds of Coleridge's criticisms of Wordsworth's poetry in the *Biographia* are present here, as are the clear indications that Coleridge had serious disagreements with Wordsworth's theory of poetry in the preface to *Lyrical Ballads*. His attitude was shaped by the fall of 1800, when "Michael" was completed and when, perhaps in a moment of impatience with Wordsworth's poetry in the second volume, Coleridge belittled "Michael" in a letter to Humphry Davy: "Wordsworth has nearly finished the concluding Poem. It is of a mild unimposing character; but full of beauties to those short-necked men who have their hearts sufficiently near their heads— the relative distance of which (according to Citizen Tourdes, the French Translator of Spallanzani) determines the sagacity or stupidity of all Bipeds & Quadrupeds" (*STCL* 1: 649).

1. Butler's account of the construction of "The Pedlar" (1802) is presented in his introduction (Butler 24–30). His transcript of the 1802 work is on pages 327–67.

One week after Coleridge's arrival, Wordsworth wrote "My heart leaps up," and the following day Dorothy wrote in her journal, "At Breakfast Wm wrote part of an ode" (*DWJ* 106), which is generally agreed to be the opening stanzas of "The Immortality Ode." He had once been able to see nature "apparell'd in celestial light," but that ability has been lost, and thoughts of grief come from that loss. His grief is a result of his lack of progress on his major poems. At the same time, there were ample sources of stress in Wordsworth's personal life. At least by February, Wordsworth had decided to marry, and in the week between Coleridge's arrival and the writing of the opening stanzas he had received and answered a letter from Annette Vallon. He was making plans for coming to an understanding with Annette, and financial problems were a constant worry. But, remarkably enough, these personal concerns do not enter into the opening stanzas. In comparison to the presence of the very private and personal concerns in Coleridge's response to the opening stanzas, his verse letter to Sara Hutchinson, there is an absence of personal reference in Wordsworth's stanzas. The subject is exclusively Wordsworth's struggle with his writing in 1802 and the unfulfilled promise of 1800.[2]

The poetry that was produced in the winter of 1801–2 did little to advance Wordsworth's major works. He resumed work on "The

2. In explanation of the dejection in "Resolution and Independence," Mary Moorman suggests that "there can be little doubt that Wordsworth's physical sufferings during the last two or three years . . . were arousing in him fears that he would not be able to continue with his poetic vocation" (1:539). She adds, however, that the spring of 1802 "was a time of lyric creation never again equalled by Wordsworth," that "March to early June 1802 were unsurpassed for the frequency with which poem followed poem, as well as for their quality," and that "the greatest of the poems had been the product of a strong uprising of his power of imaginative recollection" (1: 547–48). Jared Curtis writes that Wordsworth's "anxiety over the unresolved ties with Annette and his concern for the states of mind of Mary and Dorothy temper the picture of a happy Wordsworth so often drawn" and concludes that "the poet's problems, then, ranging in nature from practical but important concerns to a crisis of the imagination, pressed in upon him" (*Wordsworth's Experiments with Tradition: The Lyric Poems of 1802* [Ithaca: Cornell University Press, 1971] 4–5). William Heath identifies Wordsworth's uncertainty and indecision in 1802 as a doubt about the grounds for his poetry: "Notions of beneficial nature seemed to be as illusory as his hopes for becoming a great public poet. In spite of being unable quite to say what it was that kept him going, in spite of the fact that everything that could be *said* seemed to deny any optimism, and all his rhetoric finally amounted to little that could stand the test of analytic reason, Wordsworth obviously felt that somehow his existence and vocation should be justifiable . . ."(*Wordsworth and Coleridge: A Study of Their Literary Relations in 1801–1802* [Oxford: Clarendon Press, 1970] 49).

Pedlar" on December 21, 1801, as Dorothy wrote in her journal: "Wm sate beside me and read the Pedlar, he was in good spirits, and full of hope of what he should do with it" (*DWJ* 70). The following day he "composed a few lines of the Pedlar." The manuscript on which he worked had been written in fair copy in 1799, with the history of the Pedlar as an addendum or overflow material from the story of Margaret. Two of its most important sections had been removed and placed in Part II of *The Prelude*: one passage beginning "In storm and tempest" which describes the "obscure sense / Of possible sublimity" and the other beginning "From Nature and her overflowing soul" and containing lines on the "sentiment of being" and the "one life." Thus when Wordsworth returned to "The Pedlar" at the end of January, it had been seriously reduced by the removal of some of its most exulting lines on nature's life and influence.[3] In July, when Wordsworth turned again to "The Pedlar," Dorothy recorded that the poem had reached 280 lines, of which Professor Butler has been able to reconstruct about 230 (Butler 27). Of those that he reconstructs, only a little over one hundred lines are new. The remaining lines came from earlier work. In a note to *The Excursion*, Wordsworth said that the Pedlar was modeled upon James Patrick, a Scottish pedlar (*WPW* 5: 373–74). The new lines describe the Pedlar's Scottish background, his being a favorite storyteller among the local children, his rigorous religious training, and some particulars about his trade as a pedlar. His name became Drummond, and the new composition serves mainly to remove traces of autobiography from "The Pedlar" and to make the poem into a portrait of one of the residents of the Lake Country such as the second volume of *Lyrical Ballads* was designed to dignify. Nothing was added, however, to compensate for the loss of the lines appropriated for *The Prelude*. "The Pedlar" (1802) is a relatively unimpressive poem in comparison to the work up to that time on *The Prelude* or the original collection of fragments associated with the Pedlar. When he heard it on March 20, Coleridge must have expected more work

---

3. The first, entitled "Fragment" in MS. D (1799), was first drafted in the Alfoxden notebook and later copied in MS. D after the conclusion to "The Ruined Cottage." It was later moved to *The Prelude* (1799) II, 352–71 (Butler 119, 371–72). "From Nature and her overflowing soul" was removed to *The Prelude* (1799) II, 446–64 (Butler 353–55). Other changes were also made, which are described by Jonathan Wordsworth in *The Music of Humanity* (London: Nelson, 1969) 167, and Butler 29. Jonathan Wordsworth's opinion of these changes is clear: "The Pedlar is ruined" (168).

similar to that which he had known, and he must have been disappointed.

Work on *The Prelude* was no more productive. On December 26 Dorothy noted that "Wm wrote part of the poem to Coleridge," and the next day "Mary wrote some lines of the 3d part of Wm's poem" (*DWJ* 74), most likely the third book of *The Prelude*. He worked on the first quarter of the present third book, which, like the work on Part II, incorporates more lines from the Pedlar material of 1799. Jonathan Wordsworth and Stephen Gill believe that "it is virtually certain that the point reached in December 1801 was 1805, III, 167" and that the work represents a decision to bring "his exploration of youth to the culmination that might have been predicted on the basis of *The Pedlar*." Wordsworth concludes the poem "at a more logical place," the Cambridge years of indifference to his studies and private dedication to poetry.[4] Such would have been a natural resting place for *The Prelude* in 1801, since it was intended to be prelusive to the longer philosophical poem and since its subject was to be the maturing of his imagination to the point at which he began to write poetry. Mark Reed, however, takes a more conservative view of the manuscript evidence and concludes, "that the opening of III was the first part of III written deliberately for the autobiographical poem to *STC*, and that the *DWJ* references allude to the earliest such work seem to me assumptions too vulnerable for definite ascription of the lines just mentioned to 25 or 27, possibly 28 Dec 1801" (*CMY* 633). Although the Cambridge years may have been a more logical time to conclude the autobiographical preface to the philosophical poem, the opening lines of Book III do not constitute a convincing conclusion to that work because of the imbalance between the length of the third book and that of the other two and the lack of any explicitly stated conclusion to those lines. The first 167 lines of Book III seem to imply that there is indeed more planned which he did not write in 1801–2.

Thus, much of new work in the winter of 1801-2 was on the portrait of Drummond and the lines on Wordsworth's Cambridge days, perhaps mildly comic and satiric; yet much of his composition was an attempt to revise and to reorder *The Prelude*, "The Pedlar," and "Peter Bell." None of the work seemed to contribute to the growth of either the autobiographical poem or the philosophical

4. Jonathan Wordsworth and Stephen Gill, "The Two-Part *Prelude* of 1798–99," *Journal of English and Germanic Philology* 72 (1973): 524.

poem. In the absence of new inspiration for intense lyric fragments such as prompted his work on *The Prelude* in 1798–99, Wordsworth turned to another process of composition that he knew was essential for perfect form: rearrangement. The difficult work of 1801–2 was devoted to a reordering of material already written, a process that he recognized, two years before, would give intelligibility and purpose to his poetry. But the recasting of existing manuscript material seems not to have provided the inspiration that his earlier ordering of *The Prelude* had provided a little over two years before. There were no new beginnings in intense lyric recollections and no new direction implied in reordering. It is no wonder, then, that when Coleridge and spring arrived in 1802, he should have felt a serious loss and a moment of creative frustration.

"To Me Alone": "The Immortality Ode," I–IV

With all the commentary that surrounds "The Immortality Ode," it is sometimes difficult to keep in mind that the opening stanzas existed by themselves in March and April 1802. In the Fenwick note, Wordsworth said that "two years at least passed between the writing of the four first stanzas and the remaining part" (*WPW* 4: 463). Some work was done on June 17, when Dorothy wrote that "William added a little to the Ode he is writing" (*DWJ* 137), but it is impossible to determine how much Wordsworth wrote then and what Dorothy called "a little." In addition to Wordsworth's late note and Dorothy's contemporary journal, the best evidence for the lines that were written on March 27 is Coleridge's verse letter to Sara Hutchinson of April 4. It contains a good half dozen clear references to the four opening stanzas and perhaps another half dozen allusions to and comments on the images and themes in those stanzas.[5]

5. The relation between Coleridge's "Dejection: An Ode" and Wordsworth's "Immortality Ode" has been recognized and studied for the almost one hundred years since Alfred Ainger published "Coleridge's Ode to Wordsworth," *Macmillan's Magazine* 56 (June 1887): 81–87. An extensive list of the allusions and echoes is contained in Fred Manning Smith's "The Relation of Coleridge's Ode to Wordsworth's Ode," *Publications of the Modern Language Association of America* 50 (1935): 224–34. Smith argues that Wordsworth wrote more than the opening four stanzas before April 4, 1802, for he finds echoes and allusions to Wordsworth's poem up to line 129. In the absence of other external evidence, however, it is difficult to decide, because the later stanzas of Wordsworth's poem may be echoing Coleridge's. Other connections between the two poems are noted in John D. Rea, "Coleridge's Intimations of Immor-

Dorothy refers to the poem as an "Ode," and for years it bore no other title. The familiar title, which dates from 1815, is "Ode. Intimations of Immortality from Recollections of Early Childhood," a ponderous one at best, which modern criticism has by custom agreed to shorten to "Immortality Ode" or "Intimations Ode," or more simply "Great Ode." The earliest extant manuscript, from 1804, has no title, and the first published text in *Poems in Two Volumes* (1807) was entitled simply "Ode."[6] Although we usually think of the motto, "The Child is Father of the Man . . ." as an integral part of the poem, the phrase was not directly connected with the "Ode" until 1815. In 1807 "My heart leaps up" was distanced from the "Ode" and categorized in the section "Moods of My Own Mind." As late as 1809 Wordsworth thought of using the motto to preface the entire selection of poems dealing "with the simplest dawn of the affections or faculties, as the Foresight, or Children gathering flowers, the Pet Lamb, etc. and would ascend in a gradual scale of imagination to Hartley, 'there was a Boy', and it would conclude with the grand ode, 'There was a time', which perhaps might be preceded by We are Seven, if it were not advisable to place that earlier" (*LMY* 1: 334).

The 1804 stanzas, "the remaining part," the later title, and the Fenwick note with its detailed explanation of recollections of childhood conspire to mislead the reader who wishes to consider only the 1802 stanzas by themselves. The 1804 stanzas offer a consolation for loss, but they also offer a new direction for the poem and introduce a myth that is nowhere clearly implied in the opening stanzas. The children in the 1802 lines possess no unusually privileged information, nor do they betray any. They act, as do most children in Wordsworth's poetry, with the "glad animal movements" of "Tintern Abbey." They shout, leap up, pick flowers, and twist greenery into coronals. The first line of the poem, "There was a time," does not place the vision of celestial light specifically in childhood; that location comes in 1804. Supernatural origins of the light are suggested in the word "celestial" and in the ever-obscure line "The Winds come to me from the fields of sleep," but the supernatural

tality from Proclus," *Modern Philology* 26 (1928): 201–13, and in the first publication of the verse letter of "Dejection": Ernest de Selincourt, "Coleridge's 'Dejection: An Ode,'" *Essays and Studies* 22 (1937): 7–25.

6. The early manuscripts are presented and described in Jared Curtis's *Wordsworth's Experiments with Tradition* (145–48, 164–70) and in his edition of *PTV* 361–97. I quote from Curtis's reading texts.

visitation is not located in childhood. Finally, Coleridge's verse letter to Sara Hutchinson makes no clear allusion to or criticism of such a myth of childhood. Had Wordsworth implied such a myth, Coleridge would most likely have commented on it in his verse letter, as he did later in his unfavorable comments in the *Biographia*. In Chapter 22 of the *Biographia*, he quotes lines from stanza VIII on the child as prophet to ask "in what sense can the magnificent attributes, above quoted, be appropriated to a *child*, which would not make them equally suitable to a *bee*, or a *dog*, or a *field of corn*; or even to a ship, or to the wind and waves that propel it? The omnipresent Spirit works equally in *them*, as in the child; and the child is equally unconscious of it as they" (*BL* 2: 140). In the verse letter he boldly questions Wordsworth's nature myth by saying that what we receive from nature we give ourselves, but he has nothing to say about the celestial light prevailing in early childhood, as he most likely would have had if he had read the opening stanzas of the "Ode" as claiming that this special grace was granted solely to children. The references to his own joyous childhood prove only a youthful buoyancy that cannot be permanently grieved. Elsewhere in the letter he refers to the cries of a child who has lost its mother and to his own "Angel Children," who bring him pain. None of these references affirm or deny a myth of visionary childhood. Coleridge's verse letter does not read Wordsworth's opening stanzas as an exploration of an origination myth.

One piece of surrounding text for the later "Ode" is significant both for Wordsworth's 1802 work on the poem and for his earliest work on *The Prelude*. The epigraph for the 1807 text, "paulo majora canamus," "let us sing a nobler song," comes from Virgil's Fourth Eclogue, which announces the miraculous birth of a child whose coming will restore the golden age, a poem traditionally taken to be a pagan foreshadowing of Christ's birth.[7] It is thus an appropriate epigraph for the later text, but it also applies in a different way to the 1802 work if its translation is slightly altered to "let us sing a loftier song." Wordsworth had used the phrase "loftier song" in his 1798 work on *The Prelude*; he denies that while he is tracing the influence of external nature on his mind he will

7. For an examination of the relationships between Virgil's and Wordsworth's poems see Peter Manning's "Wordsworth's Intimations Ode and its Epigraphs," *Journal of English and Germanic Philology* 82 (1983): 526–40.

Forget what might demand a loftier song
How oft the eternal spirit, he that has
His life in unimaginable things
And he who painting what he is in all
The visible imagery of all the worlds
Is yet apparent chiefly as the soul
Of our first sympathies.

(Parrish 126)

In 1798 the phrase may refer to Wordsworth's projected *Recluse*, but if the following lines hint at its subject matter, *The Recluse* appears suspiciously like Coleridge's Conversation Poems. In 1802 the phrase "loftier song," or "nobler song," has a similar meaning. Wordsworth's writing turns from the composition of short pastoral poems to a more serious subject, not the "loftier song" of four years before, but to an explanation as to why he has not been able to get on with that "loftier song" that Coleridge expected him to write.

Dorothy's reference on March 27 to these lines, so long left fragmentary, as an "Ode" is curious. Her usual references are to poems by their subject, but Wordsworth thought of the poem as an ode from its very inception, as a "loftier" song than those he had been writing. His manuscripts usually tell us an entirely different story of the genesis of poems from fragments that are moved from context to context, changing their purposes. But he seems never to have wavered from considering this poem an ode even before its structure was clear or its conclusion evident. Why, at this point in his career, should he turn to the ode?

Each of the first four stanzas turns with an abrupt transition. The first turns from the phrase "There was a time" to "It is not now," in which the turn is implied in the opening phrase. To define a time that was is to distinguish it immediately from the present, and to evoke it in memory is to acknowledge its distance. "It is not now" comes as the anticipated moment whose arrival is nevertheless suddenly depressing. The second stanza turns with a more conventional signal: "The Rainbow comes and goes . . . But yet I know . . ." The rainbow may or may not be an allusion to "My heart leaps up," written the previous day, but its range of reference is wider than the scope of that effusion and the covenant of Genesis. The sign of the rainbow accompanies Ezekiel's vision and calling, and it overarches the throne of judgment in Revelation. From the vanished past of the first stanza, Wordsworth has turned to the transient present and empty beauty of the second stanza. The passing rainbow signals only a past glory. Although the "sunshine is a glorious birth," it is an image inadequate to represent the glory that has past. Naked singleness render rainbow, rose, moon, water, stars, and sunshine lifeless signs of remembered glory. The turn in "But yet I know" separates past from present and nature invested with celestial light from nature that is merely memorial. The blindness implied by the phrase "Turn wheresoe'er I may'" in the first stanza is borne out in the second, because the turns function differently here than they do in conventional lyrics. In the sonnet or ode, they often mark a progress and indicate the way toward, or announce, a conclusion or consolation. While they seem to divide, they unify, returning to their beginnings at the same time that they resolve initial complications. The turns in the first two stanzas do not unify, but divide. They create a gap, a vacancy between Wordsworth's past and his present.[8]

The second stanza laments the inadequate representation of a lost glory, and the third and fourth stanzas announce that the loss is "To me alone." His mood is a false echo of spring because it is an opposite and discordant one. His plight is deeply individual, in contrast to the generalized note of consolation in the 1804 stanzas. The abrupt turn of mood early in the third stanza separates the poet from the festive community of May celebration: "To me alone there came a thought of grief: / A timely utterance gave that thought relief." Coleridge's counterstatement in the verse letter provides the best gloss on Wordsworth's meaning:

> A Grief without a pang, void, dark, & drear,
> A stifling, drowsy, unimpassion'd Grief
> That finds no natural Outlet, no Relief
>   In word, or sigh, or tear.

(STCL 2: 790)

Wordsworth's "timely utterance" is rich in reference, while Coleridge's is quite specific. Using the same rhymes, Coleridge complains of having "no natural Outlet" in expression. Wordsworth's "timely utterance" is a "natural Outlet" that lends strength for a while. The "thought of grief" resulting from discontinuity becomes,

8. Frances Ferguson sees Wordsworth's "Ode" as confronting the discontinuities in memory, metaphysics, and logic (*Wordsworth: Language as Counter-Spirit* [New Haven: Yale University Press, 1977] 96–125).

for Wordsworth, a willed joy, a turn of mood compressed between the words "grief" and "relief" and unmarked by any conventional signs of a turn. Nature becomes the echoing fields of joy, and he hears the tumult of natural activity. The stanza's final utterance is the encouragement to the child: "Thou Child of Joy / Shout round me, let me hear thy shouts thou happy Shepherd Boy!" These lines are Wordsworth's true, as opposed to false, echo of the jollity of May. Half gleeful celebration and half blessing, they mark a turning outward, the first public utterance in the poem and an utterance that is in harmony with the festival and thus timely, a reversal of the lament earlier in the stanza, "To me alone." His "timely utterance" is his public statement that reverses his private grief, and it is an echo of the joyous celebration of childhood and nature.[9]

The fourth stanza continues the formalities of public utterance: "Ye blessed Creatures, I have heard the call / Ye to each other make . . . ," but his formal apostrophe ends with the line "I hear, I hear, with joy I hear!" Had the stanza concluded with this line, Wordsworth would have written an ode of four irregular stanzas that would have been extraordinarily Coleridgean in theme and structure. The melancholy knowledge that the poet is isolated in nature and secluded from his own past is partially relieved by an outward turning and a blessing upon others similar to the mariner's blessing of the water snakes or Coleridge's blessings in the Conversation Poems. But the fourth stanza turns also, more abruptly than any of the previous stanzas, to his private voice that repeats his sense of loss: "But there's a Tree," a phrase that echoes "There was a time" and returns to the elegiac tone of the beginning. Spring renewal is celebrated, but personal grief returns with images of singleness, previously anticipated in "To me alone."

The first four stanzas are, in the spring of 1802, an irruption of doubt and an interruption of the joyous pastorals that he had been

9. Many critics have assumed that the "timely utterance" is the short poem "My heart leaps up," the last three lines of which preface the later poem. Lionel Trilling takes it to refer to "Resolution and Independence" (*The Liberal Imagination* [New York: Viking Press, 1950] 138–41). Geoffrey Hartman suggests that the utterance is a responsive echo of joy (*Wordsworth's Poetry, 1787–1814* [New Haven: Yale University Press, 1964] 275). Jared Curtis's edition of *PTV* suggests that when the first extant manuscript was prepared in 1804 for Coleridge to take to Malta the phrase "Child of Joy" was uttered by a shepherd, not the poet (362–63) and was corrected to final form on the fair copy. Thus, originally the lines may not have contained the explicit outward blessing in 1802 that they did later. However, the gesture of blessing is clearly present in the following lines.

writing. The lament that "There was a time" contradicts the simple and untroubled pleasure of "To a Cuckoo," in which he recollects childhood:

> And I can listen to thee yet;
> Can lie upon the plain
> And listen, till I do beget
> That golden time again.
>
> (*PTV* 215)

The opening stanzas seem to have no textual precedent for doubt and seem to be a new beginning. But they do have specific reference to the work done in 1799 and 1800, specifically *The Prelude* (1799) and the "Home at Grasmere" fragments. The time of "There was a time" was not specifically childhood, which in 1802 was not clearly identified as the time of the presence of the glorious light. The time was the period of great productivity and optimism two years before, and the opening stanzas allude directly to the poetry written then, a time of mature achievement and greater promise. The opening stanzas originate in that work because they turn from it. *The Prelude* (1799) and the "Home at Grasmere" fragments precede the opening stanzas as the hopeful and perhaps highly speculative strophe to the elegiac tone of the first stanzas. The totality of Wordsworth's previous writing, not just that done in the spring of 1802, provides the context in which the opening stanzas have their full significance. The time that they acknowledge has passed is a time of meaningful and responsive utterance, not the inarticulate experiences of early life. Childhood has no text and creates no text. The precedent of a time in which a significant utterance is difficult or impossible must itself be a time in which sublime utterance came without difficulty. Perhaps one of the reasons that Wordsworth did not continue "Home at Grasmere" until 1806, after the "Ode" was completed in 1804, was that the beginning of the "Ode" doubted the claims of the "Home at Grasmere" fragments by suggesting that Grasmere might not, after all, realize its promise.

The beginning of the "Ode" acknowledges a blindness that prevents an appropriate echoing utterance to joyous spring, but a light had been visible to him in *The Prelude* (1799). *The Prelude*, in December 1801, ended with a passage, composed in 1798, in which a celestial light has been and is present:

                    I had an eye
Which in my strongest workings evermore
Was looking for the shades of difference
As they lie hid in all exterior forms,
Near or remote, minute or vast—an eye
Which from a stone, a tree, a withered leaf,
To the broad ocean and the azure heavens
Spangled with kindred multitudes of stars,
Could find no surface where its power might sleep. . . .
                    (*Prel.* [1805] III, 156–64)

If these were in fact the final lines added to *The Prelude* in December 1801, then the opening of the "Ode" is a denial that the past of "saw" and "had an eye" is the present "see" and "have an eye." One further passage emphasizes the assurance of his power of sight in 1799:

                    A plastic power
Abode with me, a forming hand, at times
Rebellious, acting in a devious mood,
A local spirit of its own, at war
With general tendency, but for the most
Subservient strictly to the external things
With which it communed. An auxiliar light
Came from my mind, which on the setting sun
Bestowed new splendour. . . .
                    (*Prel.* [1799] II, 411–19)

In 1799 the light and the splendor are not only present but are at times the product of the eye itself, but in 1802 the blind eye cannot create.

The first stanzas of the "Ode" turn even more dramatically upon the "Home at Grasmere" fragments. Almost all of the major statements in the "Ode" are reversals of the affirmations in the earlier fragments. The beginning of the "Home at Grasmere" fragments claims that after the first visit to Grasmere the valley was

                    to me
As beautiful in thought as it had been
When present to my bodily eyes; a haunt
Of my affections, oftentimes in joy
A brighter joy, in sorrow (but of that
I have known little), in such gloom, at least,

Such damp of the gay mind as stood to me
In place of sorrow, 'twas a gleam of light.

(44–51)

The "Home at Grasmere" fragments rejoice that the "gleam of light" is present, while the "Ode" laments its absence. That light permits Wordsworth a calculation of his blessings which precludes such consolation as the later 1804 stanzas of the "Ode" provide in the recollection of a childhood that was far richer than maturity:

> What wonder if I speak
> With fervour, am exalted with the thought
> Of my possessions, of my genuine wealth
> Inward and outward? What I keep have gained,
> Shall gain, must gain, if sound be my belief
> From past and present rightly understood
> That in my day of childhood I was less
> The mind of Nature, less, take all in all,
> Whatever may be lost, than I am now.

(88–96)

If there is an underlying anxiety in this passage, it is prospective, not retrospective. His "Shall gain, must gain" expresses an urgency that the "now," the moment of renewed promise, will not pass unfulfilled. The model of personal growth of "Tintern Abbey," which places the insight into the "life of things" in the present, still predominates in 1800 as an ideal model and as a rhetorical strategy for shaping lyric moments. The first stanzas of the "Ode," however, lament that a time existed in comparison to which the present is blind and unable to see what it has been. The present, in 1802, does not justify the promise of 1800.

Both the "Ode" and the "Home at Grasmere" fragments have their spring ceremony of joy. The Wordsworths suffered two or three bitterly cold months in the winter of 1799–1800 before

> the gates of Spring
> Are opened; churlish Winter hath given leave
> That she should entertain for this one day,
> Perhaps for many genial days to come,
> His guests and make them happy.

(277–81)

Coleridge may have had this passage in mind when in the letter version of "Dejection" he reverses the succession of the seasons with the descent of the winter storm into the April garden at Greta Hall. In the "Home at Grasmere" fragments, the spring festival is celebrated by the water birds' continuous and joyous flight. In his spirit Wordsworth joins their jubilation: "They show their pleasure, and shall I do less? / Happier of happy though I be, like them / I cannot take possession of the sky" (286–88). He concludes:

> Spring! for this day belongs to thee, rejoice!
> Not upon me alone hath been bestowed—
> Me, blessed with many onward-looking thoughts—
> The sunshine and the mild air.
>
> (315–18)

In the opening stanzas many reversals take place. In 1800 Wordsworth is joyous, but in 1802 his grief is out of tune with the season. In 1800 he finds himself among a natural company who all share the blessings of the season, but in 1802 the earlier "Not upon me alone" has become "To me alone there came a thought of grief." The reversal of the phrase indicates clearly that the lines of 1802 were written, not only with "Home at Grasmere" in mind, but also with the purpose of admitting that its optimism has not been realized. The blessings of "onward-looking thoughts' become the retrospective thoughts of grief, and the blessing received in 1800 turns to the blessing bestowed upon the "happy Shepherd Boy" in 1802. When the gates of spring open in 1802, Wordsworth cannot rejoice as he did in 1800.

There is one further piece of writing that is relevant to the first stanzas of the "Ode" and that makes explicit the loss that Wordsworth felt at the end of March. The additional paragraphs that Wordsworth added to the preface to *Lyrical Ballads* (1802) to answer the question "What is a Poet?" were most likely written in February or March (*CMY* 139). In those paragraphs Wordsworth argues that the poet is

> a man pleased with his own passions and volitions, and who rejoices more than other men in the spirit of life that is in him; delighting to contemplate similar volitions and passions as manifested in the goings-on of the Universe, and habitually impelled to create them where he does not find them. To these qualities he has added a disposition to be

affected more than other men by absent things as if they were present.
(*Prose* 1: 138)

At the end of the additions to the preface, Wordsworth says that "the sum of what was said is, that the Poet is chiefly distinguished from other men by a greater promptness to think and feel without immediate external excitement, and a greater power in expressing such thoughts and feelings as are produced in him in that manner" (*Prose* 1: 142). W.J.B. Owen has remarked that these additions reflect an aesthetic more expressionistic than the original preface of 1800.[10] The close connection between the writing of the additions to the preface and the opening stanzas suggests that the "spirit of life" that Wordsworth attributed to the poet in his prose writing he doubted in his poetry. The poet's job is to create what he does not have and cannot find, but the opening stanzas, by implication, deny that he can create what he does not see.

If work on the "Ode" ended in the spring of 1802 with the question "Whither is fled the visionary gleam? / Where is it now, the glory and the dream?" then the sense of loss announced in the first line is repeated in the final question. Wordsworth's exploration of his creative situation has moved from an indefinite past to the present and from a private lament to a public blessing, but in its abrupt turns it has consistently presented discontinuities and left gaps between past and present, and between public and private voices. His choice of the form of the ode to explore the impediments to composition of the loftier song, at the very outset of writing, suggests that the choice of form preceded the elaboration of content. The form of sublime ode furnished him with license to incorporate abrupt turns and contradictory statements thus providing a context for fragments that otherwise would be disconnected. His use of the form forsakes its earlier use as the proper form for the expression of enthusiastic emotion and wild speculation in order to present a more sober and perplexed analysis of his creativity. The opening stanzas make their connections with his previous work by their apparent break with it—by their progressively more abrupt turns—and by their denials they make a sequence of discontinuous fragments. The opening stanzas state clearly that memory and the chronology of past experience and development can no longer invest the rainbow and the rose with splendor. The order that no longer can be found

10. W.J.B. Owen, *Wordsworth as Critic* (Toronto: University of Toronto Press, 1969) 112.

in memory can, perhaps ironically, be found in a sequence of utterances, in the succession of fragments and fitful beginnings that are constituted by the uncompleted *Prelude*, especially its third part, and "Home at Grasmere." What, after all, did Wordsworth's writing consist of in 1802 but a collection of splendid beginnings? At the moment of their composition the opening stanzas are themselves fragments that also confirm the fragmentary nature of the previous work.

Coleridge's "Timely Utterance": The Letter to Asra

The first four stanzas of the "Immortality Ode" possess their significance, not only in relation to Wordsworth's previous poetry, but also in the works of both poets that follow. They are the initiating verses in a poetic dialogue that includes Coleridge's "Dejection: An Ode" and Wordsworth's "Resolution and Independence." This sequence is the most studied in their dialogue. The intricate relationships among the poems have been explored since before Ernest de Selincourt first published the letter version of "Dejection" in 1937. The particular details of Coleridge's composition are well known. The day after Wordsworth wrote the opening stanzas of the "Ode," he went to Keswick to visit Coleridge. On April 4 Coleridge wrote the earliest version of "Dejection" as a verse epistle to Sara Hutchinson, whom Coleridge called Asra. The immediate personal circumstance that prompted him to write her was a visit he had made to her on his trip back to Keswick from London. During that visit there were apparently moments of pain and anguish between the two, for Coleridge's notebook for the period contains several entries alluding to the difficulties: "Friday, March 12th / '& wept aloud'— you make me feel uncomfortable / Saturday, March 13th, left Gallow Hill on the Mail, in a violent storm of snow & Wind . . ." (*CNB* 1: 1151). Little is known about the occasion of the sadness, except that it obviously had to do with Coleridge's love for her since their first meeting in 1799. In the verse epistle he apologizes for having sent her a "complaining Scroll," apparently a letter that distressed her, for Coleridge accepts responsibility for causing her illness.[11]

11. For a study of Coleridge's relationship to Sara Hutchinson, see George Whalley, *Coleridge and Sara Hutchinson and the Asra Poems* (Toronto: University of Toronto Press, 1955). Coleridge's further reflections on his visit are contained in *CNB* 1: 1153, 1155–57. I have quoted the verse letter in its earliest extant form in *STCL*.

Even before his March visit to the Hutchinson's home at Gallow Hill, he contemplated poetry on their relationship which clearly anticipates the verse letter of "Dejection." The previous December he entered two notes that are particularly important both for the form of the poem and for his uncertainty about whether he should write such poetry at all.

> To write a *series* of Love Poems—truly Sapphic, save that they shall have a large Interfusion of moral Sentiment & calm Imagery on Love in all the moods of the mind—Philosophic, fantastic, in moods of high enthusiasm, of simple Feeling, of mysticism, of Religion—/ comprize in it all the practice, & all the philosophy of Love—(*CNB* 1: 1064)

> A lively picture of a man, disappointed in marriage, & endeavoring to make a compensation to himself by virtuous & tender & brotherly friendship with an amiable Woman—the obstacles—the jealousies— the impossibility of it.—Best advice that he should as much as possible withdraw himself from pursuits of morals &c—& devote himself to abstract sciences— (*CNB* 1: 1065)

The first entry contemplates a series of poems that would combine the passion of love with religion and morals, but the second seems to question the possibility of combining the two and the wisdom of the attempt. If love poetry is to combine passion and morals, and if he resolves to "withdraw himself from pursuits of morals," he must withdraw from poetry as well. The two notes are, on the one hand, a plan for a sequence of poems to be written and, on the other, a resolution not to write them. The personal and biographical motive to write leaves Coleridge with his mind not settled as to whether he should write or not. With such motives, writing would be a dangerous indulgence of private feelings and would exacerbate, rather than alleviate, them.

The generating impulse for the verse letter is neither his notes on the advisability of writing love poetry nor his visit to Gallow Hill, but rather the opening stanzas of Wordsworth's "Ode." It has long been recognized that there are explicit quotations and echoes of Wordsworth's stanzas throughout the verse letter. Wordsworth had written "My head hath it's coronal," and Coleridge responded, "I too will crown me with a Coronal." Wordsworth complained that "The things which I have seen I now can see no more," and Coleridge similarly complained, "They are not to me now the Things, which once

they were." Echoing the earlier "Mad Monk,"[12] Wordsworth's stan-
zas began, "There was a time when meadow, grove, and stream
. . . ," and when Coleridge contemplates his afflictions he writes,
"There *was* a time when tho' my path was rough . . ." Examples of
quotation and echo could be multiplied. These correspondences
would have been understood, of course, by Wordsworth and any-
one else who had seen his stanzas, and one may wonder that if Sara
Hutchinson received the letter, she would have understood the al-
lusions to stanzas that she might not have seen until much later.
Wordsworth is Coleridge's intended reader as much as she is. Cole-
ridge read the verse letter to Wordsworth on April 21 (*DWJ* 113).
Although Dorothy identified them as verses to Sara, Coleridge him-
self in July referred to his revisions of the verse letter as "a poem
written during that dejection to Wordsworth" (*STCL* 2: 814).

The genesis of Coleridge's verse letter resides in Wordsworth's
similar struggle through the discontinuities of his "Ode" to the ar-
ticulation of the "timely utterance" of his blessing on the children to
relieve his sense of loss. Coleridge's letter is, not only an individual
confession of his depression, not only an attempt to distinguish him-
self from Wordsworth by explaining the causes of his own grief, but
also his attempt to find his own "timely utterance" in his blessing of
Sara Hutchinson. His "genial Spirits fail," and his individual poetic
voice is almost lost in the merely unique voice of personal confession
and complaint. The risk he ran of writing at all is acknowledged in
the December notebook entries and in the opening lines in which he
admits that "this Eolian Lute / . . . better far were mute." His reluc-
tance even to write is overcome by Wordsworth's writing.

The verse letter is a turbulent poem. Although its moods vacillate
wildly from depression and the dread of inactivity to the vicarious
joy of contemplating harmony in the Wordsworth circle and the re-
lief of blessing that he can bestow upon Sara, it is not a formless col-
lection of stanzas.[13] It combines elements of an ode, an elegy, and
even an heroic epistle[14] and hovers between an incoherent outpour-

12. Stephen Parrish and David Erdman dispute authorship in "Who Wrote 'The
Mad Monk'? A Debate," *Bulletin of the New York Public Library* 64 (1960): 209–37.
13. William Heath, for example, has seen the verse letter as having no order: "The
most illuminating definition of the way the verse letter is constructed is Coleridge's
own description of the absence of Method: 'an habitual submission of the under-
standing to mere events and images as such, and independent of any power in the
mind to classify and appropriate them' " (*Wordsworth and Coleridge* 102).
14. Paul Fry has detailed the complexities of generic assimilation in Coleridge's

ing of contradictory thoughts and emotions and a unified poem, or rather, as I shall argue, "a *series*" of poems, which Coleridge originally thought of writing in December. Although it would be claiming too much to argue that each of the four sections that I will discuss in turn is in fact an individual poem, able to stand by itself, there are separate movements of thought and mood marked from each other by abrupt turns. Each turns from the previous section, just as the letter as a whole turns from Wordsworth's "Ode" and the "Ode" turns from preceding work. The first section, which concludes with line 110, "And trance-like Depth of it's brief Happiness" (*STCL* 2: 793), structurally resembles an earlier Conversation Poem; the second, which concludes with line 215, "And now screams loud, & hopes to make it's Mother hear" (*STCL* 2: 795), contradicts the blessing generated by pleasant recollection in the first and laments that a blessing was replaced by a complaint; the third section, which concludes with line 295, "They are not to me now the Things, which once they were" (*STCL* 2: 797), is perhaps the bleakest in the poem and faces the knowledge that the speaker himself is in dire need of some blessing to remove his depression; and, finally, the poem concludes with a more joyous blessing, which ends "Thus may'st thou ever, evermore rejoice!"

The verse letter begins with a sequence of stanzas that could stand independently as a lyric poem on the pattern of the Conversation Poems. It begins in a "heartless Mood" with Coleridge's blank eye gazing on a landscape devoid of feeling. Gradually his emotional deadness, lack of activity, and severe reluctance to speak at all are overcome, at first "feebly" when he thinks of Sara and more forcefully when he recollects, as he did in "Frost at Midnight," his school days in London, when he recalls the "secret Yearnings on my Soul. / At eve, sky-gazing in 'ecstatic fit'." Thoughts of Sara and of his former idealizations relieve the weight from his breast. With his blessing upon her, he feels his "spirit moved." The sequence ends with recollections of a peaceful evening with her: "Such Joy I had, that I may truly say, / My Spirit was awe-stricken with the Excess / And trance-like Depth of it's brief Happiness."

The relief that his utterance brings is dependent, not only upon the allusions to his own poetry, but also upon its relation to Words-

---

poem (*The Poet's Calling in the English Ode* [New Haven: Yale University Press, 1980] 162–85). Gene Ruoff delivered a paper at the Wordsworth-Coleridge Association meeting in 1982 that discussed the affinities of the verse letter with the erotic epistle.

worth's "Ode." Coleridge's reading of Wordsworth's utterance activates Coleridge's public voice of blessing to redeem his private voice of suffering, which he believes ought to be silent. His first direct allusion to Wordsworth's stanzas comes in his definition of his dejection, which has no voice: "A stifling, drowsy, unimpassioned Grief / That finds no natural Outlet, no Relief." Coleridge interprets Wordsworth's couplet to mean that his loss is the loss of the ability to write and that the public utterance relieves, partially, that loss. At first it appears that Coleridge wishes to distinguish himself from Wordsworth by citing his own incurable depression. Wordsworth is strong, and he is weak.

But the echo is only a prelude to a temporary relief through the utterance of a blessing. Before reviving that blessing, however, Coleridge must discard the notion in the opening stanzas of the "Ode" that relief is to be discovered in nature. Coleridge's second echo responds to Wordsworth's "I see / The heavens laugh with you in your jubilee." Coleridge cannot see a community of man and nature in sympathy, and his response to these lines laments that "I see them all so excellently fair! / I see, not feel, how beautiful they are." In both of these echoes Coleridge differs by negation, "no Relief" and "not feel," but these negations serve two purposes. They deepen his isolation, yet also correct what Coleridge must have considered a misdirection in Wordsworth's turn to nature. Coleridge would well have known that it was a misdirection, because in 1802 Wordsworth was moving toward a recognition of the mind's supremacy over nature and had admitted several times in *The Prelude* the power of the "auxiliar light" of his own imagination. Coleridge's lines are not only a philosophical statement; they are also a reference to Wordsworth's previous poetry. True depression, for Coleridge, is the inability to feel and the loss of "genial spirits," a phrase that echoes Milton's Samson, who complains that "my genial spirits droop."[15] Coleridge's more explicit comment on the value of nature

15. Samson's entire speech is relevant:

> All otherwise to me my thoughts portend,
> That these dark orbs no more shall treat with light,
> Nor th'other light of life continue long,
> But yield to double darkness nigh at hand:
> So much I feel my genial spirits droop,
> My hopes all flat, nature within me seems
> In all her functions weary of herself:

emphasizes his point: "I may not hope from outward Forms to win / The Passion & the Life whose Fountains are within!" In the first stanza he had hoped "that the Gust ev'n now were swelling, / And the slant Night-shower driving loud & fast," but that wish is now admitted to be fruitless for him. The natural world is significant only because it may be the object of Sara's contemplation. The thought that she may be looking at the moon as he does, "stirs my Heart."

Partial relief comes with thoughts of Sara, and his desire recalls the desire that he experienced at school sitting at the "barr'd window" and on the "leaded School-roof" when he then dreamed of "a Maiden's quiet Eyes" contemplating "Moon, or Evening Star" and associating them with "sweet Dreams." The thought that Sara is now contemplating the heavens that he sees realizes the promise of his childhood fancy and confirms the awakening of his yearning. Thoughts of Sara and the renewal of desire relieve the "stifling" grief of the opening stanzas:

> I feel my spirit moved—
> And wheresoe'er thou be,
> O Sister! O Beloved!
> Those dear mild Eyes, that see
> Even now the Heaven, *I* see—
> There is a Prayer in them! It is for *me*—
> And I, dear Sara—*I* am blessing *thee*!
>
> (*STCL* 2: 792)

His blessing brings with it the thought of the present calm, still evening before the storm descends and of an evening with Mary and Sara described in "A Day Dream," in which love is similarly expressed as a blessing:

> O ever—ever be thou blest!
> For dearly, Asra! Love I thee!
> This brooding warmth across my breast,
> This depth of tranquil bliss—ah, me!
> Fount, tree and shed are gone, I know not whither,
> But in one quiet room we three are still together.
>
> (19–24)

My race of glory run, and race of shame,
And I shall shortly be with them that rest.

Samson Agonistes (590–98) in *John Milton: Complete Poems and Major Prose*, ed. Merritt Y. Hughes (New York: Odyssey Press, 1957).

"A Day Dream" acknowledges a reality that is not present, suggests that its life is solely in memory, and thereby makes the dream and its warmth in his breast, which takes the place of the smothering weight, into a genuinely comforting fiction. The recollection of precisely the same moment in the verse letter brings much joy "that I may truly say, / My Spirit was awe-striken with the Excess / And trance-like Depth of it's brief Happiness." The value of the sweet dream in "A Day Dream" is not questioned, and the poem ends, not with any disillusionment, but with a gesture intended to preserve the privacy of the dream:

> But let me check this tender lay
> Which none may hear but she and thou!
> Like the still hive at quiet midnight humming,
> Murmur it to yourselves, ye two beloved women!
>
> (33–36)

The allusion to the same moment in the verse letter, a different context, changes the pleasant memory stored in inviolable security in a private recollection to a more public moment of "brief Happiness," that emphasizes its transience. The "trance-like" happiness has a twofold meaning. It is an ecstasy that banishes all disquieting thoughts, but it is also a moment that is defined by transience, transition, impermanence, and even unreality, all of which are suggested in Coleridge's earlier use of the phrase in the "trances of the blast" in "Frost at Midnight." At the end of this first sequence Coleridge implies a comparison to Wordsworth's loss of "the glory and the dream." To Coleridge the dream is present, yet it possesses the quality of illusion and transience, which he says later in the verse letter is the "Poison in the Wine." The dream itself becomes a moment of passage from happiness to pain and from one movement in the verse letter to another.

There are some important implications for a reading of poetry as a series of poems or as a poetic sequence in Coleridge's emphasis upon the "trance-like" happiness.[16] Transience implies a transition that makes what has come before a mere moment among many moments of change. What has been said and written may lose its full authority in the transience of its utterance. As Wordsworth said in

16. John Beer notes the various uses of the word "trance" in "Coleridge, the Wordsworths, and the State of Trance," *The Wordsworth Circle* 8 (1977): 121–38, where he comments upon the connection between "entrance" (entry) and "entrance" (transport of feeling).

the fourth stanza, the tree and "single Field" speak of "something that is gone." A transition may emphasize the "trance-like" qualities in what has come before by placing it within a sequence, and the reverse is equally true. A trance usually implies a transition to its opposite. The burden of Coleridge's lyrics is that frequently they lead to a trance that implies transition.

The second section, beginning with line 111, reverses the temporary joy with which the first concludes. It turns from the dream of his presence in Sara's company to his distance from her and his own isolation. It contemplates her future joy with the Wordsworth circle from which he excludes himself because he has no wish to be a temporary member of it or an intruder. It also turns from the blessing he has uttered upon Sara to an admission that the letter he sent her ought to have been a blessing but was exactly the opposite. He has caused her pain and tries, throughout this second part of the poem, to reactivate a voice that can bless her, but his attempts to bless are lost in the turbulence of his private pain and end with the voice of Lucy Gray crying in "utter grief & fear," which echoes his own utterance. When the turn occurs from the first section to the second, the depression of the beginning of the verse letter returns with its resolve that the best course would be to remain silent. The "smoth'ring Weight" of the first section, which was "somewhat lifted from my Breast," returns in the second when the thought of transience "weighs down the Heart." Similarly, in the first section the grief that can find no "natural Outlet" becomes a blessing, but in the second the blessing is effaced by the letter of complaint that he has sent her. The second section ends with a "Trance of deepest Silence" in the storm in which Lucy Gray's cry is heard, whereas the first had ended with a recollection of their listening "to the Stillness of the Air." This "Trance of deepest Silence" in the storm reverses the "trance-like Depth of it's brief Happiness," and this reversal establishes the transience of utterance in the first section.

The second section begins on an elegiac note. It again invokes the "fair Remembrances" that provided solace in the first, but it invokes them only to reproach them for their absence:

> Ah fair Remembrances, that so revive
> The Heart, & fill it with a living Power,
> Where were they, Sara?—or did I not strive
> To win them to me?— on the fretting Hour

Then when I wrote thee that complaining Scroll
Which even to bodily Sickness bruis'd thy Soul!

(*STCL* 2: 793)

The question repeats the conventional reproach of elegy: "Where were ye Nymphs when the remorseless deep / Clos'd o'er the head of your lov'd *Lycidas*?"[17] Coleridge's nymphs are the "fair Remembrances" whose return in the first sequence cannot atone for their absence at the crucial moment when he sent her "Pain & Sorrow." For Wordsworth in the opening stanzas of the "Ode," memory serves only to confirm the loss that he has suffered, and for Coleridge memory in the second section is a fickle and transient visitant. The "fair Remembrances" that offer a consolation and relief from the depression of the opening lines offer, in the context of the second section, only a temporary relief from the thoughts of grief. What might have been conclusive is inconclusive and contains within it the limitations on its power of permanent consolation.

The first sequence had concentrated upon Coleridge's state of mind, and the second turns to his hopes for her happiness and his wish for her comfort and joy. He hopes to spare her the painful implications of the "trance-like Depth" of happiness, the merely temporary joy. He tries to renew his blessing, to replace the "complaining Scroll" with a hope that she will remain permanently at rest in "one Happy Home, / One House, the dear *abiding* Home of All." Coleridge conceives of the perfection of their home in words that are very close to those Wordsworth used in the "Home at Grasmere" fragments to praise the valley:

'Tis (but I cannot name it), 'tis the sense
Of majesty and beauty and repose,
A blended holiness of earth and sky,
Something that makes this individual Spot,
This small abiding-place of many men,
A termination and a last retreat.

(161–66)

The tranquillity and permanence that he forsees for William, Mary, Dorothy, and Sara is expressed in terms of Wordsworth's text, which assures him momentarily that even though Sara is distant from him and "not in sight" he will be able to bless her:

17. "Lycidas" (50–51) in *Milton: Complete Poems*.

Be happy, & I need thee not in sight.
Peace in thy Heart, & Quiet in thy Dwelling,
Health in thy Limbs, & in thine Eyes the Light
Of Love, & Hope, & honorable Feeling—
Where e'er I am, I shall be well content!
Not near thee, haply shall be more content!
To all things I prefer the Permanent.
And better seems it for a heart, like mine,
Always to *know*, than sometimes to behold,
    Their Happiness & thine—
For Change doth trouble me with pangs untold!

(STCL 2: 794)

The perfection implied by the "Home At Grasmere" fragments permits no change. Coleridge's fear of change excludes him from the joyful confidence of the Wordsworth circle. Wordsworth's "To me alone" has become Coleridge's, and transience is uniquely Coleridge's:

The transientness is Poison in the Wine,
Eats out the pith of Joy, makes all Joy hollow,
All pleasure a dim Dream of Pain to follow!
My own peculiar Lot, my house-hold Life
It is, & will remain, Indifference or Strife.
While *ye* are *well & happy*, 'twould but wrong you
If I should fondly yearn to be among you—

(STCL 2: 794)

Transience changes the "fair Remembrances" to a "dim Dream of Pain." The tyranny that time imposes upon joy is that it necessarily calls forth its opposite.

In the second sequence, reality to Coleridge is transience, and consequently his happiness at contemplating Sara's is also subject to change. The transition from the hope for her happiness to a meditation upon her possible dejection is almost inevitable in the verse letter and is compounded by a number of intertextual ironies. If, as he fondly hopes, she is truly at home in Grasmere's utter perfection, she will have no need of his blessing, because in the "Home at Grasmere" fragments, those who dwell there do not need a blessing. As Wordsworth had suggested in those fragments, to bless those who do not need blessing is to intrude with the utterance that violates the sanctity of the valley by offering a blessing that assumes that the valley is less than perfection. If she dwells in perfect happiness, his voice of blessing is an intrusion; she has no need of it. On the other hand, if the intertextual references are to Coleridge's preceding lines and Wordsworth's opening stanzas of the "Ode" rather than to "Home at Grasmere," upon which the "Ode" turns, then the frame of reference becomes change, not permanence. Thus happiness, no matter how great, must imply its opposite, and sorrow must follow "trance-like" happiness. Sara must, at some time, suffer and have need of the comfort of a blessing.

The consolation of the first section was that joy came from recollection of his being with Sara; now temporary consolation comes from hoping that she will be happy in his absence. The most depressing note, however, comes from both the fond fiction that his voice is not needed in her happiness and the even more depressing realization that if her happiness requires his absence, his voice of consolation in any future distress will be similarly absent:

> But (let me say it! for I vainly strive
> To beat away the Thought) but if thou pin'd,
> Whate'er the Cause, in body or in mind,
> I were the miserablest Man alive
> To know it & be absent!
>
> (*STCL* 2: 794)

He vainly strives to banish thoughts of her suffering without his comfort, but when he utters thoughts of her suffering, he knows that is a "dark distressful Dream" that negates the effect of the "sweet Dreams" of the first section.

There is no consolation for the "dark distressful Dream"; Coleridge can only attempt to divert his attention from it to the storm that has descended and now rages outside. Although he presents it as a turn from his troubled meditations, it only reflects those meditations. His turbulence is doubled by the storm, so in turning to nature he finds no release. The storm brings winter into the spring garden, and its arrival, forseen in the opening lines of the verse letter, duplicates the arrival of grief that had been briefly relieved at the end of the first section. Ironically, his counterstatement to Wordsworth's belief that the celestial light resides in nature proves true. Nature only reflects the state of the soul.

A third section of the verse letter begins with the line, " 'Tis Midnight! and small Thoughts have I of Sleep," vastly different in tone from the previous line, "And now screams loud, & hopes to make it's Mother hear!" The previous series of stanzas concludes with a cry in the "Trance of deepest Silence," and the next begins with a sigh of quiet resignation. This third series of stanzas turns from Sara's state of mind to Coleridge's own, his feelings of isolation from friends, family, and nature. He is the individual to whom nothing or no one corresponds. And although it opens with a blessing, it is a blessing that wishes upon Sara only the happiness of being free from the suffering that he experiences: "Full seldom may my Friend such Vigils keep." His hope for her peace is only a prelude to his hope that she will bless him with her sympathy:

> Healthful & light, my Darling! may'st thou rise
> With clear & cheerful Eyes—
> And of the same good Tidings to me send!
> For, oh! beloved Friend!
> I am not the buoyant Thing, I was of yore—
> When like an own Child, I to Joy belong'd;
> For others mourning oft, myself oft sorely wrong'd,
> Yet bearing all things then, as if I nothing bore!
>
> (*STCL* 2: 796)

The following five stanzas account for his own loss of imagination and joy, and they express his fear that he can receive sympathy and blessing from no other individual. The first of them is a direct response to Wordsworth's opening stanza of the "Ode":

> There *was* a time when tho' my path was rough,
> The Joy within me dallied with Distress;
> And all Misfortunes were but as the Stuff
> Whence Fancy made me Dreams of Happiness:
> For Hope grew round me, like the climbing Vine,
> And Leaves & Fruitage, not my own, seem'd mine!
> But now Ill Tidings bow me down to earth
> Nor care I, that they rob me of my Mirth
> But oh! each Visitation
> Suspends what Nature gave me at my Birth,
> My shaping Spirit of Imagination!
>
> (*STCL* 2: 796)

In explaining his loss, Coleridge, in the preceding stanza, associates joy with his childhood and models the picture of his childhood upon Wordsworth's "timely utterance" in the third stanza: "Thou Child of Joy, / Shout round me, let me hear thy shouts, thou happy Shepherd

Boy." Coleridge's phrasing applies Wordsworth's blessing to his own past: "I am not the buoyant Thing, I was of yore— / When like an own Child, I to Joy belong'd." While later in the verse letter, joy is a spiritual state of well-being, here it seems at first to be the ability to suffer personal grief and not to be permanently depressed by it, the ability to transform it from pain to "Dreams of Happiness" particular to childhood. In the verse letter these dreams allude to the "fair Remembrances" at the end of the first section and to the idealized erotic fantasies within the confining walls of school. The energy that he once possessed to play with distress and to feed hope so that it created idealizations "not my own," fantasies unproved by any reality, has been lost.

Coleridge attributes his loss of that energy to "Ill Tidings." One does not need to use biographical detail to explain the phrase, because the entire verse epistle has presented the opposition between an utterance that is a blessing and one that causes pain. "Ill Tidings' must be the reverse of a comforting blessing. The pain he has suffered seems almost a curse, and that curse has robbed him of "what Nature gave me at my Birth." The next line equates that gift with the "shaping Spirit of Imagination." It is also true that nature's gift at birth is the gift of genius in its original meaning, the individual presiding deity that defines character. It has a definite origin in sexual energy and power, although in the verse letter it is certainly not restricted to that, since it is the energy of all generation. Among other things, Coleridge's verse epistle is about a failed marriage, and his earlier complaint that "my genial Spirits fail" makes clear that his analysis of loss is that these "genial Spirits" have been depressed by the "smoth'ring Weight" and by the "Ill Tidings" that "bow me down to earth."[18] Genius is the gift of nature at birth.

In 1802 Coleridge, not Wordsworth, introduces in the dialogue the idea that genius and imagination are naturally present at birth. Wordsworth may have had some such plan for the poet at the time that he wrote the opening stanzas, but it is not explicit in 1802. When he completed the "Ode" in 1804 and elaborated the myth of preexistence and the possessions of childhood, he spiritualized what was in Coleridge's verse epistle a surprisingly natural myth of the

18. Norman Fruman argues the thesis that Coleridge's fears of his own impotence lie behind the fears in the verse letter (*Coleridge: The Damaged Archangel* [New York: Braziller, 1971] 423–29). Mario D'Avanzo analyses the word "genial" in relation to sexuality and wedding in "Wordsworth's and Coleridge's 'Genial Spirits,' " *The Wordsworth Circle* 2 (1971): 17–19.

origin of sexual desire and imaginative energy. For Coleridge, genius has nothing to do with particular spots in nature or with connections among them; it is what distinguishes him from everything else. In a July letter to William Sotheby in which he included sections of the poem, Coleridge said that "I believe that *by nature* I have more of the Poet in me" (*STCL* 2: 814, my italics). His strategy for maintaining his tranquillity, his "sole Resource," is to "steal / From my own Nature all the Natural Man," to repress the passion and its origin when it threatens to persist, not as a blessing, but as a pain. In the spring of 1802 Coleridge struggles with a recognition that his genius and poetic individuality may not be sufficient to utter an essential blessing and that he may not be able to continue to contribute his voice to their poetic dialogue. At this point his fear seems to be that the threat of amalgamation may be alleviated, not by his finding his own genius, but his loss of it.

In certain emphases, Coleridge's account of the birth of genius parallels Wordsworth's blessed-babe passage in *The Prelude* (1799). The "shaping Spirit of Imagination" that Coleridge once had is the possession of Wordsworth's child, who has received it from its mother's love. The infant's mind is

> prompt and watchful, eager to combine
> In one appearance all the elements
> And parts of the same object, else detached
> And loth to coalesce.
>
> (*Prel.* [1799] II, 277–80)

Wordsworth's child is "no outcast," and possesses "a virtue which irradiates and exalts / All objects." Just as Coleridge as a child in possession of his genius and joy cannot be depressed by pain and grief, so too Wordsworth's child can unite the energy of imagination with the external world and the great passions, so that great passions are not afflictions. Wordsworth places the origin of the "first / Poetic spirit of our human life" in the natural love of the mother, the gift given at birth. Although Coleridge's lament of the loss of his imagination is expressed in such personifications as "Joy," "Distress," "Fancy," "Hope," "Mirth," and "Imagination," the underlying process that these only half hide is one of a physical as well as spiritual generative energy. In Coleridge's terms, the loss is critical. To lose imagination is to lose one's genius, individual creativity. The entire verse epistle is troubled by that potential loss.

Wordsworth's blessed-babe passage exemplifies a fruitful binding of the child to the mother and to nature by the "gravitation and the filial bond." The child is not bound as a slave is bound to a master, but as both creator and receiver. The binding of the child antici-pates, in a narrow sense, the "inevitable yoke" of the concluding stanzas of the "Ode" in 1804. Coleridge's response to the idea of binding turns upon Wordsworth's account of the child's connec-tions to the "*active* universe." Unlike Wordsworth, Coleridge finds that he is bound "down to earth" in affliction, and this binding has the opposite effect. For Coleridge, to be bound is to be isolated from all those who could be sympathetic. His complaint is not that there is everything to fear, a kind of existential dread, but that there is nothing to hope for, and no object that holds promise for him. His "coarse domestic Life has known / No Habits of heart-nursing Sym-pathy, / No Griefs, but such as dull and deaden me." His children are a "Bliss, that still calls up a Woe":

> What a most blessed Lot mine might have been.
> Those little Angel Children (woe is me!)
> There have been hours, when feeling how they bind
> And pluck out the Wing-feathers of my Mind,
> Turning my Error to Necessity,
> I have half-wish'd, they never had been born!
>
> (*STCL* 2: 797)

Again he feels bound, certainly not in the sense of Wordsworth's "fil-ial bond," but in the sense that he is bound to earth and prevented from flight. His binding is imprisoning, and the shades of his prison house are doubly dark for their being his alone. Once again Cole-ridge has defined his condition in direct opposition to Words-worth's.

Finally, Coleridge returns to an unmistakably Wordsworthian motif only to differentiate himself:

> These mountains too, these Vales, these Woods, these Lakes,
> Scenes full of Beauty & of Loftiness
> Where all my Life I fondly hop'd to live—
> I were sunk low indeed, did they *no* solace give;

But oft I seem to feel, & evermore I fear,
They are not to me now the Things, which once they were.

(*STCL* 2: 797)

Coleridge is not at home in Grasmere. Nature provides him with no solace. Coleridge's use of "these" mountains, woods, vales, and lakes is as specific as Wordsworth's use of the words "these" and "those" at the beginning of "Tintern Abbey," but Coleridge specifies them only as things that are no longer his. As he said in reference to his domestic life, there is nothing "whence when I mourn'd for you, my Heart might borrow / Fair forms & living Motions for it's Sorrow."

The final sequence of the letter version returns to Coleridge's desire to bless Sara and turns away from his analysis of his own isolation. His blessing upon Sara at the conclusion makes it a more optimistic poem than the published ode.[19] The published ode used the epistle's concluding blessing as the measure of how much Coleridge had failed to live up to its ideals of the deified poet by moving most of those stanzas to the middle of the ode, where they preceded his analysis of his afflictions. The relief in the verse letter is achieved by his ability to find a voice, a natural outlet, for his grief and by his strength to overcome the temptation to remain mute. The blessing that he finally utters is similar in effect to those blessings at the end of earlier Conversation Poems, "Frost at Midnight," "This Lime-Tree Bower," and "The Nightingale." It is a generous gesture, but one that is by no means simple in its implications for the preservation of his public voice. In the Conversation Poems and the verse letter, the blessing does little to alleviate the speaker's distress. Coleridge knows that he must bless from a distance and hope that Sara will be happy without him. His blessing is uttered under the conditions that Sara will be able to enjoy what Coleridge himself has admitted cannot be his. Thus the blessing assumes a disjunction between the speaker of the blessing and the utterance itself which is emphasized by the abrupt transition from the final lines of the preceding section to the final section. Coleridge turns from a knowledge that for him there is "no solace" to the opposite:

O Sara! we receive but what we give,
And in *our* Life alone does Nature live.

19. David Pirie has written that "in describing Joy, Coleridge finally achieves it, and the movements towards Sara and towards Joy are one" ("A Letter to [Asra]," *WBS* 325).

> Our's is her Wedding Garment, our's her Shroud—
> And would we aught behold of higher Worth
> Than that inanimate cold World allow'd
> To the poor loveless ever-anxious Crowd,
> Ah!, from the Soul itself must issue forth
> A Light, a Glory, and a luminous Cloud
>   Enveloping the Earth!
> And from the Soul itself must there be se[nt]
> A sweet & potent Voice, of it's own Bir[th,]
> Of all sweet Sounds the Life & Element.
>
>   (*STCL* 2: 797-98)

Coleridge hopes that Sara will be the origin of that glory that warms and illuminates and that she will possess joy:

> To thee would all Things live from Pole to Pole,
> Their Life the Eddying of thy living Soul—
> O dear! O Innocent! O full of Love!
> A very Friend! A Sister of my Choice—
> O dear, as Light & Impulse from above,
> Thus may'st thou ever, evermore rejoice!
>
>   (*STCL* 2: 798)

The final lines resemble Wordsworth's blessing upon the children, but the joy that Sara is to enjoy is anything but childlike. Coleridge's blessing is his "timely utterance," which he hopes will atone for his untimely complaining letter. Having experienced a loss of another kind, Coleridge writes, not an ode, but an epistle that at first sight seems to be a very private utterance. Shortly after he wrote the first version he began to revise it to exclude the most personal references to his marriage and sent it in letters to friends. When it was published in the *Morning Post* in October it excluded all personal references and confessions of creative failure. It is not, even in its original, a totally private document. It was not written, as were many of his other letters, for Sara's eyes alone, and it was not written as a private letter or notebook entry, the most personal of which Coleridge wrote in his secret cypher system. Since he read the poem to the Wordsworths on April 21, it was intended to be a public poem among a small circle of friends.

The verse letter is doubtless written with Wordsworth's poetry in mind and, at some points, is deliberately in conflict with some of Wordsworth's most cherished ideas of the relationship between the human mind and nature. In particular, it is addressed to the "Prospectus" to *The Excursion*. Thus Coleridge's verse letter is not simply a response to the four opening stanzas of the "Ode."[20] In effect, Coleridge's letter addresses Wordsworth's entire canon, just as the opening stanzas themselves allude to his most important work. The "Prospectus" in its earliest form first presents the theme of the wedding of mind and nature:

> Paradise, & groves
> Elysian, blessed island in the deep
> Of choice seclusion, wherefore need they be
> A history, or but a dream, when minds
> Once wedded to this outward frame of things
> In love, finds these the growth of common day.
>
> (Darlington 259)

The following lines about the "spousal verse / Of this great consumation" and the mind's being fitted to the external world were added later and form no part of the text to which Coleridge responds in 1802. Nevertheless, he does respond directly to Wordsworth's lines on the mind's being wed to nature. He questions the idea of the One Life in his poetry, even though he seems to embrace it as a philosophical statement. In September 1802 he wrote to Southey that "each Thing has a Life of it's own, & yet they are all one Life" (*STCL* 2: 866), but in the spring and early summer he wrote a poem to Wordsworth in which he proclaimed that "we receive but what we give, / And in *our* Life alone does Nature live" and "I may not hope from outward Forms to win / The Passion & the Life whose Fountains are within!" What *did* Coleridge think? Is his philosophy in prose or poetry? Did he change his mind later under the influence of Wordsworth's poetry? Or did Wordsworth, after Coleridge's poetic instruction, change his mind to write in "Resolution and Independence," "By our own spirits are we deified"? Perhaps the best answer to all these questions is that the individual statement, in verse or prose, is to a large extent determined by the context of the dialogue in which it occurs and the underlying motives of the dialogue.

In responding to Wordsworth, Coleridge used the wedding met-

20. Darlington dates the "Prospectus" to *The Excursion* from 1800–1802 and reports that Mark Reed accords with those dates, although he had earlier had held for the later date of September 1806 (21–22). Reed bases his new opinion on the echoes of the "Prospectus" in Coleridge's verse letter. See also Jonathan Wordsworth, "Secession at Grasmere," *Times Literary Supplement*, Mar. 26, 1976: 354–55.

aphor twice. The first insists that nature's "Wedding Garment" and "Shroud" both are ours. While the theme of wedding alludes to the "Prospectus," the word "Garment" alludes to the earth that was at one time "apparrel'd" in celestial light at the beginning of the "Ode." Both garment and shroud allude to the act of investiture that the child makes in the first spot of time to cloak the landscape in its "visionary dreariness." The second reference to the metaphor is more detailed and may have prompted Wordsworth himself to turn upon it and elaborate it in the fourteen-line addition to the "Prospectus" when it was connected with "Home at Grasmere" in 1806:

> Joy, Sara! is the Spirit & the Power,
> That wedding Nature to us gives in Dower
> A new Earth & new Heaven
> Undreamt of by the Sensual & the Proud!
> Joy is that strong Voice, Joy that luminous Cloud—
> We, we ourselves rejoice!
> And thence flows all that charms or ear or sight,
> All melodies the Echoes of that Voice,
> All Colors a Suffusion of that Light.
>
> (*STCL* 2: 798)

The fictional paradise that Wordsworth believed could be realized by the union of mind and nature to produce the "growth of common day" becomes in the verse letter the "new Earth & new Heaven," which is exclusively the creation of joy within the poet's mind. Joy in this section is neither the joy that dallies with distress in childhood nor the joy of the children in the opening stanzas of the "Ode." In reference to Sara, it is the assurance of spiritual well-being and maturity that grants her the grace to be a nurturing presence as the "mother Dove." In reference to Wordsworth, joy is the presence of a "strong Voice," the voice that Wordsworth sought in the "Prospectus" as a prophetic voice, and it is the presence of a light that radiates from his mind, truly the glory that he claims to have lost in the opening stanzas.

That the final blessing is for both Sara and Wordsworth complicates a full reading of it. When Coleridge sent a revised version of the letter to William Sotheby in July, the final stanza was addressed to Wordsworth by name:

> Calm stedfast Spirit, guided from above,
> O Wordsworth! friend of my devoutest choice,

Great Son of Genius! full of Light & Love!
   Thus, thus dost thou rejoice.
To thee do all things live from pole to pole,
Their Life the Eddying of thy living Soul!
Brother & Friend of my devoutest choice,
Thus may'st thou ever, ever more rejoice!
                       (*STCL* 2: 817–18)

Only in the final line does the stanza turn to a blessing: may he con-
tinue as he has been, the man of genius. The preceding lines are
apostrophe rather than blessing, and they create a Wordsworth who
fulfills the image of the ideal creative genius that has been painted
for him in the previous stanza. Yet, curiously, that earlier portrait is
quite different from the image of the poet that Wordsworth himself
draws in the "Prospectus" of the poet under the influence of nature.
Coleridge is still trying to create the poet of the great philosophical
poem.

"So Firm a Mind": "Resolution and Independence"

It has been long recognized that Wordsworth's "Resolution and In-
dependence" is an answer to Coleridge's verse letter and that the
moods of that poem can be traced directly to their poetic dialogue
in the end of March and beginning of April.[21] Wordsworth began
writing the poem on May 3, and he was familiar with the verse letter
by then. On April 21 Dorothy wrote in her journal, "Coleridge came
to us and repeated the verses he wrote to Sara. I was affected with
them and was on the whole, not being well, in miserable spirits. The
sunshine—the green fields and the fair sky made me sadder . . ."
(*DWJ* 113). The first stanzas of "Resolution and Independence"
present Coleridge's moods in the verse letter and Dorothy's reaction
to them. The joy of the morning after the storm and the medley of
the birds' songs reminds Wordsworth of a day in October 1800 on
which his mood was similar, in which joyous elation was followed by
a rapid shift to deep depression. "Resolution and Independence"
opens, not with the record of the mood of one day, or even of many

21. Both George Wilbur Meyer ("*Resolution and Independence*: Wordsworth's An-
swer to Coleridge's *Dejection: An Ode*," *Tulane Studies in English* 2 [1950]: 49–74) and
H. M. Margoliouth (*Wordsworth and Coleridge, 1795–1834* [London: Oxford Univer-
sity Press, 1953] 108) read "Resolution and Independence" as a response to Cole-
ridge's poem.

days, but rather with the record of Wordsworth's response to Coleridge's poem. In May, in response to Coleridge's verse letter, Wordsworth composed the mood of an April morning.

The correspondences between "Resolution and Independence" and the verse letter are not, as they are in earlier parts of their dialogue, a matter of verbal echoes, but rather of theme. Wordsworth's opening his poem with a morning after a storm suggests that he wants to present the more optimistic view that moments of depression are also temporary and that the winter storm that has descended into the spring garden in Coleridge's poem will give way to a glorious morning. Wordsworth's poem is the sequel to Coleridge's and turns as abruptly from its depression as other moments in the 1802 dialogue turn from their preceding moments. Wordsworth's self-portrait owes much to Coleridge's poem and little to the doubts that he expressed in the opening of the "Ode":

> My whole life I have liv'd in pleasant thought
> As if life's business were a summer mood:
> Who will not wade to seek a bridge or boat
> How can he ever hope to cross the flood?
> How can he e'er expect that others should
> Build for him, sow for him, and at his call
> Love him who for himself will take no heed at all?[22]

The first lines repeat Coleridge's portrait of his childhood and youth: "all Misfortunes were but as the Stuff / Whence Fancy made me Dreams of Happiness." And the final lines have often been taken for a portrait of the heedless, impractical Coleridge. Wordsworth has appropriated the Coleridge self-portrait for his own, and he has made thoughts about Coleridge into thoughts about himself. In the opening lines of the next stanza, "I thought of Chatterton the marvellous Boy," "Coleridge" would scan as well as "Chatterton."

But the resemblances between the two poems run deeper than the superficial, and perhaps even slightly comic, portraiture. Wordsworth's identification of his "dim sadness & blind thoughts" is an interpretation of Coleridge's fear in the verse letter. Coleridge counts many pains in that letter: the loss of his imagination, the in-

---

22. *PTV* 319. For dates and textual details of the various versions see *DWJ* 123; Curtis, *Wordsworth's Experiments with Tradition* 146 n and 186–95, and his edition of *PTV* 123–29 and 316–23, which reprints Sara Hutchinson's fair copy of the first version, from which I quote.

ability to respond to the grandeur and beauty of nature, the separation of his private life from the more public and shared joys of the Wordsworth circle, and his own unhappy marriage. All of these complaints, however, reduce themselves to the dislocation he feels from incessant change, the change from joy to sadness reflected in the "trance-like Depth of . . . brief Happiness." He returns to the fear repeatedly: "To all things I prefer the Permanent," "For Change doth trouble me with pangs untold," and "The transientness is Poison in the Wine." Wordsworth's similar thought is "as high as we have mounted in delight / In our dejection do we sink as low," which echoes Coleridge's words on the failure of nature's influence: "I were sunk low indeed, did they *no* solace give." The disturbance that vexes both Wordsworth and Coleridge is the sudden and unpredictable change from the mood of joy to that of depression and the expectation, after innumerable oscillations of this sort, that depression becomes a part of the joy since it is implied by it. The rapid changes from joy to dejection come immediately from Coleridge's verse letter, and, curiously, have their origin in their poetic dialogue in the appropriation by the "Ancient Mariner" of the mood of the sailor in some unpublished fragments of the Salisbury Plain poems. Further, the vacillation is different from the cause of depression in the beginning of the "Ode," in which there are only two significant moments, a Now of blindness and loss and a Then of glorious light. The transience of the verse letter and "Resolution and Independence" is not bound to a Now and a Then but is cut free from any such temporal determinants. It is a trouble to the poetic mind for the very reason that it is totally undetermined and unpredictable, and it is a continual dislocation. For Wordsworth to recognize that he is subject to Coleridge's fears, even for a moment, is for him to question implicitly the permanence and stability of his life and work, which he had argued in "Home at Grasmere" he enjoyed and must enjoy and which Coleridge had reinforced in the verse letter by alluding to the permanence of the Wordsworth circle.

Wordsworth also recognizes in his response to the verse letter that nature has become merely landscape. Coleridge had insisted that "we receive but what we give, / And in *our* Life alone does Nature live." In his dejection Coleridge finds that the turbulence within is matched by the storm without. He finds that there are no blessings for him in nature, no influence that can counter his mood, and no sympathy or solace in the beauty he can see but not feel. Dorothy's response to hearing the verses to Sara read repeats the thought that the glory of nature may, in the words of "Lines written in early spring," "bring sad thoughts to the mind." "Resolution and Independence" begins with a plenitude of natural voices. Stock doves, jays, and magpies fill the woods with song, and "all the air is fill'd with pleasant noise of waters." Their rejoicing echoes the spontaneous shouts of children in the "Ode," to which Wordsworth replies, "with joy I hear." The "celestial light" of the "Ode" is naturalized to the mist that glitters in the sun and seems to follow the hare's race. At first the joyous activity effaces the thoughts of "all the ways of men so vain & melancholy," but the transition to dejection changes the simplicity and purity of that picture of nature to resemble Coleridge's picture of landscape. In those complex moods in which joy and depression are mixed, Wordsworth admits that "by our own spirits are we deified," implying agreement with Coleridge.

A final significant correspondence between the two poems occurs in Wordsworth's presentation of the figure of the old leech gatherer as his response to Coleridge's "sole Resource" for dealing with his depression. Coleridge's only answer to his own dejection is

> not to think of what I needs must feel,
> But to be still & patient all I can;
> And haply by abstruse Research to steal
> From my own Nature all the Natural Man—
> This was my sole Resource, my wisest plan!
> And that, which suits a part, infects the whole,
> And now is almost grown the Temper of my Soul.
>
> (*STCL* 2: 797)

It is not accidental or insignificant that for Coleridge the antidote for his pain is a detailed study of the abstractions of philosophy. It is important for him, not only because it holds authority or because it provides a structure of truth in which human actions have meaning, but because it is a defense mechanism. Coleridge's resource is to suppress the passions that he knows can only bring him pain. Although his blessing of both Sara and Wordsworth is a turning outward and an uttering, and although it brings him a vicarious joy, it does not resolve his anxiety over his own depression.

Wordsworth's reaction to the presence of the leech gatherer serves a similar purpose. The final stanza interprets the figure as a cure for the cycle of elation and depression:

With this the Old Man other matter blended
Which he deliver'd with demeanor kind
Yet stately in the main & when he ended
I could have laugh'd myself to scorn to find
In that decrepit man so firm a mind
God said I be my help & stay secure
I'll think of the Leech-gatherer on the lonely Moor.

(*PTV* 323)

The leech gatherer is to Wordsworth a person of strength, endurance, and an almost stoic stability of mind, a figure of permanence. The full significance of the figure and Wordsworth's response to Coleridge's "sole Resource," however, is complicated by the presence of several versions of the poem, which present him in different ways. The first version, which its modern editor, Jared Curtis, calls "The Leech-Gatherer," was completed on May 7 as a response to Coleridge's letter and sent to Coleridge on May 10. At the same time it must have been sent to Mary and Sara Hutchinson. Apparently they wrote to Wordsworth with some criticisms of the style of "The Leech Gatherer," because on June 14 Wordsworth and Dorothy answered their criticisms. Wordsworth's defense rests upon the criteria of the preface to *Lyrical Ballads*: "The poem is throughout written in the language of men—'I suffered much by a sickness had by me long ago' is a phrase which anybody might use" (*LEY* 365), and in another section of the letter he wrote "You speak of his speech as tedious; everything is tedious when one does not read with the feelings of the Author" (*LEY* 367).

Wordsworth's artistic problem, identified by his critics, was that he wished to present a simplicity that was incompatible with common speech and ordinary language. His comments to the Hutchinsons show the particular kind of simplicity that he tried to convey: "A person reading this Poem with feelings like mine will have been awed and controuled, expecting almost something spiritual or supernatural—What is brought forward? 'A lonely place, a Pond' 'by which an old man *was*, far from all house or home'—not stood, not sat, but '*was*'—the figure presented in the most naked simplicity possible. This feeling of spirituality or supernaturalness is again referred to as being strong in my mind in this passage—'*How came he here* thought I or what can he be doing?' "(*LEY* 366). The simplicity that Wordsworth has in mind is not the simplicity of common, quotidian reality or of the figures of humble and rustic life. It is the simplicity of a man divested of all attributes of the individually human, so that he appears as a simple, supernatural being. His words as they survive in the earliest version are simple, then, in an ambiguous way. Wordsworth took them as intensely poetic and in accord with his impression of the character as an almost supernatural being, while his readers saw only the tedious language of common life.

The ambiguity is present when he describes the speech of the leech gatherer:

> His words came feebly from a feeble chest,
> Yet each in solemn order follow'd each
> With something of a pompous utterance drest,
> Choice word & measured phrase, beyond the reach
> Of ordinary men, a stately speech,
> Such as grave livers do in Scotland use,
> Religious Men who give to God & Man their dues.[23]

On the one hand, the poem says that his speech is decidedly not ordinary; it is formal, a "pompous utterance," which seems quite the opposite of what Wordsworth in his letter called "the language of men" and very different from the "timely utterance" of the "Ode," or the "natural Outlet" of Coleridge's verse letter. It is a grave and stately utterance, neither disjointed rusticity nor the passionate utterance of either complaint or blessing. The old man is a figure who has no particularizing attributes and can have no distinct patterns of speech; he seems stripped even of those passionately personal characteristics of speech of Wordsworth's and Coleridge's earlier poems. There is implied a strange detachment of the man from his speech. It is solemn, ceremonious, and common only in the sense that it is ritualistic and shared by all who participate in that ritual; it is not common in the sense that it is characteristic of ordinary people.

Wordsworth's defense of "The Leech-Gatherer" has an imperious tone, but nevertheless his confidence in the first version is betrayed by his revising the poem to delete the old man's direct speech and by dehumanizing him to give him a supernatural presence. Jared Curtis has remarked that Wordsworth "worked his way from the ballad-like beginnings to the fable-like effect of the last ver-

---

23. The 1802 manuscript is torn at this point, and Curtis conjectures on the basis of the remaining traces that it contained this stanza, which was included in a copy of the poem that Coleridge sent to Sir George Beaumont on August 13, 1803 (*STCL* 2: 966–70) (*Wordsworth's Experiments with Tradition* 192–93 and *PTV* 320–21).

sion."[24] At the same time, his revisions make the figure of the leech gatherer a more appropriate and subtle response to Coleridge's similar defense against emotional vacillation in his "sole Resource." The change is, first of all, a movement away from the old man's natural presence in the poem to the figure of the old man as an emblem of fortitude and endurance, a supernatural presence somewhat like a religious vision. Wordsworth's attention is drawn to the figure by a "peculiar grace / A leading from above, a something given." The figure is unique and totally out of the ordinary course of nature and human life. It is odd that Wordsworth should have deliberately created such a figure, especially when there was ample precedent in his own work for natural human figures possessed of endurance and natural piety—Michael, for example. The context of "Resolution and Independence," however, required the presence of a figure who could oppose the troubled naturalism of both Coleridge's and Wordsworth's unpredictable emotional swings. The "sole Resource" that Coleridge posed as a cure for the ills of the natural man had itself become a disease, and Wordsworth could not rely on the natural man to cure his natural ills. The supernaturalism of Wordsworth's figure has to admonish both the easy, unconscious naturalism of his youth and the inevitable depression that follows joy. No natural figure, however heroic and stoic, could counter the depression or admonish the self-pitying at the beginning of the poem.

The major addition to the poem was a simile that removes the leech gatherer from the familiar setting of the actual meeting to the realm of a vision:

> As a huge Stone is sometimes seen to lie
> Couch'd on the bald top of an eminence;
> Wonder to all who do the same espy
> By what means it could thither come, and whence;
> So that it seems a thing endued with sense:
> Like a Sea-beast crawl'd forth, which on a shelf
> Of rock or sand reposeth, there to sun itself.
>
> (*PTV* 126)

Wordsworth's commentary on this stanza comes in the next stanza and in the preface to his edition of 1815. In the following stanza the old man is described as "not all alive nor dead, / Nor all asleep." He is, as many have described him, a border figure between life and

24. Curtis, *Wordsworth's Experiments with Tradition* 111.

death, but what captures Wordsworth's attention is a sense that the figure is out of place.[25] In the 1815 preface Wordsworth illustrates the workings of the imagination by reference to this stanza: "The stone is endowed with something of the power of life to approximate it to the sea-beast; and the sea-beast stripped of some of its vital qualities to assimilate it to the stone; which intermediate image is thus treated for the purpose of bringing the original image, that of the stone, to a nearer resemblance to the figure and condition of the aged Man; who is divested of so much of the indications of life and motion as to bring him to the point where the two objects unite and coalesce in just comparison" (*Prose* 3: 33). The particular explication is designed to illustrate what Wordsworth earlier calls the "abstracting" activity of imagination, described here as stripping and divesting, in sharp contrast to the child's act of investing in the first spot of time or the child's seeing the landscape "apparrel'd in celestial light" in the opening stanzas of the "Ode." The effect is to remove the old man from a particular location and to place him in a mythical prehistory prior to change and transition. He has become an abstraction because he is a more positive resource than Coleridge's "abstruse research," the attempt to escape the pressures of his individual life by living in a world of abstraction. Coleridge's "sole Resource" would kill the natural man, but the figure of the leech gatherer still retains some of his human life.

So caught up by the sight of the old man is Wordsworth that he falls into a trance:

> The Old Man still stood talking by my side;
> But now his voice to me was like a stream
> Scarce heard; nor word from word could I divide;
> And the whole Body of the man did seem
> Like one whom I had met with in a dream;
> Or like a Man from some far region sent,
> To give me human strength, and strong admonishment.
>
> (*PTV* 128)

In the trance or dream the leech gatherer is further stripped of human qualities. His voice is no longer audible but is like a "stream / Scarce heard," which is deliberately intended to contrast with the multitude of noisy, happy, natural voices in the opening stanzas of

25. Hartman 224–25 and Jonathan Wordsworth, *William Wordsworth: The Borders of Vision* (London: Clarendon Press, 1982) 3.

the "Ode" and those of this poem, where "all the air is fill'd with pleasant noise of waters." The shift in time from present to recollected past has silenced the joyous spring voices and left the poet with an encounter on the "lonely Moor." But speech, in the context of this poetic dialogue, is transient utterance. The trance is a further divesting of the leech gatherer's human quality, but, as in Coleridge's verse letter, the trance or dream asserts its domination over the poet's mind and, without the attribute of human speech, nevertheless becomes a transient thing. Suddenly, yet in the context of the dialogue, predictably,

> My former thought return'd: the fear that kills;
> The hope that is unwilling to be fed;
> Cold, pain, and labour, and all fleshly ills;
> And mighty Poets in their misery dead.
>
> *(PTV* 128)

The inevitable transition occurs from the vision that lends "human strength" to the "fear that kills," to the natural "fleshly ills."

The final picture of the leech gatherer is of an isolated being in a barren landscape:

> While he was talking thus, the lonely place,
> The Old Man's shape, and speech, all troubled me:
> In my mind's eye I seem'd to see him pace
> About the weary moors continually,
> Wandering about alone and silently.
>
> *(PTV* 129)

The old man has become a figure of imagination, a figure of speech, and a figure in a landscape that has been reconstructed in his image. The joys of spring in the opening lines are gone, and its voices silenced. He is far from home and devoid of human society. The "something given" that Wordsworth receives is a blessing of human independence, of a fortitude and endurance that creates a painful and isolated self-sufficiency. The resolution to cling to that image of the old man as an ideal, to transform him into a figure in a barren landscape, reveals a determination to become free, not only from all human pain and joy, but also from all society. The leech gatherer is comforted neither by a community nor by nature, which presents him only with trials. He is free from all dependence and influence.

Wordsworth's determination to possess the image of the old man implies the questionable gesture of denying any dependence, but the stern admonition to remain independent has a comprehensible poetic necessity and supports the myth that increasingly in his later years he fosters: that myth of himself as a self-generated poet. As he said in "Home at Grasmere":

> Possessions have I, wholly, solely mine,
> Something within, which yet is shared by none—
> Not even the nearest to me and most dear—
> Something which power and effort may impart.
> I would impart it. . . .

(897–901)

"Resolution and Independence" implies Wordsworth's struggle for his own independence, and the contrary, up to 1802, is his dependence on Coleridge's poetry. Coleridge's impulse is entirely different, and Wordsworth's drive to independence is even more marked in contrast to it. Wordsworth receives a blessing, and Coleridge acknowledges his need of one and, recognizing that it will not come, nonetheless utters one himself upon others. His blessing offers the home of both social and natural community, but Wordsworth's choice of independence precludes the public acknowledgment of a generating discourse and claims a solution to the problems of amalgamation.

While the leech gatherer is a figure of stability, he transforms his landscape from the joyous morning to the "lonely Moor," in which Wordsworth hears only the echo of the leech gatherer's speech. Both are far from home. The transformation leads Wordsworth from a location similar to that at the beginning of "The Immortality Ode" to an isolated silence. The transformation does not provide an ample recompense, because Wordsworth's independence isolates him from the dialogue with Coleridge. While "Resolution and Independence" is generated by the dialogue, it prefigures an independence from its generating conditions. At the same time, it recognizes that such independence and stability constitute a form of death in the figure of the leech gatherer, who is "not all alive nor dead." The cost of Wordsworth's determination to become his own origin is high, and when in the spring of 1804 he returns to fruitful work on *The Prelude*, he worries about the preservation of the ode, which embodies the lyric dialogue that can reestablish a ground for his poetry.

"An Ode in Passion Uttered"

Conclusion

WHEN A READER'S initial act is an unbinding of an individual poem from its context and an assumption that the poem is an integral unity, the poem resides in an emptiness in which the richness of allusion appears only as a set of signs without reference. This is true whether an individual poem is removed from a collection or a lyric passage is extracted from a longer work. Individual poems or lyric passages are merely milestones on the Bridgewater road, not the road itself. On the other hand, if poems are read in their contexts, the vacuity created by the isolation of texts is replaced by a troubling plenitude. In such fullness, individual poems lose their individual boundaries and become fragments of a dialogue. Lyrics enact a strange passage.

From 1797 to 1802 Coleridge's and Wordsworth's poetic dialogue speaks more and more explicitly about the condition of its generation. Poems continue to be about the world and their transformations of it, but at the same time they are determined by the progress of the dialogue itself. Their major poems are generated, not exclusively by the "spontaneous overflow" of individual feelings and personal memory, but also by a dialogue in which memory and emotion are shared transpersonal experiences embodied in the complexities of common utterances. The figures, turns, and transitions of dialogue become the pre-texts for later poetic utterances. Their 1802 dialogue speaks explicitly about the issues of figuration and turn present in 1798 and 1800. Problems persist in conceiving of a pure language of nature distinct from a human, natural language with its determined associations. The problems of figuration arise in their most complex manifestation as human figures in the landscape. Coleridge's interruptions of the dialogue often question figures in the landscape, which are "uncouth" and unrecognized. When landscape's figures speak, as when the composite figure of the mariner and the discharged soldier does, they sometimes do so without the fully conscious authority and urgency of individual motivation. They are not only out of place and dislocated, they are strangely detached emotionally from their narratives. Either it is no longer their narrative or they do not feel its importance. Their detachment signals a danger point for dialogue and for the continued generation of poetry in their dialogue. Their tales, once told, leave no motive for further speech and no motive for further transformation of the tales. In such detachment there is only unwitting repetition or a silent contemplation of what has passed. Dejection is seeing without feeling, possessing no motive for expression, and having no "natural Outlet."

Detachment from expression is the negative possibility in dialogue; in 1802 it is a real threat to both poets. It is partially a product of the knowledge of the transience of utterance that reveals the fragmentariness of utterance and lyric form. Transience and trance would end in utter silence were it not for the generating turns of dialogue. Transience is both the limiting and enabling condition of lyric. It breaks apart, but it also provides the form for future composition and preserves a possibility of generating further lyrics. Ironically perhaps, the instability of figures and the inevitability of turn provide both the pauses of silence and trance and the utterances that form sequence.

The poems of 1802 incorporate wild vacillation of emotion and motive in fragmentary effusions in the form of dialogue. It is not surprising, therefore, that they should finally take the form of an ode. And it is not surprising that in the spring of 1804, when Wordsworth again began to extend *The Prelude*, that he should worry about the fate of the ode and the intelligibility of figures associated with it. The full reference of the Arab dream, which confronts the possibility of poetry and the ode, becomes clear in relation to the other fragments composed in 1804 as well as those of earlier years. At the same time in 1804 that Wordsworth is completing "The Immortality Ode," he drafts a dream sequence in which the ode is imperiled by the flood of time. The worry about the preservation of the ode in 1804 is directly related to the odes of 1802.

When Wordsworth returned to work on *The Prelude* in February and March 1804, he drafted a number of important episodes at the same time that he drafted the Arab dream sequence.[1] Before the end of the first week in March, he had drafted the dedication scene, recast the meeting with the discharged soldier, and composed the Snowdon episode simultaneously with the initial drafts of the Arab dream. Read in isolation, the Arab dream does not reveal that Wordsworth is about to begin one of his greatest creative periods. It argues the terror of total loss and a halting effort to preserve what must inevitably be lost. Yet, read in the context of the surrounding episodes of 1804, it forms a sequence or set of passages that leads toward the promise of the Snowdon scene. The movement from the dedication scene through the meeting with the discharged soldier to the Arab dream and Snowdon begins with a morning of promise that duplicates the morning at the beginning of "Resolution and Independence," in which a storm of rain and a flood are followed by a glorious dawn:

> Magnificent
> The morning was, a memorable pomp,
> More glorious than I ever had beheld.
> The sea was laughing at a distance; all
> The solid mountains were as bright as clouds,
> Grain-tinctured, drenched in empyrean light;
> And in the meadows and the lower grounds
> Was all the sweetness of a common dawn—
> Dews, vapours, and the melody of birds,
> And labourers going forth into the fields.
>
> (*Prel.* [1805] IV, 330–39)

1. For a detailed discussion of the sequence of composition, see Jonathan Wordsworth, "The Five-Book *Prelude* of Early Spring 1804," *Journal of English and Germanic Philology* 76 (1977): 1–25; *Prel.* 516–20; and *CMY* 12. Recent discussions of the Arab dream include J. Hillis Miller, "The Stone and the Shell: The Problem of Poetic Form in Wordsworth's Dream of the Arab," *Mouvements premiers: Études critique offertes à George Poulet* (Paris: Librairie José Corti, 1972) 125–47; Mary Jacobus, "Wordsworth and the Language of the Dream," *English Literary History* 46 (1979): 618–44; Geoffrey Hartman, "The Poetics of Prophecy," *High Romantic Argument*, ed. Lawrence Lipking (Ithaca: Cornell University Press, 1981) 15–40; and Jonathan Wordsworth, "As with the Silence of the Thought," *High Romantic Argument* 41–76.

The discharged soldier episode begins in a similar mood:

> O happy state! what beauteous pictures now
> Rose in harmonious imagery; they rose
> As from some distant region of my soul
> And came along like dreams—yet such as left
> Obscurely mingled with their passing forms
> A consciousness of animal delight,
> A self-possession felt in every pause
> And every gentle movement of my frame.
>
> *(Prel.* [1805] IV, 392–99)

The promise of morning in the dedication scene doubles the morning that does not lead to fulfillment in the opening lines of Book 1:

> gleams of light
> Flash often from the east, then disappear,
> And mock me with a sky that ripens not
> Into a steady morning.
>
> *(Prel.* [1805] I, 134–37)

The glorious morning in "Resolution and Independence"' and the dedication scene both lead to a confrontation with an enigmatic figure that transforms the landscape into his own image. The "uncouth" soldier is the dislocated figure; he belongs nowhere, and Wordsworth's best gestures are to restore him to an appropriate place and to humanize him.

The Arab dream, which introduces another "uncouth" figure, as Wordsworth called the Arab-Quixote figure in a later revision, a figure whose presence is even more enigmatic than the soldier's, follows upon the previous figures and elaborates them. Wordsworth's early draft of the transition from the discharged-soldier episode to the Arab dream clearly connects the two episodes:

> Enough of private sorrow—longest lived
> Is transient, severest doth not lack
> A mitigation in th'assured trust
> Of the grave's quiet comfort and blest home,
> Inheritance vouchsafed to man perhaps
> Alone of all that suffer on the earth.
>
> *(Prel.* 152)

The soldier's permanent pain is merely transitory, because it is individual. An awareness of the permanence of individual pain leads to thoughts of universal destruction, to the final loss of both the medium of nature and the medium of words in which human life and its writing is inscribed. Man, thus suffering the permanent loss of a medium on which he can inscribe his spirit, is, like the discharged soldier, depressed and forlorn, a victim, not only of the transition of mood or the trance of the moment, but also of the flood of time. Facing the flood, the Arab's hope is to preserve the ode, to preserve the enabling conditions of lyric utterance, but his recourse is to preserve through burial. His "sole Resource" echoes the repression in Coleridge's denial of the natural man and Wordsworth's association of the leech gatherer with the rock and the antediluvian sea beast in "Resolution and Independence." The possible result of a burial is that the only alternative remaining for the poet is to stand in mute silence over the grave.

In its early versions, the dream is not Wordsworth's but a friend's, but there can be little doubt that the dream is related by Coleridge.[2] The friend's dream elaborates the figures of the discharged soldier at the same time that it recapitulates the anxieties of Coleridge's earlier contributions to the dialogue: the fears of transition in the early versions of "Dejection: An Ode," the alienation and the silence, and the enigmatic figure of the mariner. Wordsworth's reasons for attributing the dream to Coleridge in the course of his own poem may only be guessed. It is not enough to say simply that the dream was told to him by Coleridge. Coleridge's presence may have something to do with Wordsworth's knowledge of the generative power of their dialogue. To continue his lyric composition, Wordsworth needed, not only Coleridge's philosophy, but also his dialogue in poetry. Echo, reverberation, and dialogue itself often fragment text and intention, but the effect of fragmentation in 1804, as it was earlier, is to lead to further creativity through the play of turn and transition. Wordsworth turns from the Arab dream to the ascent of Snowdon, first drafted at the same time as the Arab dream passage. Both the Snowdon passage and the dedication scene turn from the dream and complement it with images in which the waters of the destructive flood are the waters that provide the "sweetness of the common dawn" of the dedication scene and the "roar of waters" of the Snowdon scene. The celestial light of the dedication scene and

2. Jane Worthington Smyser, "Wordsworth's Dream of Poetry and Science," *Publications of the Modern Language Association of America* 76 (1956): 269–75.

of Snowdon transforms the flood of the dream into the covenantal promise of glorious light, a promise of something about to be. Wordsworth's work on *The Prelude* in early 1804 fragments the covenantal promise so that it may generate the long poem that imitates the form of its generation.

INDEX

Library of Congress Cataloging-in-Publication Data

Magnuson, Paul.
  Coleridge and Wordsworth : a lyrical dialogue / Paul Magnuson.
  p. cm.
  Includes index.
  ISBN 0-691-06732-5 (alk. paper)
  1. Coleridge, Samuel Taylor, 1772-1834—Criticism and
interpretation. 2. Coleridge, Samuel Taylor, 1772-1834—Influence—
Wordsworth. 3. Wordsworth, William, 1770-1850—Criticism and
interpretation. 4. Wordsworth, William, 1770-1850—Influence—
Coleridge. 5. Dialogue. 6. English poetry—19th century—History
and criticism. I. Title.
PR4484.M28 1988
821'.7'09—dc 19   87-26341